50 NIFTY STATES

by
Jerry Aten

illustrated by Marilynn Barr

Cover by Tom Sjoerdsma

Copyright © Good Apple, Inc., 1990

ISBN No. 0-86653-532-2

Printing No. 9876543

Good Apple, Inc.
1204 Buchanan, Box 299
Carthage, IL 62321-0299

TABLE OF CONTENTS

GA1138

GA1138

GA1138

INTRODUCTION

The material created for *50 Nifty States* will provide the teacher with enough activities and teaching ideas to give students a comprehensive coverage of each of our fifty states plus the nation's capital. Six pages are devoted to each state and each unit contains three common elements. There is a cover page that includes a blank outline map of the state and a small map of the United States. Instructions for the use of the outline map follow later in the unit, but this page can also serve as a cover page for individual unit studies of each state, or as a divider page for those students keeping all of the states together. The small map of the United States can be used as an introduction to each state by having students first find the location of the state on a large wall map of the United States and then placing an *X* on its proper location on their small map. Using the map in this manner should help students gain a better perspective of state locations as they proceed through their study of the states. There is also a drawing of the state seal on this page, which children can color with appropriate crayons, map pencils or markers. This is a teacher option, depending on the grade level of students.

The second page contains introductory information that will give students a brief overview of the state being studied. The bottom half of this page is a short research activity where students become familiar with a few facts about the state and its symbols. Again, depending on the age level of the students, it is a teacher option to ask students to color the pictures of the state tree, state flower and state bird with appropriate colors.

At least one of the four remaining pages is an activity that makes use of the outline map. On occasion there will be more than one map activity sheet. When using those units, it is advisable to reproduce the blank outline for each activity. This will avoid clutter and overcrowding and encourage a neater finished map. Several of the map activities lend themselves to additional options for the teacher, and of course the blank map can also be used for any other purpose which the teacher may choose.

The remaining pages of each unit are consumed with a variety of high interest, single-page activity sheets, many of which will require additional research on the part of the student. There are crossword puzzles, word searches, creative writing activities, time lines and activities that focus on creative brainstorming, favorite sons and daughters, how history might have been changed if. . ., travel folders, vacation planners and sights to see, as well as a smorgasbord of other single-page activity sheets.

The main focus of the ideas in the book is centered around an improvement of U.S. geography and history skills, but much of the material also crosses over into the disciplines of language arts, math, science and art. Students may on occasion experience minor difficulties in finding all of the answers to some of the activities if classroom encyclopedias and the almanac are the limits of their available resources. It is strongly encouraged that teachers make the experience much more complete (and less frustrating) by providing as many resources as possible. This would include current atlases, travel guides and promotional materials that are created by each department of tourism. Their addresses can be found in any good almanac and their materials are free for the asking. Be certain to write well in advance of the time when materials will be needed. A brief cover letter explaining your needs will bring a packet of useful and informative flyers and brochures to you within a few days (or, in some cases weeks). Since these brochures are costly to produce, it is advisable to ask for only one set. These promotional materials can also be used to make attractive bulletin boards when highlighting a particular state. The full-color professional finish of these brochures also helps to spark student interest.

 GA1138

Perhaps it should also be noted that a wide variety of resources will on occasion lead to a discrepancy in some of the dates presented. The teacher should encourage flexibility in accepting conflicting answers. Those provided in the answer key are there for teacher convenience but may be in conflict with other resources.

As far as assignment of the material, it is suggested that the teacher create a learning center where several states can be stored and assigned to different students at the same time. This center would include all of the available resources as well as blank activity sheets for those states being assigned. It should be emphasized that all brochures from each state be stored separately in file folders and that students should return them to those folders when they are finished. Finally, there is also a blank outline map of the United States on page 305 which can be used by students to chart by color their progress as they complete their study of each state. There is also a blank outline map of just the shape of the United States to be used for whatever use the teacher chooses. The answer key is provided for the convenience of the teacher and can also be used as an aid to students who encounter difficulty in finding some of the answers.

vi

ALABAMA

The Heart of Dixie

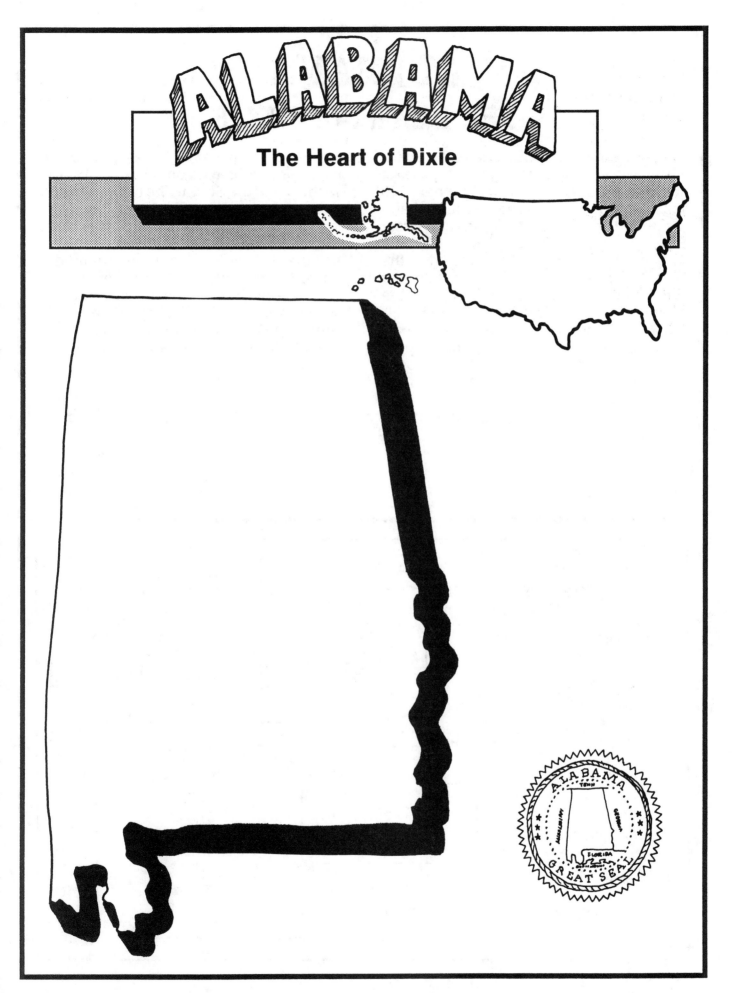

GA1138

ALABAMA
THE HEART OF DIXIE

In 1540 Hernando DeSoto planted a Spanish flag in Alabama soil, giving it its first link with European heritage. The next 200 years would see the territory shuffled and reshuffled among Spain, France and Great Britain. The fourth flag to fly over Alabama was that of the United States. During the Civil War era, dependence on cotton and sympathies toward the South led to the Republic of Alabama just prior to the Confederate States of America. Alabama's heritage has evolved from a broad spectrum of influences and cultures. Deposits of iron ore, limestone and coal helped the state to develop heavy industry, and the city of Birmingham is sometimes called the Pittsburgh of the South. The north is linked to the industry associated with the TVA, while the southern part of Alabama is close to the expanding belt of manufacturing near the Gulf of Mexico. Its one time dependence on cotton has been expanded to include lumbering, dairy farming, poultry and cattle raising. The key to Alabama's future expanded economy, however, must certainly lie with an expansion in its industrial sector.

Before continuing with your study of Alabama, identify each of the symbols called for below.

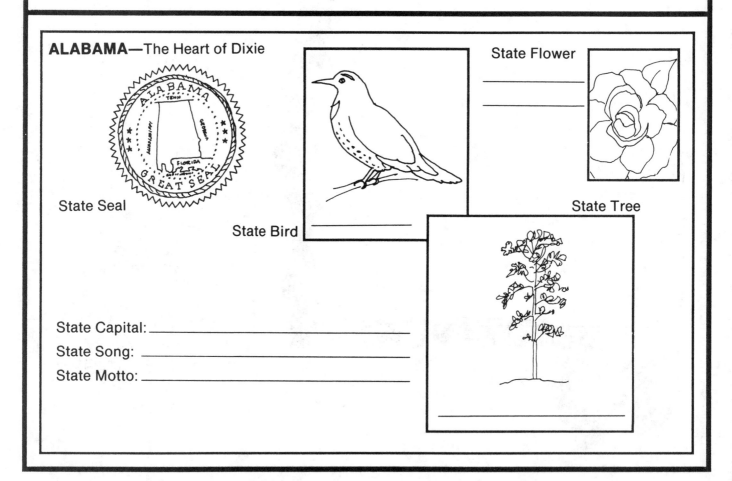

ALABAMA—The Heart of Dixie

State Seal

State Bird

State Flower
_____
_____

State Tree

State Capital: _____

State Song: _____

State Motto: _____

2

GA1138

ALABAMA ON THE MAP

Rank order the list of Alabama's largest cities below by finding their current populations; then place a #1 in the blank next to the largest, a #2 beside the next largest, etc. Pinpoint their locations on your outline map.

_____ Huntsville

_____ Tuscaloosa

_____ Mobile

_____ Decatur

_____ Dothan

_____ Birmingham

_____ Gadsden

_____ Montgomery

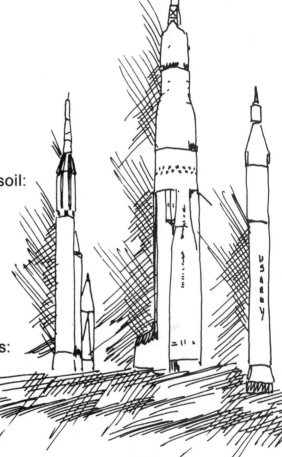

Draw in these rivers that flow through Alabama soil:

Tennessee   Mobile
Alabama   Conecuh
Choctawhatchee   Chattahoochee

Draw in these national forests:

Talladega   Conecuh
William B. Bankhead   Tuskegee

Pinpoint the locations of these tourist attractions:

Horseshoe Bend National Military Park
Alabama Space and Rocket Center
U.S.S. Alabama Battleship Memorial Park
First White House of the Confederacy
Mound State Monument
Sequoyah Caverns
Russell Cave National Monument
Gulf Shores Beach
Indian Mound and Museum

Locate two other Alabama attractions you consider important.

GA1138

SIX FLAGS OVER ALABAMA

Below are drawings of the six flags that have flown in the skies of what we now call Alabama. Identify each flag in the blank space below each flag. Then create two complete statements about each flag that will add further information about the circumstances under which that flag was flown.

Spain

_____
_____
_____
_____
_____
_____

France

_____
_____
_____
_____
_____
_____

Great Britain

_____
_____
_____
_____
_____
_____

Republic of Alabama

_____
_____
_____
_____
_____

Confederate States

_____
_____
_____
_____
_____

United States

_____
_____
_____
_____
_____

GA1138

ALABAMA RESOURCES

Below are several statements about the resources of Alabama. Expand on the information provided by each statement by adding two statements of your own to each of the resources indicated. Share your statements with the other members of your own class. For example, if the resource is Climate and the statement given is *the average is 66 degrees. . .*you could expand by adding "The average rainfall is 53 inches. The growing season is 190 days in the north and 298 days in the south."

Expand on each of the following:

Water: Alabama has 1 million acres of recreational water.

_____

_____

Forests: Forestlands occupy 22 million acres and provide employment for 67,000 Alabamians.

_____

_____

Agriculture: With a favorable climate and plenty of precipitation, Alabama is one of the nation's outstanding agricultural states.

_____

_____

Transporation: Alabama has over 57,000 miles of paved roads, ranging from market/farm roads to interstate highways.

_____

_____

Industry: Early industrial development was confined to three fields: primary metals industry, the wood-using industry and the textile industry.

_____

_____

Geography: Alabama's terrain is varied.

_____

_____

_____

Education: Alabama possesses a modern educational system with programs that ensure its continued improvement.

_____

_____

_____

NOCCALULA FALLS PARK

GA1138

NOTABLE ALABAMIANS

Accomplishment and success have long been a part of Alabama tradition. Alabama boasts a long roster of highly acclaimed people from many fields. Hidden below in the maze of letters are the names of eighteen of them. To help find those names, you should first answer the clues below the word search to identify the names you're searching out. Then simply find them and circle the letters that spell each name. Your pen can move in any direction—even around corners!

```
W G T N O T G N I H S A W E G R O E G A P R M F T
E O V C E M N E H A L M I C R N O R A A K N A H R
R N C A A H A C T W I L L I A M G O R G A S R I U
N H A R P E R L E E E C L N W A L A B A M A T R M
H T A V F I J O E L O U I S C T A A T K A O I R A
E E L E B O O K E R T W A S H I N G T O N I N A N
R H Y R A H H N O W A A M L A S A K A S A C L T C
V C H E L E N K E L L E R C N A T I K R A O U S A
O M T N A Y R B R A E B U K D H K E N B R Y T T P
N A J E S S E O W E N S F A Y K I L R Y R S H R O
B R A U N E R V O N E C U A U N N O J O C A E A T
J G E O R G E W A L L A S K I N G C G N I K R B E
```

_____ Pastor and civil rights leader—he won the Nobel peace prize before being assassinated in Memphis.

_____ He won more college football games (322) than any other coach.

_____ German-born rocket designer who lived in Huntsville and helped America's space program

_____ *The Miracle Worker* is the story of her life.

_____ He was once vice president and was one of the state's first two senators and helped develop Selma.

_____ An ex-slave who did a lot of research for the peanut and sweet potato

_____ Army doctor who helped to cure yellow fever during construction of the Panama Canal

_____ He founded Tuskegee Institute to help educate black people.

_____ Great musician and composer—among his credits are "St. Louis Blues" and "Memphis Blues"

_____ She wrote *To Kill a Mockingbird*.

_____ He surpassed Babe Ruth's home run record.

_____ Alabama's only four-time governor

_____ Undefeated heavyweight boxing champion

_____ Olympic champion who broke seven world records

_____ Famous black singer who ". . .found a million dollar baby in a 5 and 10-cent store"

_____ Alabama's most popular country music group

_____ Famous author who spent his boyhood summers in Monroeville

_____ He guided the Green Bay Packers to many championships; then he coached them.

6

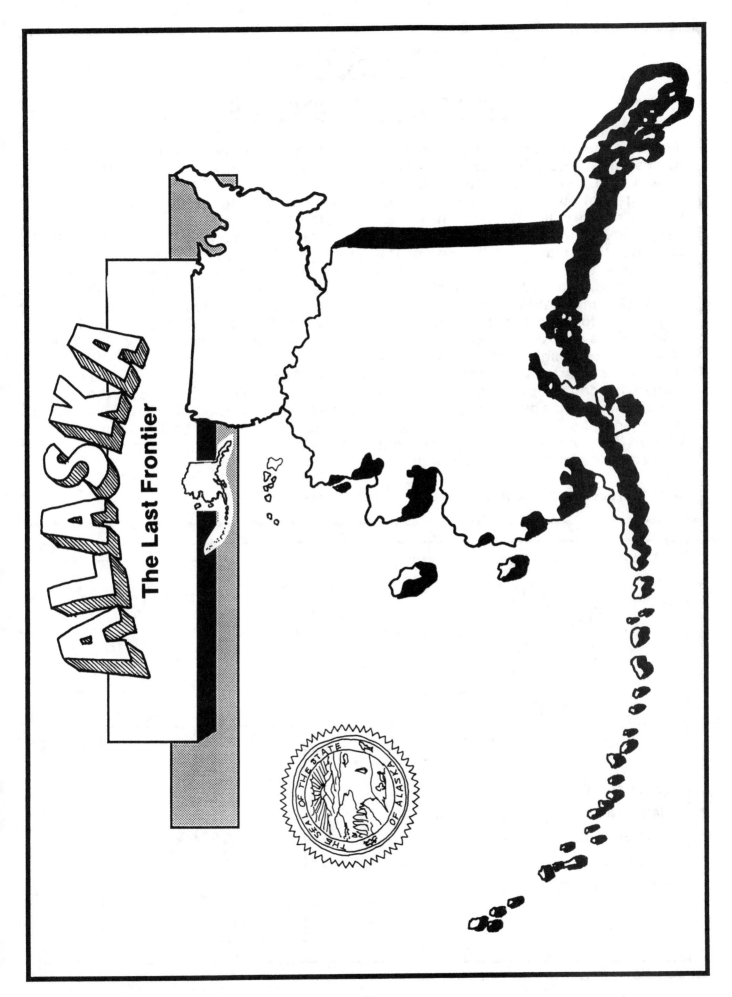

ALASKA

The Last Frontier

GA1138

ALASKA
THE LAST FRONTIER

Alayeska in the original Aleut language means "great land." The state of Alaska is indeed that! It is a land of contrasts. It is the largest of our states, covering almost 600,000 square miles. Yet Alaska has fewer people than any other state. Its coastline is longer than that of all the rest of the continental states. It contains the nation's highest mountain. Its northernmost feature is over 300 miles above the Arctic Circle. From there to Ketchikan in the southeast panhandle is almost 1400 miles. Since the United States bought Alaska from Russia in 1867 for less than two cents an acre, many who don't know Alaska think of it as little more than a huge glacier. In reality it is a land of six separate sections, each with its own climate. The southeastern panhandle is a land of forested islands and fjords with heavy annual rainfall. The interior is marked by majestic mountains, broad valleys, marshes and a climate of cold winters and very warm summers. Geologically, Alaska is a young land that is forever changing—often in dramatic ways. It is a land where wild animals found nowhere else on the continent roam freely. It is a land rich in resources. Oil is especially important because about ninety percent of the state's revenue comes from the production and export of the 63 million gallons of oil that are pumped daily through the Alaska pipeline. Alaskans, however, are carefully guarding the future of the Last Frontier in an attempt to preserve its unspoiled beauty from being swallowed up by the modern industrial world.

Before proceeding, become familiar with these Alaskan symbols:

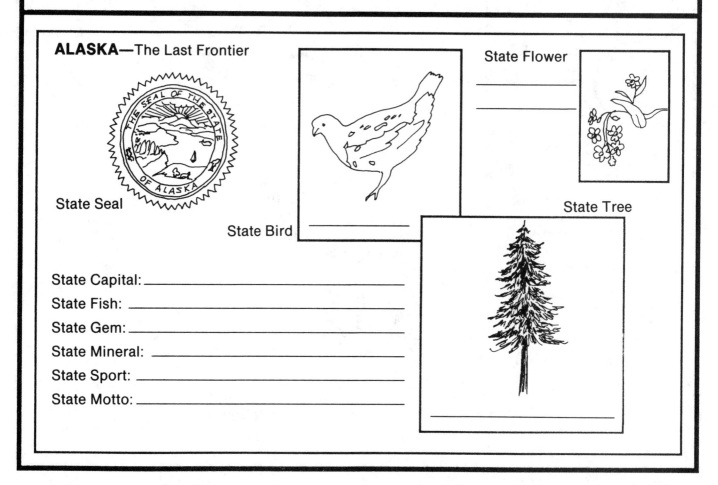

ALASKA—The Last Frontier

State Seal

State Bird

State Flower

State Tree

State Capital: _____

State Fish: _____

State Gem: _____

State Mineral: _____

State Sport: _____

State Motto: _____

8

ALASKA ON THE MAP

KATMAI NATIONAL MONUMENT

Draw in these national parks on your outline map:

Denali National Park
Glacier Bay National Park
Katmai National Park
Klondike Gold Rush National Historical Park
Sitka National Historical Park

Draw in these national forests, monuments and wildlife refuge:

Chugach National Forest
Tongass National Forest
Admiralty Island National Monument

Arctic National Wildlife Refuge
Misty Fjords National Monument

Trace the paths of the following:

Trans-Alaska Pipeline
Alaska Marine Highway System
Alaska Highway

Locate these mountain ranges with symbols (/\/\/\):

Brooks Range
Alaska Range
Aleutian Range
Talkeetna Mountains

Locate these rivers and bodies of water:

Yukon River
Kuskokwim River
Prince William Sound
Arctic Ocean

Gulf of Alaska
Norton Sound
Prudhoe Bay
Bristol Bay

Locate these peaks:

Mt. McKinley
Mt. Katmai
Mt. St. Elias

Locate these cities:

Juneau
Fairbanks
Anchorage

Barrow
Valdez
Sitka

Ketchikan
Nome
Kodiak

GA1138

TOTEM POLES

The totem pole is a document in cedar with the story carved on the totem being nothing more than a decoration. The pole or post was carved, painted with totems and often erected in front of the dwellings of Indian tribes in northwestern North America. The story behind the totems and their significance is one well worth looking into. Find out what you can about the totem pole from other sources; then look at each statement below. Some are true; others are false. Based on your research, answer each as true or false, and be prepared to tell what is incorrect about those you feel are untrue.

1. _____ Contrary to popular belief, Alaska totems have no religious significance.

2. _____ The "potlatch" is a ceremony important to the Alaskan Indians.

3. _____ Christian teachings supported totem poles, because they symbolized pagan worship.

4. _____ The coast Indian used the pole to record business dealings.

5. _____ Totems were often painted bright colors with mineral paints.

6. _____ Totem poles were registered and standardized to a maximum height of 8 feet.

7. _____ Most family totems were the creation of the family member with the greatest artistic talent.

8. _____ The memorial pole was erected for the deceased chief as a monument to his memory.

9. _____ People who could not afford totem poles often painted family crests on the fronts of their homes.

10. _____ A "shame" pole was erected to discredit someone who broke his word or behaved badly.

11. _____ Totem poles were "read" from the bottom of the pole to the top.

12. _____ In Indian lore the eagle is found on most carvings as a symbol of the creator of man and daylight.

13. _____ An oval design symbolized spirit and power.

14. _____ Various symbols were the exclusive property of clans and families and often immortalized heroes.

15. _____ The Haida Indians were outstanding carvers who lived in the Queen Charlotte Islands and in the southern areas of Prince of Wales Island.

16. _____ The actual placing of the pole in the ground was accompanied by feasts and lavish entertaining and partying by the owners.

Add more statements in the space below which you feel are important statements to make about totem poles.

BLACK GOLD

For many years after the gold rush of 1898, gold was Alaska's most important mineral source of income. This all changed with the discovery of oil in Alaska's Kenai Peninsula-Cook Inlet in 1957, which touched off further exploration that led to the discovery of the vast oil fields of Prudhoe Bay. Because of the tremendous quantities available there, it became important to transport the crude oil in something other than tankers. The result was the Trans-Alaska Pipeline—a testament to man's desire to achieve the impossible. The 48-inch pipe extends 800 miles from Prudhoe Bay to Valdez. The cost was almost $1900 per foot! It takes six days for oil to complete its journey. Oil has become so important to the economy of Alaska that it now accounts for ninety percent of the state's revenue. Sixty-three million gallons of crude oil are pumped through the pipeline daily. Careful monitoring of the system has

done little to upset the delicate balance of nature there. In fact the pipeline is high enough in places to allow caribou to pass under it, proving that man and nature can and do coexist in harmony.

However in early 1989 an incident occurred off the coast of Alaska that caused serious damage to the environment and brought on a new wave of protest from environmentalists and those who question man's ability to exploit resources without spoiling nature and the land. Investigate this incident and report the implications of what happened below. Reflect also on what you think should be done to ensure that this type of "accident" (and others similar) does not happen ever again. Do not lose sight of what oil has done for the economy of Alaska.

GA1138

FOR FURTHER RESEARCH. . .

Expand on the information provided below by further researching each of the topics. Then write down three statements below each which you consider useful and important information.

THE FIRST ALASKANS

Anthropologists now believe that most of Alaska's native peoples were descendents of nomadic hunters who crossed into North America from Siberia on a land bridge that no longer exists. These first Alaskans developed into three distinctive groups: Eskimos, Aleuts and Indians.

_____

_____

_____

LIVING IN ALASKA

Although few visitors to Alaska still expect to find Alaskans living in igloos and riding on dogsleds, many are surprised to discover that Alaskan life is much like it is in the continental United States.

_____

_____

_____

TRAVEL IN ALASKA

Towering mountains, glaciers and the wide expanses of wilderness make traveling in Alaska somewhat of a problem. Travel by car is less than satisfactory because there are not enough "paved miles" to link all points of interest. But there are several alternatives that help to overcome these natural barriers and make travel in Alaska a pleasurable experience.

_____

_____

_____

SEWARD'S FOLLY

William H. Seward, Secretary of State under Presidents Abraham Lincoln and Andrew Johnson, offered Russia $7,200,000 for Alaska following the Civil War. The offer was accepted, but many Americans criticized the purchase.

_____

_____

_____

GA1138

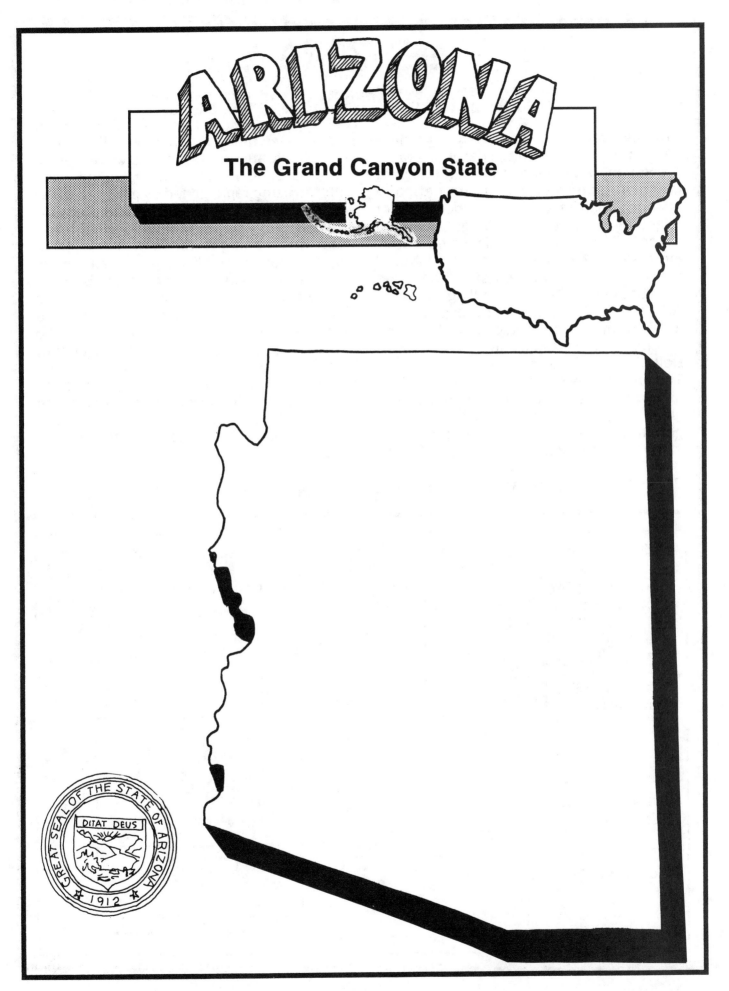

ARIZONA

The Grand Canyon State

DITAT DEUS

GREAT SEAL OF THE STATE OF ARIZONA

1912

13

ARIZONA
THE GRAND CANYON STATE

Arizona was once considered nothing much more than worthless desert. Its rapid growth in population and trend toward modern technology has dramatically changed that image. The rugged frontier image of the Wild West has given way to air conditioning and sophisticated watering systems that make Arizona a delightful place in which to live and visit. With Florida and southern California filling up fast, Arizona has in recent years experienced a flood of retired persons seeking the comfortable life associated with the Sun Belt. The populations of Phoenix and Tucson have been increasing so fast that many communities surrounding these cities have risen almost overnight. Such growth is never without its problems and in the case of Arizona the shortage of avail-able water ranks number one. Even with the dams and rivers and efficient use of underground water, more is being used than is being replenished by nature. It takes a tremendous amount of water daily to sustain such life and growth in the desert and adding huge numbers of people to these areas only makes the problem worse. During the 1800's gold and silver brought people to Arizona, but the ghost towns that dot the landscape remind us that those minerals are no longer a factor in the Arizona economy. In their place copper and oil have taken over as the mineral wealth of today. As technology continues to advance, Arizona should serve as an excellent example of man overcoming nature and turning it into a thriving environment.

Please familiarize yourself with these Arizona symbols before proceeding.

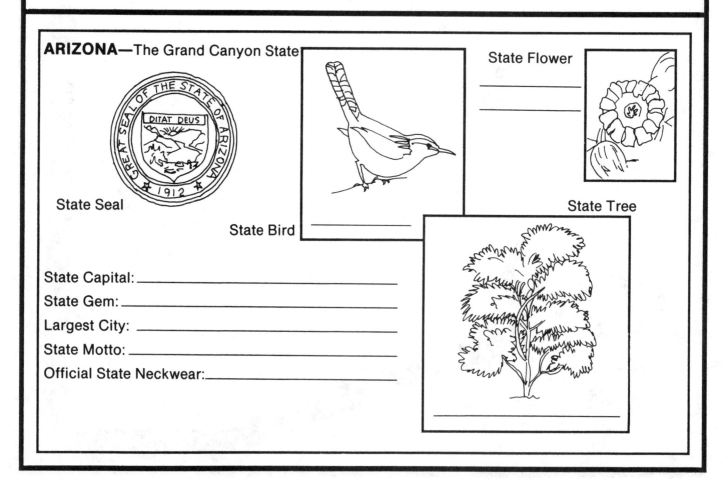

ARIZONA—The Grand Canyon State

State Seal

State Bird

State Flower

State Tree

State Capital: _____

State Gem: _____

Largest City: _____

State Motto: _____

Official State Neckwear: _____

14

ARIZONA HIGHLIGHTS

MONTEZUMA CASTLE NATIONAL MONUMENT

Below is a map of the various regions of Arizona as defined by the Arizona Department of Tourism. Roughly define each section on your outline map and label with a map pencil. Then find the following highlights of Arizona and place each in its proper location on your outline map.

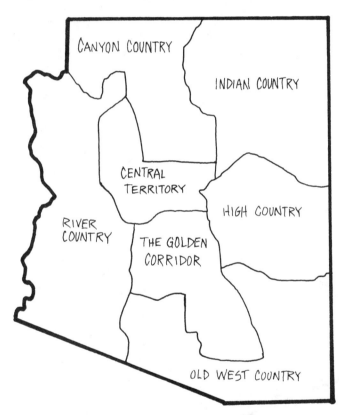

CANYON COUNTRY

INDIAN COUNTRY

CENTRAL TERRITORY

HIGH COUNTRY

RIVER COUNTRY

THE GOLDEN CORRIDOR

OLD WEST COUNTRY

Grand Canyon National Park
Kaibab National Forest
Canyon de Chelly National Monument
Oraibi
Painted Desert
Petrified Forest National Park
Besh-Ba-Gowah Ruins
Mogollon Rim
Lost Dutchman Gold Mine

Saguaro National Monument
Tumacacori National Monument
Organ Pipe Cactus National Monument
London Bridge
Colorado River
Yuma Territorial Prison
Prescott National Forest
Tombstone

GA1138

NATIVE INDIANS

Arizona has the largest American population of any of our states. Indian reservations occupy a large percentage of the state's land area. Evidence dates Indians occupying this land as far back as 25,000 years ago. The Indian heritage is very important to the Arizona culture of today. Below is a map that outlines the Indian reservations found in Arizona today. Find out the Indians that occupy each reservation and label appropriately.

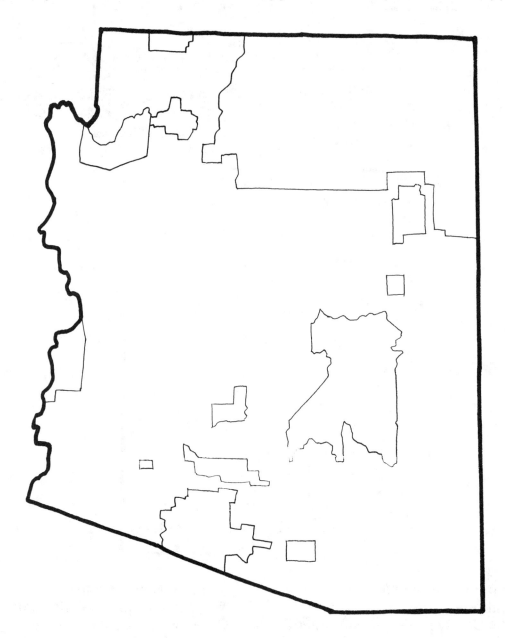

When you are finished, choose one of particular interest to you and find out all you can about that reservation. Include values, cultural beliefs, sources of income, methods used to educate children, foods and anything else you feel of interest to others. Share your findings with your class.

16

CITY CROSS

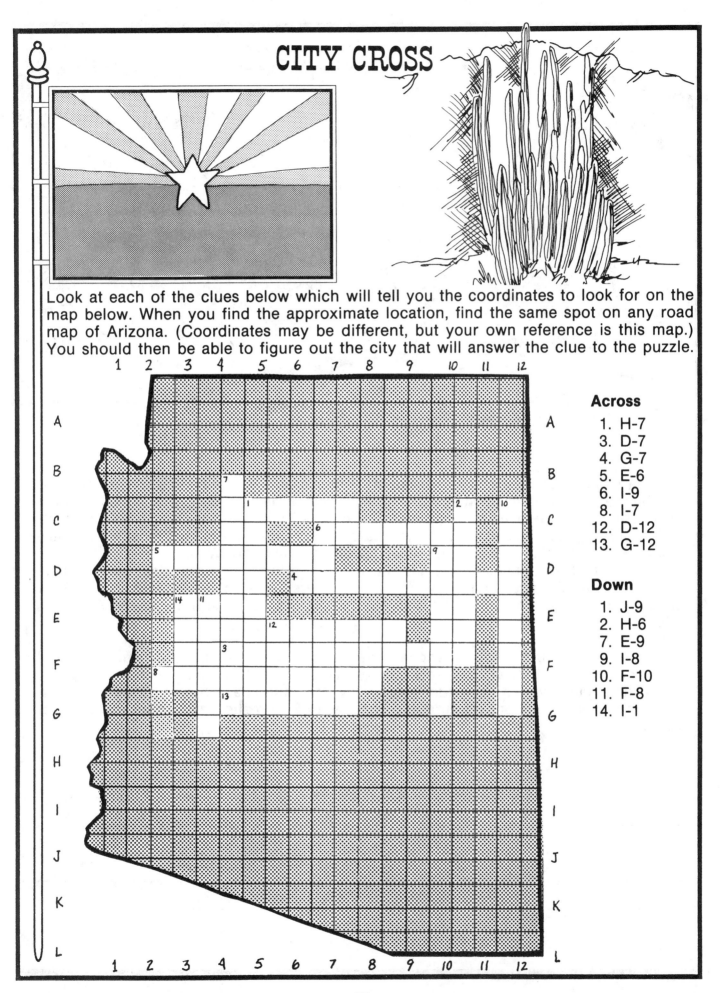

Look at each of the clues below which will tell you the coordinates to look for on the map below. When you find the approximate location, find the same spot on any road map of Arizona. (Coordinates may be different, but your own reference is this map.) You should then be able to figure out the city that will answer the clue to the puzzle.

Across

1. H-7
3. D-7
4. G-7
5. E-6
6. I-9
8. I-7
12. D-12
13. G-12

Down

1. J-9
2. H-6
7. E-9
9. I-8
10. F-10
11. F-8
14. I-1

17

GA1138

A GROWING OASIS

Arizona stands out as a shining example of man's ability to alter his environment to suit his needs and convenience. What was once worthless desert now contains some of America's most expensive real estate. An oasis of green amidst the rocks and sand of the burning desert, Arizona's growth rate is currently attracting thousands of new residents and tourists every year. How did all this happen? Water. Water is there to sustain life and make plants grow and make living in the desert a pleasant experience. Where does it all come from? How does it get there? How much water is used? What does it cost? What problems does it create? How does water hold the key to Arizona's future?

To answer these and other questions, investigate the water supply in Arizona. Read facts and statistics that will arm you with knowledge about Arizona's water supply. Jot down those statistics you consider most relevant in the space below. Draw your own conclusions about Arizona's future and share your information with other members of your class.

_____

_____

_____

_____

_____

_____

_____

GA1138

ARKANSAS

The Land of Opportunity

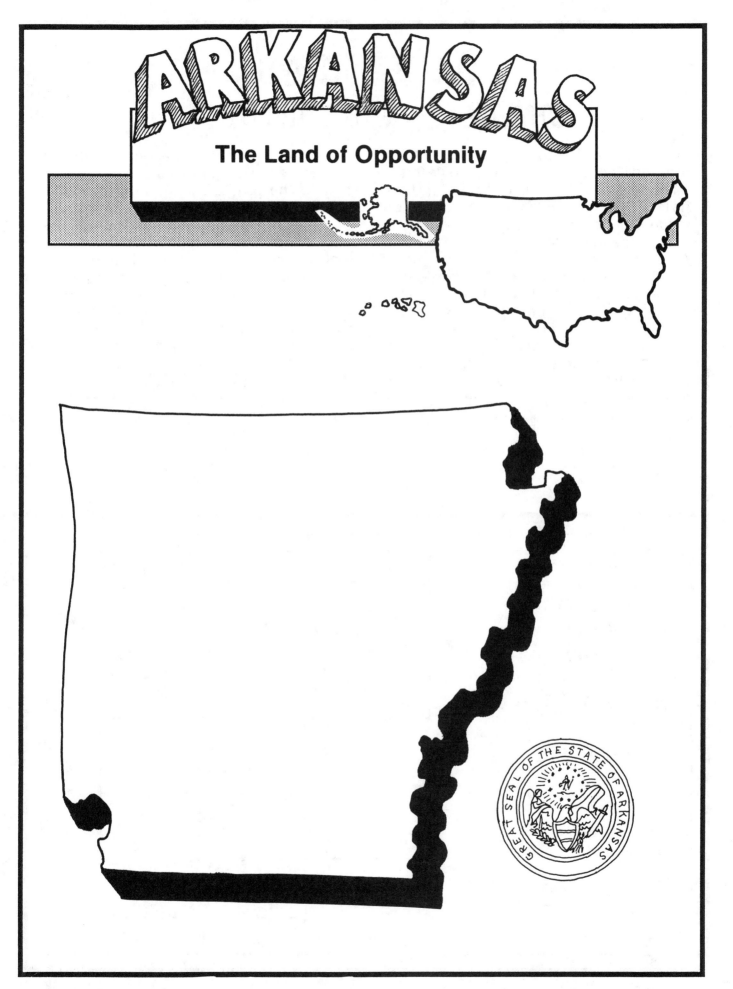

19

GA1138

ARKANSAS
THE LAND OF OPPORTUNITY

From the Ozark and Ouachita Mountains through its thick forests and on to its fertile plain, Arkansas is indeed a beautiful state. Its less-than-favorable economic condition is the product of its past, a time when the state depended almost totally on cotton. As a result, there was no focus on other resources. Cotton was king and little else mattered. But the boll weevil and a changing market caused the people of Arkansas to shift their attention elsewhere. Bauxite became important and Arkansas today remains a major supplier of the nation's demand. Farmers began to plant soybeans and rice, and they raised poultry. The production of coal, oil and natural gas be- gan to boost the state's economy, and its hardwood and pine forests became impor- tant to the furniture and wood products industries. The scenic beauty of its moun- tains began to attract thousands of visitors annually adding millions of dollars to the state's economy. But these changes were slow in coming, and the reluctance of many to accept school desegregation placed restraints on the state's progress. Arkansas today is working hard to build a more pluralistic, balanced society. Its current rank of 48th in income per capita suggests it has a long way to go, but its people have hopes for a more economically sound future.

Research the following symbols of Arkansas:

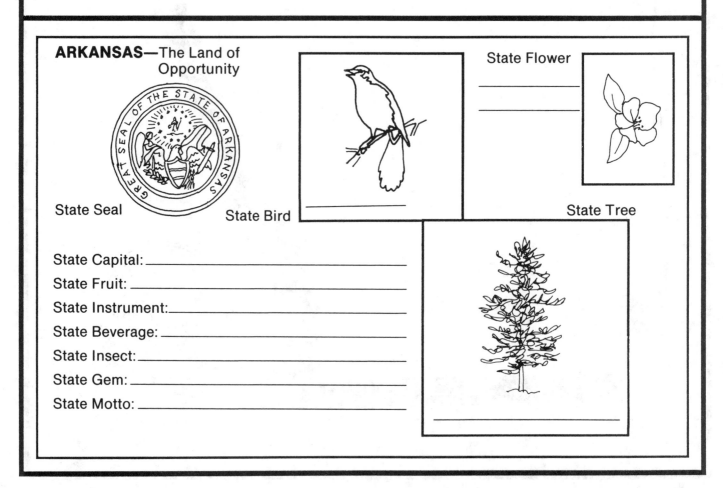

ARKANSAS—The Land of Opportunity

State Seal

State Bird

State Flower

State Tree

State Capital: _____

State Fruit: _____

State Instrument: _____

State Beverage: _____

State Insect: _____

State Gem: _____

State Motto: _____

GA1138

FUN IN ARKANSAS

Every state spends thousand of dollars annually on advertising that will lure tourists into spending their vacations and their dollars. Arkansas is no exception. There seems to be "something for everyone." Several of these attractions are cited below. Pinpoint them on your outline map and decide which three would be most important to you if you were to plan a trip to Arkansas and plan your trip on another sheet of paper. Share with other members of your class.

Shiloh Museum—preserving the rich history of northwest Arkansas, containing over 60,000 artifacts and 30,000 carefully preserved photos

Ozark National Forest—camping and fishing in one of our national forests

Fort Smith National Historic Site—the courtroom and gallows of Isaac Parker, "The Hanging Judge"

Ouachita National Forest—one of Arkansas' most popular vacation destinations includes Lake Ouachita

Talimena Scenic Drive—crosses the peaks of the scenic Ouachita Mountains on into Oklahoma

Crater of Diamonds State Park—the only place in North America where visitors can hunt through the soil and play "finders' keepers."

Texarkana—On Photographer's Island you can stand in two states at once.

Mountain Village—(near Bull Shoals) restored village of life as it was in 1890, including arts and crafts

Buffalo National River—America's first national river features 150-mile stretch popular with canoeists and campers.

Little Rock—Arkansas' state capital plus several historic sites and a zoo, the "hub" of Arkansas

Hot Springs National Park—Arkansas' vacation capital, includes a Hot Springs Resort, Historic Bathhouse Row and Magic Springs Family Attraction

Arkansas Traveler Folk Theater—19th century food and entertainment and whimsical tale of Arkansas Traveler in outdoor ampitheater

St. Francis National Forest—a wide variety of plants and wildlife

Blanchard Springs Caverns—spelunkers' paradise, often called the "cave find of the century"

Eureka Springs—Victorian resort high in the Ozarks, includes Passion Play, Beaver Lake, museums and country music

Ozark Folk Center—(Mountain View) Arkansas' largest collection of authentic working craftspeople and musicians

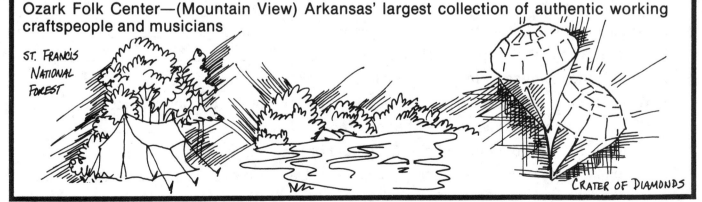

ST. FRANCIS NATIONAL FOREST

CRATER OF DIAMONDS

GA1138

CAPITAL TO CAPITAL

Below is a map of the United States that shows the locations of all the state capitals in the contiguous United States. You will also find the indicated distance of each capital from Little Rock, the capital of Arkansas. Look at the map and the list; then answer the questions that follow.

MILES FROM STATE CAPITALS TO LITTLE ROCK, ARKANSAS

AL—Montgomery - 475
AZ—Phoenix - 1325
CA—Sacramento - 2063
CO—Denver - 941
CT—Hartford - 1340
DE—Dover 1105
DC—Washington - 1011
FL—Tallahassee - 679
GA—Atlanta - 552
ID—Boise - 1769
IL—Springfield - 452
IN—Indianapolis - 609

IA—Des Moines - 560
KS—Topeka - 456
KY—Frankfort - 553
LA—Baton Rouge - 374
ME—Augusta - 1720
MD—Annapolis - 1043
MA—Boston - 1438
MI—Lansing - 750
MN—St. Paul - 818
MS—Jackson - 264
MO—Jefferson City - 355
MT—Helena - 1728

NE—Lincoln - 602
NV—Carson City - 1952
NH—Concord - 1550
NJ—Trenton - 1078
NM—Santa Fe - 873
NY—Albany - 1357
NC—Raleigh - 901
ND—Bismarck - 1318
OH—Columbus - 734
OK—Oklahoma City - 344
OR—Salem - 2186
PA—Harrisburg - 1091

RI—Providence 1369
SC—Columbia - 759
SD—Pierre - 998
TN—Nashville -346
TX—Austin - 477
UT—Salt Lake City - 1438
VT—Montpelier - 1539
VA—Richmond - 952
WA—Olympia - 2303
WV—Charleston - 730
WI—Madison - 719
WY—Cheyenne - 1065

1. Which state capital is farthest from Little Rock? _____

2. Which capital is closest to Little Rock? _____

3. How far away is Providence? _____

4. How far is it from Harrisburg to Little Rock? _____

5. Which city is the second longest in distance from Little Rock? _____

6. Which capital is the second closest in distance from Little Rock? _____

7. How far away is the capital of New Jersey? _____

8. What is the distance from Little Rock to the capital of Texas? _____

9. Which is closer to Little Rock—the capital of Nevada or the capital of Arizona? _____

10. Which is closer to Little Rock—Charleston or St. Paul? _____

11. Which is farther from Little Rock—Columbia or Lincoln? _____

12. Which is farther from Little Rock—Nashville or Des Moines? _____

GA1138

ARKANSAS AGRICULTURE

The chart below provides information on the importance of agriculture in Arkansas during a recent year. Look at the information in the chart and decide whether the statements that follow are true or false. Put T or F in each blank.

Commodity Crops	Rank	Annual Production	Unit	Commodity Truck Crops	Rank	Annual Production	Unit
Rice	1	55,120,000	Cwt.	Snap beans	9	4000	Ton
Sorghum, grain	5	40,920,000	Bu.	Tomatoes	10	400,000	Cwt.
Cotton, all	6	602,000	Bale/Lb.	Strawberries	13	1,800,000	Lb.
Cottonseed	6	228,000	Ton				
Soybeans	8	69,300,000	Bu.	**Livestock & Poultry**			
Wheat, all	16	31,980,000	Bu.	Commercial broilers	1	786,779,000	No.
Oats	22	2,211,000	Bu.	Farm chickens	4	24,382,000	No.
Hay, all	27	1,945,000	Ton	Turkeys, raised	4	16,500,000	No.
Corn, grain	32	8,480,000	Bu.	Eggs	6	3,731,000,000	No.
				Hogs & pigs	17	460,000	Head
Fruits & Nuts				Cattle & calves	21	1,840,000	Head
Grapes	8	6000	Ton	Milk	35	755,000,000	Lb.
Pecans, all	11	1,250,000	Lb.				
Peaches	19	9,500,000	Lb.				
Apples, commercial	29	10,000,000	Lb.				

Source: University of Arkansas, Crop and Livestock Reporting Service: *1986 Arkansas Agricultural Statistics.*

1. _____ The production of milk is not as important in Arkansas as is pecans.

2. _____ Arkansas leads the nation in growing rice.

3. _____ There were more bushels of wheat grown than bushels of soybeans.

4. _____ Commerical broilers rank higher on Arkansas' list than turkeys.

5. _____ There were 12,000 pounds of grapes grown.

6. _____ There were more bushels of oats grown than corn and grain.

7. _____ Peaches ranked higher than tomatoes.

8. _____ Over 300,000,000 dozens of eggs were laid by Arkansas hens.

9. _____ Snap beans rank highest on Arkansas' list of truck crops.

10. _____ There were more hogs and pigs than cattle and cows.

11. _____ Over half the nation's states grow more apples than Arkansas.

12. _____ Cotton remains "king" in Arkansas.

13. _____ There were more pounds of strawberries grown than apples.

14. _____ Farm chickens and turkeys held the same rank in importance.

15. _____ Pecans are more important to Arkansas than apples.

16. _____ There were more pounds of peaches than strawberries.

17. _____ Sorghum and grain ranked higher than turkeys.

18. _____ There were more bushels of soybeans grown than bushels of anything else.

19. _____ Arkansas ranks in the top third of the nation in the production of cattle and hogs.

20. _____ Arkansas ranks in the top ten percent of states growing snap beans.

GA1138

TRAIL OF TEARS

One of the events in the story of America which most Americans regard as a shameful deed is the Trail of Tears. A part of this tragedy took place in northern Arkansas. Even though we're not proud of some of the things that have happened, it is important to learn about them nonetheless—because they are, after all, a part of the whole story of America. Research the history behind the Trail of Tears. Why did it happen? Who was responsible? What was the *justification*? Who was most affected? How would you have felt if you had been one of the Indians forced to leave his home? Trace the story behind the tragedy and record your findings and feelings below.

TRAIL of TEARS

GA1138

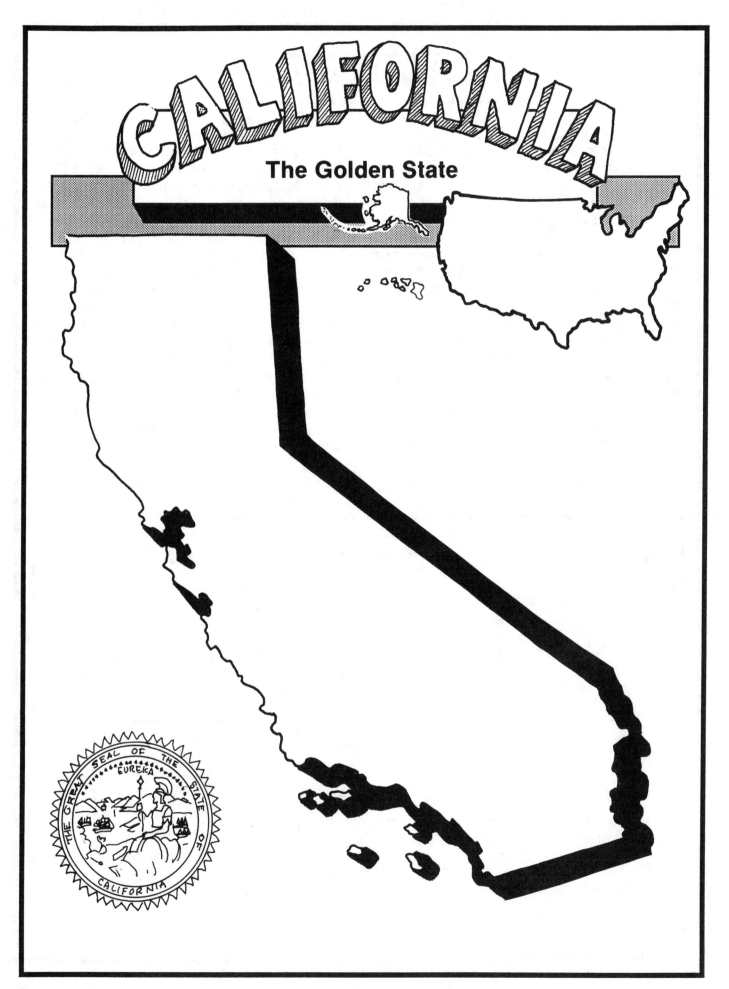

CALIFORNIA

The Golden State

25

CALIFORNIA
THE GOLDEN STATE

More people live in California than any other state. It is the third largest of our states in area with over 158,000 square miles. It stretches from north to south nearly 1000 miles and from east to west between 150 and 350 miles. It is a land with the tallest mountain in the contiguous United States (Mt. Whitney, 14,494 ft.) and the lowest point in the Western Hemisphere (Death Valley, 282 feet below sea level). More goods are produced in California than in any other state. The state is also the leader in agriculture. Lacking the resources needed for heavy industrial manufacturing, California has taken giant strides in the expansion of high technology industry. The Silicon Valley is the microchip and transistor capital of the world.

California functions almost as though it is a nation within a nation. The rugged Cascade Mountains lie across northern California with the mighty Sierra Nevadas along the east and the less severe Coast Range on the west. They form the perimeter of the long and fertile Central Valley, which makes up approximately one-fourth of the state. To the south lie the arid deserts of the Great Basin. Water continues to be California's major problem. Without enough water to support the megalopolis that is southern California, the state is constantly in search of additional sources. Its wealth of diverse wildlife, national parks, sun-drenched beaches and delightful climate make it a favorite for millions of tourists annually.

Before you begin your study of the Golden State, familiarize yourself with these symbols:

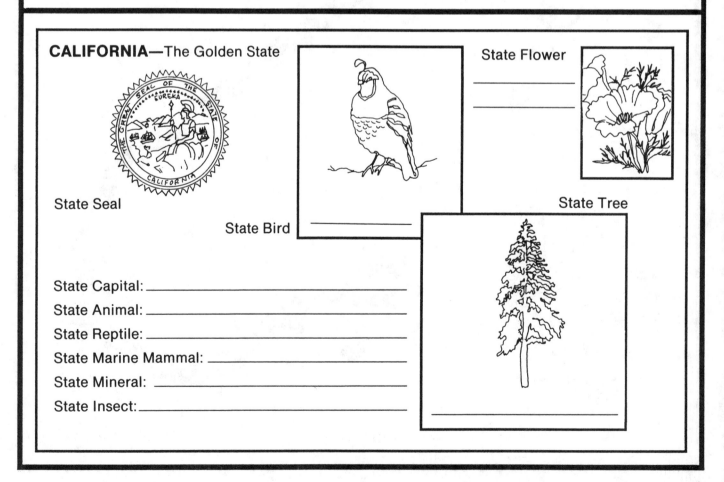

CALIFORNIA—The Golden State

State Seal

State Bird _____

State Flower
_____
_____

State Tree

State Capital: _____

State Animal: _____

State Reptile: _____

State Marine Mammal: _____

State Mineral: _____

State Insect: _____

_____

GA1138

CALIFORNIA DREAMIN'

Of all the fifty states, none is more popular as a vacation choice than California. From its redwood forests to its snow-capped mountains to its sun-splashed beaches to its many man-made attractions, California is a wonderland with something for everyone. With six national parks and twenty-two national forests, California is also a paradise for wildlife and nature lovers as well. The nearly perfect climate adds a final touch that makes it irresistible to millions of tourists annually. Below is a list of several of the "main attractions." Plot the location of each on your outline map of California.

Lake Tahoe
Disneyland
Knott's Berry Farm
Death Valley National Monument
Hanna-Barbera's Marineland
San Diego Zoo
Great America
San Simeon
Redwood Highway (U.S. 101)
These national parks:
    Channel Islands
    Kings Canyon
    Lassen Volcanic
    Redwood
    Sequoia
    Yosemite
Muir Woods National Monument
Pinnacles National Monument
Lava Beds National Monument
Napa Valley
Sutter's Mill
Big Sur
Monterey Peninsula
Squaw Valley
Fisherman's Wharf
Rose Bowl
Hollywood
Golden Gate Bridge
Locate three of California's national forests.
Locate any two of the twenty-one Spanish missions.
Locate three of California's famous beaches.

Golden Gate Bridge

When you've finished locating all of the above, decide where you would like to take your family on a two-weeks *dream* vacation to California. Include the time it will take to get there and to return home again. While you're in California, you will have to choose those attractions you feel would be most enjoyed by your family.

You obviously can't see it all. Include an itinerary of your trip and approximately what such a trip would cost.

GA1138

CALIFORNIA ON THE MOVE

Over twenty million people live over the boundary line that separates the two tectonic plates that make up the San Andreas Fault. These plates lie deep within the surface of the earth. One of the plates is called the North American Plate, and the other is the Pacific Plate. The land where the two plates meet is known as the San Andreas Fault.

1. Explain what causes an earthquake.

_____

_____

_____

2. What precautions have been taken by those who live on the San Andreas Fault?

_____

_____

_____

3. Investigate and summarize the horrible earthquake that destroyed much of San Francisco in 1906.

_____

_____

_____

4. When do seismologists predict that the next big earthquake in California will occur?

_____

_____

GA1138

THE CALIFORNIA MISSIONS

In 1769 Father Junipero Serra, the Apostle of California, traveled with a land expedition under the leadership of Governor Gaspar de Pirtola from Lower California to San Diego. The purpose of the mission was to establish missions where they could Christianize and civilize the Indians, who were taught to pray, to work, to worship and to follow the Spanish way of life. Under the direction of the Spanish overseers, the Indians did most of the work building the missions and presidios. The first of these missions was called San Diego de Alcala—near present-day San Diego. By 1823 the gray-robed Franciscans had established twenty other missions stretching as far north as Sonoma, north of San Francisco. They were connected by El Camino Real, California's first highway. The work at each mission included farming, weaving, tailoring, blacksmithing and carpentry. Conversion among the Indians was voluntary. However once the Indians became Christians, they were required by Spanish law to live at the missions. Their love to roam the forest, the regular hours imposed upon them and their fear of catching the diseases of white men made life far less than happy for the Indians. Some became ill and died. Many persons in California and Mexico wanted the missions broken up, and by 1833 the missions had been secularized. Mission lands were sold or given away to the *rancheros*, some of which became quite wealthy as a result.

Below is a listing of the locations of those twenty-one missions. Pinpoint the location of each on the outline map provided to you by your teacher.

San Diego
Carmel
Jolon
San Gabriel
San Luis Obispo
San Francisco
San Juan Capistrano
Santa Clara
Ventura
Santa Barbara
Lompoc
Santa Cruz (replica)
Soledad (partially restored)
Fremont
San Juan
San Miguel
San Fernando
Oceanside
Solvang
San Rafael (replica)
Sonoma

GA1138

C-A-L-I-F-O-R-N-I-A BRAINSTORMS

California is indeed a land of *many*— it has many people, it produces many products and it has many resources and natural (as well as man-made) wonders. Spend one minute (timed by your teacher) on each of the letters in the word *CALIFORNIA* brainstorming products, words, foods, attractions, people, whatever that start with the letter. When the signal is given (at the end of a minute) move on to the next letter. When you've gone through each letter of the word, spend time in class sharing your choices. How many did you come up with for each letter? Collectively, which letter provided the most words?

C _____

A _____

L _____

I _____

F _____

O _____

R _____

N _____

I _____

A _____

GA1138

COLORADO

The Centennial State

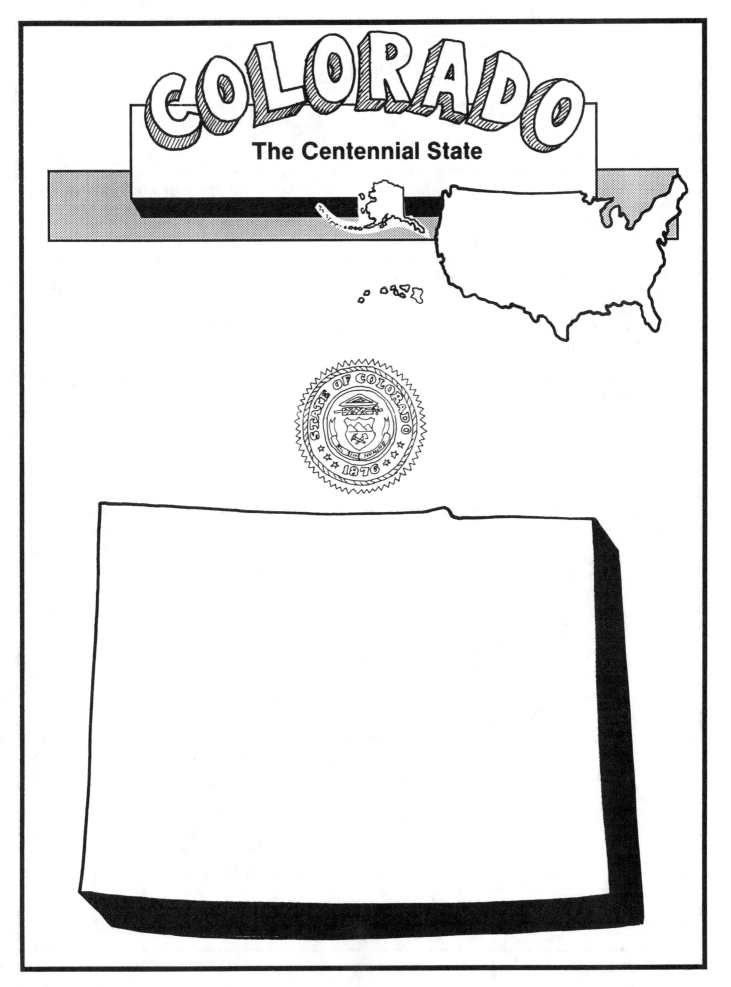

31

COLORADO
THE CENTENNIAL STATE

The delightful climate of Colorado has made it one of the fastest growing states in the United States. With almost 300 days of sunshine annually, it has become a land of enchantment for those who worship the sun as well as a paradise for skiers. Colorado is known as the "Top of the Nation" because it contains more than seventy-five percent of the area in the United States that is over 10,000 feet. It has fifty-three peaks over 14,000 feet in altitude and over one thousand peaks over two miles high. Its low humidity average of thirty-three percent creates a very desirable environment in which to live. Its diversified economy includes the manufacture of electronic instruments, steel, film, rubber products, space equipment and much more. Tourism, agriculture and mining are also very important to Colorado. Its capital city of Denver serves as the commercial, financial and retail headquarters for the Great Plains and Rocky Mountains.

To begin your study of Colorado, research its state emblems and jot down your findings in the space provided by each.

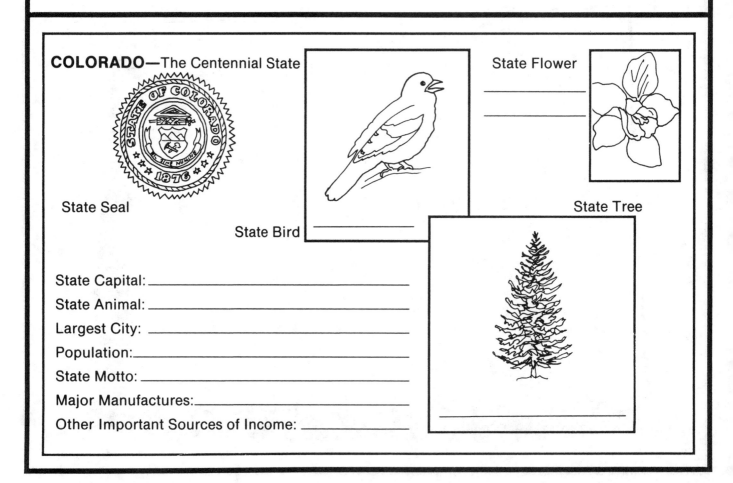

COLORADO—The Centennial State

State Seal

State Flower

_____

_____

State Bird _____

State Tree

State Capital: _____

State Animal: _____

Largest City: _____

Population: _____

State Motto: _____

Major Manufactures: _____

Other Important Sources of Income: _____

GA1138

FUN AT THE TOP

VULCAN'S ANVIL

THE BALANCED ROCK

Recreation has long been one of Colorado's most important sources of income. About one third of Colorado is owned by the people of the United States. There are national forests and two national recreation areas under control of the U.S. Forest Service. The National Park Service has jurisdiction over the two national parks listed below as well as the six national monuments, national historic site and national recreation area. Find each in an atlas and locate on your outline map of Colorado.

Rocky Mountain National Park—over 400 square miles of scenic splendor along the Continental Divide

Colorado National Monument—18,000-acre amphitheater displaying nature's finest work in deep red sandstone

Florissant Fossil Beds National Monument—fossilized impressions of insects and leaves preserved by volcanic ashfalls for over 30 million years

Mesa Verde National Park—artifacts and ruins of the Anasazi Indians of more than 800 years ago

Dinosaur National Monument—fossilized remains of prehistoric creatures more than 140 million years ago

Black Canyon of the Gunnison National Monument—deep canyon plunges to a depth of 2800 feet, narrows to 40 feet at its narrowest point of the riverbed

Great Sand Dunes National Monument—Nestled against the base of the Sangre de Cristo Mountains, the dunes are constantly changing shapes.

Bent's Old Fort National Historic Site—reconstructed adobe fur-trading post, Indian rendezvous, way station and military staging base on the Santa Fe Trail

Hovenweep National Monument—ruins of pre-Columbian Pueblo Indians

Curecanti National Recreation Area—three large reservoirs which stretch for more than 40 miles along the Gunnison River

GARDEN OF THE GODS

In addition, pinpoint the locations of these Colorado cities: Denver, Ft. Collins, Colorado Springs, Durango, Grand Junction, Gunnison, Pueblo, Boulder.

GA1138

COLORADO'S HISTORY

Below are several events that were important in shaping the history of Colorado. The order in which they occurred is all mixed up. Find out at what point in history each took place. Then place them in chronological order from 1 to 9 in the blank spaces provided.

_____ President Lincoln signed legislation creating Colorado Territory.

_____ Captain Zebulon Pike sighted the peak that bears his name.

_____ Colorado entered into the Union on August 1.

_____ Days of the Anasazi Indian civilization

_____ Exploration of Spaniards looking for gold

_____ Founding of San Luis, Colorado's oldest continually occupied town

_____ Mountain men like Kit Carson, Jim Baker, the Bent brothers and Uncle Dick Wootton blazed many a trail in the Rocky Mountains.

_____ Exaggerated reports of the discovery of gold caused Pikes Peak Gold Rush.

_____ Colorado's mining industry flourished bringing thousands of permanent settlers into Leadville/Aspen area.

From your research of the above order of events, jot down four facts about the historical incident that interests you most in the space below and share them with other members of your class.

_____

_____

_____

_____

_____

_____

_____

_____

_____

_____

GA1138

FAMOUS SONS AND DAUGHERS

Colorado has distinguished itself with many famous sons and daughters. Several are hidden in the word search below. Find each of the names in the list by moving your pencil in any direction—forward, in reverse, diagonally or vertically. You can even go around corners.

```
J  C  A  R  P  E  N  T  E  R  A  M  L  S  T  E  I  M  L  Y  O
M  T  R  B  I  B  D  C  P  U  E  W  S  Q  U  T  N  A  M  I  L
B  T  J  O  Y  U  B  B  N  W  O  R  B  Y  L  L  O  M  E  U  G
A  O  U  Y  C  F  O  G  R  O  U  C  H  O  M  I  K  I  N  P  E
B  C  P  E  Q  F  X  E  J  A  M  E  S  M  I  C  H  E  N  E  R
E  S  C  S  T  A  R  E  U  A  L  C  J  A  Z  O  L  E  D  G  D
D  N  G  P  I  L  N  K  D  A  N  C  E  R  T  U  S  I  W  G  R
I  O  R  M  E  O  S  I  Y  M  D  E  F  X  G  J  E  S  Z  Y  O
D  O  N  E  D  B  I  T  C  A  R  S  O  N  F  R  R  E  D  F  F
R  N  F  D  E  I  T  Y  O  H  J  I  M  P  Q  D  E  N  I  L  D
I  O  T  K  R  L  H  A  L  E  I  R  W  I  N  E  V  H  A  E  L
K  I  X  C  D  L  N  B  L  E  E  T  R  E  V  I  N  O  T  M  A
S  E  M  A  T  C  M  R  I  R  S  H  O  I  U  W  E  W  C  I  R
O  E  R  J  Y  O  D  Y  N  A  N  Y  J  O  H  N  D  E  O  N  E
N  Z  A  H  A  R  I  A  S  D  W  Y  A  T  T  E  A  R  P  G  G
```

Babe Didrikson Zaharias
John Denver
Judy Collins
Jack Dempsey
Kit Carson
Molly Brown

Lee Trevino
Mamie Eisenhower
Peggy Fleming
Buffalo Bill Cody
James Michener

Groucho Marx
Hale Irwin
Wyatt Earp
Scott Carpenter
Gerald Ford

GA1138

ROCKY MOUNTAIN HIGH

Below is a listing of some of Colorado's mountain peaks taller than 14,000 feet. From the information provided, decide whether each statement is true or false and write your answer in the blank space.

Wilson Peak—14,017
Pikes Peak—14,110
Grays Peak—14,270
Longs Peak—14,256
Sunshine Peak—14,001
Little Bear Peak—14,037
Mt. Massive—14,421
Mt. Lincoln—14,286
Castle Peak—14,265
Mt. Princeton—14,197
Kit Carson Peak—14,165
Mt. Eolus—14,083
LaPlata Peak—14,336
Mt. of the Holy Cross—14,005
Crestone Peak—14,294

Maroon Peak—14,156
Blanca Peak—14,345
Redcloud Peak—14,034
Mt. Elbert—14,433
Pyramid Peak—14,018
Torreys Peak—14,267
Mt. Belford—14,197
Wetterhorn Peak—14,017
Mt. Oxford—14,153
Mt. Wilson—14,246
Snowmass Mountain—14,092
Mt. Bross—14,172
San Luis Peak—14,014
Huron Peak—14,005
Humboldt Peak—14,064

T or F

1. _____ The tallest peak in Colorado is Mt. Massive.

2. _____ Humboldt Peak is taller than Grays Peak.

3. _____ Huron Peak is taller than Mt. of the Holy Cross.

4. _____ Snowmass Mountain is exactly 42 feet shorter than Mt. Wilson.

5. _____ Castle Peak is the same height as another peak in Colorado.

6. _____ Little Bear Peak is only 3 feet taller than Redcloud Peak.

7. _____ Blanca Peak is 327 feet taller than Pyramid Peak.

8. _____ Of the mountains Mt. Wilson, Torreys Peak and Mt. Bross, Mt. Bross is the tallest.

9. _____ Kit Carson Peak is not as tall as Longs Peak, but stands over 100 feet above Humboldt Peak.

10. _____ San Luis Peak stands 9 feet above Huron Peak, but is dwarfed by Mt. Elbert by over 500 feet.

11. _____ Mt. Belford stands 70 feet below Torreys Peak, but the same height as Mt. Princeton.

12. _____ Together Little Bear and Grays Peak are taller than the combination of Maroon Peak and Pyramid Peak.

13. _____ The most majestic mountain in Colorado is over 2½ miles high.

14. _____ The height above sea level of Mt. Princeton, Pikes Peak and Snowmass Mountain together totals more than 8 miles.

15. _____ The combined heights of Longs Peak and Kit Carson Peak and Mt. Eolus is 318 feet greater than the combined heights of Humboldt Peak, Wilson Peak and Mt. of the Holy Cross.

GA1138

CONNECTICUT

The Constitution State

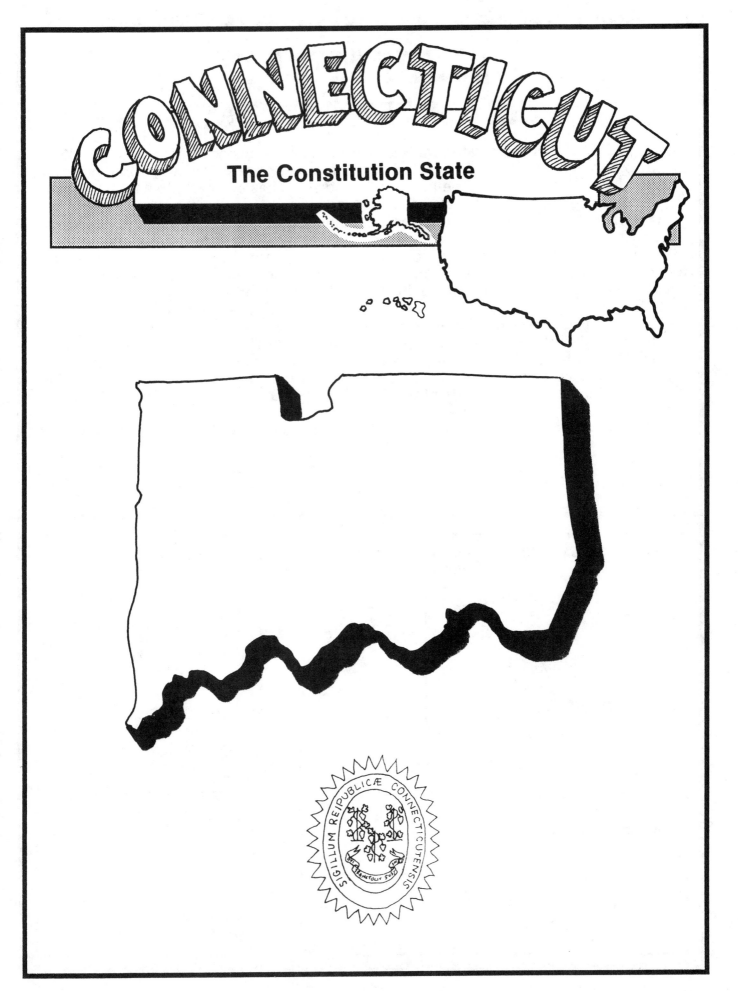

37

GA1138

CONNECTICUT
THE CONSTITUTION STATE

Although Connecticut is smaller than all of our states but two, it is an important industrial state. Its location in the heart of the eastern megalopolis gives it a close tie with both New York City and Boston. Workers can commute easily on the sophisticated network of transportation routes found in the area. Its rural areas contrast sharply with its urbanized communities that dot the state. Over fifty insurance companies have their headquarters in Hartford, making it the insurance capital of the United States. Connecticut played an important role in the early history of the United States and thousands of tour-ists visit the historic sites every year. The state was once completely rural, but over the years has evolved into a highly urbanized society. As has been the case in most other such areas of the nation, the move to the city was then followed in more recent years into the suburban land surrounding the city. Some of the most expensive real estate is found in these suburban areas. Because of this, people in recent years have started to move into the lands between the suburbs and the countryside. Its rank as second in income per capita is evidence enough of healthy economy. The future of Connecticut is bright indeed.

Before beginning your study of Connecticut, become familiar with the information called for below.

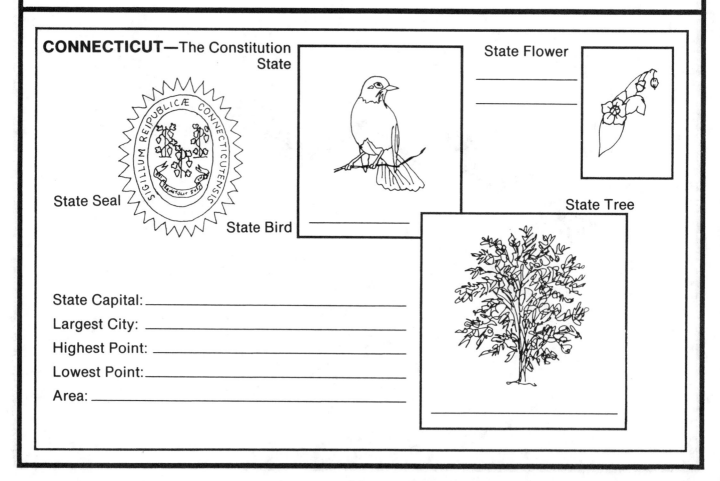

CONNECTICUT—The Constitution State

State Seal

State Bird

State Flower
_____
_____

State Tree

State Capital: _____
Largest City: _____
Highest Point: _____
Lowest Point: _____
Area: _____

GA1138

CONNECTICUT'S HERITAGE

Over 350 years of Connecticut's rich contributions to the early history of Colonial America are on display at many carefully preserved landmarks located throughout the state. Find each of the stops below on a map of Connecticut; then locate on your outline map by placing a dot and the identifying letter in the appropriate location. Place a short identifying statement beside each in the space below.

a. Fort Griswold State Park—Groton

_____

_____

b. Mark Twain Mansion—Hartford

_____

_____

c. Mystic Seaport Museum—Mystic

_____

_____

d. Ye Olde Town Mill—New London

_____

_____

e. Nathan Hale Homestead—Coventry

_____

_____

f. Nathan Hale Schoolhouse—East Haddam

_____

_____

g. Whitfield House Museum—Guilford

_____

_____

h. Stanley-Whitman House—Farmington

_____

_____

i. Nathaniel Hempsted House—New London

_____

_____

j. Pardee-Morris House—New Haven

_____

_____

k. Shoreline Trolley Museum—East Haven

_____

_____

l. Museum of Fife & Drum—Essex

_____

_____

m. Putnam Cottage—Greenwich

_____

_____

n. Jonathan Trumbull House—Lebanon

_____

_____

o. Indian Burial Grounds—Norwich

_____

_____

p. Old Lighthouse Museum—Stonington

_____

_____

q. Joseph Webb House—Wethersfield

_____

_____

r. Glebe House—Woodbury

_____

_____

s. Connecticut Fire Museum—Warehouse Point

_____

_____

t. Benton Homestead—Tolland

_____

_____

GA1138

LOOKING INTO CONNECTICUT

Research the "story" behind each of the statements below and jot down an explanation in the blank space provided.

1. The source of Connecticut's once being nicknamed The Nutmeg State _____
   _____
   _____

2. The reason for Hartford's being known as The Insurance City _____
   _____
   _____

3. Connecticut has been referred to as the Birthplace of Mass Production. _____
   _____
   _____

4. The Connecticut Compromise was the compromise that saved the Constitutional Convention of 1787. For what purpose was it written? Who was the author? What was the eventual result? _____
   _____
   _____

5. Real estate in Connecticut is among the most expensive in the United States. _____
   _____
   _____

6. The reason Connecticut is today nicknamed The Constitution State _____
   _____
   _____

We The People

CONNECTICUT HERO HUNT

Below are hidden the names of twenty people who down through the years have helped to shape the course of Connecticut history. Your problem is that you don't even know who those heroes are. To find out, identify each clue below the word search; then find that hero's name and circle it. Names can go forward or in reverse, both vertically and horizontally.

```
H L F R A N K L I N O D T M O F Y O R F O U R M
A L M A R K T W A I N I A R Y Z J M O K L P M N
R A Y D A E R E T S B E W H A O N P Y V R A E A
R W B L E W S R Y O G C W U P V K E R O M B D N
I N O O Y O I N E L L A N A H T E R O R E M N Y
E I Z N D H M B N R O B E R T I N G E R S O L L
T P Q R O S E I T S U K N F K G I L D I A M O K
B S A A O A O N I O I S R A E L P U T N A M G N
E A R T G I N N H A S A M O H T H T E S R V U D
E L P C S L N I W N A D R I A E N B L O C K D Y
C E M I E E O B I D M N D Q L M O K I O A L A S
H I F D L J R A L S A M U E L C O L T O B S R M
E N O E R K T G E J Y Y A N V A Z L N B W E R Q
R A B N A T H A N H A L E E E P K M O B B F T A
S H A E H L L N A N L R H T R O N S E M A J O M
T T E B C M O I E O C E J T Y R A N C S O T A V
O A T H O M A S H O O K E R O E B I Y O S X T R
W N C T L R O K L I T V O A U V E L R O C A V M
E R T Y E O J O N A T H A N T R U M B U L L N A
```

_____ He was the first white man to sail up Connecticut River.

_____ He helped supply food and other necessities to troops during the Revolution.

_____ He made clocks with metal works in Plymouth Hollow.

_____ He compiled the first dictionary.

_____ He developed the idea of using interchangable parts.

_____ She wrote *Little Women*.

_____ Great patriot born in Connecticut who later lived in Vermont

_____ He regretted having but one life to give for his country.

_____ He sold out his country.

_____ He vulcanized rubber.

_____ He helped to draft Fundamental Orders.

_____ He started the sleigh bell industry in 1800 in New Britain.

_____ One of Connecticut's most beloved Revolutionary War heroes

_____ He made the Dollar Watch famous.

_____ She authored *Uncle Tom's Cabin*.

_____ He developed the sewing machine.

_____ He helped Eli Whitney with new methods of production.

_____ He started silkworm culture in Connecticut.

_____ He wrote *Tom Sawyer* when he lived in Hartford.

_____ He invented the revolver.

GA1138

YANKEE PEDDLER

During Colonial America, Yankee peddlers traveled far and wide selling their wares. They spread the fame of Connecticut craftsmen by selling such products as brassware, clocks, firearms, and tinware. Some of them also sold a lot of other things, some of which were "cure-all" tonics and elixirs. The claims and "guarantees" made by these house-to-house salesmen earned them a reputation as shrewd businessmen who could seldom be trusted. For a few moments, imagine yourself back in Colonial Connecticut. Fashion yourself as one of these Yankee peddlers, except that you are completely honest. Create a dialogue below that will convince your potential customers that everything you say is true. Remember—they've dealt with peddlers before, and they don't trust them because many of them were out to make as much profit as they could possibly make. Be as creative as you can to convince those you meet that your product (whatever it may be) is truly going to help them in some way.

Tonics
CURE-ALL

Elixirs
CURE-ALL

HAND LANTERN

GA1138

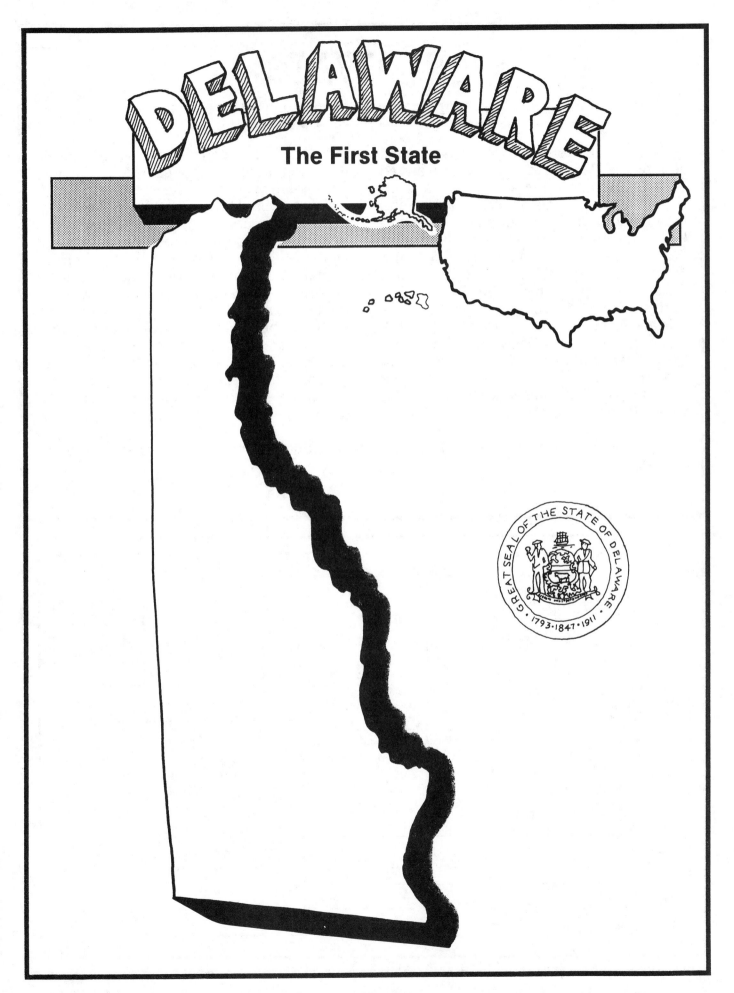

DELAWARE

The First State

GA1138

DELAWARE
THE FIRST STATE

On March 29, 1638, two merchant ships sent by the New Sweden Company landed on a rocky outcrop in an inlet off a large river. They were led by Peter Minuit and they came to the newfound land to establish a colony. The settlement was called Fort Christina, the foundation of what later would become Wilmington, Delaware. Delaware's nickname, The First State, derived from its being the first of the thirteen original states to ratify the U.S. Constitution. Today Delaware is a contrast of two very different sides of America. In the north is found one of the largest assemblies of chemical factories in the world. Its nearness to Baltimore, Washington, D.C., Philadelphia and New York places it at the core of the eastern industrial complex. Yet south of the Chesapeake and Delaware Canal, the landscape takes on a gardenlike appearance with truck farming, dairy and poultry production. Its nearness to huge eastern markets has helped to make Delaware one of the richest states in terms of per capita income. However, the two contrasting lifestyles have created a friction between the industrial and agricultural areas that has presented several problems in government, the economy and the general well-being of the state. Its sprawling suburban population has only further complicated the issues.

Before continuing your study of Delaware, find out about each of these state symbols:

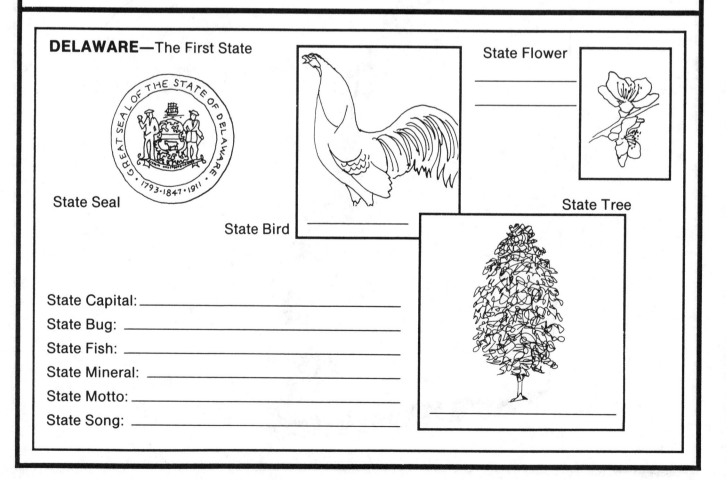

DELAWARE—The First State

State Seal

State Bird _____

State Flower
_____
_____

State Tree
_____

State Capital: _____

State Bug: _____

State Fish: _____

State Mineral: _____

State Motto: _____

State Song: _____

GA1138

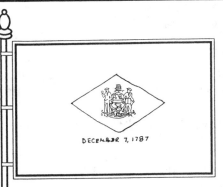

December 7, 1787

DELAWARE ON THE MAP

On your outline map of Delaware, pinpoint the locations of the following cities, bodies of water and places. To make your work more accurate, use coordinates of your own that are similar to those you find in an atlas.

Wilmington
Newark
Milford
Lewes
Harrington
Middletown
New Castle
Smyrna
Elsmere
Georgetown
Seaford
Delaware City

Bethany Beach
Slaughter Beach
Bowers Beach
Rehoboth Beach
Dewey Beach
John Dickinson Plantation
Woodland Beach Wildlife Area
Rehoboth Bay
Lums Pond State Park

Delaware River
Delaware Bay
Fenwick Island
Cape Henlopen State Park
Bombay Hook National Wildlife Refuge

TRAP POND STATE PARK / NEAR LAUREL

45

GA1138

DELAWARE'S STORIED PAST

Below are listed several of the events that are significant to its history. The order in which they are presented is all mixed up. Find out which took place first and place a #1 in the blank space that precedes the description. Do the same with all other events.

a. _____ Captain De Vries visited Zwaanendael, only to find that the settlers had been killed and their buildings burned.

b. _____ Peter Stuyvesant established Dutch authority over all of New Sweden.

c. _____ William Penn annexed the Lower Counties of Delaware to be included in Pennsylvania.

d. _____ Henry Hudson sailed the *Half Moon* along the shore of what is now Sussex County.

e. _____ Peter Minuit brought a group of Swedes into the Delaware River Valley and established a settlement at present-day Wilmington. He named the colony Fort Christina.

f. _____ At the time of the Declaration of Independence, Delaware declared itself a separate government apart from Pennsylvania.

g. _____ John Dickinson of Delaware presided over the Annapolis Convention, which led to the eventual Federal Constitutional Convention.

h. _____ Samuel Argall named the coastline cape De La Warr.

i. _____ William Penn was granted the Province of Pennsylvania by King Charles II.

j. _____ The battle of Cooch's Bridge was the only conflict in the Revolution fought on Delaware soil.

k. _____ Delaware became "The First State" when it ratified the constitution unanimously in a convention held in Dover on December 7, 1787.

l. _____ The first settlement in what is now Delaware was called Zwaanendael, located near the present site of Lewes.

m. _____ Under the leadership of Johan Rising, the Swedish colony seized the Dutch post, Fort Casmir.

n. _____ Oliver Evans of Newport, Delaware, invented automatic flour milling machinery, revolutionizing the industry.

o. _____ William Penn petitioned to the Crown to include land now in part of Delaware to avoid having his colony landlocked.

WILLIAM PENN

GA1138

DELAWARE—SMALL WONDER

In size Delaware ranks 49th in the nation with a total area of only 1982 square miles. It is 96 miles long and varies in width from 9 to 35 miles. Travelling from one place to another in Delaware is usually a matter of only a few minutes. Still travel is travel and people need to make plans on how long it is going to take for them to arrive at their destinations. Find the following distances on any good road atlas that has a scale of miles. Assuming you can average around 45 miles per hour, calculate your approximate travel time for each trip.

	Miles Traveled	**Approximate Travel Time**
1. From Wilmington to Dover	_____	_____
2. From Dover to Slaughter Beach	_____	_____
3. From Bethany Beach to Wilmington	_____	_____
4. From Seaford to Ocean View	_____	_____
5. From Georgetown to Bowers Beach	_____	_____
6. From Dover to Delaware City	_____	_____
7. From Milford to Elsmere	_____	_____
8. From Lewes to Bethany Beach	_____	_____
9. From Rehoboth Beach to Dover	_____	_____
10. From Smyrna to Wilmington	_____	_____
11. From Georgetown to Wyoming	_____	_____
12. From Slaughter Beach to Bethany Beach	_____	_____

GA1138

WHAT'S COOKING IN DELAWARE?

The early culture and history of Delaware were influenced by political changes experienced there. Evidence of the Swedish, the Dutch, the Finnish, the English and even the French all having been there resulted in a mixed cuisine that gives the visitor a wide variety of food fare. Today, Delaware's poultry industry, vegetable farms and fresh seafood add to the unique flavor of carefully prepared Southern cooking, making a meal in Delaware a memorable experience.

A FEW DELAWARE FOOD FACTS

- In 1895 the peach blossom became the state flower in honor of the state's 800,000 peach trees.
- Sussex County leads the nation in the production of broiling chickens.
- Delaware is the second largest producer of lima beans in the nation.
- The sea trout was named the state fish because of its growing abundance in Delaware Bay.

A FEW DELAWARE FOOD FESTIVALS

- Old-Fashioned Ice Cream Festival
- Delmarva Chicken Festival
- St. Anthony's Italian Festival
- Old Dover Days

Each state has its own food facts and special festive occasions that celebrate the foods that are best noted in that state. Find out about some of the "specialities" of the state where you live and the festive days set aside to celebrate them and list them in the space below.

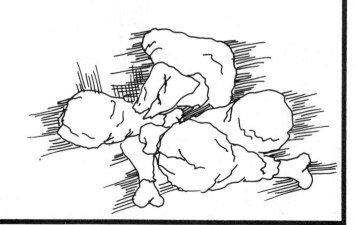

GA1138

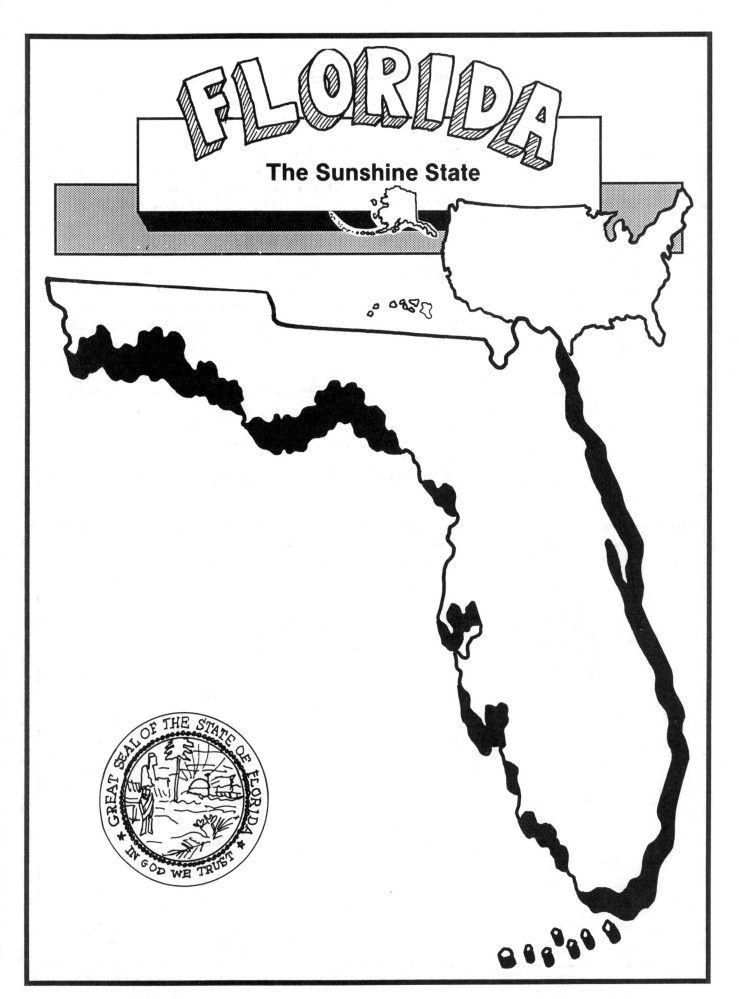

The Sunshine State

FLORIDA
THE SUNSHINE STATE

Probably Florida's greatest resource is its sunshine. It has become one of the most sought-after vacation and retirement "capitals" in the United States because of its delightfully mild wintertime climate. Because of its location, it has also become a melting pot for the exiled and the poor from Caribbean and Central American countries. While the influx is mixed with good news as well as bad, the environmental problems created have fast become a major concern. The arrival of so many newcomers has placed a heavy strain on the resources and quality of living conditions of the heavily populated areas. To accommodate the influx of both people and business, housing and office space has been increased at a record pace. The result has been erosion of the beaches and serious damage to the environment, especially along the east coast. Recognition of the problem has brought about several reclamation projects that will hopefully restore the land to its unspoiled state in the near future. Florida also lies within the hurricane belt, posing potential disaster for those who live there, but the joys of its subtropical climate seem to more than offset the risk. In fact almost every sector of Florida's economy including its citrus fruit industry is tied to its fair weather and tropical climate. The swamplands of south Florida and the four national forests found in the state serve as sanctuaries for tropical birds and other wildlife seldom found in the United States.

Before continuing with your study of the Sunshine State, familiarize yourself with these symbols:

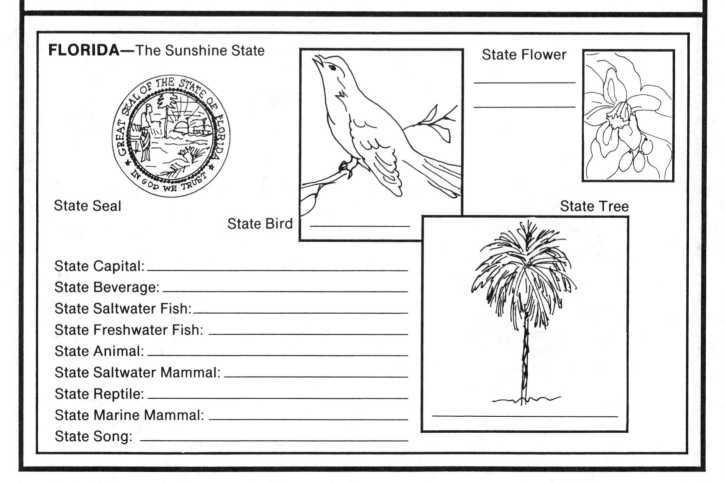

FLORIDA—The Sunshine State

State Seal

State Bird _____

State Flower _____

State Tree _____

State Capital: _____
State Beverage: _____
State Saltwater Fish: _____
State Freshwater Fish: _____
State Animal: _____
State Saltwater Mammal: _____
State Reptile: _____
State Marine Mammal: _____
State Song: _____

GA1138

VACATION PARADISE

Over thirty million out-of-state visitors enjoy Florida each year and make tourism the state's largest industry. Below are some of the more popular attractions that bring them there. Find out where each is located and pinpoint that location on your outline map of Florida. The list below will serve as your map legend. Create your own symbols that will give the attractions meaning on the map. For example, you might create a likeness of a spaceship for Kennedy Space Center.

 Kennedy Space Center

Busch Gardens

Sea World

Cypress Gardens

Apalachicola National Forest

Walt Disney World

Daytona International Speedway

Castillo de San Marcos National Monument

Merritt Island National Wildlife Refuge

Tarpon Springs

Ocala National Forest

Canaveral National Seashore

Osceola National Forest

Weeki Wachee

Alligator Alley

Lion Country Safari

Everglades National Park

Florida Keys

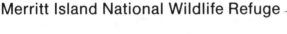

GA1138

FLORIDA TRAVEL FOLDER

Tourism is Florida's largest industry. A recent year's statistics showed that nineteen percent of the taxable sales in the state were related to tourism and recreation. Over 600,000 people in Florida are employed in tourism-related jobs. A state that depends so heavily on tourism is constantly printing literature that will advertise to others what it has to offer. Create your own advertising piece in the form of a six-page brochure that will give others good reason to spend their dollars in Florida. Each page should be four inches wide and eight inches tall. Start with a twelve-inch sheet of white paper. Fold it twice accordion-style the way maps are folded (shown below), and you will have six pages on which you can advertise the Sunshine State. Using statistics you find and facts you consider meaningful, create ad copy to go along with the pictures you either draw or cut from magazines to make your brochure more attractive. When you are finished, share your folder with others and create a class bulletin board.

FLORIDA TIME TRACK

Several dates important to the history of Florida are shown on the "time clock" below. The events which occurred on those dates are found in the clues below. Your task is to match them up by placing the letter that corresponds to an event next to the date.

a. Andrew Jackson captures Pensacola, which was being used as a base of Gulf operations by the British.

b. British General James Oglethorpe captured Castillo de San Marcos.

c. On the last day of John Tyler's administration, he signed a law making Florida the 27th state.

d. The British return Florida to Spain.

e. Ponce de Leon calls the land Pascua Florida.

f. Spain cedes Florida to England following the French and Indian War.

g. The United States launches Alan Shepard into space from Cape Canaveral.

h. Second Seminole War begins with the massacre of Major Francis L. Dade.

i. Construction is begun on $700 million Walt Disney World near Orlando.

j. The founding of St. Augustine, the first permanent colony in Florida

k. Kennedy Space Center witnesses America's worst space tragedy as *Challenger* explodes.

l. Work is begun on Castillo de San Marcos.

m. Florida comes under U.S. control.

n. The Civil War ends.

o. Sir Francis Drake, a British seafarer, conquers and burns St. Augustine.

p. Water driven from Lake Okeechobee by a hurricane causes the drowning of 1500 persons.

GA1138

FLORIDA'S FUTURE . . .

1. Florida has sometimes been referred to as the "northernmost of the Southern States." Just looking at the map would suggest that geographically speaking this is an incorrect statement. There are, however, reasons for this label. Investigate the growth patterns of Florida and jot down your explanation below for this statement.

_____

_____

_____

2. Florida's mild climate and ample rainfall make it suitable for growing a variety of food crops. Growing citrus fruits has long been one of Florida's leading industries. In recent years, however, the citrus industry has suffered a number of financial setbacks. What risks and uncertainties make citrus growing a "risky" venture?

_____

_____

_____

3. The delightful climate and beauty of Florida have combined with its "man-made" attractions to make it one of the most sought-after vacation and retirement areas in the United States. Billions of tourist dollars are pumped into the Florida economy annually. While such a windfall is healthy for Florida's financial concern, the state is experiencing several internal and environmental problems. Investigate the source of these problems and list them in the space below.

_____

_____

_____

4. Look at your list from question #3 and rank order them according to your own feeling about Florida's biggest problem. In the space below explain your choice of its greatest problem and describe how you think it can best be solved as Florida heads into the 21st century?

_____

_____

_____

GA1138

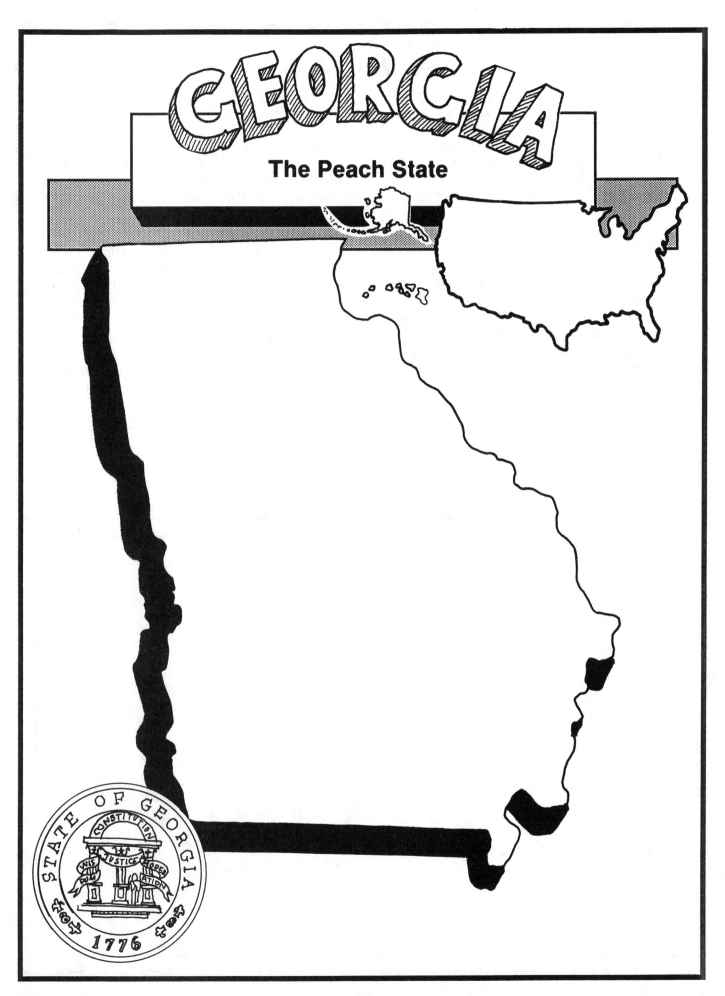

GEORGIA

The Peach State

55

GEORGIA
THE PEACH STATE

Because of its large size and leader as a southern manufacturing state, Georgia has often been referred to as the "Empire State of the South." For many years cotton was almost the sole source of its income, but during the early 1900's many Georgia farmers began growing tobacco, fruits and corn. The manufacturing industry began slowly with the weaving of cotton providing the modest beginning. Over the years more and more people turned to industry, and today Georgia's economy relies heavily upon industry, including timber and wood products. Processing of pine tar, turpentine and rosin made from the sap of pine trees contributes significantly to the Georgia economy with textile mills processing of foods, manufacture of transportation equipment and chemicals also being chief sources of income. No other state produces more peanuts, and it ranks as a leader in growing peaches. The natural beauty of Georgia's stately pines, moss-draped trees and magnolias combined with its delightful climate, its mountains, rich historical past and excitement of Atlanta make it a popular tourist favorite among millions of vacationers annually. It is indeed one of the South's most important states with a bright outlook to the future.

Before proceeding with your study of Georgia, familiarize yourself with these symbols:

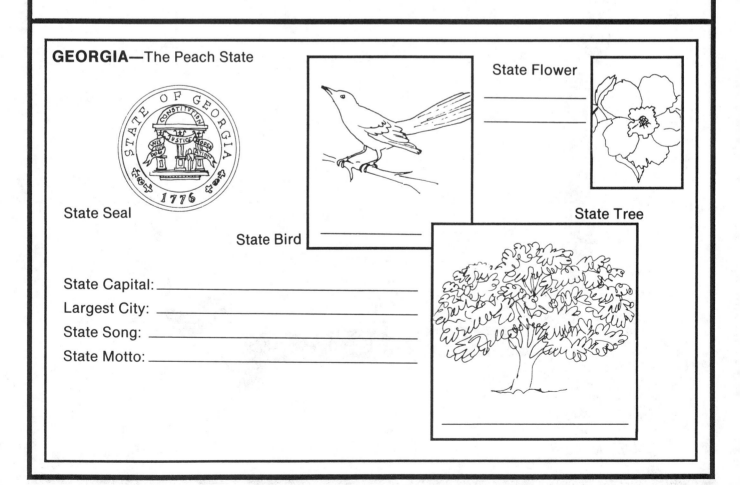

GEORGIA—The Peach State

State Seal

State Bird

State Flower

State Tree

State Capital: _____

Largest City: _____

State Song: _____

State Motto: _____

GA1138

GEORGIA ON THE MAP

Below are the scrambled names of eighteen cities found in the state of Georgia. Your task is to unscramble the letters to correctly spell those cities. Then pinpoint their locations on your outline map of Georgia.

1. TATALNA _____
2. TUUAGSA _____
3. HNVASANA _____
4. IRMAEATT _____
5. ADTLON _____
6. EMRO _____
7. UOLMTRIE _____
8. LEELLMIDVGILE _____
9. RUEDCTA _____

10. OERDCEL _____
11. NOCMA _____
12. TSOVDALA _____
13. NHTAES _____
14. YNABLA _____
15. IREAMCSU _____
16. RYCOAWSS _____
17. NIGAEVISLLE _____
18. RIFGFIN _____

Unscramble the names of these Georgia rivers and geographical features. Draw them in and label on your outline map.

1. ANAVASNH EIRVR _____
2. HAPAALA VRIER _____
3. NCOOEE RRIVE _____
4. RTSMSAY IRVER _____
5. ENWUANSE IERVR _____
6. NILFT IRVER _____
7. EEEKFOENOK WMSAP _____
8. KALE EISDNY EALNIR _____
9. EECTTHCAAHOOH ANTOINAL SOFRET _____
10. EECONO ANTINOAL RFOEST _____

57

GA1138

GEORGIA CROSSWORD

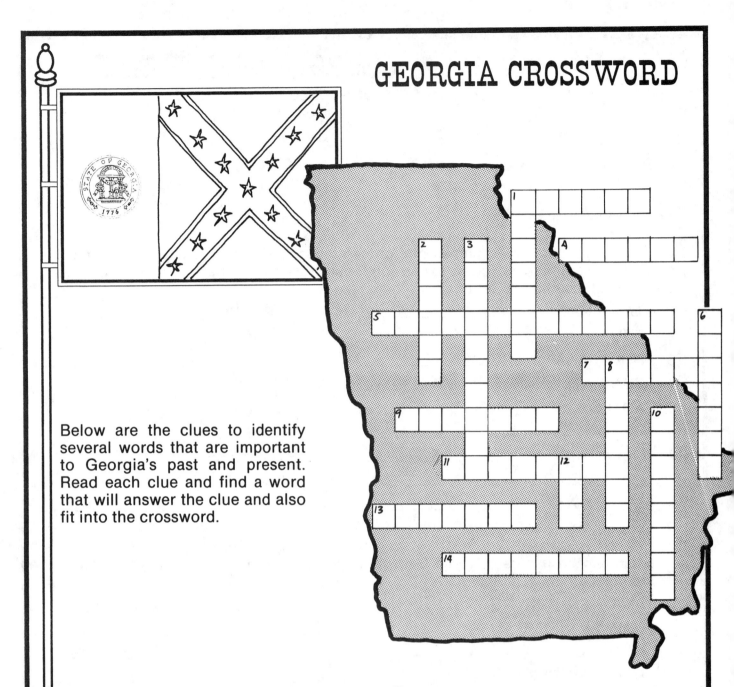

Below are the clues to identify several words that are important to Georgia's past and present. Read each clue and find a word that will answer the clue and also fit into the crossword.

Across

1. One of Georgia's most important crops
4. Georgia's "President from Plains"
5. The largest dome of exposed granite in the U.S.
7. He wrote stories about Uncle Remus.
9. He burned Atlanta.
11. Sent by Spanish King in 1565 to force the French from Georgia
13. His cotton gin helped to launch the cotton cloth industry on a large scale.
14. First permanent settlement in Georgia

Down

1. He built the first cotton mill near Athens in 1928.
2. First white man to visit Georgia
3. Englishman who made the first attempt at a permanent settlement in Georgia
6. The world's best golfers come to this tournament early in April each year.
8. Georgia's second capital
10. Her novel *Gone with the Wind* used Atlanta as the setting.
12. She founded the Girl Scouts in Savannah on March 12, 1912.

58

WHAT MIGHT HAVE BEEN

The list below contains some of the significant events that weighed heavily in the unfolding of Georgia's history. Your task is to speculate on how the course of history might have changed if the event had *not* happened at all. Be brief with your explanations, but give each enough thought that you will be able to justify the implications that might have been involved in such changes.

In 1742 James Oglethorpe defeated a band of invading Spanish soldiers at the Battle of Bloody Marsh.

_____

_____

_____

Eli Whitney invented the cotton gin near Savannah in 1793, making cotton the South's most important crop.

_____

_____

_____

In 1864 Union General William T. Sherman burned Atlanta and marched to the sea during the Civil War.

_____

_____

_____

Former Governor Jimmy Carter became the 39th President of the United States in January, 1977.

_____

_____

_____

King George II granted a charter to James Oglethorpe to create a refuge in the New World for Englishmen in prison for not paying their debts.

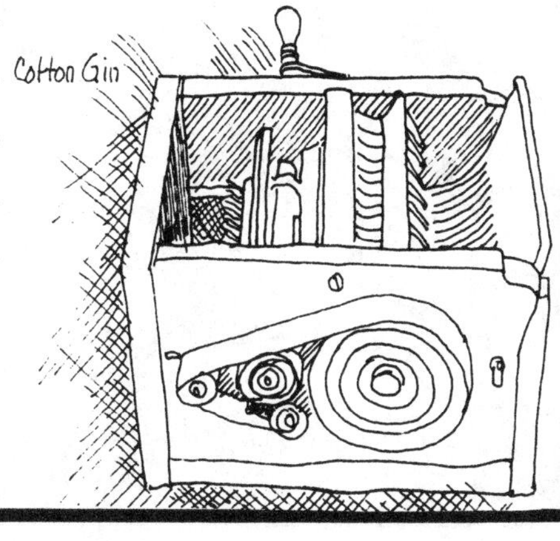

_____

_____   Cotton Gin

_____

_____

_____

GA1138

GEORGIA ON MY MIND

Read each of the clues below to help you identify some of Georgia's sites and sounds.

1. _____ "The Home of the Braves" . . . The Big A . . .

2. _____ This famous Georgia island was once called Ospo by the Indians. It was at one point the center of one sixth of the nation's wealth with "cottages" of Marshall Field, William Rockefeller, Vincent Astor, Jay Gould, J.P. Morgan, Joseph Pulitzer and William Vanderbilt.

3. _____ He wrote the music to the state song—"Georgia on My Mind."

4. _____ The acronym for Atlanta's rapid transit system

5. _____ This city claims to be "the pecan capital of the world."

6. _____ The site of the first U.S. gold rush in 1828

7. _____ Often called the South's Garden City . . . it also plays host to the annual "Celebration of Golf"

8. _____ Atlanta's most celebrated street . . . formerly an Indian trail running to the Chattahoochee River

9. _____ This city boasts America's largest National Historic Landmark District.

10. _____ The three personalites carved on the side of Stone Mountain in deep relief
    _____
    _____

11. _____ Located 225 miles south of Atlanta, it is south Georgia's largest city.

12. _____ This city has been called the Crossroads of Georgia—intersection of I-75 and US 341 and I-41.

13. _____ Famous 331-acre theme park near Atlanta with over 100 rides

14. _____ This world-famous display contains five acres of floral display and the longest inland man-made white sand beach—2500 acres in all of golf courses, rolling meadows and flowers.

15. _____ Almost 100 miles West of Macon, it is Georgia's westernmost largest city.

16. _____ In the far northwest corner of the state, this tourist attraction straddles the Tennessee-Georgia line, offering tourists a panoramic view of seven states.

GA1138

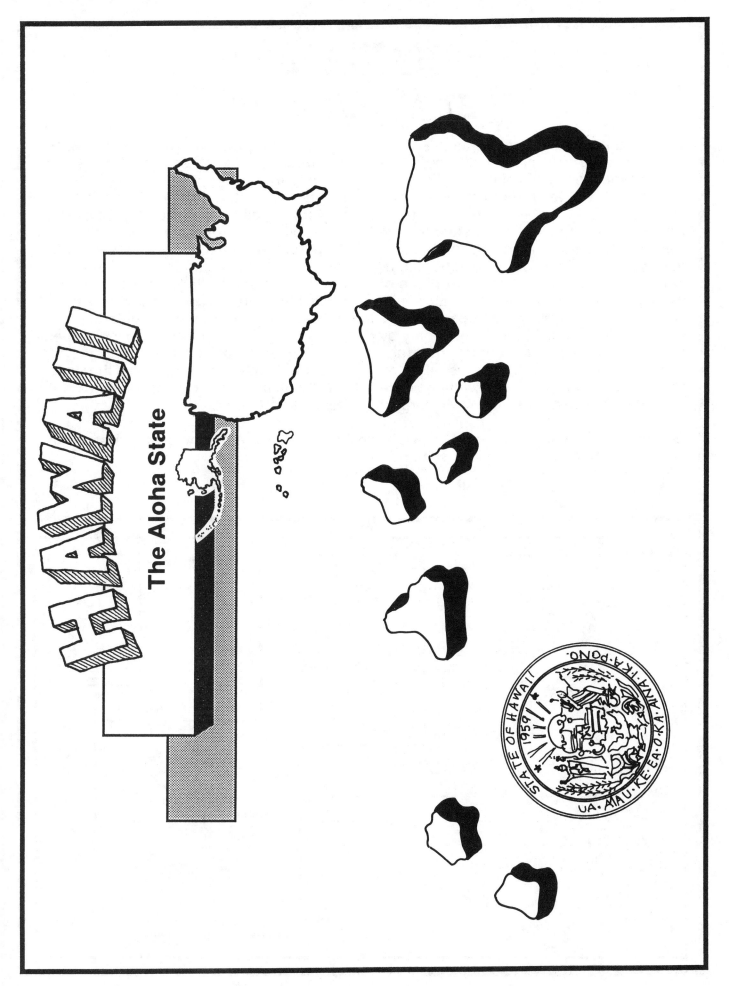

HAWAII

The Aloha State

61

HAWAII
THE ALOHA STATE

The beautiful islands of Hawaii are more than America's tropical paradise, they serve as the crossroads of the Pacific. They are the link between East and West. The cultural melting pot in Hawaii is unique from that found in any other state. Native Hawaiians, Caucasians, Japanese, Chinese, Koreans, Filipinos and Pacific Islanders all live and work together with little of the tension that is found in a number of states with fewer ethnic groups. Hawaii's location has helped to fuel its economy by making it attractive to foreign investors, especially the Japanese. It is also an important military outpost, with governmental employment making up the largest share of the Hawaiian work force. But the beautiful climate and beauty of the islands make tourism the largest source of revenue for the state. Its deep blue seas, colorful flowers, graceful palm trees and plunging waterfalls give it some of the most dramatic scenery the United States has to offer. Pineapple and sugarcane industries are also important to the state's economy. While the future of Hawaii is indeed a bright one, its distance from the mainland makes the cost of living in paradise very expensive. When it entered the Union in 1959 as our 50th state, commitment of the United States ensured its future and will no doubt help it to grow.

Before you begin your study of Hawaii, find out about the symbols of the state and report your findings in the blank spaces.

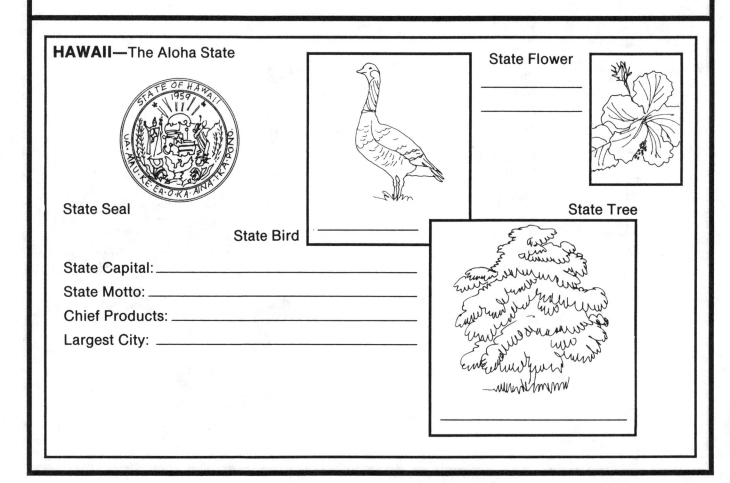

HAWAII—The Aloha State

State Seal

State Bird _____

State Flower
_____
_____

State Tree

_____

State Capital: _____

State Motto: _____

Chief Products: _____

Largest City: _____

GA1138

WHAT TO DO WITH THE MAP

Hawaii consists of a chain of 132 islands that extend a distance of over 1500 miles. The eight main islands are located at the southeastern end of the chain. Almost all of the people in Hawaii live on seven of these eight islands. These are the islands shown on your outline map. Label each island and indicate the island's nickname underneath in smaller print.

Pinpoint the locations of these Hawaiian cities:

Honolulu, Kaneohe, Kailua, Hilo, Wailuku, Kahului, Lahaina, Waipahu, Pearl City, Kekaha, Hanamaulu

Locate Pearl Harbor, Diamond Head, Waikiki Beach, Haleakala National Park, Hawaii Volcanoes National Park, Akaka Falls, Menehune Fish Pond.

Draw symbols of your own choosing that depict the important products to the economy of the Hawaiian Islands. Place each symbol on the map at the location where the product is produced in large quantity. Be certain to include map key to show meanings of your symbols.

GA1138

ISLANDS FROM THE SEA

1. Hawaiian legend tells us that the islands were formed by one of the gods, Maui, when he let down fishhooks into the sea and pulled up the islands. Science feels the islands were created in a different way. Research the scientific explanation and summarize your findings below.

_____

_____

_____

_____

_____

_____

2. When man first arrived in the Hawaiian Islands, he found a tropical environment already there. In considering Hawaii's location, which is over 2000 miles from the closest large land mass, one has to wonder just how all the plants and animals got there. Explain how you think this "land from the sea" became the island paradise it is today.

_____

_____

_____

_____

_____

3. Hawaii has been called a land "still in the making." How do you explain this statement?

_____

_____

_____

_____

_____

GA1138

TRADE WINDS AND TROPICAL BREEZES

1. While Hawaii's climate is responsible for the lush green tropical growth that adds much to the beauty of the islands, there are parts of Hawaii that receive less than ten inches of rainfall annually and thus qualify as desert. In fact on the island of Kauai lies Mt. Waialeale, considered the world's wettest spot. (One year it recorded 486 inches of rain!) Yet less than twenty miles away the rainfall averages twenty inches per year. How do you explain this phenomenon? Use the diagram below to explain your answer.

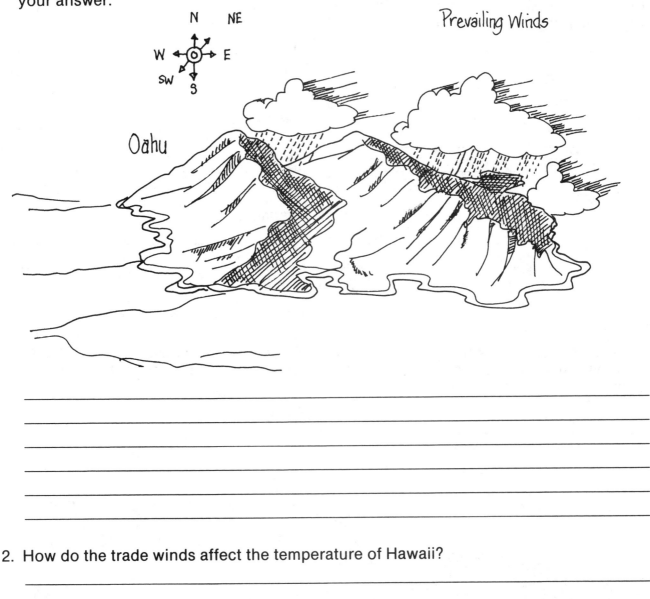

_____

_____

_____

_____

_____

2. How do the trade winds affect the temperature of Hawaii?

_____

_____

_____

_____

_____

GA1138

HAWAIIAN TALK

Most Hawaiians speak English fluently and the English language is taught in Hawaiian schools. However many Hawaiians often make use of several words that come from the Hawaiian language. These words have an almost musical sound to them and add to the charm of the islands as they are presented to tourists. The Hawaiian alphabet has only twelve letters—A, E, H, I, K, L, M, N, O, P, U, W. Every Hawaiian word and syllable ends with a vowel. The accent on most words falls on the next to last syllable.

Below are several words that are frequently used. Research the meaning of each and jot down in the space provided.

ae _____   luau _____

ai _____   mahalo _____

aloha _____   makai _____

aole _____   malihini _____

hana _____   manu _____

hiamoe _____   mauna _____

huhu _____   mele _____

hula _____   ohana _____

kaukau _____   pua _____

keiki _____   puka _____

ko _____   wahine _____

lei _____   wai _____

Create four sentences using a combination of some of the above words and English that tell a story. Exchange stories with another member of your class and *interpret* each other's stories.

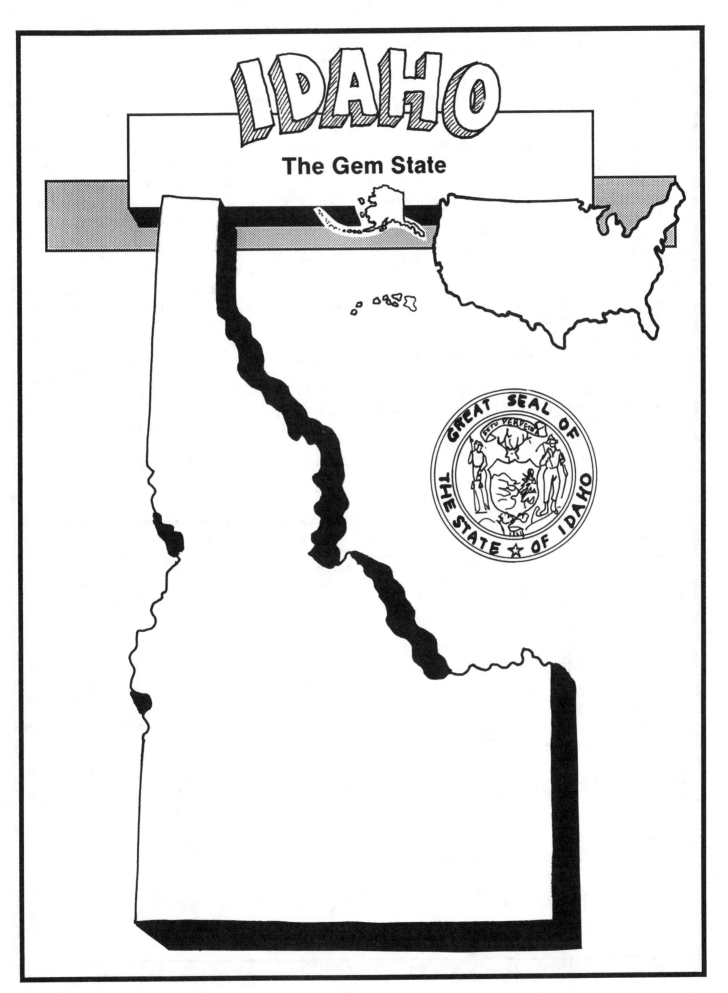

IDAHO

The Gem State

GREAT SEAL OF THE STATE OF IDAHO

GA1138

IDAHO
THE GEM STATE

With towering, snow-capped mountains, swirling wild rapids, steep canyons and peaceful lakes, Idaho is indeed a land of contrasts. The uncompromising scenery is among the most beautiful found in the United States anywhere. Although Idaho ranks 11th in size among the states, it is the smallest of the Rocky Mountain states. Blessed with many natural resources, the state until recently had relied mostly on exploitation of its natural wealth and irrigated agricultural products. In more recent years, the economy has become somewhat dependent upon industry because of the cheap hydroelectric power available there. The state remains among the leaders in the production of silver, lead and zinc, and more than forty percent of the state is covered by forests. Idaho's potato crop leads the nation and sugar beets, wheat and other crops make agriculture a significant portion of the Idaho economy. The natural beauty and rugged terrain, ample snowfall and protection from harsh winds make it a hit for thousands of vacationers annually in both summer and winter. Sun Valley continues to rank among the leaders as a ski resort. Idaho has oftentimes been referred to as "the undiscovered America." Its future is very positive as the untapped resource wealth, available hydroelectricity and natural scenic splendor await the influx of more Americans and a richer economic base.

Before continuing with your study of Idaho, familiarize yourself with these symbols:

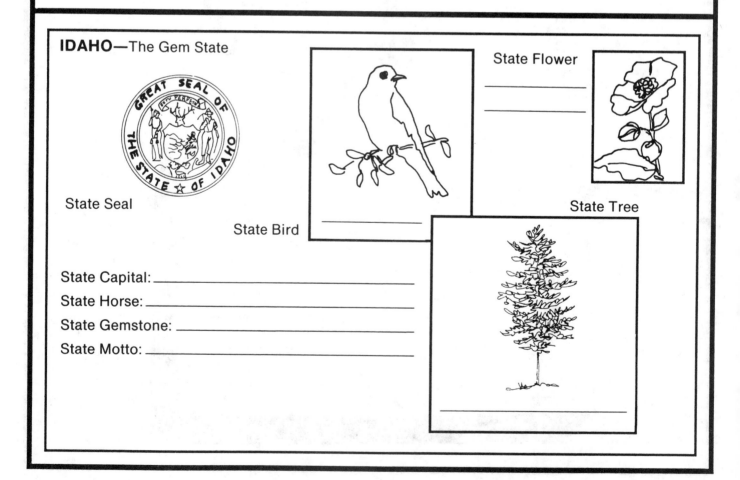

IDAHO—The Gem State

State Seal

State Bird

State Flower

State Tree

State Capital: _____

State Horse: _____

State Gemstone: _____

State Motto: _____

68

IDAHO MAP STUDY

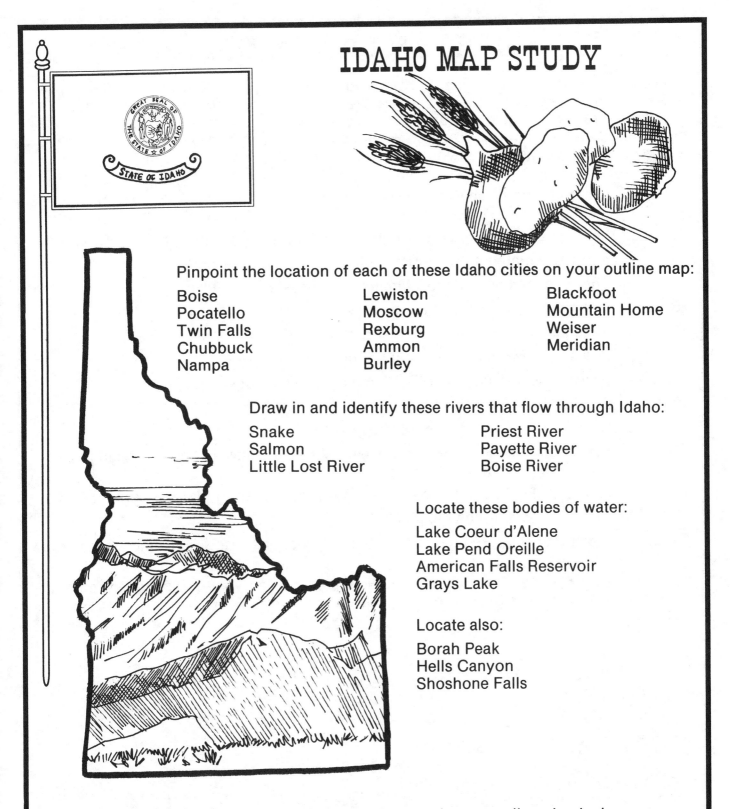

Pinpoint the location of each of these Idaho cities on your outline map:

Boise
Pocatello
Twin Falls
Chubbuck
Nampa

Lewiston
Moscow
Rexburg
Ammon
Burley

Blackfoot
Mountain Home
Weiser
Meridian

Draw in and identify these rivers that flow through Idaho:

Snake
Salmon
Little Lost River

Priest River
Payette River
Boise River

Locate these bodies of water:

Lake Coeur d'Alene
Lake Pend Oreille
American Falls Reservoir
Grays Lake

Locate also:

Borah Peak
Hells Canyon
Shoshone Falls

Idaho has been blessed with vast resources. Among them are silver, lead, zinc, copper, forest products, limestone, phosphate, vanadium, gypsum, shale, mercury, gold. Find out where these resources are found in greatest quantity in Idaho and create little symbols of your own choosing that will identify these locations. The Idaho economy also leans heavily on agricultural products, such as raising beef cattle and sheep, wheat, barley, hay, potatoes, sugar beets. Create symbols for these products as well and locate on the map. Be certain to provide a legend to explain your symbols. These symbols can be colors, drawings or whatever else you choose to make them.

GA1138

IDAHO'S STORY RETOLD

Below is a list of historic events that occurred in helping to shape Idaho's story. The order in which they are presented is not the order in which they took place nor are any dates provided to give you any clues. To write the story of Idaho's past, you will first need to find out through research when each event occurred. Then, when you have all the facts, rewrite the story in your own words on another sheet of paper.

1. ____ Chief Joseph, leader of the Nez Percé Indians, surrendered to U.S. troops ending the Nez Percé War.

2. ____ Lewis and Clark passed through the region on their way to the Pacific Coast.

3. ____ Idaho celebrated its territorial centennial.

4. ____ The Mormons built Idaho's first irrigation system.

5. ____ Idaho became the 43rd state on July 3.

6. ____ Violence broke out between union miners and mine owners.

7. ____ David Thompson built the first trading post in Idaho.

8. ____ Gold was discovered by E.D. Pierce on Orofino Creek.

9. ____ Franklin became Idaho's first permanent settlement.

10. ____ Gold was discovered in the Boise Basin.

11. ____ Fort Hall on the Snake River was established . . . later to become an important trading post on the Oregon Trail.

12. ____ Governor Frank Steunenberg was murdered, drawing international attention.

13. ____ Congress established the Idaho Territory.

14. ____ Electricity was produced from nuclear energy for the first time near Idaho Falls.

15. ____ Brownlee Dam, Oxbow Dam and Hells Canyon Dam were completed to generate vast quantities of hydroelectric power.

70

GA1138

IDAHO'S NATURAL TREASURES

Idaho has three distinct land regions. The Rocky Mountains begin in the extreme north in the Panhandle and extend through much of the eastern and central portions of the state. The land is characterized by rugged mountains, steep canyons and swift mountain streams. The Columbian Plateau follows the sweep of the Snake River across southern Idaho. The same plateau extends along the far western area of Idaho into the Panhandle. The land includes a broad fertile plateau and valley on which most of the agricultural products are grown. The Basin and Range Region lies to the southeast of the Columbian Plateau and is characterized by deep valleys, grassy plateaus, and much of the area is used for sheep grazing. The map below shows the rough boundaries of these three regions.

Over forty percent of the state is covered with forests, providing a major industry to Idaho's economy. The U.S. Department of the Interior closely monitors the lumbering activity in its millions of acres of national forests. There are in fact no fewer than fifteen national forests in Idaho. Locate the approximate area where each is found on the map below.

Bitterroot
Boise
Cache
Caribou
Challis
Clearwater
Coeur d'Alene
Kaniksu
Kootenai
Nezperce
Payette
St. Joe
Salmon
Sawtooth
Targhee

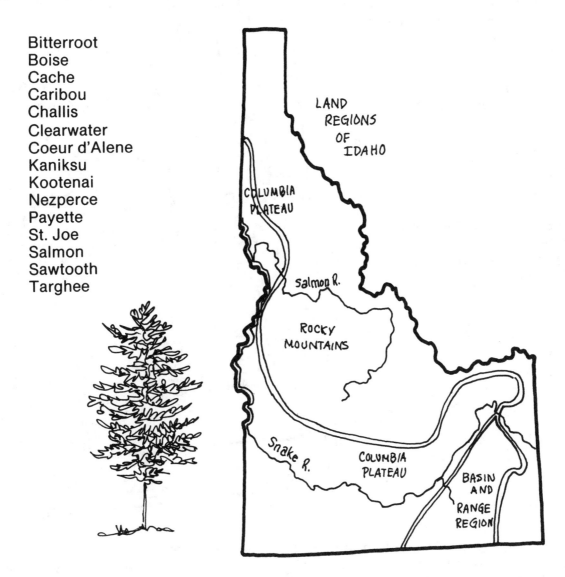

GA1138

DISCOVER THE UNDISCOVERED AMERICA

The Idaho Travel Council has adopted the above catch phrase in its travel brochures and advertising in an attempt to lure tourists and businesses to explore the many opportunities found there. The dramatic and often spectacular scenery provide an unparalleled beauty found in very few other places in the United States. With some of the highest mountains, deepest canyons and wildest rivers, Idaho is a vacationer's paradise. Even though the population is growing and tourists are arriving at a healthy rate, Idaho would like to see more! Help them out by creating a poster that reflects much of the natural beauty, charm and fun Idaho has to offer. Your poster should be 22" x 34" in size and can be either vertical (if you want to include a rough outline of Idaho) or horizontal. Include photos or pictures cut from magazines or travel folders that will help to portray the highlights of your poster. The choices are yours, but the following are some suggested possibilities:

Balanced Rock
Cataldo Mission
Nez Percé National Historical Park
Lake Pend Oriello
Snake River Canyon
American Falls
Shoshone Falls
Craters of the Moon National Monument
Boise
Sawtooth National Recreation Area
Lava Hot Springs
Hells Canyon
Old Fort Hall
Lake Coeur d' Alene
Selway Bitterroot Wilderness
Sun Valley
Bear Lake Recreation Area

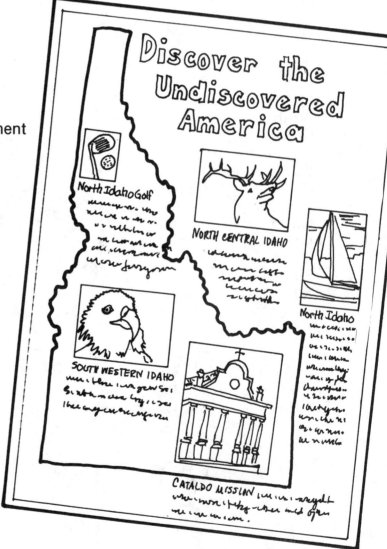

Create an ad for each of the attractions you plan to highlight. When you have completed your poster, share with other members of your class with a brief explanation of your choices. Then display all posters on a bulletin board or post around the perimeter of the room.

GA1138

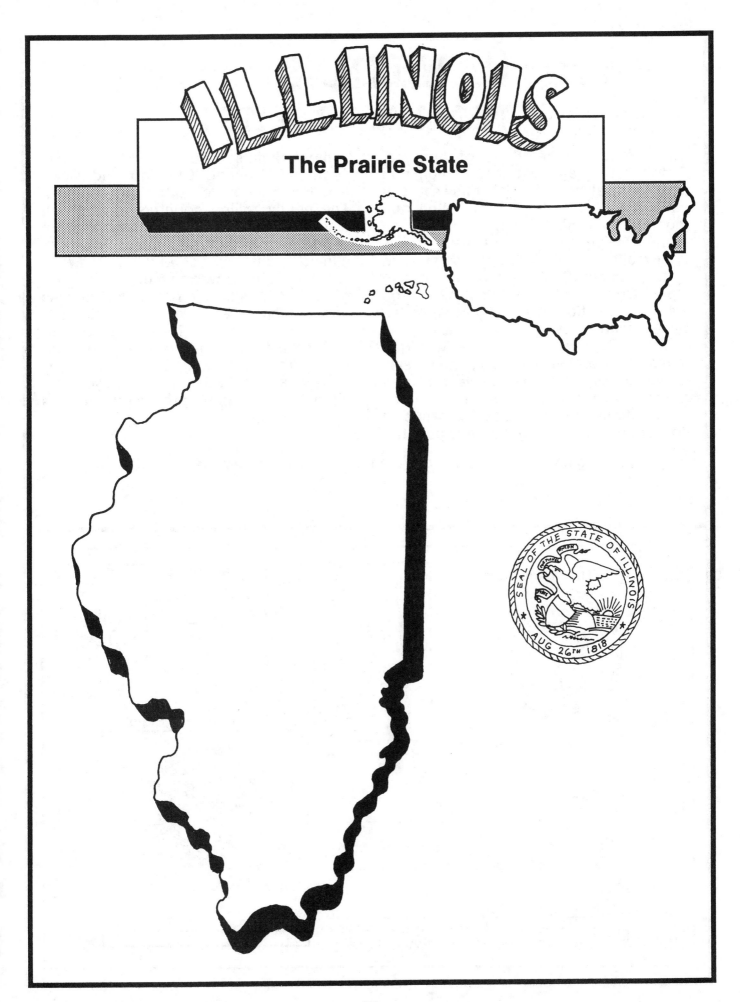

ILLINOIS

The Prairie State

SEAL OF THE STATE OF ILLINOIS
AUG 26TH 1818

ILLINOIS
THE PRAIRIE STATE

Situated in the heartland of America, Illinois serves as the transportation hub and financial center of the Midwest. But yet not far from the sophistication and nightlife of Chicago can be heard the gentle whisper of a prairie stream. Illinois is in reality almost like two separate and distinct states. Chicago and surrounding Cook County contain almost half the state's population. It is a city often called the Gateway to Everywhere because of its location. Its position on Lake Michigan makes it accessible to oceangoing vessels as well as having downstate water access to link it with the Mississippi River and all its tributaries. Hundreds of thousands of convention attendees and visitors pour billions of dollars annually into the Illinois economy. Beyond Chicago and Cook County lie the state's other 101 counties. The gently rolling countryside and rich black soil make it one of the nation's most important agricultural states. Southern Illinois is different yet with the Shawnee National Forest covering much of that part of the state. Its scenic beauty and dozens of sparkling lakes make it a vacationer's paradise. Illinois is indeed a land of contrasts. Its economic wealth, its location and its role in helping to "feed America" make it a state with not only a rich and cherished past, but a promising future as well.

Before you begin your study of Illinois, identify the following Illinois symbols:

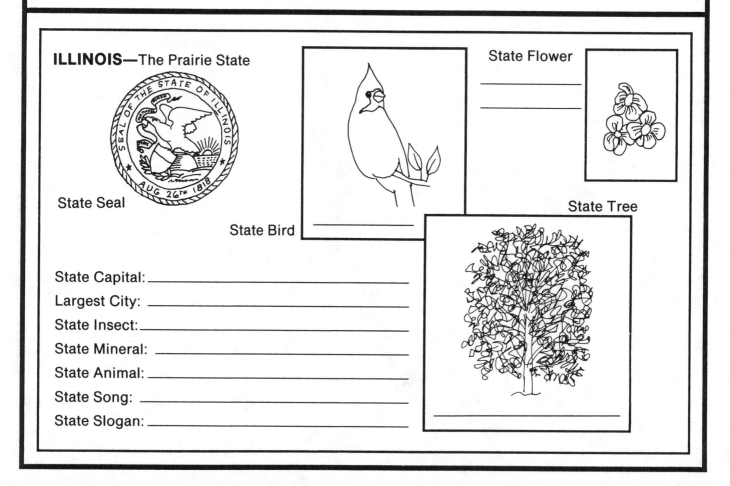

ILLINOIS—The Prairie State

State Seal

State Bird _____

State Flower _____

State Tree _____

State Capital: _____
Largest City: _____
State Insect: _____
State Mineral: _____
State Animal: _____
State Song: _____
State Slogan: _____

74

TIME TRAVELER

CAHOKIA MOUNDS STATE HISTORIC SITE

The following sites that are operated by the state of Illinois will give the Illinois traveler a broad perspective of the state's rich and cherished history. Following the listing of each site is its location. Find each on an Illinois map; then pinpoint the site on your outline map and identify with corresponding letter. Sites have been arranged in chronological order based upon the history of Illinois.

a. Cahokia Mounds—near Collinsville
b. Fort Kaskaskia—near Chester
c. Black Hawk Historic Site—Rock Island
d. Cahokia Courthouse—Cahokia
e. First State Bank of Illinois—Old Shawneetown
f. Lincoln's New Salem—Petersburg
g. Vandalia Statehouse—Vandalia
h. Old State Capital—Springfield
i. Postville Courthouse—Lincoln
j. Lincoln-Herndon Law Offices—Springfield
k. Lincoln Log Cabin—Lerna
l. Old Market House—Galena
m. Bishop Hill—Bishop Hill
n. Mount Pulaski Courthouse—Mount Pulaski
o. Bryant Cottage—Bement
p. Ulysses S. Grant Home—Galena
q. Douglas Tomb—Chicago
r. David Davis Mansion—Bloomington
s. Lincoln's Tomb—Springfield
t. Carl Sandburg Birthplace—Galesburg
u. Dana-Thomas House—Springfield
v. Illinois Vietnam Veterans Memorial—Springfield

After locating each site, choose one that is of interest to you. Research its history and prepare a short summary of your findings to share with the rest of the members of your class.

GA1138

A SWEEP THROUGH HISTORY

Below is a list of events that have helped to shape the rich history of Illinois. The date when each occurred is indicated on the time line. Your task is to look at each event in the list, find out when it took place, and then record the letter that corresponds to that event at the end of the line indicating the date.

a. Illinois country ceded to Britain by France.
b. Northwest Ordinance makes Illinois a part of Northwest Territory.
c. Illinois becomes 21st state on December 3.
d. Marquette and Joliet are first Europeans to reach Illinois country.
e. Black Hawk War
f. Lincoln-Douglas debates; Lincoln loses election.
g. Civil War ends and Lincoln is buried.
h. Springfield becomes state capital.
i. Lincoln is elected President for a second term.
j. Great Chicago Fire
k. World's Columbian Exposition in Chicago
l. Haymarket Riot
m. Capital is moved from Kaskaskia to Vandalia.
n. George Rogers Clark secures Illinois country for Virginia.
o. Cahokia, Illinois, first permanent settlement is founded.
p. Illinois Territory is organized by Congress.
q. Joseph Smith, leader of the Mormon Church, is murdered in Carthage.
r. Lincoln is nominated and elected President.
s. First McCormick reaper plant is built in Chicago.
t. New state constitution forbids slavery.
u. Illinois celebrates its 150th year as a state.
v. Illinois country becomes part of French Colony of Louisiana.
w. Treaty of peace forces Britain to recognize Illinois as part of the United States.
x. Illinois becomes part of the Indiana Territory.
y. Jane Addams opens Hull House.

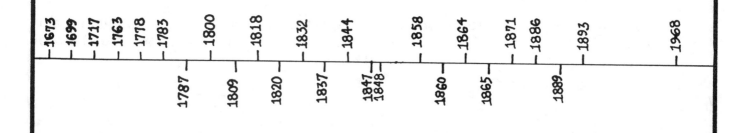

GA1138

TOURISM IN ILLINOIS

The tourism industry represents an important segment of the total Gross State Product, accounting for over $8 billion annually in income. Travelers to Illinois generate over 150,000 jobs and account for over four percent of the total state income. Illinois currently ranks seventh among all states in travel expenditures. Look at the charts and graphs that tell part of the story of tourism in Illinois and answer these questions.

1. For what reason do most people travel in Illinois according to the information supplied?

_____

2. What percent of Illinois travelers go there for business or convention? _____

3. Which state in the U.S. is the most widely traveled? _____

4. Express the number of dollars spent in Illinois during the year portrayed on the graph.

_____

5. Approximately how much more did travelers spend in Illinois in 1985 than in 1979?

_____

6. How much did the average traveler in Illinois spend in 1985? _____

7. What approximate percentage increase did the traveler spend in 1985 compared to 1979? _____

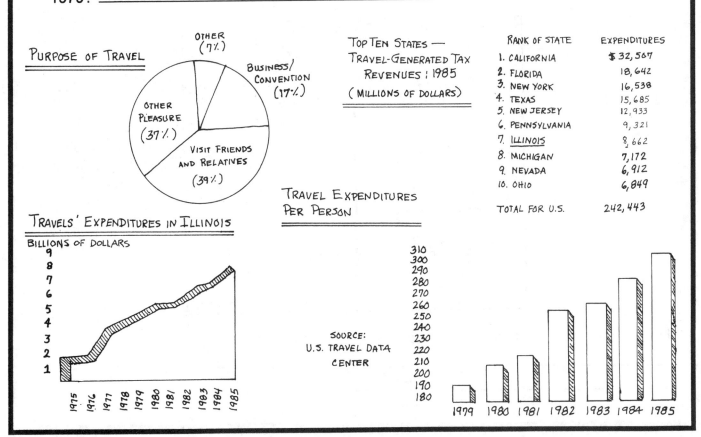

PURPOSE OF TRAVEL

OTHER (7%)
BUSINESS/ CONVENTION (17%)
OTHER PLEASURE (37%)
VISIT FRIENDS AND RELATIVES (39%)

TOP TEN STATES — TRAVEL-GENERATED TAX REVENUES: 1985 (MILLIONS OF DOLLARS)

RANK OF STATE	EXPENDITURES
1. CALIFORNIA	$ 32,567
2. FLORIDA	18,642
3. NEW YORK	16,538
4. TEXAS	15,685
5. NEW JERSEY	12,933
6. PENNSYLVANIA	9,321
7. ILLINOIS	8,662
8. MICHIGAN	7,172
9. NEVADA	6,912
10. OHIO	6,849
TOTAL FOR U.S.	242,443

TRAVELS' EXPENDITURES IN ILLINOIS

BILLIONS OF DOLLARS
9 8 7 6 5 4 3 2 1
1975 1976 1977 1978 1979 1980 1981 1982 1983 1984 1985

TRAVEL EXPENDITURES PER PERSON

310 300 290 280 270 260 250 240 230 220 210 200 190 180

SOURCE: U.S. TRAVEL DATA CENTER

1979 1980 1981 1982 1983 1984 1985

77

GA1138

THE WINDY CITY

Chicago, the nation's third largest city with a population in excess of three million, is the financial and transportation center of the entire Midwest. The distinctive landmarks and the skyscrapers that compose the Chicago skyline make it one of the most dramatic found anywhere. Below are five of the most recognizable symbols of Chicago that visitors easily remember. There are, of course, many more. Identify each landmark on the line beneath each picture.

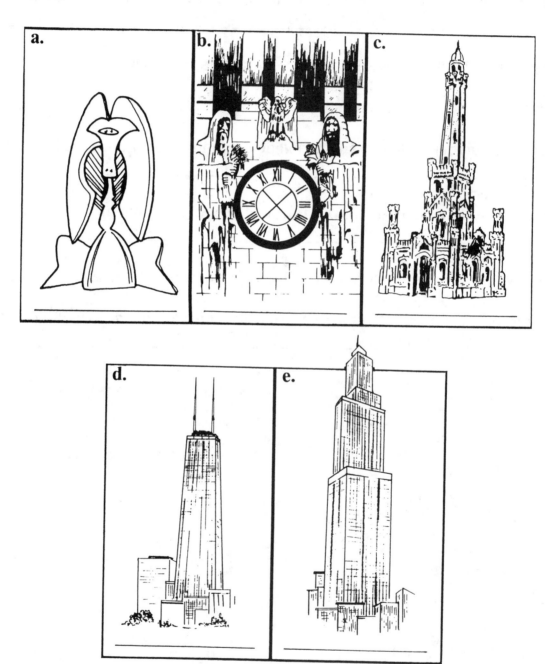

a. _____

b. _____

c. _____

d. _____

e. _____

Name three other landmarks in Chicago you consider important.

_____

_____

78

GA1138

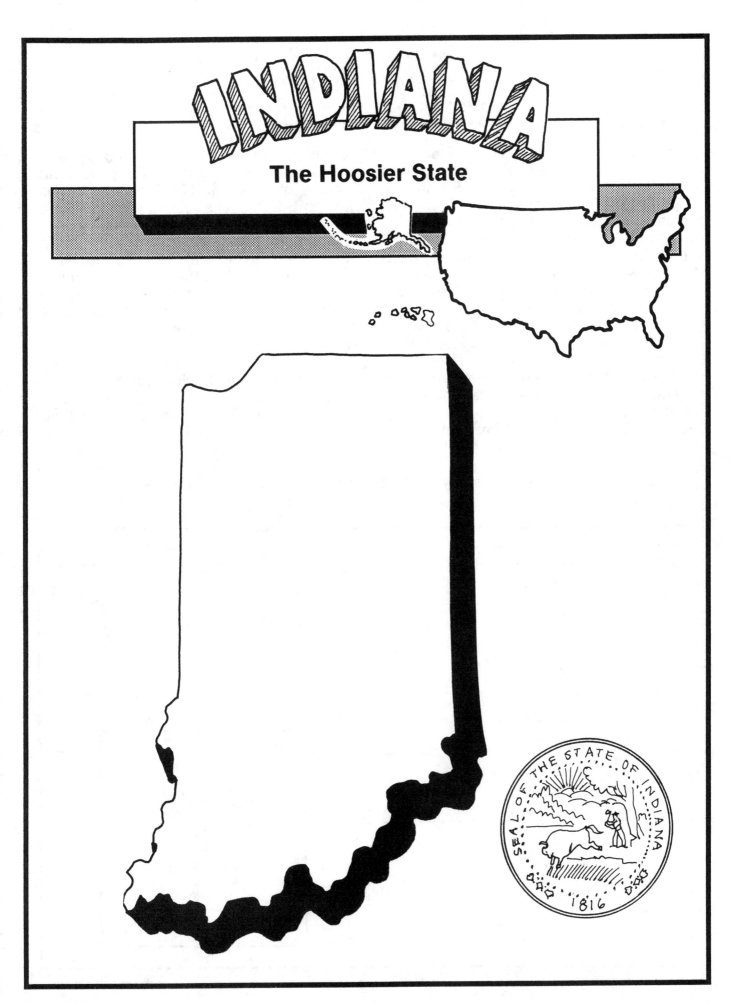

INDIANA

The Hoosier State

SEAL OF THE STATE OF INDIANA
1816

INDIANA
THE HOOSIER STATE

Indiana is the smallest state in size of any state west of the Appalachian Mountains except Hawaii; however, its 5.5 million people rank it as the twelfth most populous state. Its motto "The Crossroads of America" is significant because of its location in the heartland of America. Its northwestern area contains some of the heaviest industry in America and provides a big boost to the state's economy. Much of the state lies in the heart of America's rich and fertile corn belt with corn being its leading crop. Indiana also grows a lot of wheat and soybeans. Tourists enjoy the more than fifteen thousand acres of terrain in the Indiana Dunes National Lakeshore along Lake Michigan. The state's lakes and streams also provide boating, fishing and swimming. The geographic and cultural patterns found in Indiana mirror the great variety of American life. It can claim ties to the South by its location on the Ohio River. It served as a path to the West in the historic settlement of America. And in the center of the state is Indianapolis, a major metropolitan, that is the very heartland of the state. Its famous Indianapolis Motor Speedway plays host annually to the Indianapolis 500, the greatest event in auto racing. Recent downward turns in the economy have hurt Indiana, and the state has been plagued with water pollution problems. But the resourceful people and the determination to move forward will no doubt put Indiana back into a more favorable position soon.

Before continuing with your study of Indiana, find out about these symbols:

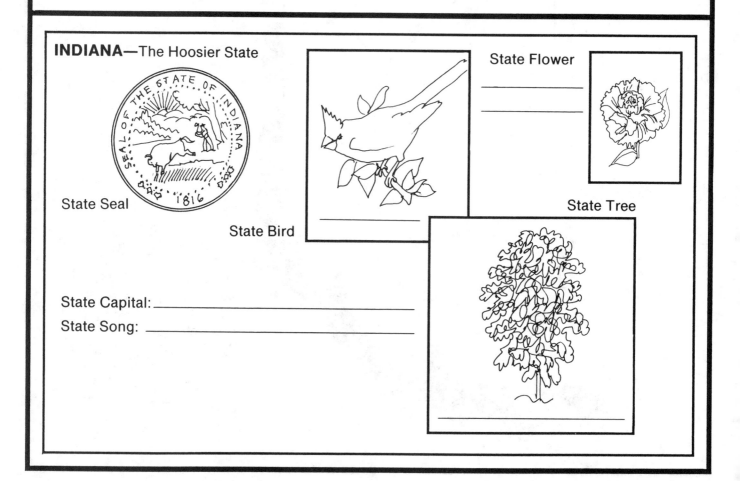

INDIANA—The Hoosier State

State Seal

State Bird

State Flower

State Tree

State Capital: _____

State Song: _____

GA1138

INDIANA ON THE MAP

Locate these cities on your outline map of Indiana:

Indianapolis
Gary
Fort Wayne
Evansville
Kokomo
South Bend

Lafayette
Terre Haute
Bloomington
Columbus
Michigan City
Marion

Draw in these Indiana rivers:

Wabash
Ohio
White
Kankakee
Tippecanoe
Eel
Salamomie

Label the following:

Lake Michigan
Norman Upland
Mitchell Plain
U.S. 40 (formerly the National
   Road)

Indianapolis is often referred to as Circle City. The reason for this name is that its location in the center of the state makes it the hub of the entire state. Looking at an Indiana road map will give you the impression that "all roads lead to Indianapolis," much as the spokes of a wheel lead from the center to the outside perimeter. Draw in and label these interstate highways: I-65, I-74, I-70 and I-465.

GA1138

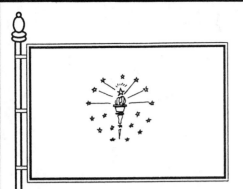

WANDER INDIANA

Even though Indiana is one of the smaller states, it has a lot of places to visit and places to see. In fact tourism in Indiana is a $3 billion industry annually. What do people come to Indiana to see? Below is a list of some of its more popular attractions. Find out about each and write a brief one-sentence description. In the blank space preceding the name of each attraction, create a small symbol you might use to pinpoint its location on the map. For example, a ⬭ could be used to identify the Indianapolis Motor Speedway. Create symbols for the other attractions. Then after you've finished your identifying statements, go back to your outline map and draw in the symbols on your map. You need no other means of identifying the meaning of the symbols as this page will serve as the map's legend.

Indianapolis Motor Speedway _____

_____

Indiana Dunes National Lakeshore_____

_____

New Harmony _____

_____

French Lick _____

_____

Lincoln Boyhood National Memorial _____

_____

George Rogers Clark National Historical Park _____

_____

Hoosier Dome_____

_____

Wyandotte Cave _____

_____

Hoosier National Forest_____

_____

Tippecanoe Battlefield and Museum _____

_____

Studebaker National Museum _____

_____

Clifty Falls State Park _____

_____

GA1138

INDIANA TIME LINE

Below are several events important to the history of Indiana. There is also a list of dates that correspond to the events as they took place. Your task is to match them.

a. 1679	e. 1794	i. 1825	m. 1906
b. 1731	f. 1800	j. 1850	n. 1911
c. 1763	g. 1811	k. 1886	o. 1933
d. 1778	h. 1816	l. 1889	p. 1956

1. _____ The Northern Indiana Toll Road was completed.

2. _____ The French lost Indiana after the French and Indian War.

3. _____ Congress established the Indiana Territory.

4. _____ Robert Owen founded the experimental community of New Harmony.

5. _____ Standard Oil built one of the world's largest oil refineries in Whiting.

6. _____ The French explorer Robert de la Salle was the first white man to reach Indiana.

7. _____ The state's first gas well was drilled at Portland.

8. _____ The first Indianapolis 500-mile Memorial Day race was held.

9. _____ Fort Wayne was founded by General Anthony Wayne to protect settlers from hostile Indians.

10. _____ Indiana's first permanent settlement Vincennes was founded.

11. _____ William Henry Harrison's troops defeated the Indians in the Battle of Tippecanoe.

12. _____ Indiana became the 19th state on December 11.

13. _____ George Rogers Clark seized Vincennes, but the English recaptured it in 1779.

14. _____ United States Steel Corporation built a large steel plant in Gary.

15. _____ The National Road was completed across Indiana.

16. _____ The state government was reorganized and the governor given more power.

GA1138

THE GREATEST SPECTACLE IN SPORTS

Every year on Memorial Day over 350,000 people jam their way into the middle of and around the perimeter of a two and one half mile oval to watch 33 of the world's most skillful drivers find out which one can make 200 laps around that oval in the least amount of time. The site is Indianapolis Motor Speedway and the event is the Indianapolis 500. There is no other event in sports that attracts so many people. Below are the names of some of the drivers who have etched their names into sporting history by their performance at Indy. Research each clue and fill in the appropriate spaces with the names that satisfy the clues.

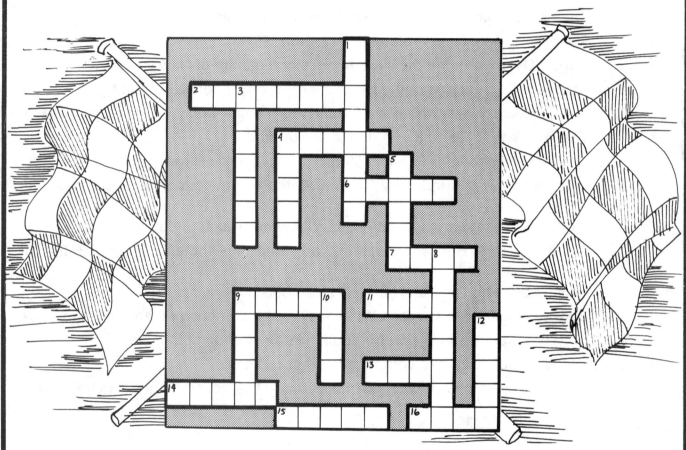

Across

2. His winning speed was 162.029 mph.
4. He finished behind Johnny Rutherford in 1980.
6. He was the first to win in a Lotus Ford.
7. His first of three victories was in 1937.
9. He drove to victory in the first Eagle-Offenhauser.
11. He won in 1959.
13. He first won in 1961.
14. He won in '79, '84 and '88.
15. He was the 1957 champion.
16. His Lola-Ford won in 1966.

Down

1. He won in both 1953 and 1954.
3. He won the first Indy.
4. He finished second in 1961.
5. Victory was his in 1957.
8. He won in 1969.
9. His first two victories were in a P.J. Colt-Ford.
10. He won in 1947 and 1948.
12. He broke the speed record in 1986.

GA1138

IOWA

The Hawkeye State

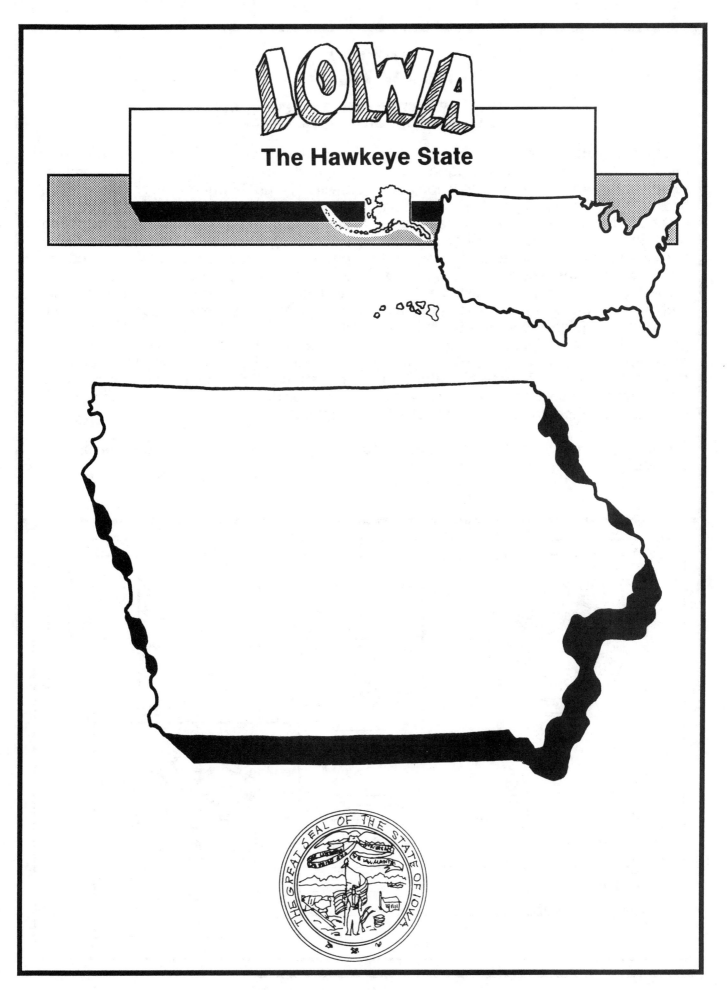

85

GA1138

IOWA
THE HAWKEYE STATE

Nestled in the heartland, Iowa is in the very midst of the most productive agricultural region in the world. This favorable location has helped to place it first in the nation in the production of corn and soybeans and third in pork production. Nearly all of Iowa's soil is cultivable, and its proximity to Midwest industrialization puts it in a favorable position for future expansion. In fact, many might be surprised to know that Iowa's industrial production is three times greater than its agricultural output. Also more Iowans live in cities (58%) than on farms (42%). Even with these statistics that point toward its diversification, the state's total output is far below its more industrial-ized neighbors. Its future will probably depend upon the ability of Iowans to diversify the economy even more. The many farmers who live in Iowa are constantly caught up in the wedge of dwindling prices for grain and livestock and the rising costs of farm machinery, fuel and feed. As a result an increasing number of farmers fail every year. Others tire of the continual battle they wage against such prices. Iowa now is attempting to expand its economy into new markets and product areas. Its future may well be a combination of more industrialization that will help to stabilize and provide better markets for its agricultural output.

To begin your study of Iowa, research the following and write the answers in the spaces provided.

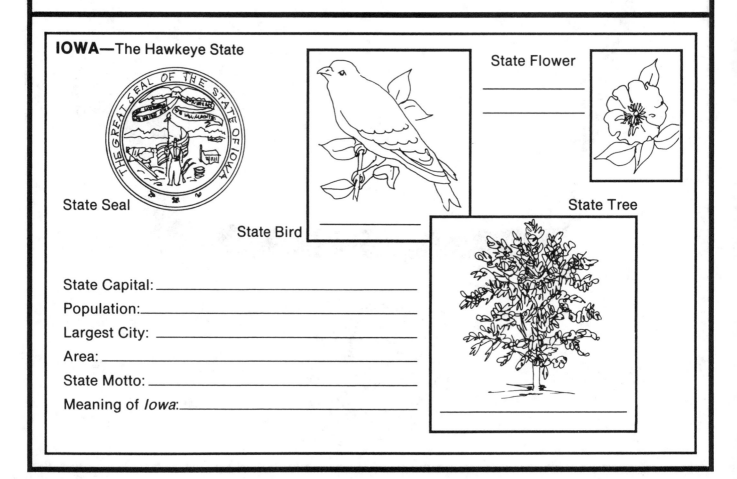

IOWA—The Hawkeye State

State Seal

State Bird

State Flower

State Tree

State Capital: _____

Population: _____

Largest City: _____

Area: _____

State Motto: _____

Meaning of *Iowa*: _____

GA1138

IOWA TRIVIA

Below are some questions that will require some research. With the help of a few travel brochures on Iowa, you should be able to find the answers.

1. How many villages make up the Amana Colonies? _____

2. What Indian tribe holds a powwow near Tama each year? _____

3. In what city is Snake Alley—"The Crookedest Street in the World"? _____

4. How many state parks and recreation areas are there in Iowa? _____

5. Davenport holds a jazz festival each summer in honor of what famous musician? _____

6. There are six bridges in Madison County that are listed on the National Register of Historic Places. What type of bridges are all six? _____

7. Which Iowa community hosts the National Hobo Convention? _____

8. What does the acronym RAGBRAI mean? _____

9. Where in Iowa are the National Hot Air Balloon Championships held? _____

10. The sprint car capital of the world is _____.

11. In what month is the Iowa State Fair held each year? _____

12. This city hosts the nation's largest action exhibits of steam engines and steam-powered farm machinery each summer with its Midwest Old Threshers Reunion. _____

13. Des Moines plays host to one of the nation's premier track meets each year in April. This classic event is called _____

14. Which city hosts the Grant Wood Art Festival? _____

15. The largest Amish settlement west of the Mississippi River is near _____.

16. Name either of the two Iowa communities which hosts an annual Tulip Festival in May. _____

87

GA1138

"IQ"—IOWA QUOTIENT

Test your "Iowa Quotient" by looking at the clues below the crossword puzzle. If you need extra help, consult other sources.

Across

2. This river serves as the western boundary of Iowa.
6. One of the team of "first explorers" to investigate Iowa's western border
7. It served as the inspiration for Meredith Wilson's *The Music Man*.
10. This city is one of the nation's insurance centers.
11. Iowa's Big 8 team from Iowa State University
12. The number of greyhound racetracks in Iowa
13. The home of Maytag
14. The nickname for the athletic teams from the University of Iowa

Down

1. This famous Iowan was born in Winterset.
2. This river serves as the eastern boundary of Iowa.
3. The birthplace of our 31st President
4. Ronald Reagan was an amateur radio announcer for this station.
5. The national scholastic test in which Iowa seniors rank first
8. One of the team of explorers to "discover" Iowa in 1673.
9. Johnny Carson was born here.

GA1138

LOCATING IOWA CITIES

When travelers are trying to locate a city on a road map, they usually look at the coordinates index in preference to a random search of the entire map. The coordinates index provides the user with a method of pinpointing a location that is based on an intersection of an east/west line with a north/south line.

For example, in the sample below, the city of Oakland would be indicated as B-2 on the index. If a map user did not know where Oakland was on the map, he could look in the index. Then after finding B-2, he would run one pointer down an imaginary line straight south from B. The other pointer (fingers will do) should follow a path from the 2 straight east. Where the two imaginary lines intersect should be the city of Oakland. Sometimes the coordinates are not precisely correct as they must each serve more than a single point of reference, but they will at least get the user in the "vicinity" so his search will be easier.

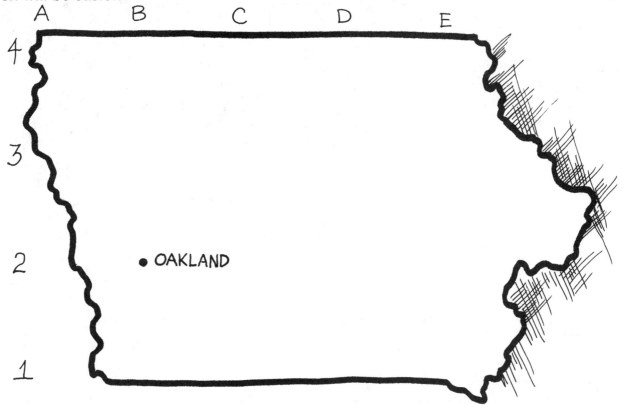

Test your own ability to use coordinates by locating the following Iowa cities and towns given in the index below. Do not look at a road map of Iowa. Using the map above, locate each city as best you can, place a dot where you think it should be and print the name of the city. When you've finished locating all the cities, exchange your map with a friend and check your accuracy with a road map of Iowa.

Des Moines C-2	Cedar Rapids E-2
Keokuk E-1	Mason City C-4
Iowa City E-2	Ottumwa D-1
Sioux City A-3	Council Bluffs A-2
Cedar Falls D-3	Dubuque E-3

GA1138

IOWA'S GREATEST RESOURCE—HER LAND

Iowa farmland is among the richest and best in the world. The rich black topsoil provides the perfect environment for corn and soybeans as well as several other crops. The amount of soybeans and corn an area can produce per acre largely determines the value of the land. Man can help that production increase by applying herbicides and pesticides. Nature has provided the level terrain, the soil and proper heat and moisture. Below is a map showing Iowa farmland values in a recent year, according to what was paid for farms purchased during that year. From the information provided, calculate the problems which follow.

Key

☐	$800-1200/acre
▨	$1200-1600/acre
▩	$1600-2000/acre
▦	$2000-2500/acre
⣿	over $2500/acre

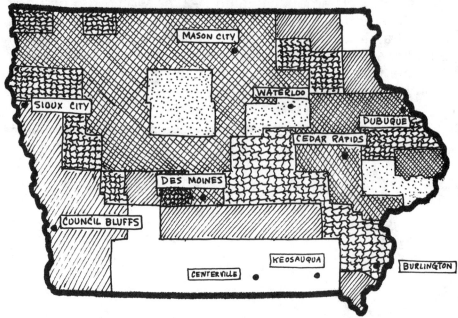

1. Would you rather own a farm near Cedar Rapids or Council Bluffs? Justify your choice.

   _____

   _____

2. How much more per acre could a farm near Mason City be worth than one near Sioux City? _____

3. How much more could a 460-acre farm near Burlington be worth than one near Dubuque? _____

4. What would be the minimum a farmer near Centerville could expect for his 280-acre farm? _____

   _____

5. At the very minimum how much more would a farmer near Waterloo expect to get for his 320-acre farm than one who owns a farm near Keosauqua?_____

6. How much could a farmer near the capital of Iowa expect to get for his 160-acre farm if he gets top dollar for his land? _____

7. Your choice: Owning a 1000-acre farm near Council Bluffs or a 600-acre tract of land near Cedar Rapids? _____

GA1138

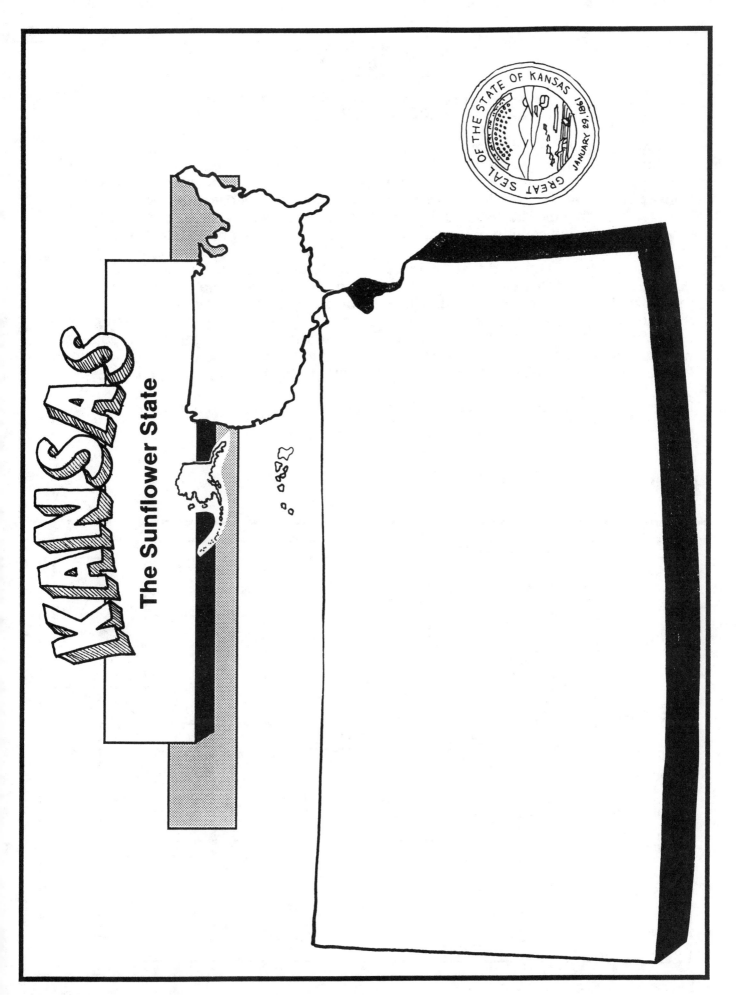

KANSAS

The Sunflower State

91

KANSAS
THE SUNFLOWER STATE

During the days when pioneers were settling in California and the Oregon Territory, the land which is today called Kansas was regarded as little more than a place through which to pass. Its importance grew with the coming of the railroad and the connection it served between the cattle ranches of Texas and their markets in the East. Dodge City became known as the Cowboy Capital of the World. When the nation became divided over the issue of slavery, both the North and the South wanted this strategic state. Open warfare erupted as the two sides attempted to set up state governments without success. Kansas was eventually admitted as a free state that prohibited slavery. The Homestead Act helped to further populate the land, and a hardy strain of wheat brought by a group of Mennonites from Russia soon became a highly successful crop that was well-suited for Kansas soil and climate. Today, Kansas is one of our top producers of grain. But industry has become important to Kansas, too, and the manufacture of aircraft, camping gear, snowmobiles and air-conditioning equipment are all significant to the Kansas economy.

Before continuing with your study of Kansas, become familiar with these symbols:

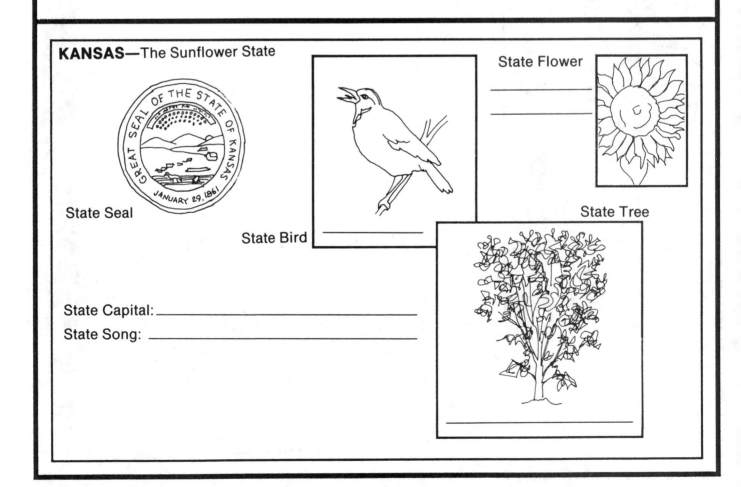

KANSAS—The Sunflower State

State Seal

State Bird _____

State Flower
_____
_____

State Tree

State Capital: _____
State Song: _____

GA1138

KANSAS ON THE MAP

Locate these cities on your outline map of Kansas:

Emporia	Salina	Lawrence
Pittsburg	Kansas City	Leavenworth
Garden City	Topeka	Manhattan
Hutchinson	Wichita	Great Bend
Abilene	Hays	

Draw in these rivers that are important to Kansas:

Arkansas	Missouri
Kansas	Smoky Hill

Identify the historic significance of each of the following with a brief statement. Then pinpoint the location of each on your outline map.

Fort Larned National Historic Site
Fort Riley
Hollenberg Station
Dodge City
John Brown Memorial State Park
Dwight D. Eisenhower Boyhood Home

Draw in the route followed by the Old Chisholm Trail and the Santa Fe Trail.

AMERICA'S CENTRAL PARK

Place yourself in the role of working for the Kansas Travel and Tourism Bureau. You have just been designated to create a new travel brochure that will attract tourists to the state. The main thrust of the new advertising campaign will be "Kansas—America's Central Park." Your task will be to design a logo using this theme—then create a four-page brochure that will carry this theme and emphasize the good points of Kansas. Include historical, recreational and high interest places and things to do that will make a trip to Kansas a worthwhile experience. Make each page of the folder 4" x 8" and create copy that will accompany your pictures (cut from magazines or hand drawn). Share your folder with other members of your class.

GA1138

KANSAS, CROSSROADS OF AMERICA

Answer each of the clues below with a name (or word) that fits into the spaces provided.

Across

2. This river is part of the northeastern boundary of Kansas.
3. Favorite son of Kansas
5. Well-known abolitionist
6. He led an early expedition across Kansas.
8. Persons who fought to make Kansas a free state
11. Home of the University of Kansas
13. The grandson of an Indian chief, he was once vice president of the United States.
14. Highest point in Kansas

Down

1. He was made marshall of Abilene.
2. They brought Turkey Red wheat to Kansas.
4. He wrote the words to the state song.
7. The Indian word for "People of the South Wind"
9. The first governor of Kansas
10. Kansas' #1 grain
12. He surveyed the Oregon Trail.

GA1138

FOR FURTHER RESEARCH. . .

Find out about each of the following through researching other resources and add two complete sentences that will better explain each.

JOHN BROWN

1. Explain the meaning of the term *Bleeding Kansas*.

   _____
   _____
   _____
   _____

2. Explain why Kansas is sometimes referred to as "America's Central Park."

   _____
   _____

3. Explain how towns like Abilene, Wichita and Dodge City sprang up almost overnight.

   _____
   _____

4. Explain how Kansas' position in the geographic center of the United States should not be equated with middle-of-the-road conservatism.

   _____
   _____

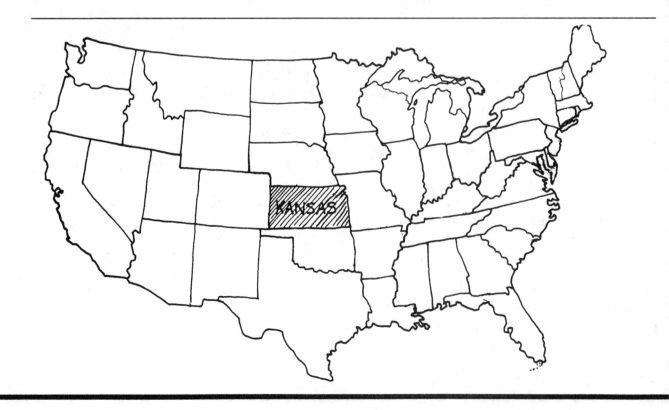

GA1138

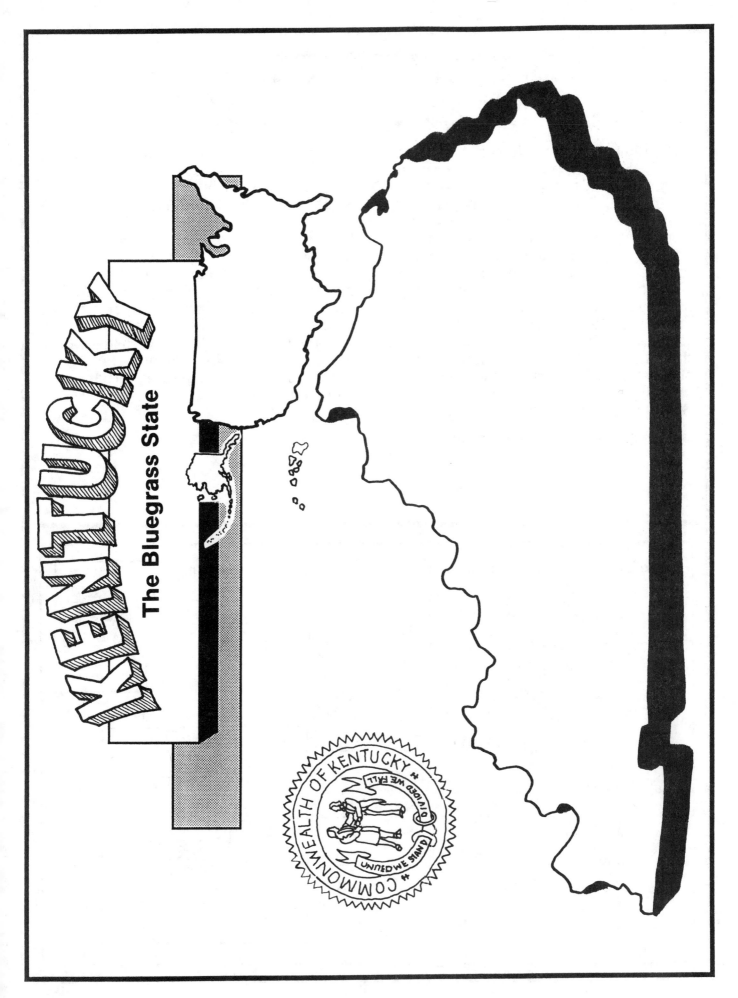

KENTUCKY

The Bluegrass State

GA1138

KENTUCKY
THE BLUEGRASS STATE

Both tradition and location have combined to make Kentucky one of those "crossroads of America." During the early expansion of America, it was the land between the eastern seaboard and America's western frontier. With the Appalachians on the east and the Mississippi to the west, it remains today a crossroad between east and west. It also served as a boundary between North and South during the Civil War at which time it tried to remain neutral. Its nostalgic touch with the past stimulates romantic thoughts—Daniel Boone, vast plantations, stately mansions, distinguished gentlemen in white suits and the familiar strains of Stephen Foster's "My Old Kentucky Home"

just preceding the running of the Kentucky Derby. Kentucky is all of that and more. Its production of bituminous coal in the Appalachian Highlands and Tennessee River Valley rank it among the nation's leaders. Tobacco, whiskey and timber products are also important to the Kentucky economy. A sprinkling of industrial cities along the Ohio River have boosted Kentucky's rank as an industrial state in recent years, but there is still a lot of poverty in Kentucky that ranks it low (46th) in income/capita. A rise in future rank must surely come from greater urban and industrial development.

Before continuing on further with your study of Kentucky, find the following symbols:

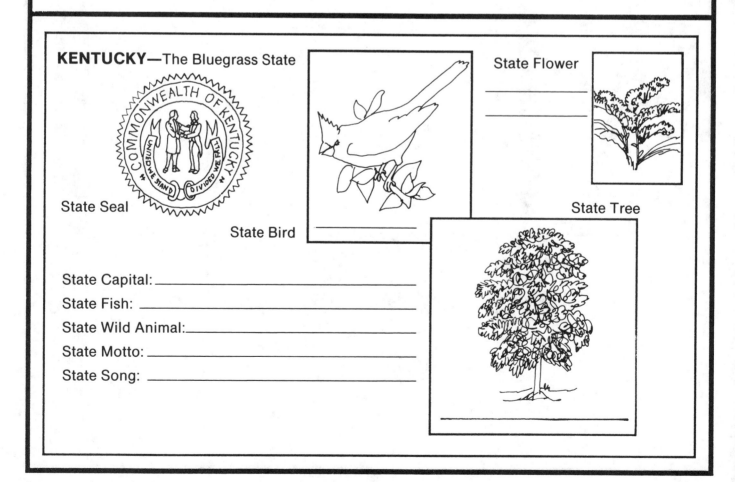

KENTUCKY—The Bluegrass State

State Seal

State Bird

State Flower

State Tree

State Capital: _____

State Fish: _____

State Wild Animal: _____

State Motto: _____

State Song: _____

GA1138

KENTUCKY TIME LINE

Below are several significant events that have helped to shape the rich history of Kentucky. The events are all out of order. Find out when each took place and record the letter that corresponds to that event on the time line at the bottom next to the appropriate date.

a. Harrodsburg, the first permanent Kentucky settlement, was established.
b. Kentucky became the 15th state on June 1.
c. The *Enterprise*, the first steamboat to travel up the Mississippi and Ohio Rivers, reached Louisville.
d. Thomas Walker made the first thorough exploration of Kentucky.
e. The loose-leaf tobacco market was established in Lexington.
f. Federal law passed to require strip mine owners to restore the land.
g. Daniel Boone made his first journey into Kentucky.
h. Kentucky remained loyal to the Union in the Civil War.
i. Daniel Boone founded Boonesborough.
j. America's 16th President, Abraham Lincoln, was born near Hodgenville.
k. Kentucky lowered the voting age to 18.
l. Kentucky farmers broke a tobacco monopoly during the Black Patch War.
m. Kentucky Dam was completed to create Kentucky Lake, one of the largest artificial lakes in the United States.
n. The U.S. Treasury established a gold vault at Fort Knox.
o. The state legislature reapportioned the senate and the house to provide for representation based on population.

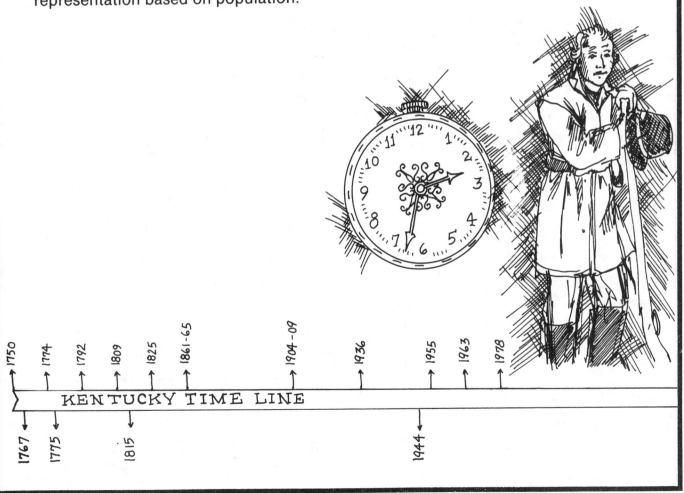

Time line marks (above the line): 1750, 1774, 1792, 1809, 1825, 1861-65, 1904-09, 1936, 1955, 1963, 1978

KENTUCKY TIME LINE

Time line marks (below the line): 1767, 1775, 1815, 1944

99

KENTUCKY FARE

There are indeed a lot of sights to see in Kentucky. There's a lot of history and tradition, and there is also the beauty of the land itself, from its majestic mountains in the east, to the vast sparkling lakes in the west, to its deep lush forests that are preserved for hiking and camping. Listed below are some of the main attractions. Pinpoint the location of each on your outline map of Kentucky. You may need to do some research to find out where the attractions are to be found. You may also need to abbreviate some of the names of the attractions.

My Old Kentucky Home
Mammoth Cave National Park
Daniel Boone National Forest
Land Between the Lakes
Cumberland Gap National Historical Park
Churchill Downs
Abraham Lincoln Birthplace National Historic Site
Lake Barkley
Kentucky Lake

Big South Fork National River
Shaker Village of Pleasant Hill
Fort Knox
Lincoln Heritage House
Colonel Sanders Museum
Old Washington
Harrodsburg
Jefferson Davis Monument State Historic Site

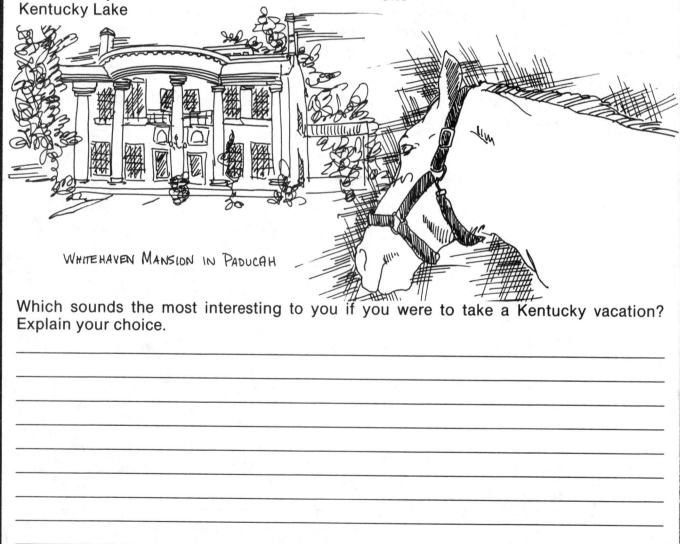

WHITEHAVEN MANSION IN PADUCAH

Which sounds the most interesting to you if you were to take a Kentucky vacation? Explain your choice.

_____
_____
_____
_____
_____
_____
_____
_____
_____
_____

GA1138

A FRONTIER LEGEND

Daniel Boone was perhaps the most famous pioneer of colonial times. His love for Kentucky, his knowledge of the ways and crafts of the great outdoors, his courage in fighting Indians and his skills as a trailblazer have made him a favorite of young and old alike. Read about the life of this great frontiersman and you will see why Kentucky is so justly proud of his accomplishments, his personality and his lifestyle that have made him a shining example of what early Kentucky was all about. Then fill in the blanks below that highlight his life.

1. His birthplace _____

2. The religion of his parents _____

3. The name Boone gave his favorite rifle _____

4. The man from whom Boone first heard about Kentucky _____

5. Where the Boones moved when Pennsylvania became *too crowded* _____

6. When Boone was 21, he married a neighbor girl named _____

7. When Daniel Boone did finally reach Kentucky, he followed a path through the mountains called _____

8. The name of the fort and settlement Boone established in Kentucky _____

9. The route Boone made famous to Kentucky _____

10. Describe how you think Boone would have described his *first look* at Kentucky _____

_____

_____

_____

DANIEL BOONE

GA1138

THE MOST EXCITING TWO MINUTES IN SPORTS

Every year on the first Saturday in May, Kentucky hosts the most famous horse race in the world, the Kentucky Derby. Held at Louisville's Churchill Downs, the Derby has become a yearly pilgrimage for thousands of horse race fans. Below are the names of some of the Derby's past winners and the jockeys who rode them. Research Derby history to find the correct answers. Then find those names in the maze of letters below and circle each.

The 1948 winner of the Triple Crown
1955 champion
1937 champion
He rode both Riva Ridge and Secretariat.
1958 champion
He rode Decidedly.
1923 champion
1977 champion
Jockey aboard Swale
1966 champion
1956 champion
1987 champion
He rode Foolish Pleasure.
1988 champion
Eddie Arcaro won his first Derby aboard this horse.
1978 Triple Crown champion
1984 champion
1944 champion
1951 champion
1980 champion

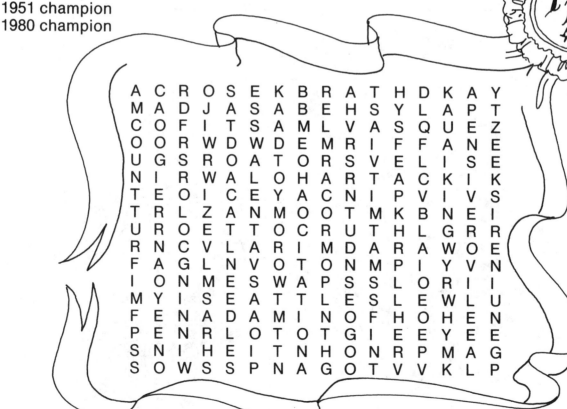

```
A C R O S E K B R A T H D K A Y
M A O D J A S A B E H S Y L A P T
C O F I T S A D M L V A S Q U E Y
O O R S W D S W A E M R I F L A N Z
U G R R O A T O H R S N F E C K E E
N I E O I C A L E Y H A T A P B I K
T R L Z A N E N M O C R I M L N V S
T O O E V T T O C R U T K A G E I
U N C G L A R I M D N H R P R O R
R A G N L N V O T O N A M L I V E
F O I M E S W A P S S L O W Y R N
I Y N M S E A T T L E S L E W H I
M E A A D A M I N O F H O E E A U
F N R L O T O T G I E Y M E A N
P I H E I T N H O N R P L A E G
S W S S P N A G O T V V K L P
```

102

GA1138

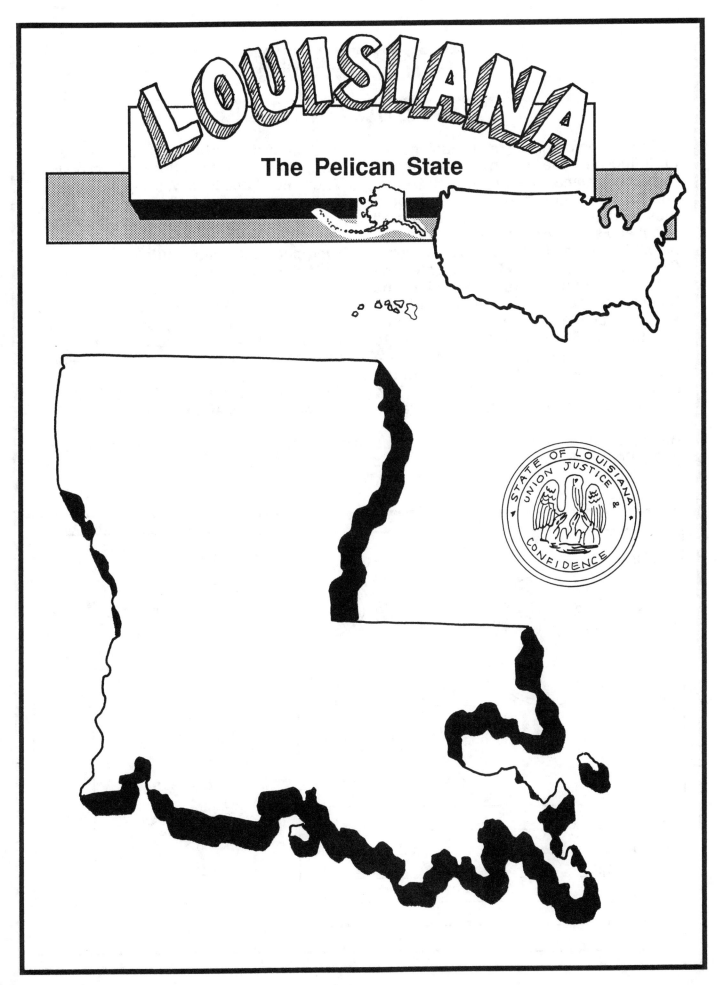

LOUISIANA

The Pelican State

STATE OF LOUISIANA
UNION JUSTICE & CONFIDENCE

103

LOUISIANA
THE PELICAN STATE

Perhaps in no other U.S. state can one see the influence of the French and the Spanish than in Louisiana. The art, the architecture and the culture of those European countries is what the city of New Orleans is all about and shows dramatically their importance in the early history of the area. Originally settled by the French, Louisiana fell under Spanish rule following the French and Indian War. French settlers in a part of Canada called Acadia were forced out by the British. Many migrated to Louisiana. These Cajuns, as they were called, have preserved the French culture ever since. In 1800 Louisiana was given back to the French. The emperor of France sold all of the territory called Louisiana to the United States for fifteen million dollars. The state at one time was dependent upon agriculture to sustain its economy. Today cotton, rice, sugarcane and sweet potatoes are important agricultural products; however, petroleum and natural gas, commercial fishing, trapping and manufacturing far outreach agriculture in their importance to the economy. Forests that cover almost half of the state supply pine to sawmills for pulp and lumber and hardwoods that are used in furniture. The broad delta of the Mississippi River as it empties into the Gulf of Mexico has made New Orleans one of America's great port cities.

Before continuing with your study of Louisiana, become familiar with these symbols of the Pelican State:

LOUISIANA—The Pelican State

State Seal

State Bird _____

State Flower
_____
_____

State Tree

State Capital: _____
State Gemstone: _____
State Insect: _____
State Fossil: _____
State Dog: _____
State Motto: _____

_____

GA1138

LOUISIANA ON THE MAP

Pinpoint the locations of these Louisiana cities on your outline map:

New Orleans   Kenner
Shreveport   Lafayette
Alexandria   Monroe
Lake Charles   Houma
Baton Rouge   Bossier Ctiy
Metairie

Draw in these Louisiana rivers:

Mississippi   Sabine
Ouachita   Pearl
Red   Calcasieu

Label these bodies of water:

Gulf of Mexico   Lake Borgne
Lake Pontchartrain   Breton Sound

Locate these tourist attractions:

Jean Lafitte National Historical Park
Kisatchie National Forest
Avery Island
Grand Isle
Acadiana

GA1138

LOUISIANA'S PAST

Read each clue below and find a word (or words) associated with Louisiana history that fits into the puzzle and also satisfies the clue.

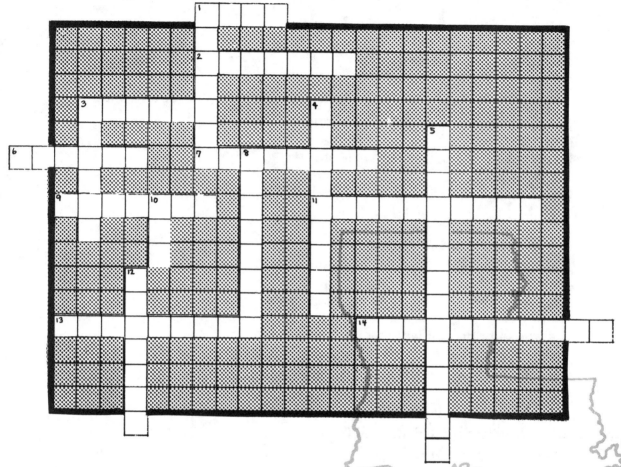

Across

1. Style of music born in New Orleans
2. Colorful descendents of the Spanish and French in Louisiana
3. French-Acadians who came to southern Louisiana
6. He was probably the first white man in Louisiana.
7. He sold all of Louisiana to the United States for $15 million.
9. He gave Louisiana its name.
11. Famous concert pianist born in Louisiana
13. New Orleans' festival held prior to Lent
14. It empties into the Gulf of Mexico at New Orleans.

Down

1. He won the Battle of New Orleans after the War of 1812 had ended.
3. He developed a profitable fur trading business with the Indians.
4. He founded the city of New Orleans.
5. New Orleans' most famous jazz musician
8. Louisiana's parallel to counties of all other states
10. Scotch banker and developer
12. He won fame for his remarkable paintings of American birds.

NEW ORLEANS—THE CRESCENT CITY

New Orleans, that never-ending festival of fun, attracts millions of tourists annually to the many sights and sounds amidst a charming Old World atmosphere. It is the nation's largest seaport on the Gulf of Mexico and is one of the the South's most important cities. But perhaps more important to its economy is its reputation as one of the most fun cities to visit in the United States.

You have just been hired as a tour guide to help tourists see and enjoy this great city. To do a good job, you will have to do some researching and "exploring" to make certain tourists get to see the "high spots" and get their money's worth. You'll want to blend the history of some of the more important landmarks with the jazz music that has made the city famous. Don't forget about the Spanish and French architecture and certainly you won't want to forget the food and nightlife that have helped to earn the city its reputation. Decide what you're going to say about each of the following as well as other sites you feel should be included in a tour of the Crescent City. Prepare your narrative and exchange your tour with a fellow student.

Stops you'll probably want to include:

Lake Pontchartrain Rain Causeway
Preservation Hall
Royal, Bourbon, Burgundy,
    Dumaine, Chartres Streets
St. Charles Streetcar Line

French Quarter
Jackson Square
St. Louis Cathedral
Cabildo
Audubon Zoo

French Market
Garden District
Presbytére
Riverwalk

GA1138

CAJUN COOKIN'

South Louisiana was settled by a people whose zest for life has flavored the swamps and bayous with lively music and spicy foods. The Cajuns are descendents of French-Acadian exiles who came to this land from eastern Canada during the 1700's. They have preserved their culture and heritage in a unique lifestyle that is celebrated daily. Among the most distinctive features of the Cajun heritage is their cooking. No visit to New Orleans and south Louisiana is complete without a meal fixed "Cajun style." Find out about this unique way of cooking that has become well-known throughout the United States and brings millions of dollars into the economy of south Louisiana annually. Report your findings below and list several foods that are prepared this way. Finally describe two recipes in detail that involve Cajun cooking. Include the names of the dishes and ingredients and instructions that go into their preparation.

GA1138

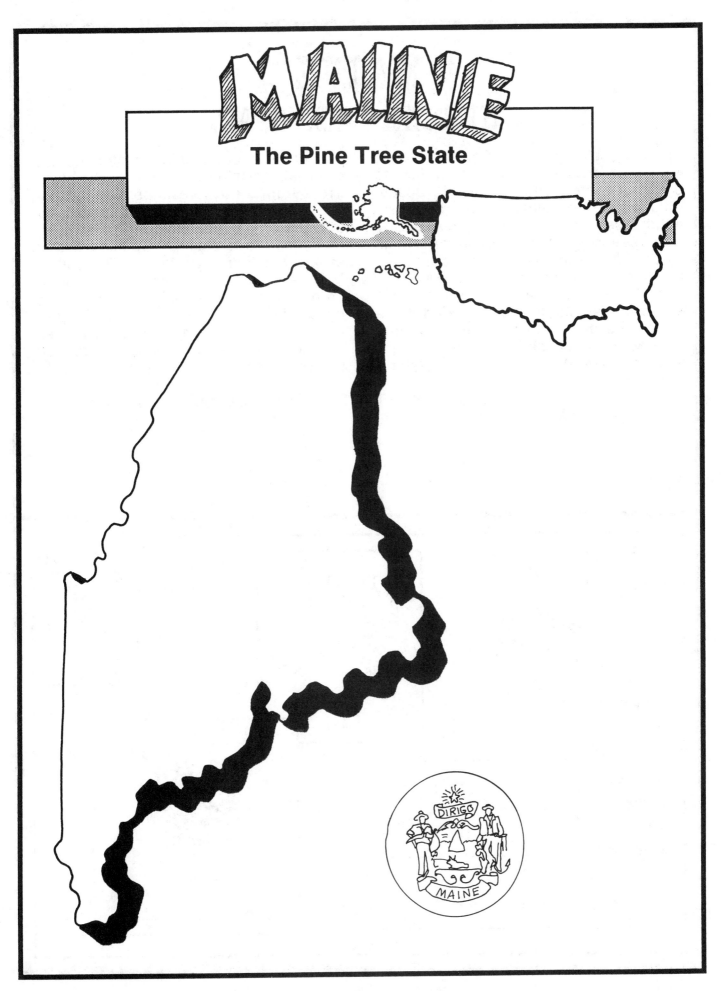

MAINE

The Pine Tree State

GA1138

MAINE
THE PINE TREE STATE

The largest of the New England states, Maine, is perhaps best known for its beautiful shore along the Atlantic Ocean. This famous coastline has several classic lighthouses, small fishing villages, sandy beaches and thousands of offshore islands. Rocky cliffs and jagged rock formations add to the rugged beauty of Maine's coastline. Acadia National Park draws thousands of tourists annually, making it the nation's second most popular national park. Maine's location in the extreme northeast corner of the United States makes it our nation's easternmost state. Forests cover almost ninety percent of the state. Trees from these forests provide the raw materials for the giant wood-processing industry. The people involved have wisely replanted the forests they've harvested to ensure the industry's future. The soil of Maine is carefully cultivated to support crops such as potatoes. The state has declined significantly in economic importance since its early days, but the Yankee traditions of Maine embody the rugged self-reliant essence of early America.

Before continuing your study of the Pine Tree State, familiarize yourself with the symbols of Maine called for below.

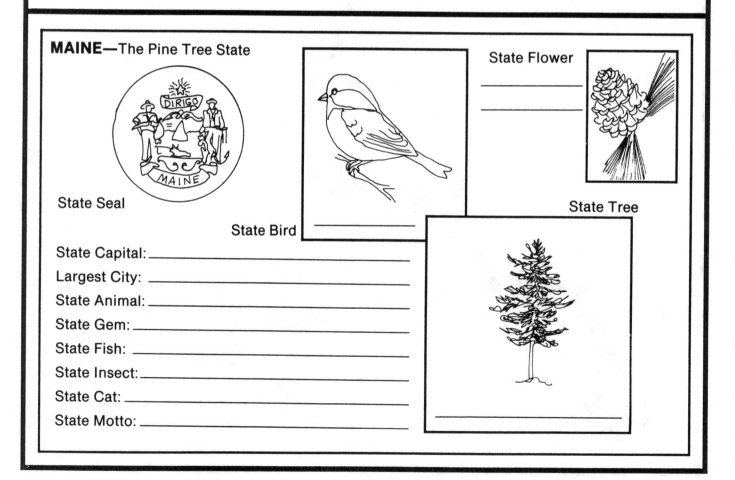

MAINE—The Pine Tree State

State Seal

State Bird

State Flower

State Tree

State Capital: _____

Largest City: _____

State Animal: _____

State Gem: _____

State Fish: _____

State Insect: _____

State Cat: _____

State Motto: _____

GA1138

CROSSING MAINE'S HISTORY

1. He arrived in 1614 to explore Maine's coast from Penobscot to Cape Cod.
2. He was governor in 1857, then became vice president.
3. He probably explored the coast of Maine in 1498.
4. He was the first Democrat elected to the U.S. Senate by the voters of Maine.
5. Massachusetts bought Maine from his heirs for $6000.
6. He led the American army through the Kennebec Valley to attack Quebec.
7. He was the 14th U.S. President educated at Bowdoin College.
8. He probably explored the coast of Maine around 1000 A.D.
9. One of the early white English sailors who wrote about his experiences in the New World
10. The state's first settlement founded in 1607
11. He arrived in 1605 to explore Maine.
12. He invented the doughnut hole.

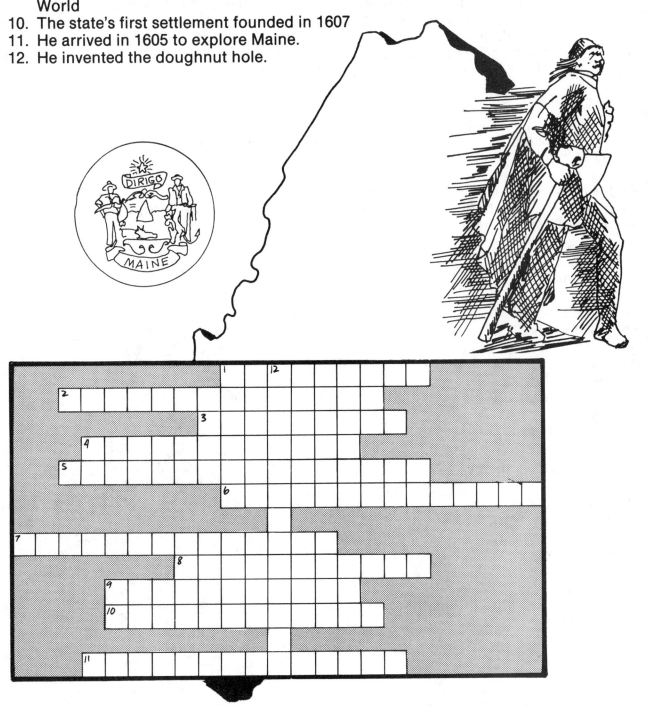

GA1138

MAP MASTER

As many state departments of tourism have done, the Maine Publicity Bureau has developed specifically defined regions of Maine. These regions are often determined by an area of a state that has a landform/geography that is unique to the rest of the state. Another method of "dividing" the state makes use of historical events that have occurred in a well-defined area. Find out about these regions found in Maine and draw them in on your outline map. Be certain to label them properly.

South Coast
Mid Coast
Downeast-Acadia
Sunrise County

Western Lakes and Mountains
Kennebec Valley
Katahdin Moosehead
Aroostook

Each of these regions has several attractions that bring thousands of tourists to Maine annually. Find out the location of each on the list below and print in its proper place on the outline map.

Kennebunk
Sebago Lake
Portland
Penobscot Marine Museum
Rangeley Lakes
Rockport
Bar Harbor
Allagash
Mount Desert Island
Millinocket
Moosehead Lake

Old Orchard Beach
Augusta
Boothbay Harbor
Acadia National Park
Eastport
Winthrop Lakes
Calais
Baxter State Park
Bangor
Presque Isle

GA1138

A SEARCH THROUGH MAINE

BENEDICT ARNOLD

Following the maze of letters below are the names of several cities and people who helped to shape the history of Maine. "Search" them out. You may move your pencil in any direction, including diagonally. You may even turn corners.

```
I  D  L  O  N  R  A  P  R  E  W  E  R  B  M  J
N  F  V  B  A  N  G  O  R  M  T  O  C  R  A  E
E  V  U  S  R  P  M  R  H  I  P  X  K  P  S  S
D  L  A  M  X  S  I  T  Y  T  M  N  L  Q  O  D
M  E  T  S  D  N  A  L  E  T  E  A  A  A  A  G
A  W  A  T  S  U  G  U  A  U  Y  B  N  A  I  C
C  I  W  H  T  I  M  S  N  Y  M  T  D  N  O  H
S  S  R  A  I  Y  T  T  D  P  M  Y  Y  D  T  A
E  T  Z  X  I  P  T  S  A  R  U  C  I  S  M  M
G  O  D  R  O  F  N  A  S  O  E  K  V  A  L  P
R  N  B  R  N  S  T  W  I  E  K  N  F  U  W  L
O  V  T  R  O  S  S  S  G  F  L  E  L  O  C  A
G  M  B  L  C  T  O  T  N  K  U  U  T  I  M  I
T  Y  R  M  F  O  Y  T  O  T  A  H  S  P  Y  N
B  U  E  C  R  E  I  P  L  A  A  C  Y  P  U  R
A  M  T  Y  L  O  R  I  W  X  F  E  Y  M  U  T
```

Bangor	Eastport	Bath	Gorges	Popham
Portland	Brunswick	Sanford	Mason	Longfellow
Augusta	Rockland	Camden	Champlain	Pierce
Lewiston	Brewer	Waymouth	Smith	Arnold

GA1138

MAINE FACTS

Below are several facts and opinions about Maine which you can make use of in helping you to create an advertising brochure that will attract tourists to Maine. Your task is to make the copy so appealing that tourists will be lured into a "Maine Vacation." First "rough out" your copy on another sheet of paper. Then create a genuine four-page 8½" x 4" folder on Maine. Use appropriate photos or drawings that will help to illustrate your message. You may find that you cannot use some of the statements.

Maine. . .

- is recognized as one of the most healthful states in the nation with summertime temperatures averaging 70⁰ F and winter temperatures averaging 20⁰ F.

- is about 320 miles long and 210 miles wide with a total area of 33,215 square miles.

- has 16 counties with 22 cities, 424 towns, 51 plantations and 416 unorganized townships.

- has one mountain, Mt. Katahdin (5268 ft. above sea level) almost a mile high.

- has 6000 lakes and ponds, 32,000 miles of rivers and streams, 17 million acres of forestland, 3478 miles of beautiful coastline and 2000 islands.

- has 60 lighthouses including Portland Head Light commissioned by George Washington.

- has 542,629 acres of state and national parks, including Allagash Wilderness Waterway, Acadia National Park (the second most-visited national park in the United States).

- is America's largest blueberry-growing state, raising ninety-eight percent of the low-bush blueberries in the United States.

- is nationally famed for its shellfish; over 20 million pounds of lobster are harvested annually.

- is blessed with an abundance of cherished landmarks that link us to its romantic past.

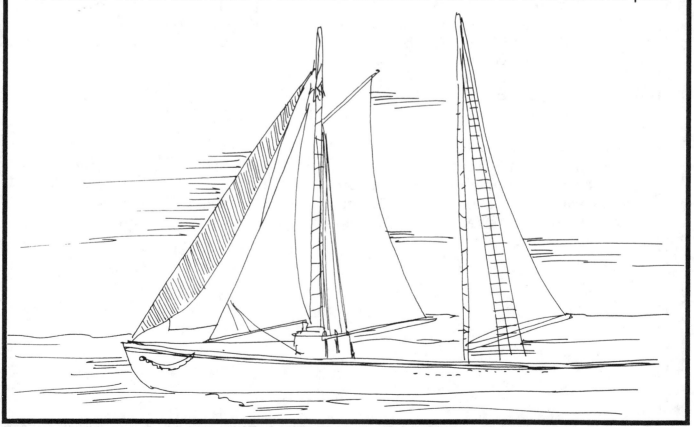

GA1138

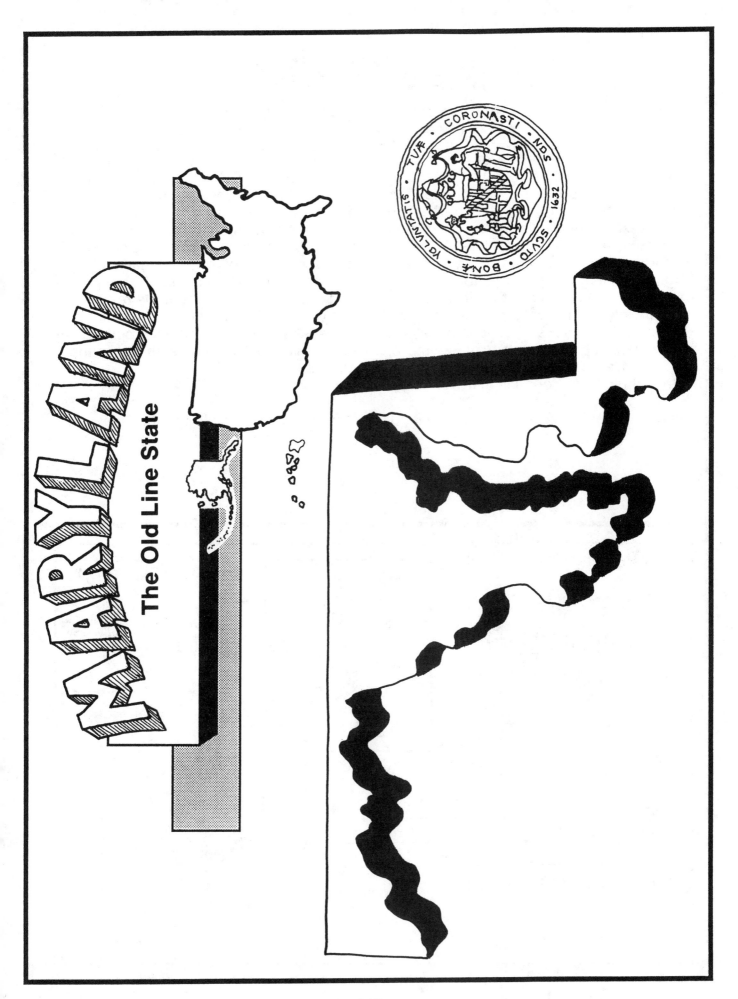

MARYLAND

The Old Line State

115

GA1138

MARYLAND
THE OLD LINE STATE

Although Maryland is one of the smaller states in size (ranking 42nd), it is a state of several different areas, each reflecting a different tradition of American life. The eastern shore lies within the Delmarva Peninsula, a narrow strip of land shared by three states (Delaware, Maryland and Virginia). This region is primarily an agricultural and fishing area that finds ample markets along the eastern coast of the United States. Across Chesapeake Bay on the western shore lies the city of Baltimore, the state's largest city. Baltimore has much of the ethnic flavor found in many of America's large cities. The suburban areas that border on the District of Columbia form another region, one that contains a large segment of military and civilian government installations. In the far northwest corner lies a narrow panhandle of land that is Maryland's area of the Appalachian hill country. This land is a mix of rural poverty and tourism. Thus each of the regions has its own identity, assets and problems. In few states do we find the wide cultural and economic differences as those found in Maryland.

Before continuing your study of Maryland, identify the symbols called for below.

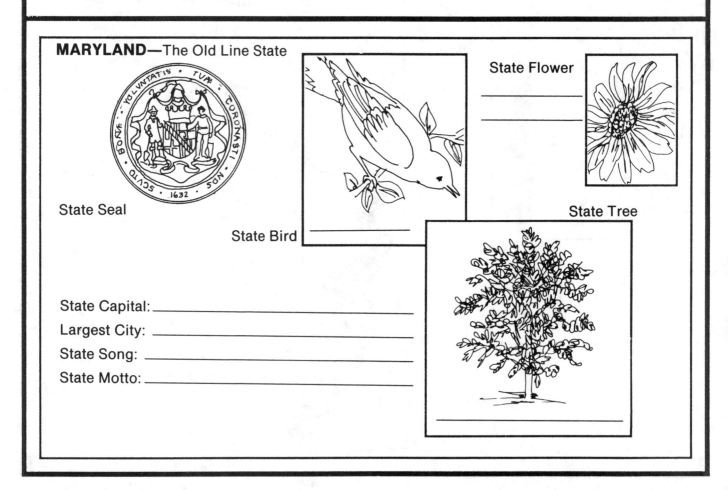

MARYLAND—The Old Line State

State Seal

State Bird _____

State Flower
_____
_____

State Tree

State Capital: _____

Largest City: _____

State Song: _____

State Motto: _____

GA1138

USING THE MAP

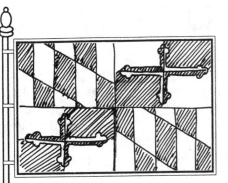

In 1791 Maryland gave up seventy square miles for the purpose of establishing a national capital that was not a part of any state. The result was the city of Washington, D.C.

Show where Washington, D.C., is on your outline map.

Label the areas that are parts of the four states that touch the boundaries of Maryland.

Pinpoint the location of each of these Maryland cities:

Baltimore	Laurel
Hagerstown	Bowie
Cumberland	Silver Spring
Annapolis	Dundalk
Frederick	Bethesda
Rockville	Columbia
College Park	Towson

Draw in and label these bodies of water:

Potomac River	Gunpowder River
Chesapeake Bay	Patapsco River
Patuxent River	Susquehanna River

Show the location of each of these historic sites found in Maryland:

Antietam National Battlefield
Fort McHenry
Harpers Ferry
Barbara Fritchie House
Flag House

LOY'S STATION BRIDGE
IN FREDERICK COUNTY

GA1138

"... THE BOMBS BURSTING IN AIR ..."

During the War of 1812, the British defeated the young American militia at Bladensburg, captured Washington, D.C., and burned the Capitol Building, the President's house and other government buildings. Afraid of being cut off from their supplies, the British left the city and returned to their ships. They then focused their attention on Baltimore, the country's third largest city. The Americans had expected this and had strengthened the city's defenses. Fort McHenry, guarding the approach by sea, had been fortified and old ship hulls placed in positions where they could be easily sunk and thus block the main channel to the city.

On Sunday, September 11, the British fleet arrived at the mouth of the Patapsco River and the church bells of Baltimore called the militia to arms. On September 12, the British landed at North Point and began moving toward the city. It was the British plan to take the city by both land and sea, but Fort McHenry stood in the path of their approach by sea. Because the river was too shallow for the larger British ships (and the ships' hulls had been sunk by this time), they moved sixteen smaller vessels into position. At dawn on September 13 the British began bombarding Fort McHenry. The firing continued all day. At 1:00 a.m. on September 14, the British attempted to land a force of men to attack the fort from the rear. But they were discovered and retreated down river. The bombardment continued all night. After twenty-four hours of shelling the fort without making any real headway, the British finally gave up and withdrew around 9:00 a.m. on September 14. Miraculously only four Americans had been killed and twenty-four were wounded. Because the British felt that taking the city without naval support would prove too costly, they gathered up all their troops and sailed toward the open Atlantic. The attempt to take Baltimore had failed.

While the War of 1812 accomplished absolutely nothing for either the Americans or the British (the reasons the war began were not even mentioned in the Treaty of Ghent), the United States did get something totally unexpected out of the war: a national anthem. The events at Fort McHenry were all a part of it, and this is how it happened.

GA1138

When the British withdrew from Washington, D.C., they had arrested Dr. William Beanes, a physician, for interfering in military matters. He had broken a vow of neutrality. Francis Scott Key, an experienced attorney and friend of Dr. Beanes, went to plead with the British on his behalf. He took with him John Skinner, a U.S. agent in charge of prisoner exchange. Key took along letters from wounded British men attesting to the excellent care they had received from Dr. Beanes. Because of these letters and the method in which Key presented his case, the British released Beanes from custody. However, they refused to allow any of the three Americans to leave at the moment because of their knowledge of the plans to attack Baltimore. Thus the three were kept on board the *H.M.S. Torrant* during the attack on Fort McHenry. At dawn on September 14, Key saw a flag hanging limply over the fort, but he assumed it was a British flag. As the flag slowly unfurled in the early morning breeze, he saw that it was the stars and stripes! He was so moved that he wrote a poem which was called "The Defense of Fort McHenry." We all know that the rest is history. The words were set to the music of an old tune and later became "The Star-Spangled Banner" and was adopted as the national anthem. While the words to the song are indeed poetic and were the outpouring of a deeply moved man, Francis Scott Key no doubt also felt the realism of what was going on as that long night wore on. Your task is to take a long look at the words he wrote and describe how it might have been to have spent that night in darkness listening to the bombardment of Fort McHenry. Describe your feelings as a journal entry in the space below. Be certain to include your reactions to your learning that the British failed.

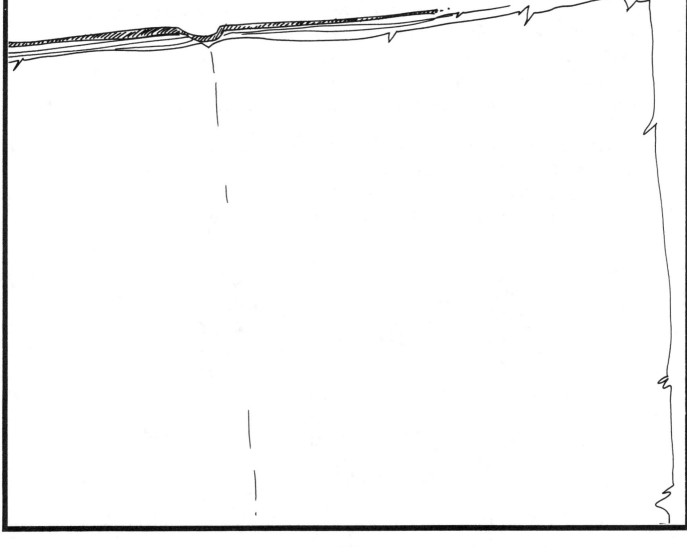

GA1138

MARYLAND'S PAST

Below you will find a list of events that helped to shape the story of Maryland. The order in which they are presented is wrong. Find out when each occurred and arrange the events in sequential order by placing a #1 in the blank beside the event which took place first, etc.

_____ Maryland passed a religious toleration act allowing the free worship of all religions.

_____ Lord Baltimore regained control of the colony from William Claiborne.

_____ Marylanders burned the *Peggy Stewart* and its cargo of tea.

_____ King Charles I granted the Maryland charter to Cecil Calvert, second Lord Baltimore.

_____ The Second Continental Congress met in Baltimore.

_____ Captain John Smith explored Chesapeake Bay.

_____ Mason and Dixon completed their survey of the Maryland-Pennsylvania boundary.

_____ Maryland became the seventh state on April 28.

_____ The first settlers began arriving in Maryland.

_____ George Washington resigned his commission as commander in chief at Annapolis.

_____ Federal troops drove back the Confederates from Antietam Creek.

_____ A constitution abolishing slavery was adopted by the Maryland legislature.

_____ William Claiborne established a trading post on Kent Island.

_____ William Claiborne seized control of the colony.

_____ Maryland gave land for the District of Columbia.

_____ Maryland resisted the nation's prohibition laws and became known as the "free state."

_____ Voters approved a state lottery to raise money for the state.

_____ Maryland declared its independence.

_____ Francis Scott Key wrote "The Star-Spangled Banner."

_____ Maryland reapportioned its legislative and congressional districts.

CAPTAIN JOHN SMITH

FRANCIS SCOTT KEY

GEORGE WASHINGTON

GA1138

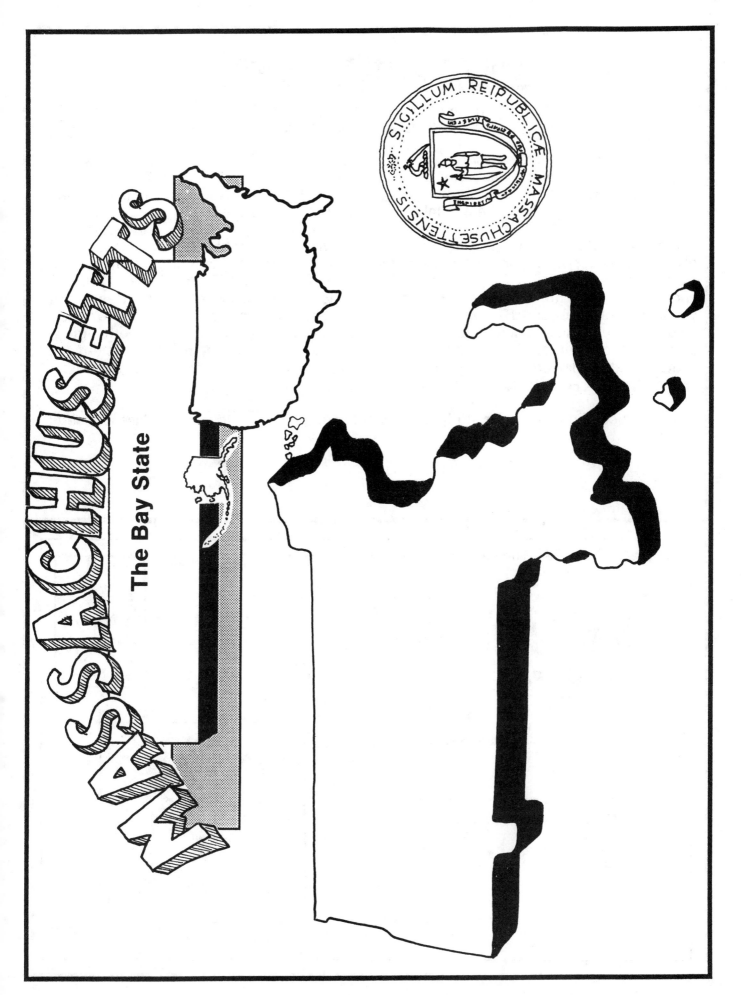

MASSACHUSETTS

The Bay State

121

MASSACHUSETTS
THE BAY STATE

Massachusetts is a state small in size, but ranks near the top in population density. It is one of our most important manufacturing states, and Boston, the capital and largest city, is a major U.S. seaport. Its role in the early history of Colonial America has given it a number of historic landmarks that make it one of America's favorite tourist spots. The many great colleges and universities in and around Boston qualify it as one of the world's educational, medical and research centers. The state's sea routes, roads and rivers cover not only New England, but reach out to the rest of the nation. Many of these transport systems center on the Boston area like spokes in a wheel giving it the nickname the Hub. Even though some of the nation's industry has left the Northeast for the South and the West, Massachusetts remains a leader in high-technology industry. The land itself goes from sea level along the Atlantic Coast to over 3500 feet near its western border. Massachusetts has given the nation three U.S. Presidents and many other great American statesmen, research scientists, engineers, sports heroes and entertainers.

Before proceeding with your study of Massachusetts, find the following Massachusetts symbols:

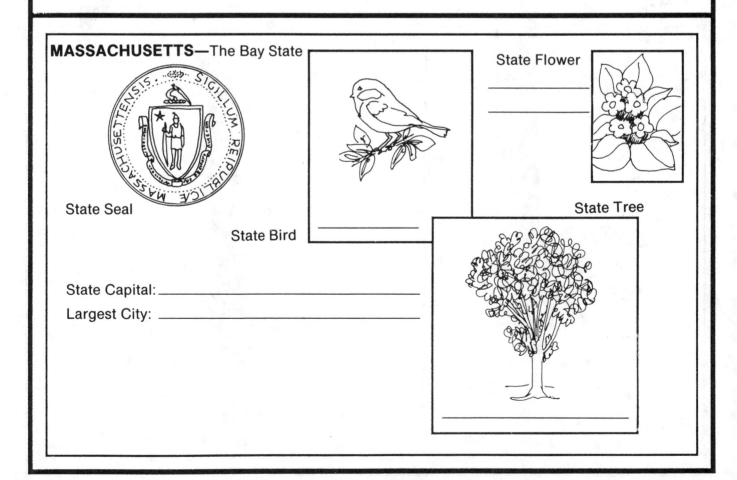

MASSACHUSETTS—The Bay State

State Seal

State Bird

State Flower
_____
_____

State Tree

State Capital: _____
Largest City: _____

GA1138

MASSACHUSETTS ON THE MAP

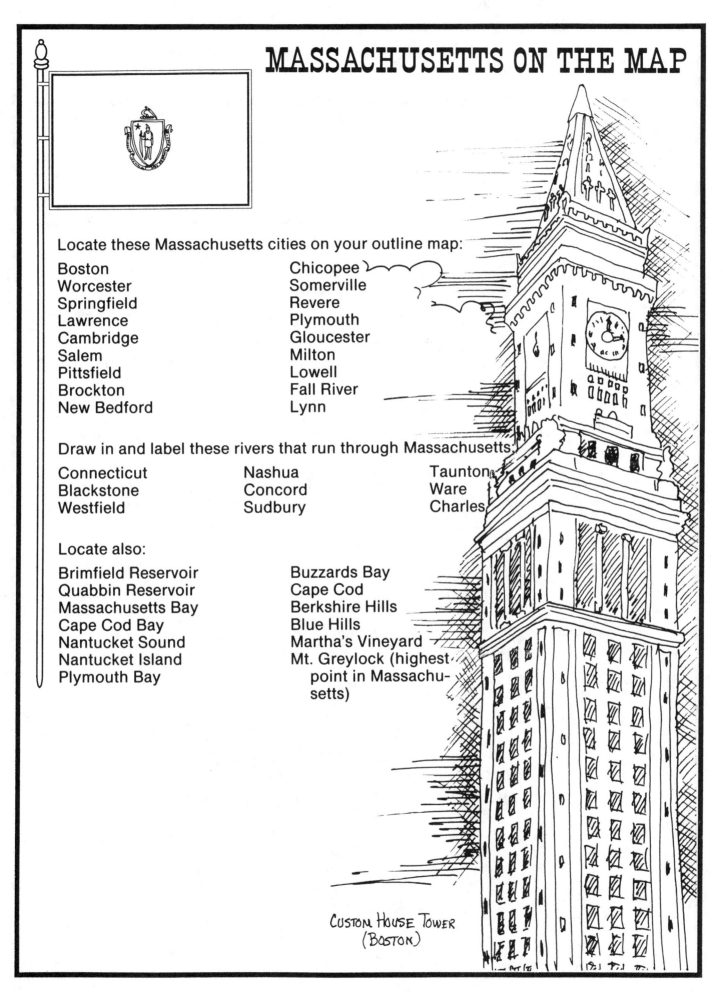

Locate these Massachusetts cities on your outline map:

Boston	Chicopee
Worcester	Somerville
Springfield	Revere
Lawrence	Plymouth
Cambridge	Gloucester
Salem	Milton
Pittsfield	Lowell
Brockton	Fall River
New Bedford	Lynn

Draw in and label these rivers that run through Massachusetts:

Connecticut	Nashua	Taunton
Blackstone	Concord	Ware
Westfield	Sudbury	Charles

Locate also:

Brimfield Reservoir	Buzzards Bay
Quabbin Reservoir	Cape Cod
Massachusetts Bay	Berkshire Hills
Cape Cod Bay	Blue Hills
Nantucket Sound	Martha's Vineyard
Nantucket Island	Mt. Greylock (highest
Plymouth Bay	point in Massachu-
	setts)

CUSTOM HOUSE TOWER
(BOSTON)

GA1138

MASSACHUSETTS TIME LINE

Below are several important events in the history of Massachusetts. However they are not presented in proper choronological order. Your task is to rearrange them (by number) in proper sequence. To do this you will no doubt need to find out when each took place.

a. _____ The Puritans founded Boston.

b. _____ British soldiers killed several colonists in the Boston Massacre.

c. _____ The American Revolution began at Lexington and Concord.

d. _____ Massachusetts colonists helped the British win the French and Indian Wars.

e. _____ Bartholomew Gosnold visited the Massachusetts region.

f. _____ Patriots dumped British tea into Boston Harbor during the Boston Tea Party.

g. _____ John Adams became the President of the United States.

h. _____ The Embargo Act destroyed Massachusetts shipping and led to manufacturing.

i. _____ William Lloyd Garrison published the antislavery newspaper, *The Liberator*.

j. _____ The Pilgrims landed at Plymouth.

k. _____ Massachusetts adopted its first code of law, the Body of Liberties.

l. _____ Massachusetts became the sixth state on February 6.

m. _____ A strike of textile workers at Lawrence led to improved conditions in the textile industry.

n. _____ Massachusetts colonists won King Philip's War.

o. _____ Settlement of the Boston police strike brought national prominence to Governor Calvin Coolidge.

p. _____ John Quincy Adams became President of the United States.

q. _____ Harvard became the first college in the Colonies.

r. _____ Massachusetts adopted its constitution.

s. _____ John F. Kennedy became President.

GA1138

MASSACHUSETTS NAME HUNT

Hidden below are the last names of thirty-six famous people associated with Massachusetts history. Find the name of each and circle the letters. Choose five of interest to you and jot down on the back of this page a statement about each that identifies the person with Massachusetts.

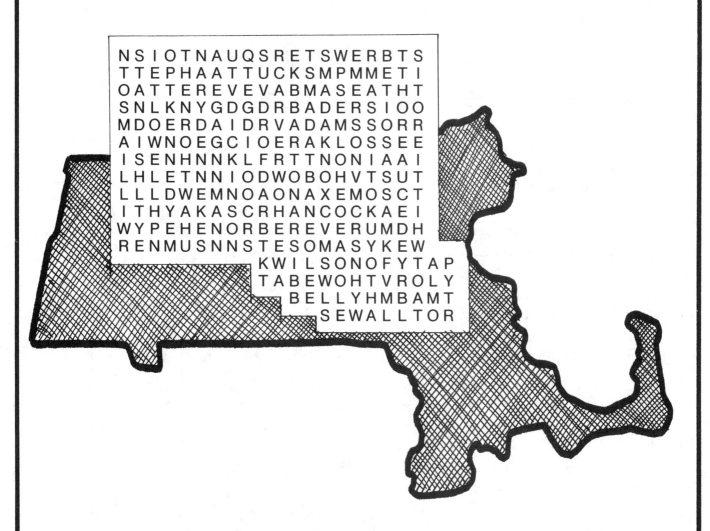

```
N S I O T N A U Q S R E T S W E R B T S
T T E P H A A T T U C K S M P M M E T I
O A T T E R E V E V A B M A S E A T H T
S N L K N Y G D G D R B A D E R S I O O
M D O E R D A I D R V A D A M S S O R R
A I W N O E G C I O E R A K L O S S E E
I S E N H N N K L F R T T N O N I A A I
L H L E T N N I O D W O B O H V T S U T
L L L D W E M N O A O N A X E M O S C T
I T H Y A K A S C R H A N C O C K A E I
W Y P E H E N O R B E R E V E R U M D H
R E N M U S N N S T E S O M A S Y K E W
        K W I L S O N O F Y T A P
        T A B E W O H T V R O L Y
        B E L L Y H M B A M T
        S E W A L L T O R
```

John Adams	John Carver	Elias Howe	Samoset
John Q. Adams	Calvin Coolidge	John F. Kennedy	Samuel Sewall
Samuel Adams	Emily Dickinson	Robert F. Kennedy	Squanto
Crispus Attucks	Ralph Waldo Emerson	Henry Knox	Miles Standish
Clara Barton	Edward Everett	James Russell Lowell	Charles Sumner
Alexander Graham Bell	Thomas Gage	Horace Mann	Henry David Thoreau
James Bowdoin	John Hancock	Massasoit	John G. Whittier
William Bradford	Nathaniel Hawthorne	James Otis	Roger Williams
William Brewster	Oliver Wendell Holmes	Paul Revere	Henry Wilson

GA1138

FREEDOM TRAIL

There is perhaps more early American history in Boston than in any other single U.S. city. In the early 1950's a canny Boston newspaperman, William G. Schofield, realized the near proximity of Boston's many landmarks. He planned out a two-and-one-half mile walking tour of the area and the Freedom Trail was born. The trail is marked by nine wide, red lines painted on city sidewalks, cobblestones and brick paths that guide thousands of Americans annually past some of her most cherished symbols and landmarks. Below are the sixteen landmarks encountered along the trail. Find out the significance of each and jot down a brief statement about each.

1. Faneuil Hall _____

2. Boston Massacre Site _____

3. Old State House _____

4. Benjamin Franklin Birthplace _____

5. Old South Meeting House _____

6. Old Corner Book Store _____

7. America's First Public School _____

8. Statue of Benjamin Franklin _____

9. Old Granary Burying Ground _____

10. Park Street Church _____

11. State House _____

12. King's Chapel _____

13. Paul Revere's House _____

14. Paul Revere's Mall _____

15. Old North Church _____

16. Copp's Hill Burying Ground _____

FANEUIL HALL
OLD SOUTH MEETING HOUSE
COPP'S HILL BURYING GROUND
OLD NORTH CHURCH
PAUL REVERE MALL
PAUL REVERE'S HOUSE
FREEDOM TRAIL
OLD STATE HOUSE
FANEUIL HALL
OLD GRANARY BURYING GROUND
BOSTON MASSACRE SITE
KING'S CHAPEL
OLD CORNER BOOK STORE
BENJAMIN FRANKLIN STATUE
BIRTHPLACE OF BENJAMIN FRANKLIN
OLD SOUTH MEETING HOUSE
PARK STREET CHURCH
SITE OF FIRST PUBLIC SCHOOL
STATE HOUSE

GA1138

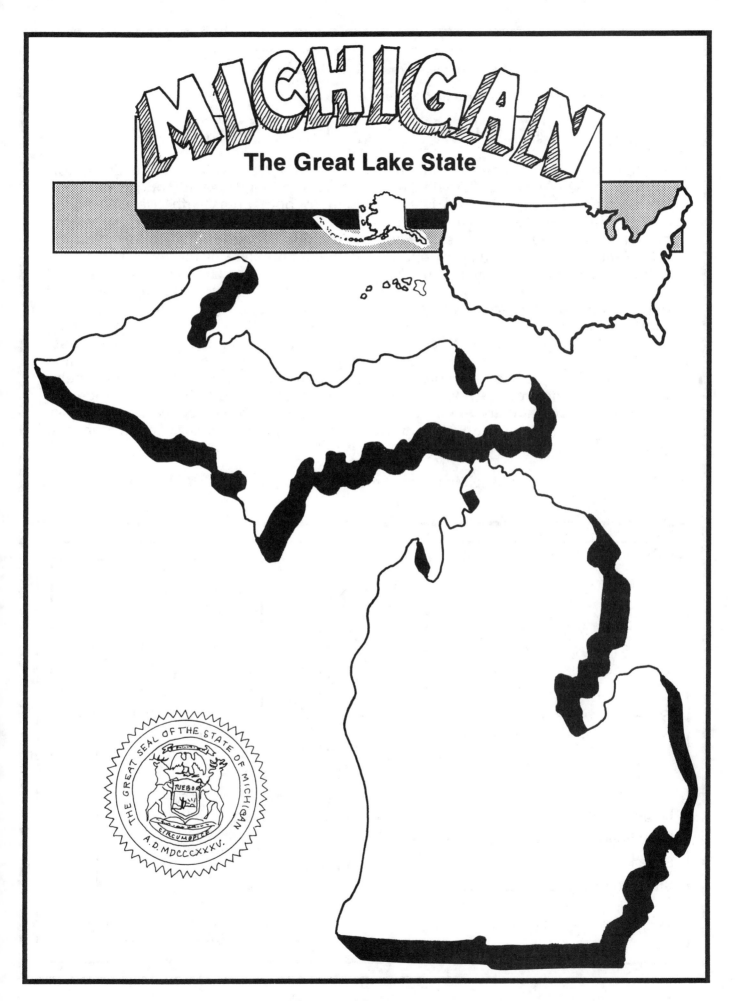

MICHIGAN

The Great Lake State

GA1138

MICHIGAN
THE GREAT LAKE STATE

Michigan, whose name comes from the Algonquian Indians' word for "great lake," is formed by two peninsulas nearly surrounded by the greatest body of fresh water in the world—the Great Lakes. It is rimmed by a 3200-mile shoreline, which is longer than the entire Atlantic seaboard of the United States. Michigan's course in the modern history of the world was set a hundred and fifty centuries ago when the glaciers of the Ice Age began to dredge the basins that border the state and form this long shoreline. The Lower Peninsula, larger in size and more densely populated, is the home of heavy industry with Detroit, the automobile capital of the world, and the industrial cities of Flint and Lansing.

The Upper Peninsula contains dense forests and mineral wealth. Tourism is important to both areas with over 20 million travelers annually, making it the eighth most popular travel destination. With the longest shoreline of the forty-eight lower states, around 11,000 inland lakes and 19 million acres of forests, travelers find plenty of places to go. While its income per capita ranks sixteenth, Michigan is facing problems with the decline of heavy industry. That, along with a serious depletion of natural resources, has caused unemployment and technological changes in Michigan. Its future success will largely depend upon its ability to change and weather the economic storm.

Familiarize yourself with these Michigan symbols:

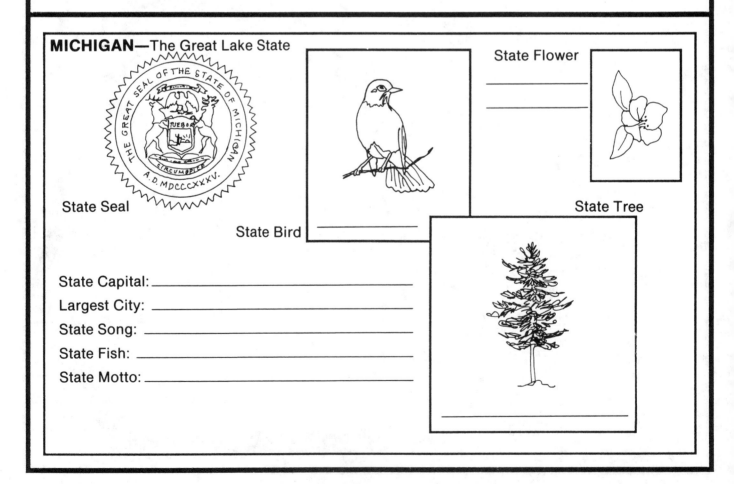

MICHIGAN—The Great Lake State

State Seal

State Bird _____

State Flower

State Tree

State Capital: _____

Largest City: _____

State Song: _____

State Fish: _____

State Motto: _____

GA1138

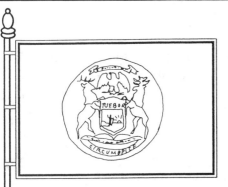

TOUCHING THE PAST

There is indeed a lot of history in Michigan. Beginning with the Indians who lived there many years ago, through the era of Henry Ford and the automobile, its space center, even beyond today, Michigan continues to live its past through its many museums. Millions of dollars have been spent to keep America in tune with its cherished past. While there are literally hundreds of museums and historical places to visit in Michigan, those listed below are some of the more noted. Find out about each and pinpoint its location on your outline map.

Frankenmuth Historical Museum
Henry Ford Museum
Sloan House
Cranbrook Institute of Science
Detroit Institute of Arts
Grand Rapids Art Museum
Kalamazoo Aviation History Museum
Fort Michilimackinac
Michigan Space Center
Art Center of Battle Creek
1839 Courthouse Museum
Quincy Mine Hoist
Impression 5, Michigan's Science Museum
Greenfield Village
Gerald R. Ford Museum
Cobblestone Farm Museum
Michigan's Own, Inc., Military and Space Museum
Michigan Transit Museum
Detroit Antique Toy Museum
Ella Sharp Museum
Historic Fort Wayne

Henry Ford

Once you've located each on the map, go back through your list a second time and decide which you think you would find most interesting. Perhaps you've already been there. Discuss your choice below.

_____
_____
_____
_____
_____
_____
_____

GA1138

MICHIGAN'S PEOPLE

Below are clues that will help you fill in the missing letters that identify some of those who helped to shape both the history of Michigan and the United States.

1. __ __ n __ __   __ __ r __   A name in the auto industry we associate with Detroit

2. __ __ __ q __ __ __   __ __ __ q __ __ __ __ __ __   A Jesuit missionary who lived among the Indians while searching for the Mississippi River

3. __ __ __ u __ __ __ __   Famous Indian chief

4. __ __ b __ __ __ __   __ i __ __ __ __ __   He helped to rebuild Detroit after the fire of 1805.

5. __ __ __ s __ __   O __ __ __   Another associated with the auto industry

6. __ l __ __ __   __ e __ __ __ __ __   He won the Nobel prize for chemistry.

7. __ __ r __ __ __   __ o __ __   Our 38th President

8. __ __ h __   __ a __ __ __   __ __ __ o __   He became one of America's wealthiest men through his fur-trading business on Mackinac Island.

9. __ __ __ p __   __ __ n __ __ __   The first black man to win the Nobel peace prize

10. __ __ l __ __ __ __   __ __ a __ __ __ __ __ __   He observed the digestive process through an unhealed gunshot wound.

11. __ __ l __ __ __   C __ __ __ __ __ __ __ __   One of the founders of the Big Four

12. __ o __ __ __ __ __ __ __ __   __ r __ __ __   She spent much of her time and energy helping to free slaves on the Underground Railroad.

13. __ r __ __ __   __ a __ __ __ __ __   He won a Pulitzer prize for his work *A Stillness at Appomattox.*

14. __ __ __ l __ __ __   __ __ r __ __ __   Industrial pioneer

15. __ __ a __ __ __ __   __ i __ __ __ __ __ __ __ __   He was the first man to fly solo across the Atlantic.

Sojourner Truth

GA1138

MICHIGAN TIME TABLE

Arrange these events in the order in which they helped to shape the history of Michigan.

_____ The Straits of Mackinac Bridge was opened to traffic between Mackinaw City and St. Ignace.

_____ Michigan became a part of the Northwest Territory.

_____ Michigan workers formed the United Automobile Workers union.

_____ Congress created the Territory of Michigan.

_____ The Soo Canal was completed.

_____ Michigan's first railroad between Erie and Kalamazoo was completed.

_____ Father Marquette founded Michigan's first settlement at Sault St. Marie.

_____ Antoine Cadillac founded what is now Detroit.

_____ Michigan became a part of the United States after the Revolutionary War.

_____ Michigan's legislature adopted a state income tax.

_____ The British gained control of the land that is now Michigan.

_____ Ransom Olds built the first automobile factory in Detroit.

_____ Voters approved spending $435 million in bond issues to expand recreational areas and fight water pollution.

_____ Michigan became a part of the Indiana Territory.

_____ Michigan entered into statehood on January 26, 1837, as the nation's 26th state.

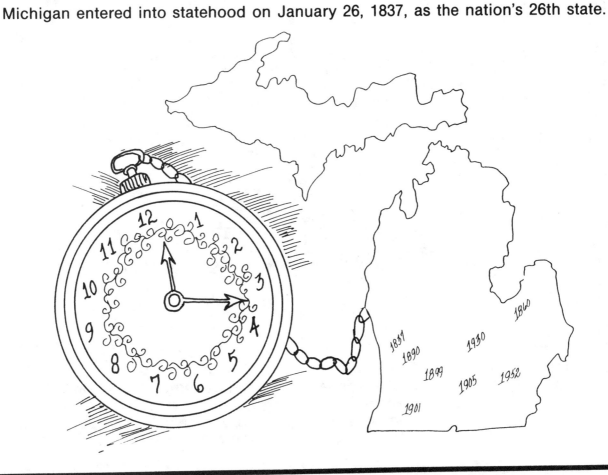

GA1138

CENTER STAGE

Michigan not only produces the wheels that move America, it also produces much of the talent that moves this great nation. Hidden below are the names of twenty of the state's native-born entertainers. Find as many as you can. Your pencil may move in any direction.

```
I  L  M  O  T  Y  L  I  L  B  Y  N  N  O  S  G
N  F  R  A  N  C  I  S  C  O  P  P  O  L  A  E
H  T  O  L  R  A  L  M  N  N  O  D  A  M  V  O
O  K  C  E  L  L  E  C  M  O  T  R  O  B  E  R
M  S  T  U  E  L  C  A  R  N  G  A  W  T  R  G
A  S  H  M  E  I  A  R  J  R  S  O  I  A  N  E
S  O  D  S  I  N  R  W  A  E  I  L  U  J  O  P
I  R  E  D  N  C  W  C  E  V  E  T  S  R  T  P
M  A  L  I  V  R  H  H  O  P  E  R  D  P  S  A
E  N  I  V  X  E  T  R  A  L  T  O  N  H  E  R
S  A  A  G  C  A  H  T  U  G  R  E  N  I  P  D
E  I  G  M  L  M  O  N  O  N  U  N  D  E  T  B
E  D  M  L  A  D  M  Y  E  Y  L  L  E  R  B  U
R  A  L  L  D  E  O  N  Y  G  Y  T  S  R  U  V
```

Piper Laurie	Ellen Burstyn	Max Gail	Charlton Heston
Francis Coppola	Stevie Wonder	Ted Nugent	Della Reese
Sonny Bono	Madonna	Lily Tomlin	George Peppard
Diana Ross	Tom Selleck	Ed McMahon	Julie Harris
Lee Majors	Robert Wagner	Marlo Thomas	Alice Cooper

GA1138

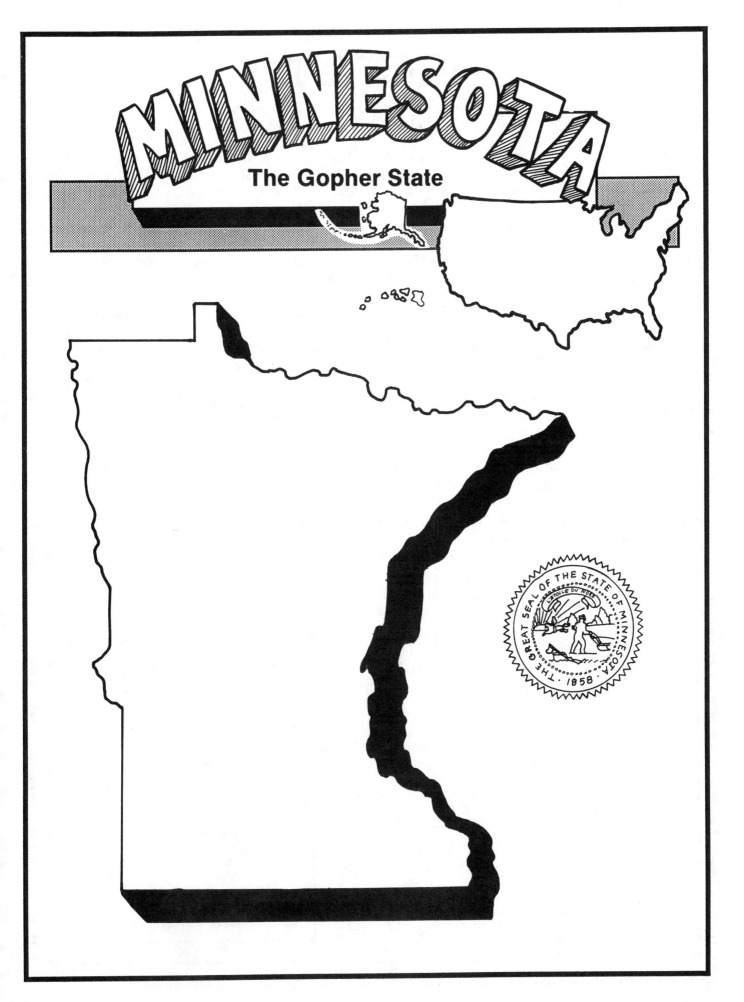

MINNESOTA

The Gopher State

133

GA1138

MINNESOTA
THE GOPHER STATE

Beautiful blue lakes, fertile farmland and rich deposits of iron make Minnesota perhaps the most pronounced example of the glacial impression left by the Ice Age. In the northern part of the state, retreating ice exposed the iron-rich bedrock of the Canadian Shield, making Minnesota a major supplier for the steel industry. As the glaciers melted, streams and lakes were carved out of the land, leaving the state with an abundance of waterways and recreation areas. Dairy and grain farms add to Minnesota's wealth as well as qualify it as part of America's heartland region. The scenic beauty of its thousands of sparkling lakes and deep pine woods makes it a vacation paradise for thousands annually.

The state's history is centered around the development of its natural resources. First the furbearing animals found that they were an attraction to fur traders from the East Coast. Its thick forests attracted lumberjacks from Maine and Michigan. The rich and fertile soil brought farmers from New England. Finally, the vast deposits of iron ore brought miners to Minnesota. The Minnesota of today is less dependent on these raw resources as changes in farming techniques and the availability of the rich iron ore have declined. But the people have adjusted well and the economy of Minnesota is still strong and has a bright outlook for the future.

Before beginning your study of this beautiful state, familiarize yourself with the symbols of the Gopher State called for below.

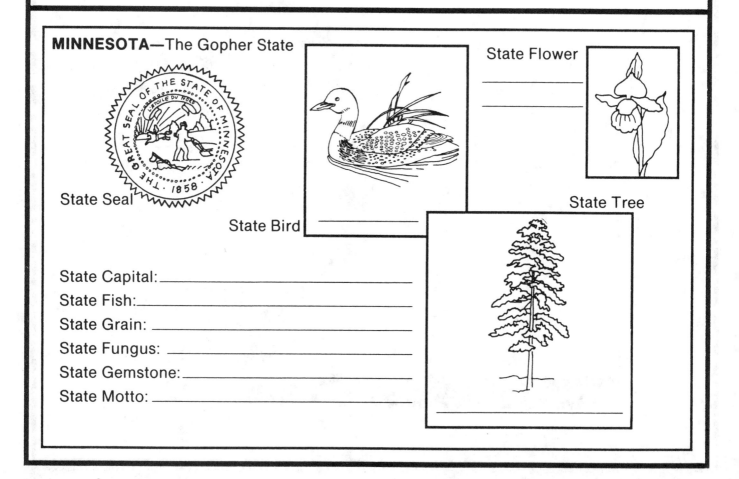

MINNESOTA—The Gopher State

State Seal

State Bird _____

State Flower
_____
_____

State Tree

State Capital: _____
State Fish: _____
State Grain: _____
State Fungus: _____
State Gemstone: _____
State Motto: _____

GA1138

Split Rock
Lighthouse

WHAT TO DO
WITH THE MAP

Historic sites are found all over Minnesota. Charting the location of some of its most important ones is what this assignment is all about. Find out about the significance of each, jot down an identifying statement and locate on the outline map.

1. Split Rock Lighthouse _____

_____

2. Lindbergh House _____

_____

3. James J. Hill House _____

_____

4. Forest History Center _____

_____

5. Jeffers Petroglyphs _____

_____

6. Oliver H. Kelley Farm _____

_____

7. Comstock House _____

_____

8. Fort Snelling _____

_____

9. North West Company Fur Post _____

_____

_____

10. Grand Mound _____

_____

_____

Lindbergh House History Center

FAMOUS MINNESOTANS

Across

1. He was vice president and he ran for President, but he did not win.
3. She was Dorothy in *The Wizard of Oz.*
7. Artist of the day who has done many paintings on contemporary athletics.
8. She played a large role in *King Kong.*
9. He created "Peanuts."
10. Pioneers in medicine, a famous clinic
11. He flew the first solo transatlantic flight in 1927.
13. He built the Great Northern Railroad.
15. Famous television journalist
16. Supreme Court Chief Justice

Down

2. Famous rock star
4. Actress, country singer
5. Novelist, screenwriter F. Scott _____
6. Poet
12. U.S. senator and vice president under Lyndon Johnson
14. A winner of the Nobel prize in literature

GA1138

BEFORE MINNESOTA WAS MINNESOTA

The history of Minnesota can be traced in the lakes, streams and landforms created millions of years ago by the glaciers of the Ice Age. Perhaps no other state serves as such an example of the effects of the Ice Age as the physical geography of Minnesota. Minnesota has more than 90,000 miles of lake and river shoreline, 25,000 miles of rivers and streams, over 12,000 inland lakes that are 10 acres or larger. Just how did all this happen? On the drawing of Minnesota below you see four major land regions created by the Ice Age.

Land Regions of Minnesota

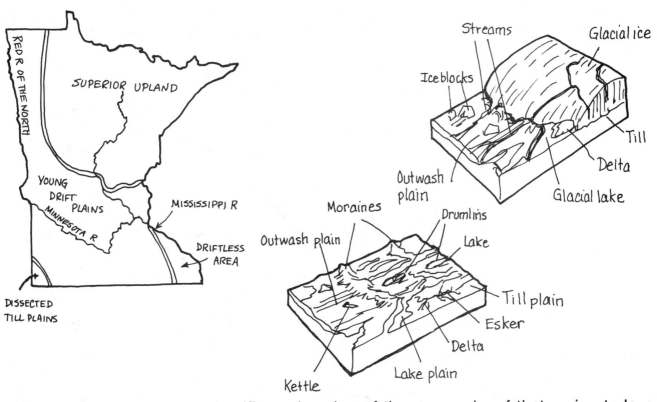

Present for each area the scientific explanation of the geography of that region today.

Superior Upland _____

_____

Young Drift Plains _____

_____

Dissected Till Plains _____

_____

Driftless Area_____

_____

GA1138

PICTURE POSTCARD

Tourism accounts for several million dollars each year of the state's income. Its natural beauty makes the "Land of Sky-Blue Waters" a favorite on the vacation list of thousands of tourists every year. The main ingredient in the tourism industry is advertising. Getting out the good word about all the good things a state has to offer is what attracts people to that state. Your task in this assignment is to create a poster on Minnesota that will depict this state in its finest hour. Use blocks similar to those shown below. You'll have to read elsewhere about Minnesota to be able to write convincing, legitimate ad copy. Cut out the blocks and arrange them attractively on an 18" x 24" sheet of white poster board. Find pictures from magazines or travel brochures that will add to the attractiveness of your poster.

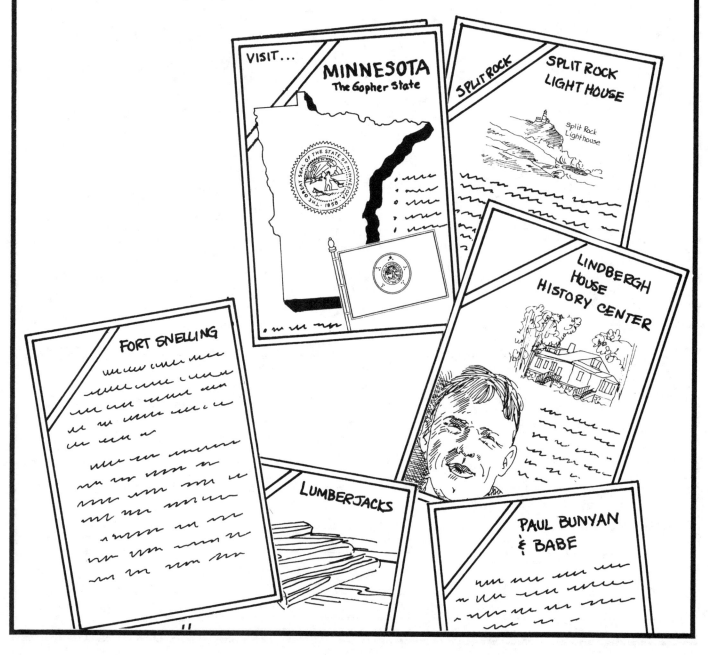

GA1138

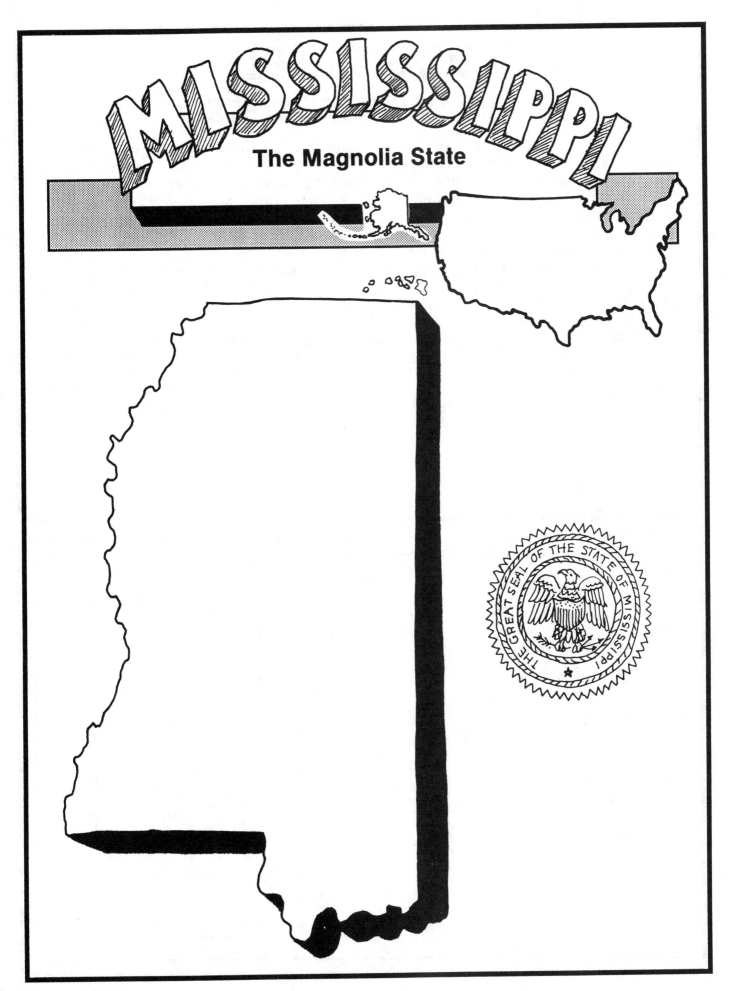

MISSISSIPPI

The Magnolia State

GA1138

MISSISSIPPI
THE MAGNOLIA STATE

Once a state of farmers and small towns, the Mississippi of today is becoming one of factory workers and busy cities. Agriculture is still important to Mississippi and its natural resources are best suited for farming. But the trend toward industry has helped put the state's economy into a more favorable position even though many problems remain. Tradition is very important to the people of Mississippi, and reminders of the Old South are found all over the state. Economic and cultural differences are sometimes magnified by Mississippi's political conflict. Even before the Civil War, the people were divided politically and some of their differences remain unsolved. Steps have been taken in recent years toward political equality among the wealthy, the white farmers and the rural Blacks. The state and liberal tax laws and the inexpensive labor found there have lured many businesses into relocating in Mississippi. The mild climate attracts thousands of tourists to Mississippi, especially during the winter months. The Mississippi Gulf Coast has many large, sunny beaches lined with fine hotels that bring millions of dollars into Mississippi each year.

Before you begin your study of the Magnolia State, familiarize yourself with its symbols and information called for below.

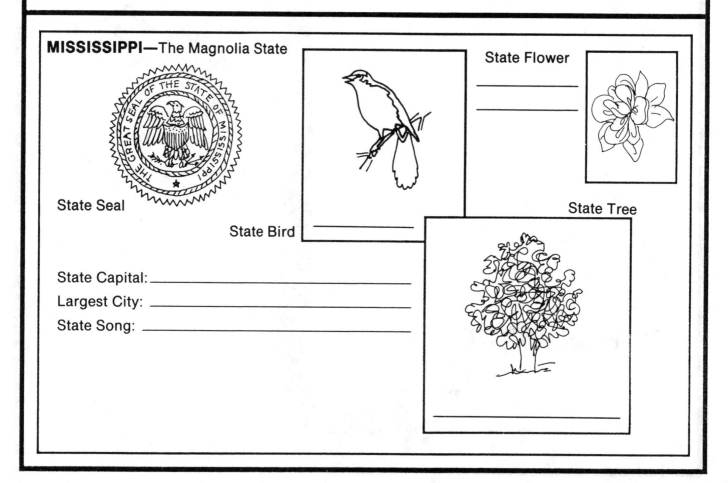

MISSISSIPPI—The Magnolia State

State Seal

State Bird

State Flower

State Tree

State Capital: _____

Largest City: _____

State Song: _____

GA1138

ALL ROADS TO JACKSON

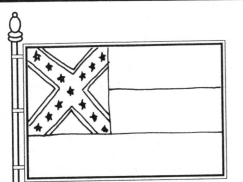

Jackson, Mississippi, is the capital of Mississippi, the largest city and the very lifeblood of this southern state. Its centralized location makes it a natural for serving as the state's hub of government, business and industrial affairs.

Below is a list of Mississippi's twenty largest municipalities. Pinpoint the location of each on your outline map.

Cleveland	Jackson
Greenwood	Pearl
Clarksdale	Meridian
Southaven	Laurel
Tupelo	Hattiesburg
Greenville	Moss Point
Starkville	Biloxi
Columbus	Gulfport
Vicksburg	Pascagoula
Clinton	Natchez

Once you've located each, find the distance (by highway) each lies from Jackson, the state capital. Consult any good atlas and either calculate the distances using the scale of miles provided or use the "highway distances" guide found on most highway maps.

Cleveland-Jackson _____

Greenwood-Jackson _____

Clarksdale-Jackson _____

Southhaven-Jackson _____

Tupelo-Jackson _____

Greenville-Jackson _____

Starkville-Jakcson _____

Columbus-Jackson _____

Vicksburg-Jackson _____

Clinton-Jackson _____

Pearl-Jackson _____

Meridian-Jackson _____

Laurel-Jackson _____

Hattiesburg-Jackson _____

Moss Point-Jackson _____

Biloxi-Jackson _____

Gulfport-Jackson _____

Pascagoula-Jackson _____

Natchez-Jackson _____

GA138

THE FLAGS OF MISSISSIPPI

Below are drawings of the seven flags that have flown over Mississippi. Research the story behind each. Jot down a brief statement of identification under each flag and arrange them in chronological order according to their place in Mississippi history (for example, place a #1 in the box beside the earliest flag, etc.).

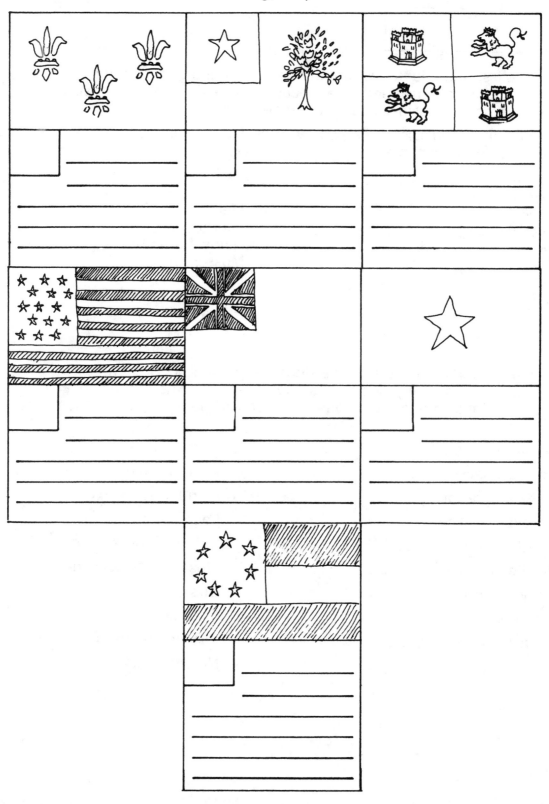

GA1138

MISSISSIPPI TIME LINE

Below is a list of events that are significant to the history of Mississippi. Find out when each event occurred and place the corresponding letter of identification on the time line in its proper place.

a. _____ Mississippi seceded from the Union.

b. _____ Mississippi became English territory after the French and Indian War.

c. _____ Atomic scientists set off the first nuclear test explosion east of the Mississippi at Baxterville.

d. _____ Oil was discovered at Tinsley.

e. _____ Hernando de Soto explored the Mississippi region.

f. _____ Union forces captured Vicksburg during the Civil War.

g. _____ The Mississippi Territory was first organized.

h. _____ Mississippi was readmitted to the Union.

i. _____ Spain occupied the Gulf Coast.

j. _____ The first French colony was established at Old Biloxi.

k. _____ The legislature passed laws that broadened the tax-free privilege of industrial properties.

l. _____ Mississippi adopted laws to encourage manufacturing.

m. _____ Mississippi became the 20th state on December 10.

n. _____ Charles Evers became the mayor of Fayette, thus becoming the first black mayor in Mississippi.

o. _____ Mississippi started a swamp drainage program on the Delta.

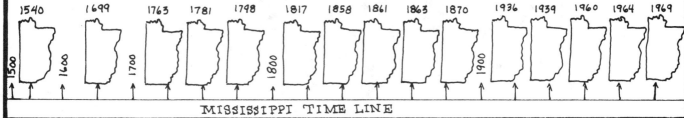

1540 1699 1763 1781 1798 1817 1858 1861 1863 1870 1936 1939 1960 1964 1969

1500 1600 1700 1800 1900

MISSISSIPPI TIME LINE

143

MOLDERS OF MISSISSIPPI

Below are descriptions of several men and women from Mississippi who helped to shape not only the history of Mississippi, but the history of the United States as well. Read the description of each; then unscramble the letters that correctly spell his/her name.

1. _____ FNOEJFSRE ADSVI—He was the first and only president of the Confederate States of America.

2. _____ NETHSPE D. ELE—He ordered the first shot fired at Fort Sumter.

3. _____ HOJN A. QUTIMNA—Mexican War hero and governor of Mexico and Mississippi

4. _____ LAWIILM KFLENAUR—Winner of 1950 Nobel prize for literature, he was one of the greatest fiction writers of first half of 20th century. He lived in Oxford and wrote about the South.

5. _____ VLSEI SLRPEEY—"The King," born in Tupelo, went from "rags to riches" and was the hero of millions of teenagers. His records topped sales of 100,000,000 copies.

6. _____ EDUAOR YLWET—Winner of every major award for literature including a Pulitzer prize. She has written successful Broadway plays as well as novels.

7. _____ ENEALURC EOJNS—Founder of Piney Woods Country Life School, a school to help black children to become better educated.

8. _____ MMJIEI RRGEODS—The "father of country music," his records sold over 20 million copies.

9. _____ YNLOETNE CRPIE—The first black American woman to achieve international stardom in the field of opera

10. _____ L.Q.C. RALMA—Famous Mississippi congressman who later served on the Supreme Court and was in Grover Cleveland's cabinet

11. _____ NJEA SPBATITE NIEVBILEL—Founder of Natchez, New Orleans and Baton Rouge

JEFFERSON DAVIS

ELVIS PRESLEY

GA138

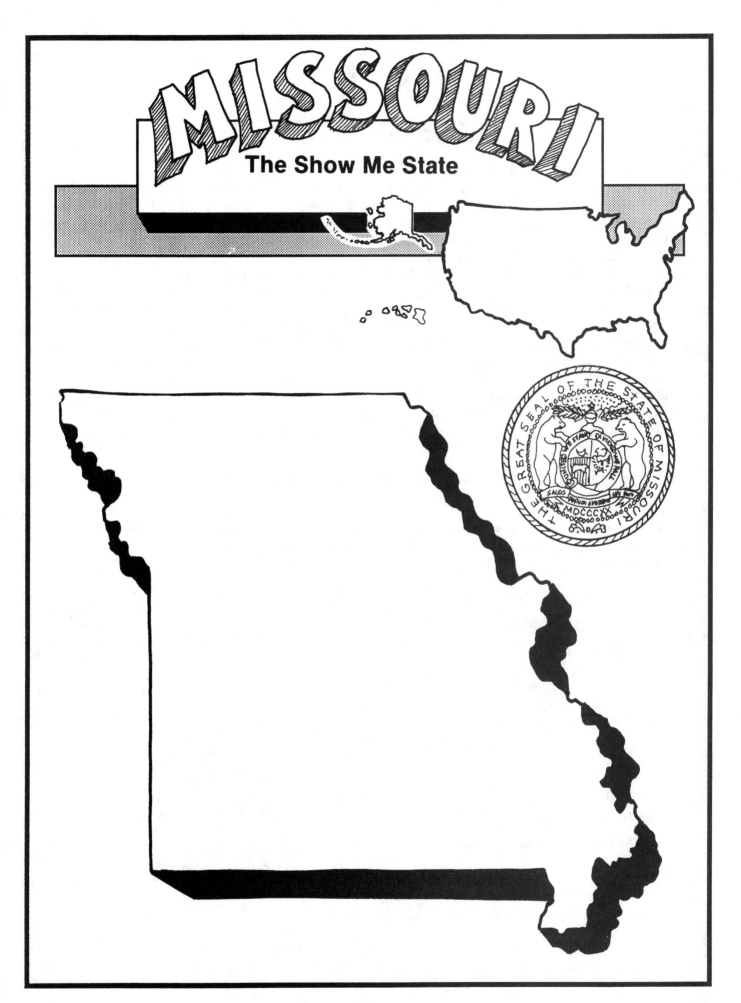

MISSOURI
The Show Me State

MISSOURI
THE SHOW ME STATE

The Gateway Arch in St. Louis was built to commemorate the spot where Lewis and Clark embarked on their exploration into the Louisiana Territory. The symbol also serves as a constant reminder that Missouri has long been regarded as the Gateway to America's West. Both the Oregon Trail and the Santa Fe Trail originated in Missouri. Its key location as the supply center for those heading west helped to settle the area and bring about an early need for manufacturing furs brought from the Northwest and made St. Louis the fur capital of the world. Missouri's rolling plains and favorable growing season soon made the state a farming state with vast fields of golden grain and green pastures. The scenic region in southern Missouri called the Ozarks is characterized by rugged plateau and fast-moving streams. Kansas City and St. Louis are major industrial cities with aerospace and transportation equipment heading the list. Its considerable mineral wealth, combined with a balance of agriculture and industry, gives the state a healthy economy. The Ozarks remain an important drawing card to millions of summertime vacationers and over $5.5 billion to Missouri. In more recent years, the state has added a new dimension to its economy with a push toward urban renewal projects and more strength in professional and service industries.

Before continuing with your study of Missouri, research these Missouri symbols:

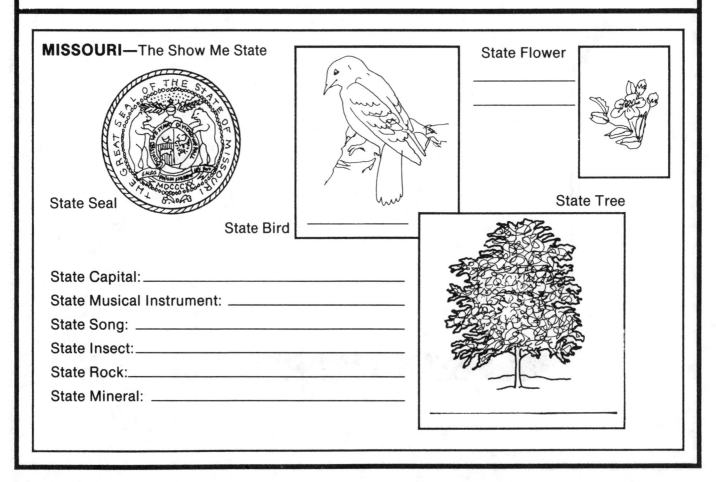

MISSOURI—The Show Me State

State Seal

State Bird

State Flower _____

State Tree

State Capital: _____

State Musical Instrument: _____

State Song: _____

State Insect: _____

State Rock: _____

State Mineral: _____

GA1138

MAPPING MISSOURI

Look at a good map of Missouri and find the following cities and sites. Note the coordinates (those letters and numbers found on the top, bottom and both sides of maps that best approximate the location of the city or site) you are trying to find. Relocate these cities on the map below, using the coordinates that have been provided. Then go back to the list of cities and indicate the coordinates that would be used in a listing of cities and locations (for example, St. Louis—D-3, etc).

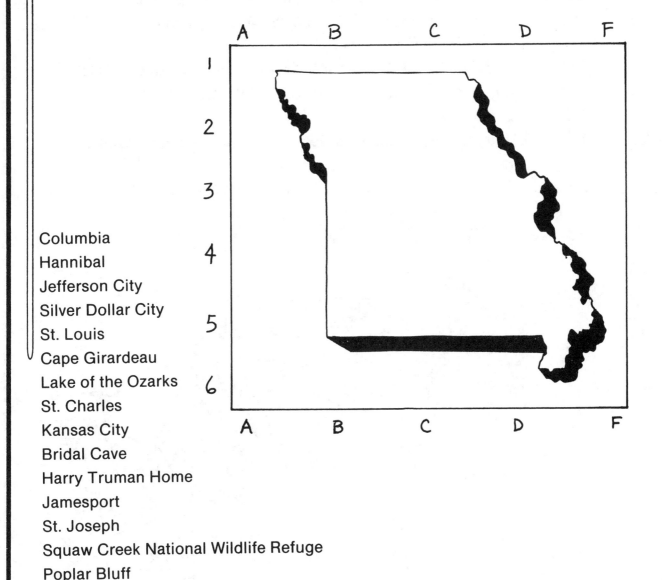

Columbia

Hannibal

Jefferson City

Silver Dollar City

St. Louis

Cape Girardeau

Lake of the Ozarks

St. Charles

Kansas City

Bridal Cave

Harry Truman Home

Jamesport

St. Joseph

Squaw Creek National Wildlife Refuge

Poplar Bluff

GA1138

MISSOURI HISTORY

Below are several dates that are significant to the history of Missouri. The order in which they are presented is not the order in which they occurred. To correct the proper sequential order, find out when each took place; then number the events in proper chronological order.

a. _____ La Salle claimed the Mississippi Valley for France.

b. _____ Spain returned Louisiana to France.

c. _____ Lewis and Clark started their famous journey to the Pacific Northwest from St. Louis.

d. _____ Marquette and Jolliet were probably the first white persons to see the mouth of the Missouri River.

e. _____ Missouri became the 24th U.S. state.

f. _____ Gateway Arch (the nation's tallest monument) was completed.

g. _____ The first permanent settlement at St. Genevieve was established.

h. _____ Congress made Missouri a territory.

i. _____ The Pony Express linked St. Joseph, Missouri, and Sacramento, California.

j. _____ Harry S. Truman became the 33rd President of the United States.

k. _____ France ceded Louisiana to Spain.

l. _____ The Louisiana Purchase Centennial Exposition was held in St. Louis.

m. _____ France sold Louisiana to the United States.

n. _____ Missouri was a part of the battleground during the Civil War.

GA1138

FAMOUS MISSOURIANS

Hidden below are the names of fourteen of Missouri's most famous sons and daughters. Answer first the clues below the maze of letters to find out who they are. Then circle the letters that locate their names in the maze of letters.

```
R R E D L I W S L L A G N I A R U A L J A H E
J O H T Y A T M A H G O H E C F O Y T O O R L
O G S A C S K H D A N I E L B O O N E H V D G
S G E O U N L M A R K T W A I N S T C N N L L
E I M M O M A R B R A D L E Y S D R E J I E Y
P M A R O S O N W Y S N H F U S H E M P L I R
H P J R T H T I A S E S O J I N O E P E P F A
S R E V R A C N O T G N I H S A W E G R O E G
M K S S P G G E O R G E B I N G H A M S J N D
I A S A V O M F R U H H O U H S T W K H T E T
T I E O E P E W E M H Y K E E L L A S I T G A
H L J D A V I D R A T C H I S O N D W N O U T
R R V H A C N O U N T N H O W S O W N G C E A
I W H N O T N E B T R A H S A M O H T S S T J
```

_____ He was the father of ragtime.

_____ He was "President for a Day" in 1849.

_____ He was unsuccessful in his attempt to find peace for his followers in Independence.

_____ She wrote all her "Little House" books from a simple frame house at Rocky Ridge Farm.

_____ In World War II he commanded 1.3 million troops—the largest American force ever united under one war.

_____ His home in Arrow Rock is a historic site to honor this great artist who painted life on the Missouri frontier.

_____ "The Man from Independence," 33rd President of the United States

_____ Hannibal's most famous citizen

_____ He was born a slave and later became one of America's greatest scientists helping farmers make a better living.

_____ Missouri's most "infamous citizen"

_____ He came to Missouri in 1799 as governor of the Missouri Territory and later became more famous as an Indian fighter and scout.

_____ He commanded the American forces in Europe during World War I.

_____ Author, newspaper reporter, columnist who is best remembered for his famous children's poetry including "Little Boy Blue" and "Wynken, Blynken, and Nod"

_____ Famous artist from Neosho who painted a panorama of Missouri history in the state capital

SPIRIT OF ST. LOUIS

St. Louis, Missouri, is indeed a fun place to visit with many sights to see. Many are described below by simple one-line clues. Read each clue carefully, do a little research on St. Louis and you should be able to unscramble the letters that will correctly spell the attraction in question.

1. _____ WGEAYTA HRAC—Symbol of St. Louis' role as the "Gateway to the West"

2. _____ EDLLCAES DLNAIGN—Shopping, dining and nightlife area on historic St. Louis waterfront

3. _____ HUBSC LRMIOMEA DTSAUIM—Home of the St. Louis Cardinals

4. _____ TS. UILSO OZO—One of the world's finest zoos

5. _____ OINUN NATSTOI—Unique redeveloped downtown shopping center

6. _____ NEEPRSDTI—America's largest river excursion boat

7. _____ RSTNGA ARFM—Outdoor beauty, home of the famous Clydesdales and site of a former U.S. President's cabin

8. _____ XIS SAFLG EOVR DIM-AAERMCI—Famous theme park with over 100 rides, shows and adventures

9. _____ ETH YUMN—12,000-seat outdoor theater in Forest Park where Broadway plays and musicals are presented every summer

10. _____ EEWJL XBO—Floral conservatory in Forest Park

11. _____ UOSSMIRI LTBOACINA RGAEDN—World famous botanical extravaganza founded by Henry Shaw

12. _____ OSSIMURI SICHTORIAL ISOCETY—Museum featuring exhibits on Lewis and Clark and Charles Lindbergh

GA1138

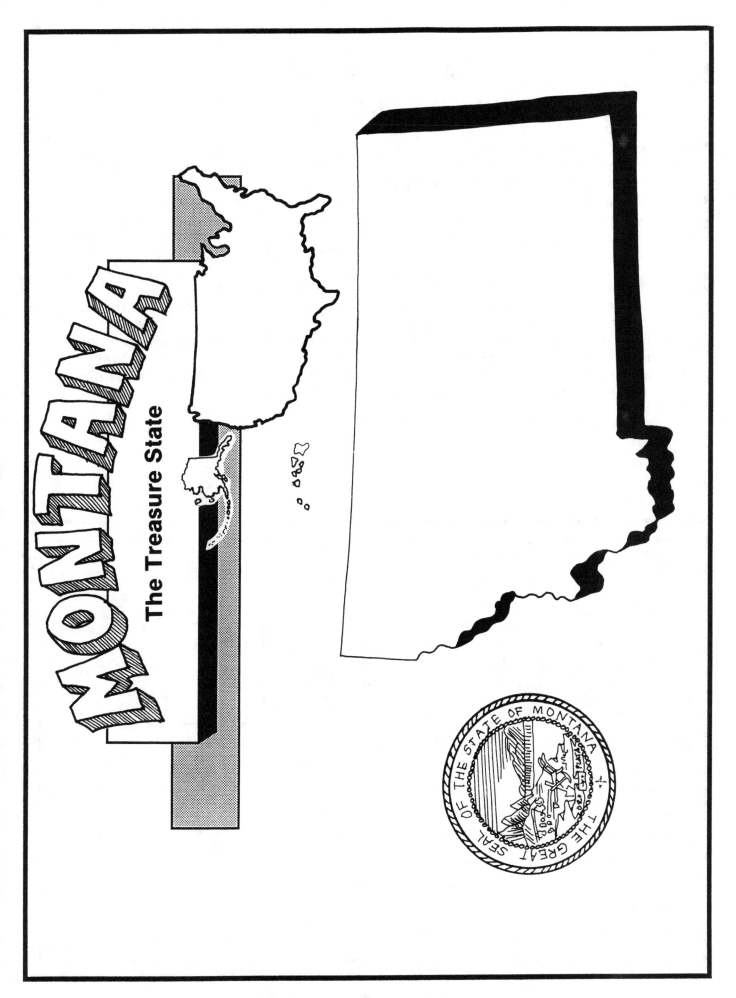

MONTANA

The Treasure State

THE GREAT SEAL OF THE STATE OF MONTANA

151

MONTANA
THE TREASURE STATE

Montana is a word derived from the Latin meaning "mountainous." It is our fourth largest state, averaging 550 miles long and 275 miles wide. The eastern third is plains country, the central third, plains and isolated mountains and the western third, mountains and valleys. It is an agricultural state with livestock production as well as crops of wheat, hay, sugar beets and barley providing most of the agricultural income. Revenue from oil, copper and coal account for most of the mineral income. In addition are ample supplies of timber, gold, silver and natural gas. Most of the state's power is hydroelectric. Montana is the home of seven North American Indian tribes. The people of Montana are proud of its wide open spaces. Outdoor recreational areas make the state a haven for hunters, campers, skiers, fishermen and those who love the atmosphere of the Old West. Glacier National Park draws thousands of tourists annually and three of the five entrances to Yellowstone (our oldest and largest national park) are found in Montana. The people of Montana are environmentally aware of their state and will continue to protect its unspoiled wilderness and unique character that set it apart from all other states.

Before continuing your study of Montana, familiarize yourself with its symbols as called for below.

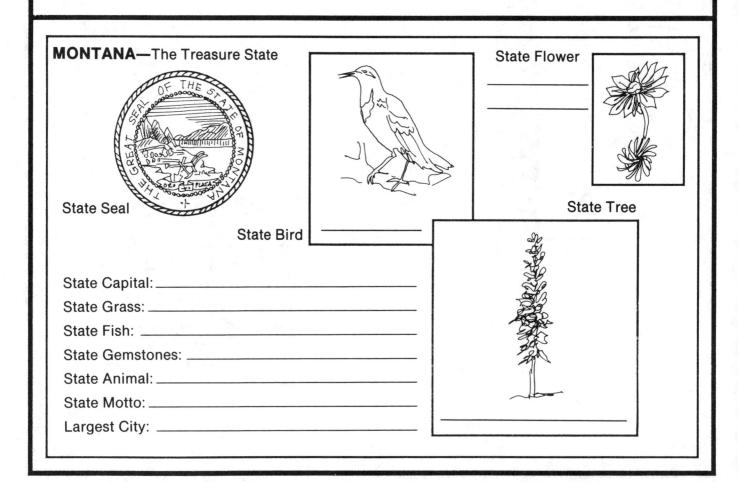

MONTANA—The Treasure State

State Seal

State Bird _____

State Flower
_____
_____

State Tree

State Capital: _____

State Grass: _____

State Fish: _____

State Gemstones: _____

State Animal: _____

State Motto: _____

Largest City: _____

GA1138

MONTANA MATH

Below are several facts and statistics that are relevant to the state of Montana. Read each statement carefully and decide exactly what is needed; then perform the math functions that will lead to the desired answers.

1. There are 11 national forests, including 12 wildernesses in Montana with 16,798,274 acres of public lands for outdoor recreation; 7 state forests containing 213,000 acres; 276,157 acres of individual tracts of state forest land. What is the "average size" of a national forest in Montana? _____

2. The highest point in Montana is Granite Peak, 12,799 feet; the lowest point is 1800 feet in northwest Montana where the Kootenai River leaves the state. What is the difference in feet between Montana's high and low points? _____

3. In a recent year cash receipts from the marketing of agricultural products totaled $1.22 billion. Cash from leading commodities were cattle and calves $689,000,000; dairy products $44,000,000; sheep and lambs $23,000,000; hogs $22,000,000; wheat $249,000,000; barley $62,000,000, sugar beets $29,000,000; hay $48,000,000; all other crops and livestock $55,000,000. What percentage (to the nearest tenth) was accounted for by dairy products? _____ by cattle and calves? _____ by sugar beets? _____ by barley? _____ by hay _____ by hogs? _____ by wheat? _____ by sheep and lambs? _____ by all other crops and livestock? _____. Add all your percentage calculations together. What is your total? _____

Once you've completed all calculations and figured all the percentages, show your statistics in the form of a circle graph in the space below.

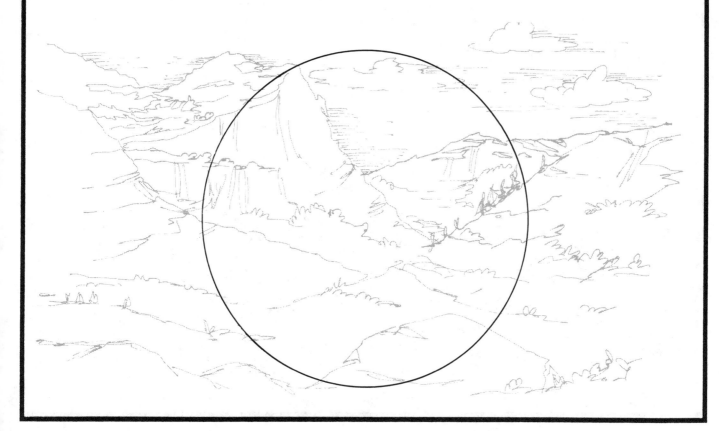

GA1138

MONTANA MATH

4. There are 597 elementary schools (k-8) serving 104,267 students; 10 accredited junior high schools (7-9) for 6078 students; and 170 high schools (9-12) for 43,727 students. What is the average size school at each level? Elementary _____ junior high _____ high school _____ What is the average size of all schools in Montana? _____

5. Tourism ranks among Montana's top industries with more than $600 million flowing into the state's economy during a recent year. If there were 2.75 million out-of-state visitors during that year, about how much did each spend while in Montana? _____

6. In 1984 the estimated population of Montana was 824,057. Its six largest cities and their populations were Billings 69,836; Great Falls 58,769; Butte 34,462; Missoula 33,447; Helena 24,643; Bozeman 23,462. What percentage (to the nearest tenth of a percent) of Montana's population lives in these six cities? _____

7. In 1970 the U.S. Census Bureau recorded 649,409 persons living in Montana. In 1980 there were 786,690 inhabitants there. What percentage increase (to the nearest tenth of a percent) did the population increase during the 1970's? _____

Should the rate experienced during the 1970's continue, during what census can Montana's population be expected to top the million mark? _____

154

GA1138

WHAT TO DO
WITH THE MAP

There are many sights to see in Montana. Its wide open spaces and dramatic mountains bring thousands of vacationers every year. The "Big Sky" of Montana is firmly grounded in the Montana mind-set. Some of its most scenic grandeur is visible in these designated areas of Montana. There are also several historical locations and protected areas of notation. Locate and identify each on your outline map.

Yellowstone National Park

Glacier National Park

Flathead National Forest

Chief Joseph Battleground

Custer Battlefield National Monument

Bannack

Lewis and Clark Caverns

Big Hole National Battlefield Monument

Custer National Forest

Fort Peck Indian Reservation

Lewis and Clark National Forest

Kootenai National Forest

Beaverhead National Forest

Blackfeet Indian Reservation

Deerlodge National Forest

Old Faithful

Lower Falls of Yellowstone National Park

GA1138

CUSTER'S LAST STAND

One of the most famous Indian campaigns in American history was fought in Montana near the Little Bighorn River. Research the drama and background behind this legendary page of America's past. Describe the scene below from the standpoint of a member of the news media who might have been there to observe and report the entire incident. Be as convincing as you can in piecing together the events as they occurred.

156

NEBRASKA

The Cornhusker State

GA1138

NEBRASKA
THE CORNHUSKER STATE

The first white men who explored the land we now know as Nebraska looked beyond to the riches of land and minerals farther to the West. In fact this region of the country was so-called the Great American Desert because it had little in the way of forests, very few minerals and nothing but a vast expanse of grassland stretching from one end of the region to the other. Today that image has changed. Nebraska is one of our leading agricultural states. This transition happened because of the resourceful people who turned the semiarid land into productive farm country by building irrigation ditches and practicing scientific farming methods. The development of the steel plow helped them to break the thick prairie sod, and the settlement of Nebraska was on its way. The first wave of homesteading poured into Nebraska during the 1860's. Although Nebraska continues to be a leader in agriculture, the technology of today allows for fewer people needed to till Nebraska farms with the result being a shift toward the cities and more jobs in manufacturing in the future. Nebraska is the only state to employ a unicameral state legislature. The future economy of the state seems to be headed toward a continued strength in ranching and agricultural products and an increase in the meat packing and food processing industries.

Before continuing with your look at Nebraska, identify the symbols called for below.

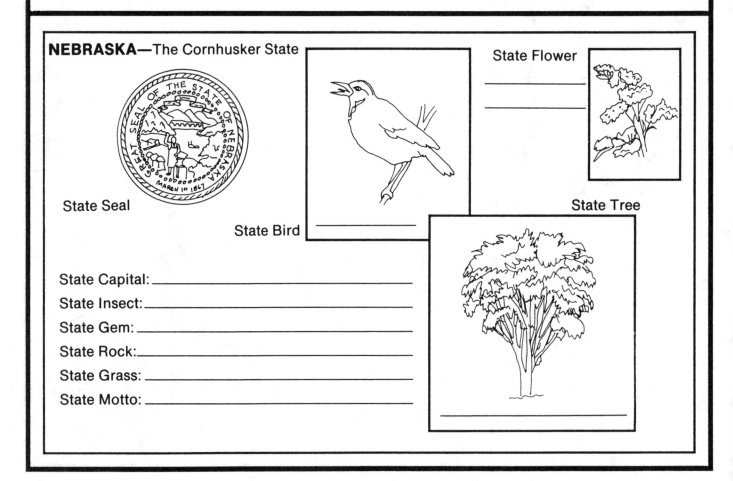

NEBRASKA—The Cornhusker State

State Seal

State Bird _____

State Flower _____

State Tree

State Capital: _____

State Insect: _____

State Gem: _____

State Rock: _____

State Grass: _____

State Motto: _____

GA1138

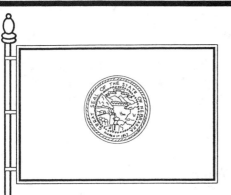

NEBRASKA MAP STUDY

Locate these Nebraska cities on your outline map:

Beatrice	Norfolk	North Platte
Fremont	Omaha	Ogallala
Hastings	Lincoln	Tecumseh
Grand Island	Kearney	West Point
Scottsbluff	Nebraska City	Lexington

Locate these national forests:

Nebraska
Samuel R. McKelvie

Draw in these rivers that flow through Nebraska:

Missouri	Loup	Republican	White
Platte	Calamus	Big Nemaha	Little Blue
Wood	Elkhorn	Little Nemaha	

Draw in Interstate 80—the main overland artery in Nebraska.

Draw in and label the roads you would take to get from. . .

Kearney to Greeley	Lincoln to Rushville
Valentine to McCook	Lexington to Omaha
Loup City to Minden	Butte to Tecumseh

GA1138

NEBRASKA'S PAST

Below are several events significant to the history of Nebraska. The order in which they are presented is not the order in which they occurred. Your task is to place them in proper chronological order by placing the proper number sequence in the blank spaces provided.

_____ Nebraska celebrated its territorial centennial.

_____ Union Pacific Railroad began building its line from Omaha.

_____ Robert Cavelier, Sieur de la Salle, claimed the region drained by the Mississippi for France.

_____ Lewis and Clark traveled up the Missouri River and explored eastern Nebraska.

_____ Congress passed the Kansas-Nebraska Act.

_____ France gave the Louisiana Territory to Spain.

_____ Nebraska became the 37th state on March 1.

_____ Congress authorized the Missouri River Basin Project.

_____ The United States bought the Louisiana Territory from Napoleon.

_____ Zebulon Pike first visited Nebraska.

_____ Spain returned Louisiana to France.

_____ Swarms of grasshoppers destroyed Nebraska farm crops.

_____ The "Great Migration" along the Oregon Trail began.

_____ Pierre and Paul Mallet were probably the first white men to cross Nebraska.

_____ The North Platte River Project was begun to help irrigate Nebraska farmland.

GA1138

NEBRASKA'S TREASURES

While many people drive across Nebraska from east to west (or west to east) on their way to somewhere else, there are many sites to see besides those visible from Interstate 80. On the map below, several of these sites are pinpointed. Your task is to find out the location of each attraction listed below the map and then jot down the corresponding letter on the map in its proper place.

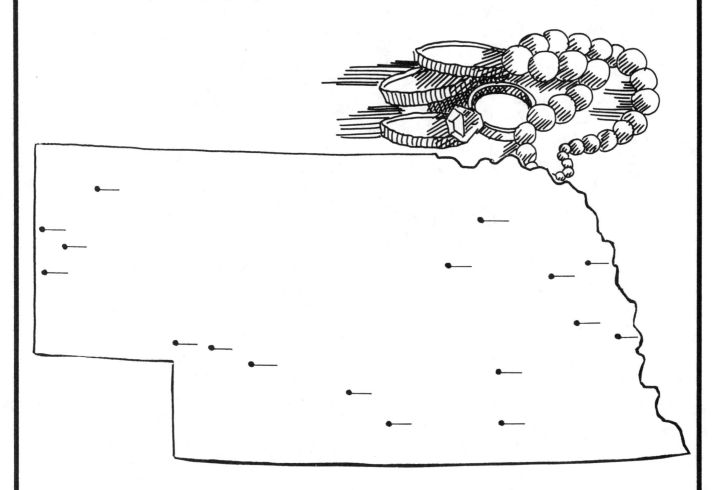

a. State Capital
b. Scotts Bluff National Monument
c. Buffalo Bill's Ranch State Historical Park
d. Harold Warp's Pioneer Village, Minden
e. Museum of the Fur Trade
f. Front Street
g. DeSoto National Wildlife Refuge
h. Chimney Rock National Historic Site
i. Neligh Mills

j. Boys Town
k. Fort Atkinson State Historical Park
l. Wild Horse Holding Facility
m. Oregon Trail Wagon Train
n. Lake McConaughy—Nebraska's largest reservoir for water recreation
o. Homestead National Monument
p. Fort Kearny State Historical Park
q. Strategic Air Command Museum

NEBRASKA SEARCH

Hidden below are several words that answer the clues below. Perhaps the best strategy would be to find the answers to the clues through your own research and remembering and then to find those words in the search. Words can be found horizontally, vertically and forward or in reverse.

```
L  T  O  M  P  A  G  O  M  O  N  K  L  U  T  O  N  Y  L  E
O  R  E  G  O  N  T  R  A  I  L  D  T  Z  S  W  A  R  S  D
W  E  Y  F  R  A  B  C  Y  A  O  E  T  T  A  L  P  H  E  O
E  S  G  R  O  C  P  M  A  H  C  K  L  C  D  N  N  C  R  R
S  E  A  G  H  G  E  R  M  A  N  M  O  A  A  K  L  M  P  P
T  D  T  I  L  L  A  D  U  M  I  A  P  A  E  T  E  A  O  F
E  N  R  P  N  I  C  R  Y  O  L  F  R  K  B  A  X  N  N  C
R  A  O  C  O  T  T  O  N  W  O  O  D  S  A  L  I  A  E  H
N  C  P  A  O  T  R  F  Z  B  M  A  C  A  N  D  S  I  K  I
M  I  W  G  O  L  D  E  N  R  O  D  I  R  U  O  S  S  I  M
E  R  L  A  R  E  M  A  C  I  N  U  E  B  U  R  T  I  P  N
A  E  U  C  S  B  L  R  M  A  B  E  Y  E  A  J  Y  U  N  E
D  M  O  U  Z  L  G  B  O  F  N  N  I  N  V  E  L  O  O  Y
O  A  V  V  P  U  A  A  M  O  H  G  A  S  A  M  I  L  L  R
W  T  M  W  L  E  W  I  S  M  S  K  N  A  H  P  N  G  U  O
L  A  E  G  A  S  L  E  N  L  A  R  S  S  O  A  G  G  B  C
A  E  C  O  N  T  I  N  E  N  T  A  L  N  G  F  T  A  E  K
R  R  N  Y  H  E  O  I  F  Y  O  L  H  A  A  B  O  N  Z  A
K  G  F  M  K  M  F  T  A  K  P  C  I  K  C  Y  N  M  T  I
```

_____ The leading national origin of Nebraska's people

_____ The state native grass

_____ Official state flower

_____ Official state tree

_____ Largest city

_____ Capital of Nebraska

_____ Type of state legislature unique to Nebraska

_____ Thirty-eighth U.S. President born in Omaha

_____ Type of climate found in Nebraska characterized by hot summers and cold winters

_____ 1854 act of Congress that organized Nebraska Territory

_____ Important minerals to Panhandle region of Nebraska

_____ Explorers who investigated regions in 1804

_____ Valuable mineral to western part of Nebraska

_____ The river that flows through the heart of Nebraska

_____ Nebraska was called this before it was bought by the U.S. in 1803.

_____ Famous explorer in early Nebraska

_____ Famous trail through Nebraska

_____ Nebraska was called this during the "Great Migration."

_____ The state bird of Nebraska

_____ This river is the eastern boundary of Nebraska.

_____ National historic site in western Nebraska

GA1138

NEVADA

The Silver State

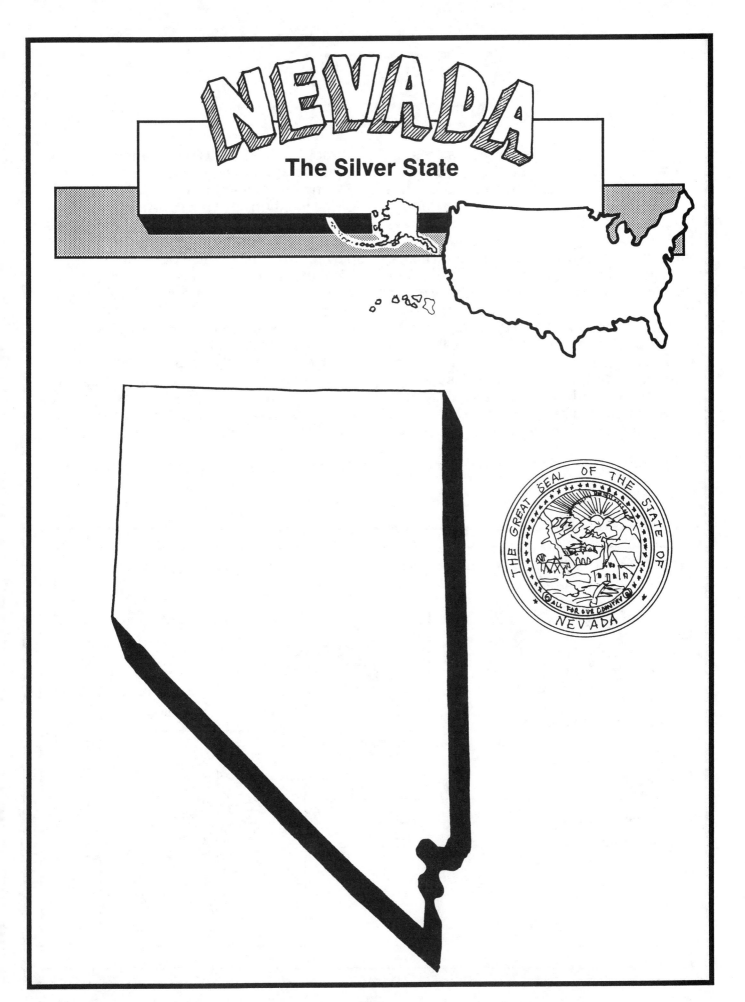

163

NEVADA
THE SILVER STATE

Nevada is one of the driest states in America. Much of the land is so dry that sagebrush, cactus and yucca are about the only plant life found in areas not under irrigation. But gigantic Hoover Dam was built and as a result Lake Mead, one of the world's largest artificially created lakes, supplies much of Nevada, Southern California and Arizona with water. Those areas that are irrigated provide a welcome relief from the desert that surrounds them. Nothing more than a quiet meadow 150 years ago, Las Vegas today is a brilliant array of neon, glitz and first class entertainment. In the 1930's state laws in Nevada allowed legalized gambling in the Las Vegas and Reno-Lake Tahoe areas. Today they attract millions of visitors annually. The nightlife of Las Vegas has helped to make it a major convention city. In fact in view of its location, it isn't surprising to learn that gambling is the mainstay of the state's economy. The federal government has also played a role in the development of Nevada with the testing of many of its nuclear weapons in the deserts away from populated areas. There is also mineral wealth in Nevada with deposits of copper, barite, gold, silver, gypsum and stone. Its current small population and large area make it one of the least densely populated states. But the Las Vegas area alone is growing at the rate of several thousand each year and prospects for the future are looking good.

To begin your study of Nevada, research the symbols below and record your answers.

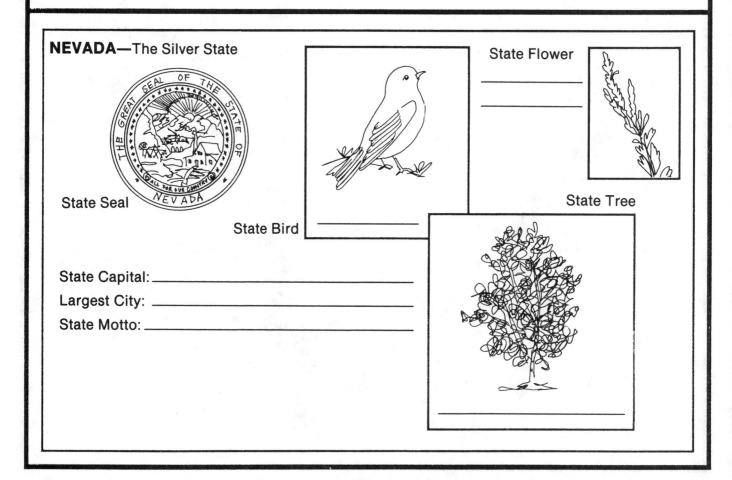

NEVADA—The Silver State

State Seal

State Bird

State Flower

State Tree

State Capital: _____

Largest City: _____

State Motto: _____

164

CHARTING THE MAP

Nevada is a contrast of bleak deserts, the Old West and bright city lights. The Nevada Commission on Tourism has divided the state into these five "territories"—Covered Wagon Territory; Reno-Tahoe Territory; Pony Express Territory; Pioneer Territory; and Las Vegas Territory. Locate each on your outline map and color each territory with a pencil of a different color. Be certain to create a key that will add significance to your colors. For the tourist who wants to spend his entire vacation in Nevada, the Commission has provided a listing of "musts" to visit in each territory. Locate each of the following on your map with a dot and label:

Covered Wagon Territory
Battle Mountain
Carlin
Unionville
Northeastern Nevada Museum
Lovelock

Reno-Tahoe Territory
Genoa
Reno
Harrah's Automobile Museum
Fleishmann Planetarium
Virginia City/Comstock Lode
Ponderosa Ranch
Lake Tahoe
Carson City

Las Vegas Territory
Las Vegas
Hoover Dam
Ripley's Believe It or Not Museum
Liberace Museum
Boulder City

Pony Express Territory
Fernley
Sand Mountain
Grimes Point/Hidden Cave
Eureka

Pioneer Territory
Ione
Schurz
Goldfield
Pioche
Rhyolite

GA1138

A DAY IN THE LIFE OF . . .

During the 1860's, the Pony Express helped to connect the East with the West by providing the rapidly growing West with its first reliable mail service. There are many exciting stories about brave young men who were a part of this service. Many of the stations were located along present-day Nevada Highway 50. Look into the early history of this daring and valuable link of the East to the West. Then imagine yourself one of the riders and create a single day's entry into your daily diary. Include distance traveled, adventures encountered, and any other "information" that will make your entry of interest to others.

GA1138

NEVADA HISTORY

Below are several events that have helped to shape Nevada's history. After reading each, find out the date it occurred and jot that date in the blank to the right as a reminder to you. Then when you've found all the dates, arrange the events in chronological order by placing numbers in the blanks to the left.

_____ Nevada became the 36th state on October 31. _____

_____ Hoover Dam was completed. _____

_____ John Frémont and Kit Carson explored the Great Basin. _____

_____ The first federal irrigation project (The Newlands Project) was completed. _____

_____ The discovery of silver near Virginia City brought a rush of prospectors to western Nevada. _____

_____ The Atomic Energy Commission began testing nuclear weapons at Yucca and Frenchman flats. _____

_____ The Nevada legislature made gambling illegal. _____

_____ Francisco Garcés may have been the first white man to enter the Nevada region. _____

_____ The Southern Nevada Water Project was completed. _____

_____ Congress created the Nevada Territory. _____

_____ The price of silver fell and caused the closing of many Nevada silver mines. _____

_____ Nevada state legislature made gambling once again legal in casinos. _____

GA1138

OUR DRIEST STATE

Nevada lies almost entirely within the Great Basin, a huge desert area that extends into Idaho, Wyoming, Utah and California. The region consists mainly of an upland area that is broken by several north-south mountain ranges. The elevation varies from only about 500 feet above sea level (near the Colorado River) to more than 13,000 feet in the southwest. An average of only 7.4 inches of rain falls annually in Nevada, making it one of the very driest states. The Lake Tahoe region of the Sierras gets as much as 25 inches of rain, but most of the state is very dry. Thus the state has been forced to look to irrigation to satisfy its water needs. To familiarize yourself with how a state solves such problems, investigate the following and jot down your findings.

1. Nevada has several small rivers that flow only during the wet season (December to June). Most of these, however, are of no value to man. Find out why.

_____

_____

_____

2. Find out the history behind the construction of Hoover Dam. What uses have been made of this massive structure? How has it helped the economy of the Southwest?

_____

_____

_____

3. Find out about the "desert farming" that has become a small part of the Nevada economy.

_____

_____

_____

HOOVER DAM

GA1138

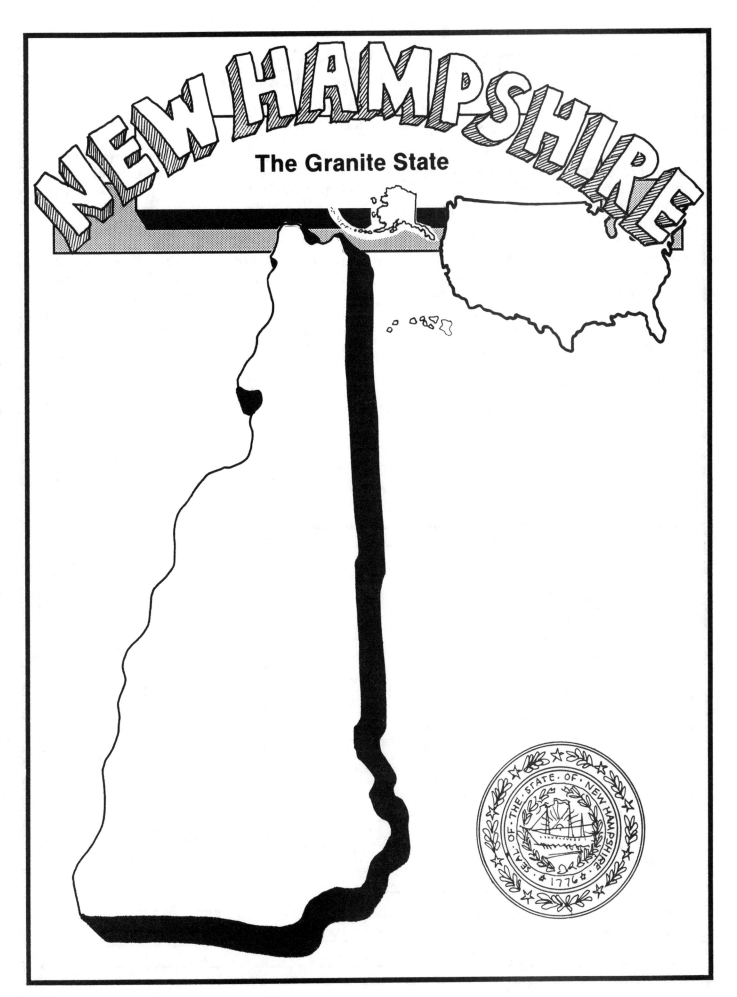

NEW HAMPSHIRE

The Granite State

GA1138

NEW HAMPSHIRE
THE GRANITE STATE

Although small in size, possessing few natural resources, and located in a remote corner of America, New Hampshire has retained its character as a shining example of Yankee independence. Its historic significance to the early stages of the industrialization of America is still evident today with the manufacture of electronic products supplying jobs for thousands of New Hampshire workers. Its 9304 square miles place it 44th in size, and its population of over 900,000 ranks it 42nd, but the per capita income of New Hampshire residents is very near the top half of American states. Triangular in shape, New Hampshire extends almost 200 miles from north to south and varies in width from only a few miles near the Canadian border to approximately 100 miles at the New Hampshire-Massachusetts state line. New Hampshire's Atlantic Coastline between Maine and Massachusetts is only 17.5 miles long. The state's boundaries also include the three southernmost offshore Isles of Shoals. Portsmouth, at the mouth of the Piscataqua River, is the state's only seaport. Except for the narrow coastal plain along the Atlantic, most of New Hampshire is either hilly or mountainous with altitudes ranging from sea level to over 6200 feet. Its natural rugged beauty makes it a favorite among millions of New England vacationers annually.

Before continuing your study of New Hampshire, become familiar with these symbols and other important information:

NEW HAMPSHIRE—The Granite State

State Seal

State Bird

State Flower

State Tree

State Capital: _____

State Gem: _____

State Rock: _____

State Motto: _____

State Animal: _____

State Insect: _____

State Amphibian: _____

GA1138

NEW HAMPSHIRE MAP STUDY

Place these cities on your outline map of New Hampshire:

Portsmouth	Claremont	Somersworth
Nashua	Berlin	Laconia
Manchester	Keene	Rochester
Concord	Exeter	Salem

Locate these colleges and universities:

University of New Hampshire
Dartmouth College
Nathaniel Hawthorne College
Daniel Webster College
New England College

Draw in these rivers and bodies of water:

Merrimack River	Mascoma Lake
Lake Winnipesaukee	Piscataqua River
Connecticut River	Blackwater Reservoir
Lake Wentworth	Pleasant Lake
Cold River	
Hopkinton Lake	
Sugar River	

Draw in these mountains:

White Mountains	Moose Mountain
Long Mountain	Mt. Lafayette
Blue Mountain	Sandwich Range
Crescent Range	
Percy Peaks	
Presidential Range	

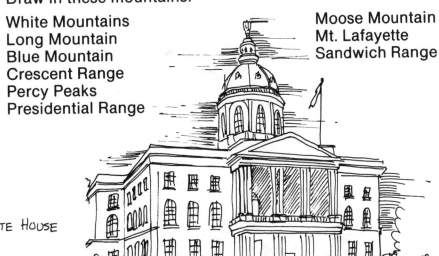

STATE HOUSE

GA1138

FAMOUS SONS AND DAUGHTERS

Below are the scrambled names of some of the men and women from New Hampshire who have distinguished themselves through their accomplishments. Unscramble the letters to identify each personality.

1. _____ EADINL RBWESET—Famous statesman who was Secretary of State under three Presidents

2. _____ NLNAFRKI EEPRIC—14th U.S. President

3. _____ EOALNDR OOWD—Governor General of the Philippines

4. _____ ARANLH TNESO—Chesterfield native who became Chief Justice of the Supreme Court

5. _____ LAAN DHRSEAP—The first American in space

6. _____ AEND NEDA RTCPOOR—Famous poet

7. _____ WTEALR IKTRTDEGE—Author of "Tenting on the Old Campground"

8. _____ RECAHO RGELEYE—Founder of the *New York Tribune*

9. _____ YRAM EKBAR DEDY—Founder of Christian Science

10. _____ OAMLSN HCSAE—Cornish native who became Chief Justice of the Supreme Court

11. _____ DAEWRD LCMDAWOEL—Famous composer

12. _____ RBEROT SFOTR—Although born in San Francisco, he wrote many of his poems in, or about, New Hampshire.

13. _____ OHNJ SMANO—He gave New Hampshire its name.

ROBERT FROST   FRANKLIN PIERCE

HORACE GREELEY

GA1138

NEW HAMPSHIRE TIME CAPSULE

Below are some of the important milestones in New Hampshire's storied past. Guide each capsule to its proper place in history by numbering them in the order in which they occurred.

a. _____ John Mason named the land New Hampshire.

b. _____ John Smith explored the shoreline of New England and what was later to be New Hampshire.

c. _____ New Hampshire became the 9th state to ratify the U.S. Constitution.

d. _____ New Hampshire became a separate province after thirty-eight years of control by Massachusetts.

e. _____ Alan Shepard became the first American in space.

f. _____ The state's first cotton mill was founded at New Ipswich.

g. _____ The state legislature adopted a tax on business profits.

h. _____ Franklin Pierce became the 14th U.S. President.

i. _____ New Hampshire was made a part of the Massachusetts Colony.

j. _____ The first railroad in New Hampshire was completed.

k. _____ The provincial congress adopted its own constitution.

l. _____ Martin Pring explored the mouth of the Piscataqua River.

m. _____ Benning Wentworth became the last royal governor of the province.

n. _____ Dartmouth College was founded at Hanover.

GA1138

WILDLIFE IN NEW HAMPSHIRE

The forestlands of New Hampshire and the wide differences in the geography of the land from the White Mountains to the Coastal Lowlands make it a paradise for wildlife. Hidden below in the "wild" are the names of twenty-nine of these animals. Find each and circle the letters that spell the word correctly.

white-tailed deer
cottontail rabbit
grey squirrel
otter
mink
skunk
beaver
wood duck
rainbow trout
harbor seal

weasel
muskrat
red fox
black bear
wildcat
moose
golden-eye duck
whitefish
ruffed grouse
landlocked salmon

grey fox
Canadian lynx
porcupine
fisher
elk
brook trout
cusk
pickerel
white perch

```
N W O O D D U C K M L A E S R O B R A H U W
O K O P O T T E R A G H L E R E K C I P B H
M C U S K W U M O L S B E A V E R M C T E I
L U H O Y A K N U K S S A A D S R H U U S T
A D M K N I M E T K B B L E S A E W O O U E
S E C O T T O N T A I L R A B B I T R R O T
D Y A F A E R I C O N A E R O S B T E T R A
E E N O C T O P N O H C D C E S O O M W G I
K N A R D A W U N T S K F W R U I O R O D L
C E D A L I R C G A I B O P U V D C K B E E
O D I F I L E R R R F E X O F Y E R G N F D
L L A Y W D T O V K E A S K E O R F E I F D
D O N P R E V P X S T R E H S I F H I A U E
N G L G R E Y S Q U I R R E L K K N T R R E
A T Y Q Y B U L T M H C R E P E T I H W B R
L O N A M G I B L U W W X M P I R I T L Y J
I M X Z B R O O K T R O U T C V T M O R V E
```

174

GA1138

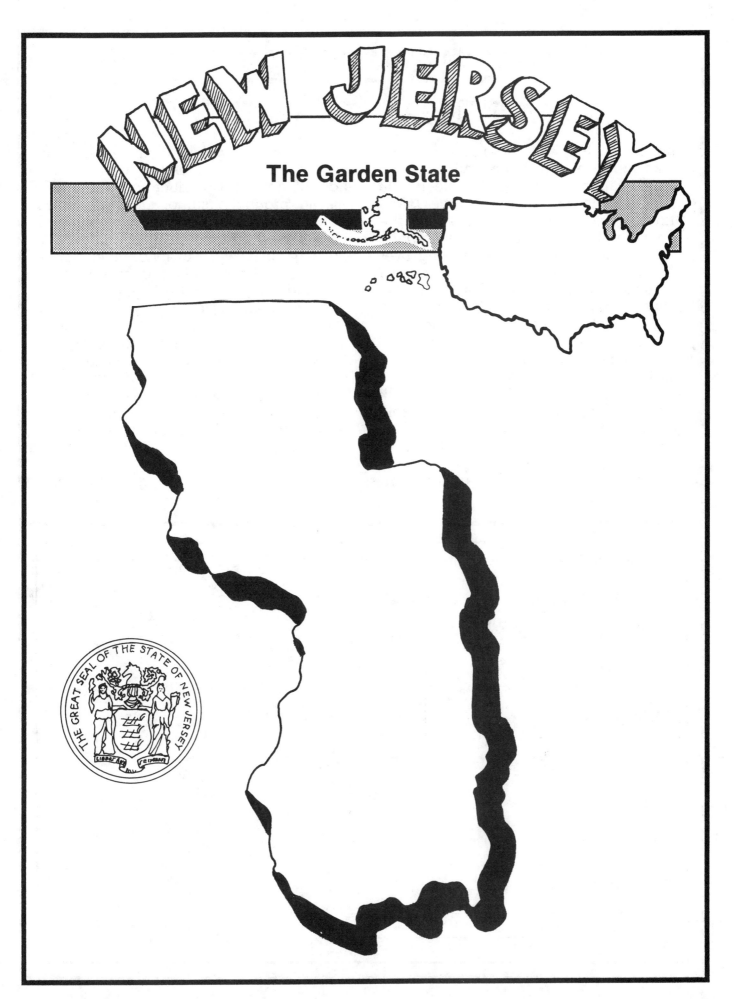

NEW JERSEY

The Garden State

THE GREAT SEAL OF THE STATE OF NEW JERSEY

NEW JERSEY
THE GARDEN STATE

Though small in size (46th), New Jersey ranks ninth in population and fourth in income/capita, reflecting its role in the economy of the eastern coast of the United States. Almost ninety percent of the population lives in urban areas with parts of northeastern New Jersey having over 12,000 persons per square mile. This area of intense population is due to its location between Philadelphia and New York City. Despite all this, two thirds of the state remains open farms, forests and salt marshlands. New Jersey's nickname, The Garden State, was coined to identify the state with its large number of small truck farms that supply many of the vegetable demands of the urban East Coast. Poultry products are also important to the rural farmers. Industry plays the most vital role in New Jersey's economy with high technology, chemical production; rubber and plastic products; stone, clay and glass products leading the way. Thousands of New Jersey citizens also commute daily and work in New York City or other places in the megalopolis. Giant tunnels beneath the Hudson River and bridges above the water connecting New Jersey to New York City are among the busiest traffic lanes in the world during rush hour. Not to be overlooked is Atlantic City as a popular vacation resort area and gambling capital of the East. New Jersey's role in America's early history creates further interest in its becoming the choice of thousands of vacationers annually.

Before beginning your study of this important state, identify the following symbols and other important information:

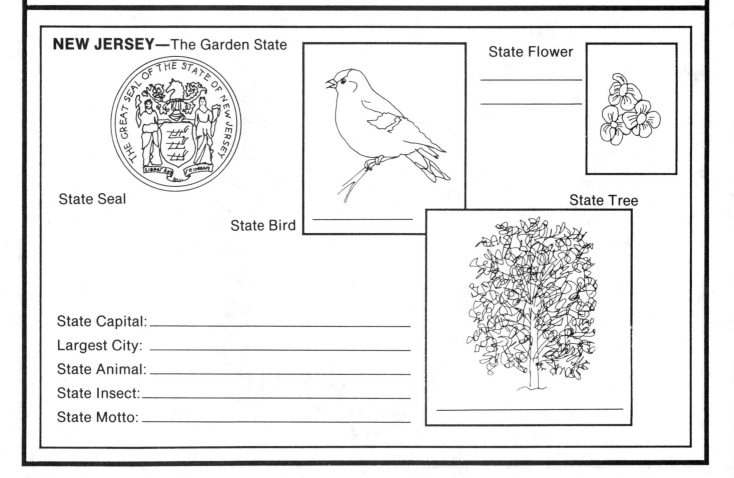

NEW JERSEY—The Garden State

State Seal

State Bird _____

State Flower
_____
_____

State Tree

State Capital: _____
Largest City: _____
State Animal: _____
State Insect: _____
State Motto: _____

GA1138

NEW JERSEY
MAP MYSTERIES

STATE HOUSE
TRENTON, NJ

Below are clues that describe several of New Jersey's cities. Decide the solution to each clue, write the name of the city in the blank space provided and pinpoint the city's location on your outline map.

1. _____ Hessian troops were entrenched here on Christmas night in 1776 when they were attacked and defeated by Washington's men. . .currently the state capital.

2. _____ In his little wooden shack in this city, Thomas Edison made some of the most important scientific advances of mankind.

3. _____ John D. Rockefeller began refining petroleum around 1900.

4. _____ The largest city in New Jersey

5. _____ Home of Seton Hall University

6. _____ It lies at the western end of the Holland Tunnel.

7. _____ The largest of the "Oranges"

8. _____ The first planned industrial city in the United States

9. _____ Located just north of Jersey City, it derives its name from the Dutch words meaning "land of the tobacco pipe."

10. _____ Located just across the Delaware River from Philadelphia, this city has extensive shipyards, food processing and canning factories.

11. _____ The state's oldest English settlement built in 1664; also the city where Isaac Singer made the first sewing machine.

12. _____ South of Paterson—a city with great woolen mills, textiles, rubber goods, radio and railroad equipment, founded by the Dutch in 1676

13. _____ Old city founded in 1683, long noted for its china and tiles made from a special clay, located south of Elizabeth

14. _____ The home of Rutgers, The State University

15. _____ The "Home of the Boardwalk" Miss America Pageant, Gambling Casino capital of the East

16. _____ The fourth oldest university is located here.

Also draw in the following: Delaware River, Hudson River, Atlantic City Expressway, Garden State Parkway, New Jersey Turnpike, I-195, I-78, I-80, the Appalachian Trail, the Kittatinny Mountains, the Scotts Mountains, Bearfort Mountains and the Pohatcong Mountains.

GA1138

FIRST IN NEW JERSEY

The spirit of innovation has been very much alive in New Jersey from colonial times to the miracles of technology today. Twenty of those innovations are listed below. Your task is to match the innovation or invention on the left with its proper identification on the right.

1. _____ first smokeless gunpowder
2. _____ first submarine
3. _____ first phonograph
4. _____ first steam locomotive to pull a train on a track
5. _____ first Colt Revolver
6. _____ first town lighted by electricity
7. _____ first direct distance dialing, coast to coast
8. _____ first yacht club
9. _____ first successful glass factory
10. _____ first incandescent lamp
11. _____ first boardwalk in the world
12. _____ first log cabin in U.S.
13. _____ first organized baseball game
14. _____ first intercollegiate football game
15. _____ first celluloid
16. _____ first motion picture
17. _____ first national historical park
18. _____ first salt water taffy
19. _____ first ferry service
20. _____ first drive-in movie

a. invented by Thomas Edison in 1879
b. built in Atlantic City in 1870
c. built in Gibbstown, Gloucester County in 1640's
d. at Englewood on November 10, 1951
e. at Morristown in 1933
f. developed in 1890 at Maxim
g. built by John Holland in 1878
h. Roselle, New Jersey
i. developed by Thomas Edison at West Orange in 1889
j. developed by Thomas Edison at Menlo Park in 1877
k. operated between Hoboken and Manhattan in 1811
l. founded by John Cox Stevens in 1884
m. built by John Stevens in Hoboken in 1824
n. developed in Paterson in 1836
o. played in Hoboken in 1846
p. played in New Brunswick between Princeton and Rutgers
q. opened by Caspar Wistar in Salem County in 1739
r. produced at the Jersey Shore in 1870's
s. invented by John Wesley Hyatt
t. build on 10-acre plot in Camden County in 1933

GA1138

CROSSING IN NEW JERSEY

Below are clues that will help to identify several of New Jersey's heroes. Read each clue, identify the personality that fits the clue and place that person's name in the appropriate boxes.

Across

2. He wrote *The Red Badge of Courage.*
4. He was president of Princeton, governor of New Jersey and later President of the U.S.
8. He surprised the Hessian troops at Trenton on Christmas night in 1776.
11. The "Poet of the Revolution"
14. He began refining petroleum in Bayonne around 1900.
15. Famous 19th century landscape painter
17. He showed the style of colonial life in his *Journal.*
19. He was born in Caldwell, lived in Princeton and became President twice.
20. Dutch explorer who founded Fort Nassau
21. He invented the electric bulb and motion pictures.

Down

1. The first New Jersey landowner to be appointed as governor of the colony.
3. In 1664 he gave "New Jersey" to his friends.
5. He founded a porcelain factory in Trenton that has made the name famous worldwide.
6. He wrote *The Leatherstocking Tales.*
7. He made the sewing machine a household appliance and built a sewing machine factory in Elizabeth.
8. Famous poet who lived in Camden
9. The first white man in New Jersey
10. In 1609 he sailed the *Half Moon* into Sandy Hook Bay.
12. He and Sir George Carteret received land in New Jersey from the Duke of York.
13. He designed the Brooklyn Bridge.
16. He did much of his work at the Institute for Advanced Studies at Princeton.
18. He developed a code for the telegraph.

THE WIZARD OF MENLO PARK

Thomas Alva Edison was one of the greatest inventors America has known. Although he was born in Ohio, many of the more than one thousand inventions he patented were invented in his laboratories in Menlo Park and later West Orange, New Jersey. Research the life of this great American in other sources. Then prepare a short biography of his life and record a history of his accomplishments you feel were his most important in the space that follows.

Thomas Alva Edison
1847-1931

Biographical Facts:

_____
_____
_____
_____
_____
_____
_____
_____
_____

Accomplishments and Inventions:

_____
_____
_____
_____
_____
_____
_____
_____
_____

GA1138

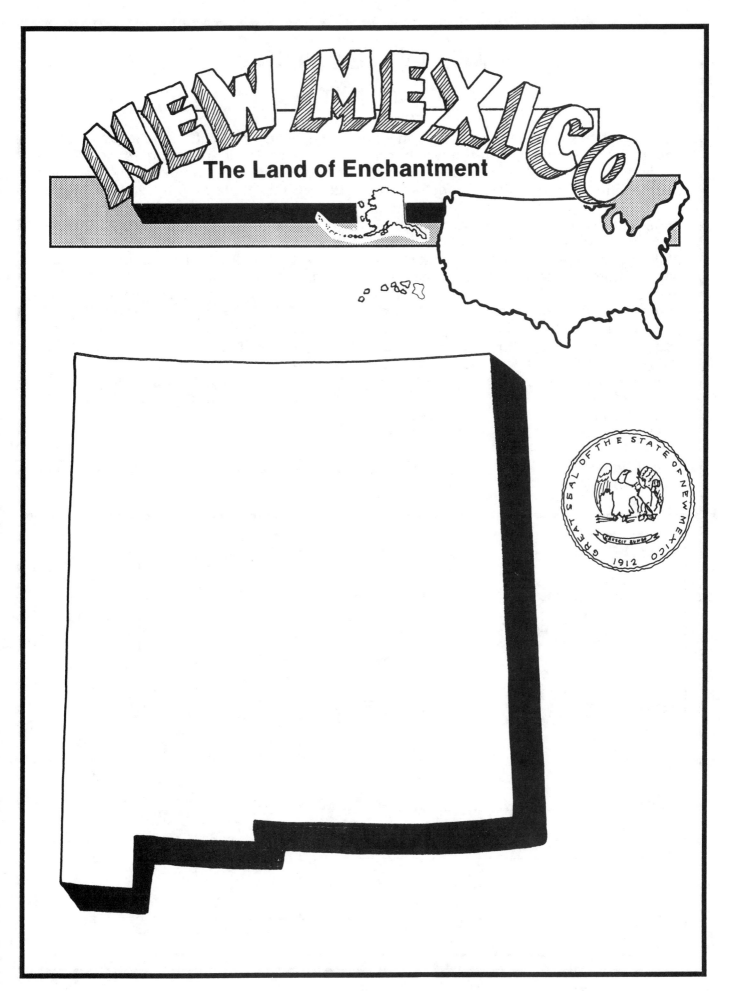

NEW MEXICO

The Land of Enchantment

NEW MEXICO
THE LAND OF ENCHANTMENT

New Mexico is a unique combination of assets and problems that have been defined by the state's geography and its people. Blending the high technology of the nuclear age with irrigated croplands, huge cattle ranches, the natural beauty of its rugged mountain deserts and the charm of its Hispanic past make it a complex and highly interesting land for study. It has few natural resources, but does have deposits of uranium, oil, natural gas and potash that play a major role in the strength of its economy. Ranking fifth in total land area but thirty-seventh in population places New Mexico among the sparsely populated states of America. Most of its current population is concentrated in the valley of the Rio Grande, but thousands of tourists and new residents attracted to the Sun Belt find other areas appealing as well. These new arrivals have pumped millions of new dollars into the economy of New Mexico but have caused problems with the poor Native American and Hispanic cultures who live there. Lack of water hampers the growth of industry and there is thus a competition for the jobs that do exist. In recent years the federal government has created many new jobs in its military and research installations here, but the problem still exists to a degree. As the influx of new residents continues, New Mexico will have to adjust to the population mix and blend the ancient past with the technology of today.

Before you begin your story of The Land of Enchantment, find the symbols and data called for below.

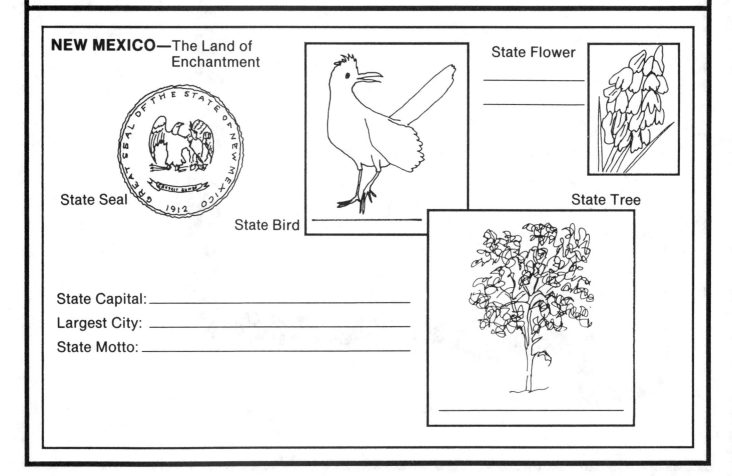

NEW MEXICO—The Land of Enchantment

State Seal

State Bird _____

State Flower
_____
_____

State Tree

State Capital: _____
Largest City: _____
State Motto: _____

182

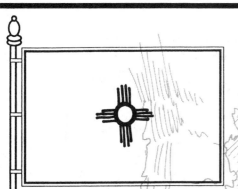

A TRIP BACK IN TIME

The Land of Enchantment, with its spectacular landscape, vibrant culture and history, has eleven National Park Service areas. Find each as described below on a map of New Mexico; then identify each location on your outline map. Once you've located each of the sites, look at a road map of New Mexico and decide the order in which you would visit each if you were planning such a trip. Number in the order in which you would visit them.

Aztec Ruins—The impressive Anasazi ruins on the banks of the Ánimas River. Intact they appear much as they did during the occupation by the Anasazi.

Bandelier—Ancient ruins of cliff dwelling Indians who lived amid the canyons cut into the slopes of Jémez Volcano

Capulin Mountain—The viewer can see over ninety miles from the top of this classic cinder cone volcano.

Carlsbad Caverns National Park—A series of huge caves in southeastern New Mexcio; one of the world's great natural wonders

Chaco Culture—The site of major ruins of Indian culture. Recent excavations reveal much about this high point of Anasazi culture.

El Morro—Great rock towers above a rare, hidden waterhole, vital to the ancient travel route that passed this way. Travelers carved messages here—a register of the pageant of history that passed by.

Fort Union—A once-great fort that served as the first sign settlers had crossed the plains and reached New Mexico along the Santa Fe Trail.

Gila Cliff Dwellings—Located deep in a national forest is this canyon with its spectacular cliff dwellings.

Pecos—Perhaps the greatest of the pueblos when Europeans arrived, Pecos was a trading center with the Plains Indians.

Salinas—Three Indian villages each with its Spanish mission. Missions and villages alike were abandoned in the 1660's.

White Sands—A geological oddity creates a valley of great gypsum sand dunes—a geological classroom.

GA1138

A LAND OF CONTRASTS

New Mexico, ranking fifth in size in total land area, is indeed a land of contrasts. Its total area of over 120,000 square miles stretches almost 400 miles from north to south and over 350 miles from east to west. The land itself can be described as having four distinct regions, each a product of millions of years and various geological phenomena and each contributing to the overall enchantment and appeal of a state full of contrasts. The locations of the four regions are shown on the map to the right. Read from other sources about each and describe in detail in the identification below.

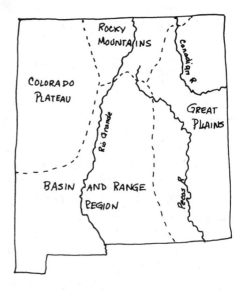

Great Plains _____
_____
_____
_____
_____

Rocky Mountains _____
_____
_____
_____
_____

Basin and Range Region _____
_____
_____
_____
_____

Colorado Plateau _____
_____
_____
_____
_____

GA1138

A SPANISH PAST

Read each of the clues below. Then fill in the blanks with names that correctly answer the clues to some of New Mexico's early history.

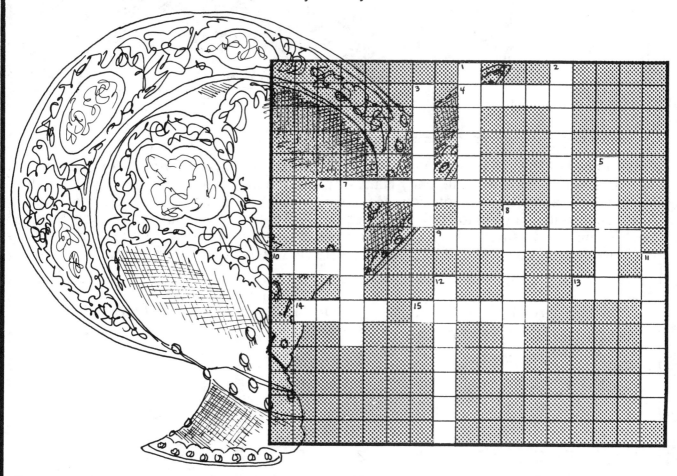

Across

4. His was the first name on Inscription Rock, now a national monument.
6. Spanish viceroy who sent an exploring party into New Mexico in 1539
9. He followed Coronado's expedition with an expedition in 1581 along the Rio Grande.
10. He was the first explorer from the United States sent to explore the Southwest held by Spain.
13. He led a successful Pueblo Indian attack against the Spaniards in 1680, killing over four hundred settlers.
14. His journey in 1792 to New Mexcio followed the path that later became the Sante Fe Trail.
15. He subdued a Pueblo Indian attack in 1696.

Down

1. Spanish explorer who arrived in the area in 1540 and captured the Zũni pueblo of Hawikuh
2. He and his men chased the bandit Pancho Villa into Mexico.
3. Franciscan friar chosen to lead the 1539 exploration
5. He was most responsible for colonizations of New Mexico.
7. Black guide of 1539 expedition killed by Indians
8. Coronado's name for Hawikuh
11. He founded the city of Santa Fe.
12. The first territorial governor of the New Mexico Territory

GA1138

LOST PUEBLOS

TAOS PUEBLO

While many of the pueblos in New Mexico are the ruins of ancient Indian civilizations who lived there, there are still many Native Americans in the Southwest living in pueblos. In fact over eight percent of New Mexico's population is composed of these Native Americans, and many inhabit those "active pueblos" that dot the landscape of New Mexico. Lost in the word search below are the names of several of those pueblos. Look at the list below the search and find the pueblo names in the maze of letters below.

```
A  S  A  N  J  U  A  N  J  O  N  C  F  O  P  H  R  A
O  A  T  O  M  D  A  C  O  M  A  Q  L  K  I  F  P  R
G  N  P  A  C  E  D  O  E  H  M  P  J  M  C  A  O  A
N  I  A  V  O  O  I  C  I  F  B  Z  E  E  U  O  J  L
I  L  N  A  N  S  S  H  U  S  E  M  M  R  R  T  O  C
M  D  U  N  R  D  A  I  D  N  A  S  E  D  I  N  A  A
O  E  G  E  A  Y  T  T  Z  D  C  A  Z  R  S  W  Q  T
D  F  A  T  E  L  S  I  A  E  A  N  U  E  S  A  U  N
A  O  L  J  T  T  A  D  R  U  N  F  N  D  S  T  E  A
T  N  R  E  N  O  O  N  O  Q  W  E  I  D  A  E  H  S
N  S  A  N  T  A  A  A  N  A  U  S  L  L  D  O  L  F  K
A  O  T  H  A  N  M  O  P  S  E  I  A  P  O  M  U  T
S  U  S  E  T  K  N  U  S  E  M  P  F  S  V  P  Y  O
P  H  D  V  N  Q  A  Z  R  T  T  E  F  L  J  M  R  E
```

Picurís	Sandia	San Juan
Taos	Isleta	Jémez
Santa Clara	Nambé	Laguna
Santa Domingo	Acoma	Cochití
Tesuque	Pojoaque	San Felipe
Zia	Santa Ana	San Ildefonso
Zuñi		

GA1138

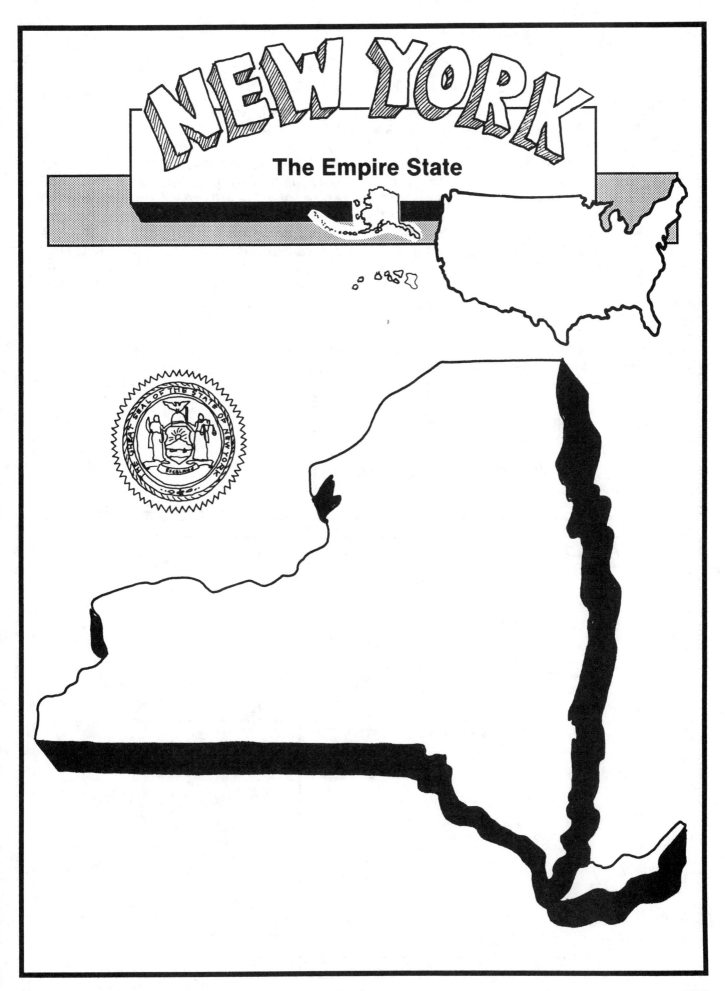

NEW YORK

The Empire State

187

GA1138

NEW YORK
THE EMPIRE STATE

From the earliest Indians who came into what is now New York State 10,000 years ago when the glaciers melted, to the European and Africans who arrived and established permanent settlements during the 1600's, New York has long fulfilled the nation's motto—E Pluribus Unum—one from many. A wide variety of rich, cultural heritages and a myriad of ethnic languages have melted together in today's family of New Yorkers. The Statue of Liberty and the symbolism of opportunity and challenge she represents are what living in America is all about. New York City is our nation's largest and most important city. But the Empire State is much more than just New York City. There is a rich tapestry of people and places that combine to make the New York we know today.

In 1977 the above logo slogan was developed to promote tourism in New York. The use of the heart as a symbol for the word *love* has since been copied for use in other slogans ranging from cities to states to animals to events. In the space to the right, design your own logo that will promote your own state and be unique from all other logos.

To begin your exploration of New York State, research these state emblems:

NEW YORK—The Empire State

State Seal

State Bird

State Flower
_____
_____

State Tree

State Capital: _____
State Fruit: _____
State Fish: _____
State Gem: _____
State Animal: _____
State Motto: _____
Population: _____
Area: _____
Largest City: _____

TIME CAPSULE: NEW YORK

Below are several dates that are important to New York's history. Find each event and in the appropriate place on the time line place its corresponding number.

1. Samuel de Champlain/Henry Hudson discover parts of New York.

2. Indians joined forces with Irish settlers to defeat French at Lake George.

3. Acquital of John Peter Zenger for publishing the truth—the basis for first amendment to U.S. Constitution

4. Ellis Island began serving as entry point for millions of European immigrants.

5. All black slaves are freed by state law.

6. Duke of York took control of the colony, renaming it New York.

7. Giovanni da Verrazano entered the mouth of the Hudson.

8. End of the Revolutionary War drove those loyal to England from United States.

9. Iroquois confederacy

10. New York becomes 11th state.

11. President William McKinley is assassinated in Buffalo.

12. Completion of Erie Canal

13. First industrial research lab built in U.S.A.

14. NBC began transmitting TV images from atop the Empire State Building.

15. Completion of first railroad in New York

16. French and Indian War came to an end.

17. Dutch West India Company began bringing in black slaves.

18. Establishment of trading post at Fort Nassau

19. Dutch settlers began building New Amsterdam.

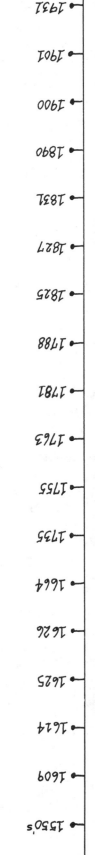

WILLIAM McKINLEY

1931 • 1901 • 1900 • 1890 • 1831 • 1827 • 1825 • 1788 • 1781 • 1763 • 1755 • 1735 • 1664 • 1626 • 1625 • 1614 • 1609 • 1550's • 1524 •

GA1138

NEW YORKERS OF THE 20TH CENTURY

Listed below are the names of New York's more famous sons and daughters. The clue should help you to fill in the missing letters that will identify each.

1. __ __ e __ __ __ r __   __ o __ __ __ __ __ l __ President of the United States from 1901-1909

2. __ __ __ r __ __   __ __ a __ y President of AFL-CIO from its merger until 1979

3. G __ o __ __ __   __ a __ __ m __ __ He developed roll film.

4. S __ __ a __   __ n __ __ __ __ y She organized women into a fight for voting rights.

5. __ r v __ __ __ __   __ e __ __ i __ He wrote "God Bless America."

6. __ r __ h __ __   M __ l __ __ __ Playwright who wrote *Death of a Salesman*

7. L __ __ __ s __ __ __   __ u __ __ e __ Famous black poet

8. __ a __ __ e __   G __ __ p __ __ __ Powerful president of the American Federation of Labor

9. J __ __ o __ __   __ e __ n He wrote the successful Broadway musical *Show Boat.*

10. __ a r __ __ __ __ __ __   __ e a __ World famous anthropologist at the Museum of Natural History from 1926-1978

11. __ e __ n __ __ __   __ __ __ __ s t __ __ __ He wrote the score for *West Side Story.*

12. F __ __ __ __ __ __ i __   R __ __ __ __ v __ __ __ He was President longer than any man.

13. __ __ l __ o __   __ o __ __ __ f __ __ __ __ __ __ Vice president from 1974-1976

14. __ e __ e   __ a r __ z __ __ He won the U.S. Open in 1922 and 1932.

15. J __ n __ __   S __ l __ He discovered a vaccine for polio that bears his name.

16. __ u a __   __ a y   __ o __ __ __ s __ Five-time world boxing champion

17. D __ __ e   E __ l __ __ __ __ __ __ __ __ Famous jazz pianist and composer

Choose one from the above and research the life of that famous New Yorker. Share your findings with the rest of the class.

THE REGIONS OF NEW YORK

HENRY HUDSON

New York has many fun and fascinating places to visit. Its Department of Tourism has divided the state into several different regions, each of them with several attractions all its own. Look at the map below showing the regions clearly defined. Draw the lines of definition and label on your outline map. The clue to the name of each will be the city that is listed beside the name of each region. Simply find the location of each city on a map of New York and label in the region in which it is located.

Region/City

Long Island/Islip

Hudson Valley/Poughkeepsie

Catskills/Kingston

Capital-Saratoga/Albany

Adirondacks/Plattsburgh

Thousand Islands-Seaway/Watertown

Central-Leatherstocking/Utica

Finger Lakes/Syracuse

Niagara Frontier/Buffalo

Chautauqua-Allegheny/Jamestown

191

ATTRACTING TOURISTS TO NEW YORK

There are many tourist attractions all over New York State which bring thousands of visitors into the state each year. Look at the list below of major regions. Each has several attractions of interest to tourists. One of the most important found in each region is listed below. Your task is to match each attraction to the resource in which it is listed.

1. _____ Adirondacks
2. _____ Capital-Saratoga
3. _____ Thousand Islands-Seaway
4. _____ Central-Leatherstocking
5. _____ Hudson Valley
6. _____ Catskills
7. _____ Long Island
8. _____ Chautauqua-Allegheny
9. _____ Finger Lakes
10. _____ Niagara Frontier

a. Fort Ticonderoga
b. National Baseball Hall of Fame
c. Woodstock
d. Erie Canal Museum
e. Saratoga Battlefield
f. Fire Island National Seashore
g. Niagara Falls
h. Vanderbilt Mansion, Hyde Park
i. Allegany State Park
j. Dwight D. Eisenhower Lock, Massena

The greatest attraction in all of New York is New York City itself. It is our nation's largest city, and it stands as perhaps our best example of the melting pot this nation has become. It is a kaleidoscope of lights and sounds where the pace never slows down and the day never ends. Below you will find a list of its stand-out attractions. Find out about each. Then find the location of each on a good map of New York City and then rank order the five you consider a "must" on your list if you were visiting New York City for the first time.

_____ South Street Seaport
_____ Greenwich Village
_____ Chinatown
_____ Central Park
_____ Carnegie Hall
_____ Rockefeller Center
_____ Broadway
_____ Statue of Liberty
_____ Bronx Zoo

_____ United Nations
_____ Ellis Island
_____ Lincoln Center for the Performing Arts
_____ Wall Street
_____ St. Patrick's Cathedral
_____ Empire State Building
_____ World Trade Center
_____ Staten Island Ferry

New York has long been referred to as "The Big Apple." Find out the derivation of this nickname for our nation's largest city.

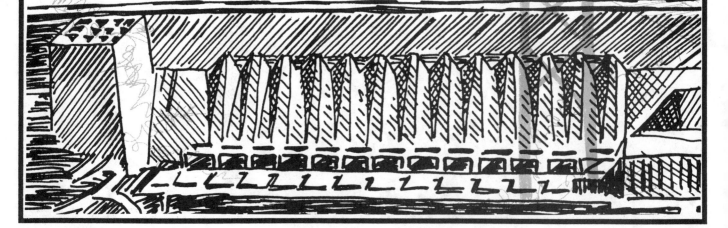

GA1138

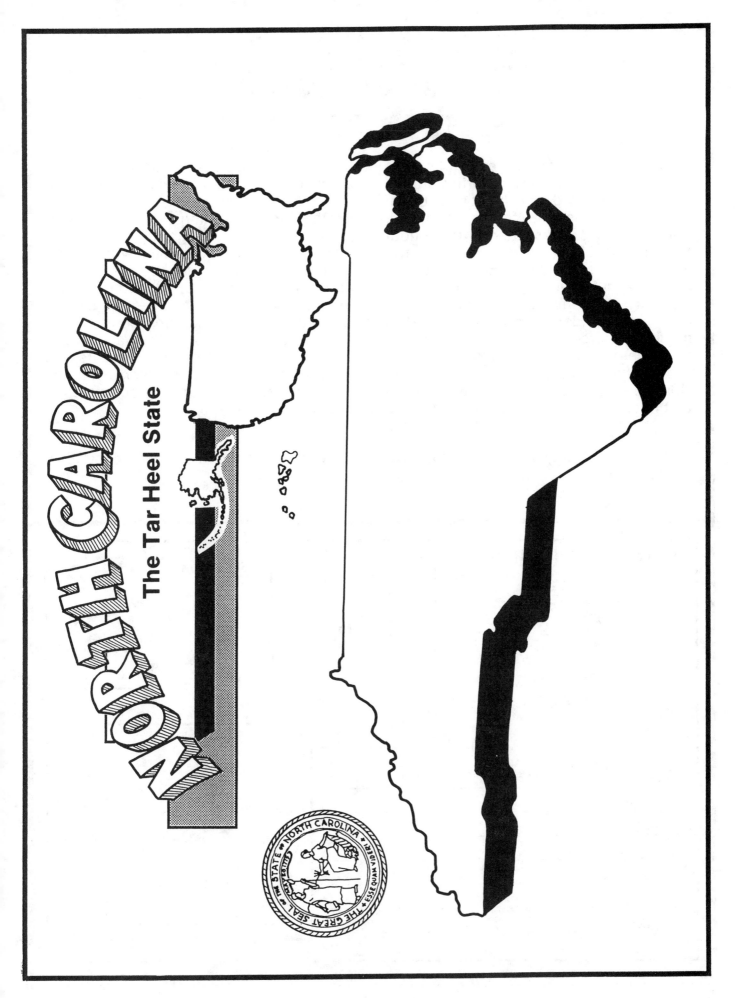

NORTH CAROLINA

The Tar Heel State

GA1138

NORTH CAROLINA
THE TAR HEEL STATE

Rising through lovely sand hills into industrial cities and towns, North Carolina stretches westward from the Atlantic Coast across swamps and fertile farmland. Tobacco farms are scattered throughout the state making North Carolina the nation's leader in the production of tobacco. Manufacturing provides more jobs than any other industry in the state, with a strong dependence on use of the state's natural resources for raw materials. These resources include its rich forests and fertile soil for the growth of tobacco and cotton. North Carolina has played several important roles in the story of America from the first groups of English settlers who came here in 1585 and again in 1587 to its serving as an important battleground during the Civil War to Kitty Hawk and the Wright Brothers to its position today as a leader in the South. Its delightful climate and beautiful scenery combined with its fair share of "landmarks" in American history have made it a popular vacation spot for tourists. Premier golf courses, ski slopes, rustic lodges and charming country inns have certainly added to the vacationer's delight in choosing North Carolina. Its land area ranks it 28th in size, but North Carolina currently ranks 10th among our states in population.

To begin your study of this beautiful southern state, research the following and jot down your findings.

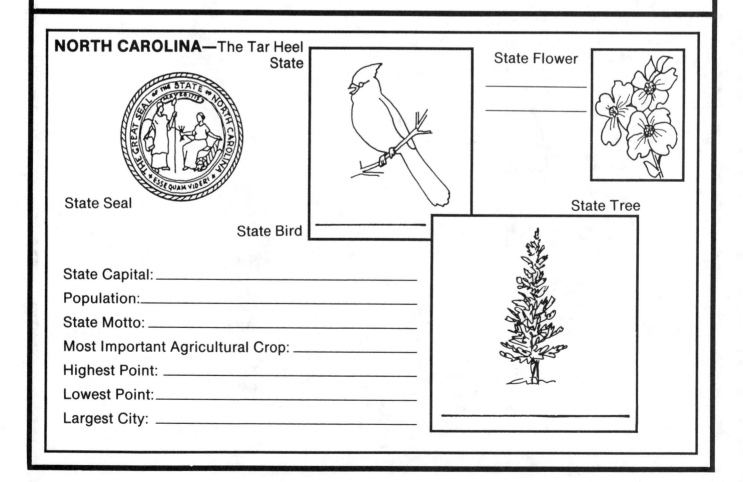

NORTH CAROLINA—The Tar Heel State

State Seal

State Bird _____

State Flower
_____
_____

State Tree

State Capital: _____

Population: _____

State Motto: _____

Most Important Agricultural Crop: _____

Highest Point: _____

Lowest Point: _____

Largest City: _____

GA1138

ON YOUR MAP . . .

Locate the following cities in North Carolina:

Winston-Salem
Durham
Charlotte
Greensboro
Wilmington
Raleigh
Asheville
Greenville
Fayetteville
Burlington
Chapel Hill
High Point

Trace these rivers in North Carolina:

Tar
Yadkin
Neuse
Catawba
Hiwassee
Roanoke
Cape Fear

Create your own map key to locate the following farm, mineral and forest products of North Carolina:

Tobacco   Beef Cattle

Soybeans   Dairy Products

Cotton   Mica

Corn   Stone

Peanuts   Feldspar

Forest Products

Show the location where each of these is found by drawing in your symbol on the outline map.

North Carolina has three mainland regions. Shade the area of the Atlantic Coastal Plain with a light-blue pencil or crayon and label. Label the area known as the Piedmont and color a light tan. Indicate the area of the state containing the Blue Ridge Mountains (the state's largest range) as well as the Great Smoky, Iron, Bald, Black, Brushy, South, Stone, Unaka Mountains with /\/\/\/\ symbols. Then label and color with a light green.

GA1138

EARLY HISTORY OF NORTH CAROLINA

Below are some important dates of events that have helped to shape the history of North Carolina. Your task is to match the event in the first column with the year (in which the event occurred) found in the second column.

1. ____ King Charles I granted Carolina to Sir Robert Heath.

a. 1664

2. ____ North Carolina's first government was established in Albemarle County.

b. 1524

3. ____ North Carolina became the 12th state on November 21.

c. 1663

4. ____ Giovanni da Verrazano visited the North Carolina coast.

d. 1629

5. ____ North Carolina seceded from the Union.

e. 1903

6. ____ King Charles II granted the Carolina colony to eight lords proprietors.

f. 1650

7. ____ Three North Carolina universities joined in the Research Triangle program for industry.

g. 1958

8. ____ North Carolina was readmitted to the Union.

h. 1868

9. ____ The Wright brothers made the first successful powered airplane flight at Kitty Hawk.

i. 1789

10. ____ The first permanent settlers came to the Albemarle region from Virginia.

j. 1781

11. ____ The state took over the support of public schools.

k. 1861

12. ____ British forces withdrew from North Carolina during the American Revolution.

l. 1933

In the space below, build your own time line of North Carolina's early history. Include the events above, but shorten the explanation to fit the space available.

GA1138

FOR FURTHER RESEARCH . . .

1. North Carolina is called the Tar Heel State. Find out the origin of the term and report your findings on these lines.

_____

_____

_____

_____

2. Cape Hatteras is often called the "Graveyard of the Atlantic." How did it get this name?

_____

_____

_____

_____

3. In 1585 a group of English settlers arrived in the New World on Roanoke Island off the coast of North Carolina. The region was inhabited by hostile Indians, and the colony abandoned the island and went back to England. In 1587 another group landed on the same island. Find out what happened to this colony and report your findings below.

_____

_____

_____

_____

4. North Carolina is a "forward-looking state" that spends a lot of money on the research of its future. In fact there is an area commonly referred to as its "research triangle." Find out the location of this cradle of research and describe the reason for its name.

_____

_____

_____

GA1138

MILEAGE MASTER

Road maps usually have a grid similar to the one below that will help the travelling motorists to know how far it is from one city to another. Obviously all the towns and cities in North Carolina cannot be included in such a grid. In those cases the motorist can look at the distance between the two cities on the grid that are closest to where he has been and where he is going. He can then look at the map and add on (or subtract from) any additional miles as needed. To see how all this works, look closely at the grid below and answer each question.

1. What is the distance between Greensboro and Charlotte? _____

2. How far is it from Kitty Hawk to Charlotte? _____

3. How far is Raleigh from Chapel Hill? _____

4. How many miles between Winston-Salem and Asheville? _____

5. How far to High Point if you are now in Raleigh? _____

6. How many miles from Statesville to Greenville? _____

7. What is the distance from Greensboro to Asheville? _____

8. How far to Charlotte when in Wilmington? _____

9. How far from Raleigh to Kitty Hawk? _____

10. How far from Winston-Salem to Durham? _____

11. What is the distance from Statesville to High Point? _____

12. If Burlington is only 21 miles northeast of Greensboro, how far is it from Burlington to Asheville? ___

13. If Monroe is 26 miles southeast of Charlotte, how far is Statesville from Monroe? _____

14. If Hickory is 28 miles west of Statesville, how many miles from Hickory to Asheville? _____

15. Look on the map to find Gastonia. After locating it on the map, find the city on the grid closest and calculate the miles from Gastonia to Greensboro?

_____

Asheville	Chapel Hill	Charlotte	Durham	Greensboro	Greenville	High Point	Kitty Hawk	Raleigh	Statesville	Wilmington	Winston-Salem
224											
115	127										
231	12	140									
178	48	91	54								
336	116	228	103	163							
165	61	73	70	17	174						
460	237	352	227	282	138	299					
241	28	143	23	78	85	93	215				
103	122	43	129	69	220	63	343	136			
318	151	203	146	184	117	192	251	123	229		
144	74	81	81	27	195	19	308	104	42	210	

198

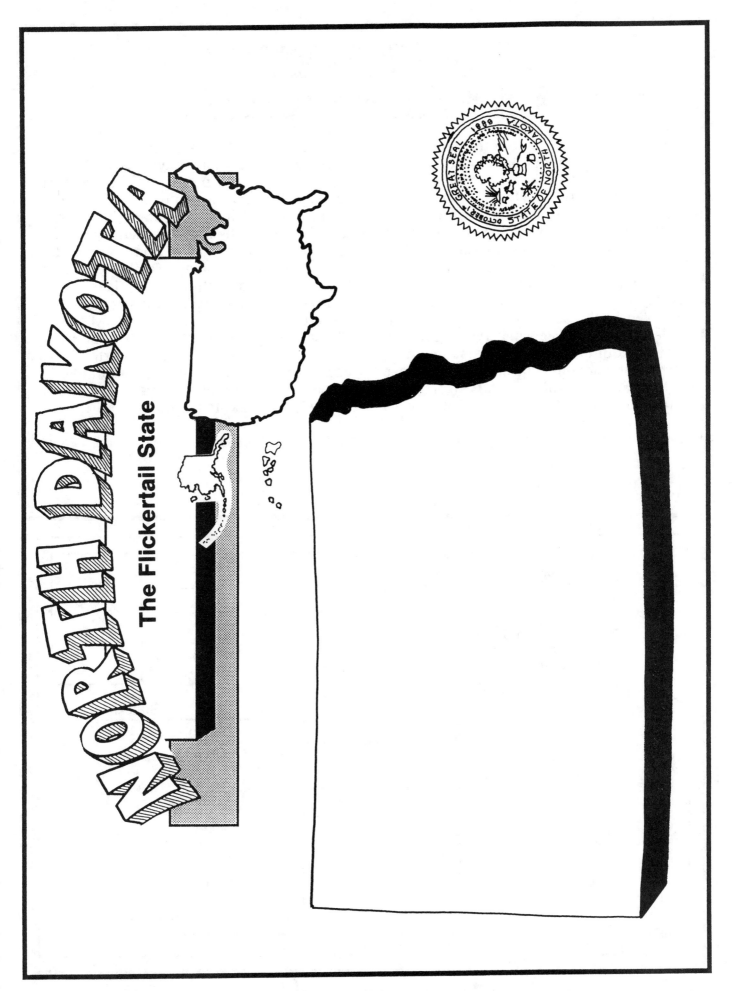

NORTH DAKOTA

The Flickertail State

NORTH DAKOTA
THE FLICKERTAIL STATE

Only the economy of South Dakota depends more heavily on farming than does the midwestern state of North Dakota. About 51 of every 100 North Dakotans live in rural areas and many of those who live in cities work in factories that produce farm products or farm equipment. Ranches and farms are found all the way from the Red River Valley in the east to the rugged Badlands of the west. Wheat is the major crop with flaxseed, sunflower seeds, barley, oats, pinto beans, rye and sugar beets accounting for most of the remaining agricultural income. Its long, sometimes bitterly cold winters and short, hot summers with little precipitation provide a climate for only the hardiest of people. But those who live there have made adjustments and have a per capita income that ranks just below the top half in the nation. Nature has divided the state into three distinct areas. The Red River Valley, which separates North Dakota from Minnesota, is a broad green valley. To the west is a Drift Prairie of rolling hills, lakes and valleys that stretch west to just east of the Missouri River. From there is the Missouri Plateau and the Badlands, a region of treeless hills and soft clay earth. Vast deposits of lignite and significant oil reserves may well play a role in the future of the North Dakota economy.

Before continuing with your study, find the following symbols of the Flickertail State:

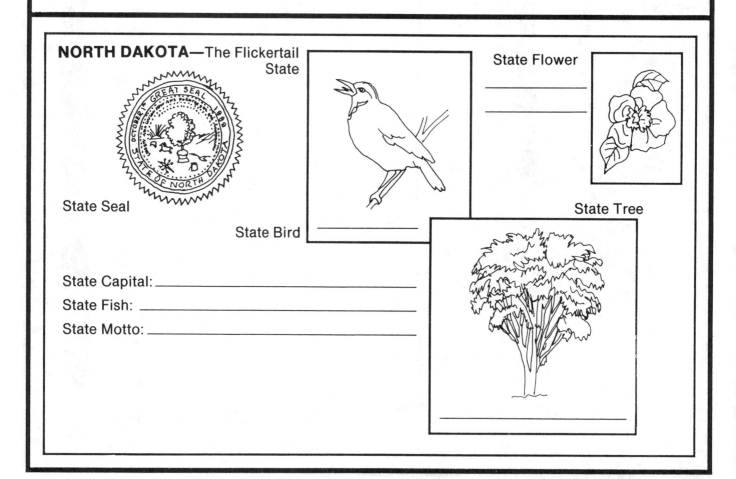

NORTH DAKOTA—The Flickertail State

State Seal

State Bird _____

State Flower
_____
_____

State Tree

State Capital: _____

State Fish: _____

State Motto: _____

GA1138

NORTH DAKOTA ON THE MAP

Hidden in the word search below are the names of thirteen cities, two rivers and one national park you should locate and label on your outline map of North Dakota. Look at each clue below the maze of letters, use a road map to find the city, river or park, locate and circle the letters that spell that word in the word search. Then pinpoint its location on your outline map.

```
T S I S K R O F D N A R G E T K B
A H O N A D E D T O N I M G R M Y
H Y B N L L F E N S T A S F E I T
N O I K L L O V O N W B C F D V L
M I S S O U R I R I V E R U R U D
P R M M R T T L U K H A O O I L N
B M A O A C Y S R C I C S N V O L
O G R A F T A L U I I H B W E P E
W O C P I S T A L D E T Y T R A U
M R K S E E E K L S E T D S A M C
A A N W O T S E M A J B O Y B T T
N A P O L E O N D O Y S A W O I T
T H E O D O R E R O O S E V E L T
```

_____ The University of North Dakota is located here.

_____ River cuts a path from northwest to south-central part of state

_____ Capital city of North Dakota

_____ 193 miles east of Bismarck along highway 29

_____ 67 miles south of Bismarck on Standing Rock Indian Reservation

_____ On Route 2, 89 miles west of Grand Forks

_____ On Route 94, this city is 98 miles west of Bismarck.

_____ This city lies 164 miles northwest of Jamestown at the intersection of Routes 281 and 30.

_____ Located at intersection of Routes 83 and 52

_____ 171 miles south of Williston, this city is located on Route 12.

_____ City at the intersection of Routes 281 and 94

_____ 200 miles north of Dickinson

_____ Western city near Montana on Route 94

_____ 75 miles southeast of the capital city

_____ It serves as the border between North Dakota and Minnesota.

_____ The U.S. President after whom North Dakota's only national park is named.

GA1138

NORTH DAKOTA TIME CAPSULE

Below are several events that are significant to the history of North Dakota. The dates when the events occurred are given on the time line at the bottom of the page. Find out when each occurred and place the number that corresponds to that event on the time line in its proper place.

1. Lewis and Clark passed through North Dakota on their way to and from the Pacific Ocean.

2. Congress created the Dakota Territory.

3. North Dakota became the 39th state.

4. French Canadian La Vérendrye explored North Dakota.

5. Nonpartisan League was founded.

6. Oil was discovered near Tioga.

7. U.S. acquired northeastern North Dakota by treaty with Great Britain.

8. Construction began on Garrison Diversion Project.

9. U.S. acquired southwestern North Dakota through Louisiana Purchase.

10. Dakota Territory was opened for homesteading.

11. North Dakota Centennial

12. The first attempt at a permanent settlement was made at Pembina.

13. La Salle claimed for France all land drained by Mississippi.

14. The first generator at Garrison Dam began to produce electricity.

15. Congress approved modified version of Garrison Diversion Project.

1682 — 1738 — 1803 — 1804-1806 — 1812 — 1818 — 1861 — 1863 — 1889 — 1915 — 1951 — 1956 — 1968 — 1986 — 1989

GA1138

TRAVELLING NORTH DAKOTA

For purposes of promoting tourism in the state of North Dakota, the State Department of Tourism has divided the state into five travel regions. Each has certain features and attractions that make it distinctive from the other regions. The map below shows the lines of various regions. Below that is a list of the sites and attractions that bring thousands of tourists to North Dakota every year. Find the location of each and place its corresponding letter in the appropriate spot on the map.

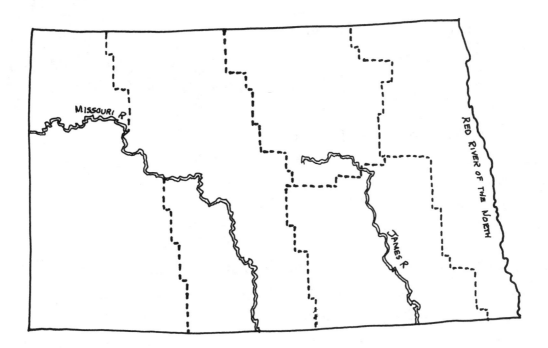

a. Pembina Historic Site

b. Bonanzaville, USA

c. Chateau de Mores

d. International Peace Garden

e. Lake Sakakawea

f. Writing Rock

g. Theodore Roosevelt National Park

h. Fort Abercrombie

i. Knife River Indian Villages National Historic Site

j. Battle of the Little Bighorn

k. Roger Maris Museum

l. Fort Totten Indian Reservation

m. Fort Seward

n. Geographical Center Pioneer Village

o. Fort Buford

p. Sully's Hill National Game Preserve

Draw a circle around the letters of the five sites you would find most interesting if you were visiting North Dakota. On the back of this paper, jot down a brief description of each that identifies your interests.

GA1138

NORTH DAKOTA TRIVIA

Find the answers to each of the interesting bits of North Dakota trivia below.

1. What is unique about the state capital?

   _____

   _____

2. The state's nickname is The Flickertail State. What is a flickertail?

   _____

   _____

STATE CAPITAL

3. The three major land regions found in North Dakota: _____

   _____

4. Top three agricultural products:

   _____

5. State Dimensions—Greatest North-South Distance: _____

   Greatest East-West Distance: _____

   Rank in Land Area: _____

6. Land Elevations—Highest Elevation: _____

   Lowest Elevation: _____

7. Population: _____

   Rank: _____

8. Government—Number of U.S. Senators: _____

   Number of U.S. Representatives: _____

   Number of Members in the State Senate: _____

   Number of Members in House of Representatives: _____

9. Name of railroad built from Fargo to Bismarck completed in 1873: _____

10. State's greatest mineral resource: _____

OHIO

The Buckeye State

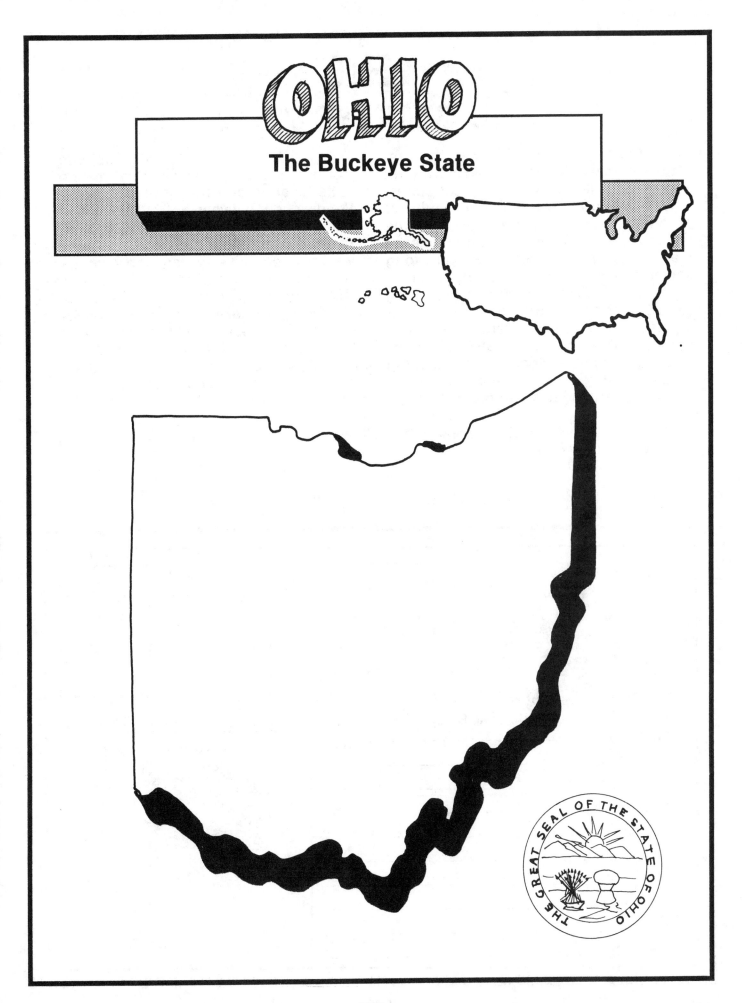

GA1138

OHIO
THE BUCKEYE STATE

Since the days when Ohio was the first state to be carved out of the old Northwest Territory, it has been a leader of states. Ohio's manufacturing and agricultural production is among the highest in the nation. The ethnic mix found there makes it a microcosm of America. Ohio has long served as a sounding board for politicians looking for public opinion and marketing experts testing new products and marketing strategies. Its large deposits of high-quality coal, oil, natural gas and stone have helped to make it one of the leading industrial states. Its location within the nation's heartland has also made it a state with significant agricultural production. But perhaps its greatest natural resource is its location and transportation system. Sandwiched between Lake Erie and the Ohio River and densely covered with railroads, interstate highways and waterways, Ohio is able to transport raw materials and finished products all over the world. Its location on the eastern edge of the Midwest makes it a heavily traveled overland connection between the Midwest and the heavily populated East. With all this, Ohio remains a beautiful state of rolling hills and upland plateaus.

To begin your study of Ohio, research the following emblems and jot down your findings in the space provided.

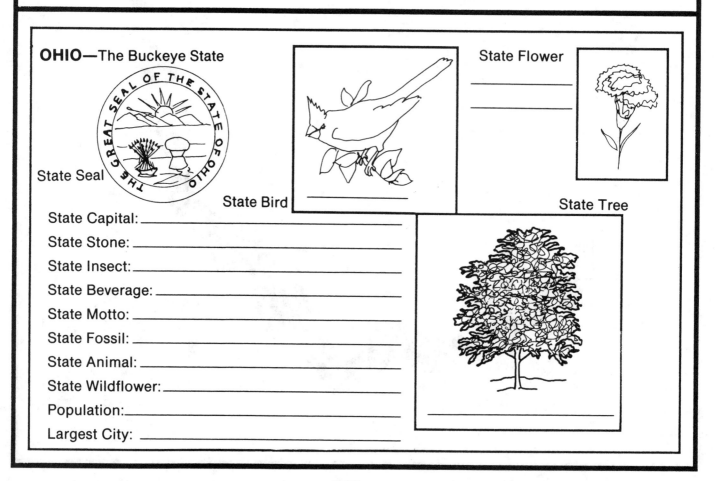

OHIO—The Buckeye State

State Seal

State Bird

State Flower

_____

_____

State Tree

State Capital: _____

State Stone: _____

State Insect: _____

State Beverage: _____

State Motto: _____

State Fossil: _____

State Animal: _____

State Wildflower: _____

Population: _____

Largest City: _____

GA1138

FAMOUS OHIOANS

Below are clues that describe accomplishments of some of Ohio's more famous sons and daughters. Read each clue and try to fill in the missing letters that will spell the name of the famous Ohioan. If you cannot identify the personality, research the event from other resources to get the information you need to identify that personality.

1. C __ Y __ __ __ __   Famous baseball immortal; name of an award for the best pitcher in baseball each year

2. __ d __ __ __ M. S __ __ __ __ __ n   He was Lincoln's Secretary of War.

3. __ l y __ __ __ __ S. __ r __ __ __   Civil War general, later U.S. President

4. H __ __ __ __ y S. F i __ __ __ __ __ __ __   Rubber manufacturer

5. __ i l __ __ __ __ M __ __ __ __ __ e __   24th U.S. President

6. __ o __ __ __ __ M __ __ __   Famous educator

7. A n __ __ __ __ a __ __ __ __   Famous markswoman

8. Z __ __ __ __ G __ __ __   Famous novelist

9. __ a __ __ __ __ G. __ a __ __ __ n __   U.S. President from Blooming Grove

10. J __ __ __ __ __ __ o __ __   Famous abolitionist who was hanged

11. J o __ __ C __ __ __ __ __ __ __   Johnny Appleseed

12. __ __ __ i e __ B __ a __ __   He founded the Boy Scouts.

13. __ __ r __ __ y O __ d __ __ __ __ __   Famous auto racer

14. T __ __ __ __ __ __ h   Indian chief

15. B __ n __ __ __ __ __ __ __ r r __ __ __ __   U.S. President from North Bend

16. __ a __ __ s G __ __ __ i __ __ __   20th U.S. President

17. __ o __ __ D. __ o __ k __ __ __ __ __ __ __   Industrialist, philanthropist from Cleveland

18. __ o __ n __ h __ __ __ a __   Coauthor of antitrust act

19. J __ s __ __ h __ t __ __ u __ __   He built the Golden Gate Bridge.

20. __ i __ l __ m H __ __ __ y H __ r __ __ __ __ __   U.S. President

21. __ u __ h __ __ __ __ __ __ B. __ a __ e __   19th U.S. President

22. __ __ o __ __ __ __ __ u __ t __ __   Famous general

23. C l __ __ __ __ __ __ __ __ a r __ __ __   Famous trial attorney

24. J __ h __ B __ n __ __ __ __   He prosecuted Lincoln's assassins.

25. __ o __ __ __ l __ m   He was the drummer boy at Shiloh.

OHIO COUNTIES

Below is an outline map of Ohio's 88 counties. Some of them are shaded. From the clues given below, identify the names of those requiring identification in the blank spaces. Then label on shaded areas. You will need a map of Ohio counties to locate county names once you've solved clues.

1. _____ named for the river which flows through it. . .comes from an Indian word *Scionto*, meaning "deer"

2. _____ named for a river which flows through it. . .derived from an Indian word meaning "crooked"

3. _____ named in honor of the Indians who lived there

4. _____ named for the town in Arabia to which Mohammed fled from Mecca

5. _____ named for the French word meaning "a plain"—so called because of the level terrain

6. _____ named for the fort built there by General "Mad Anthony" Wayne

7. _____ named for the river so named from an Indian word meaning "fallen timbers"

8. _____ named for the early salt licks found in this county

9. _____ named for Christopher Columbus and Anna

10. _____ named for the victorious American leader who won the Battle of Lake Erie

PRESIDENTIAL TOUR

Ohio claims to be the "Mother of Presidents" because eight of her sons have risen to the highest office in the land. Seven Presidents were born in Ohio and the eighth moved into this state before it was admitted to the Union. Most of the homes and burial places of these great men are now public memorials. Below is the outlined route for a motor tour that covers several Ohio cities where the homes, tombs, memorials and other memorabilia of these great leaders are located. Find out the names of these famous sons of Ohio and pencil in the name of the President we associate with each of the cities on the map below.

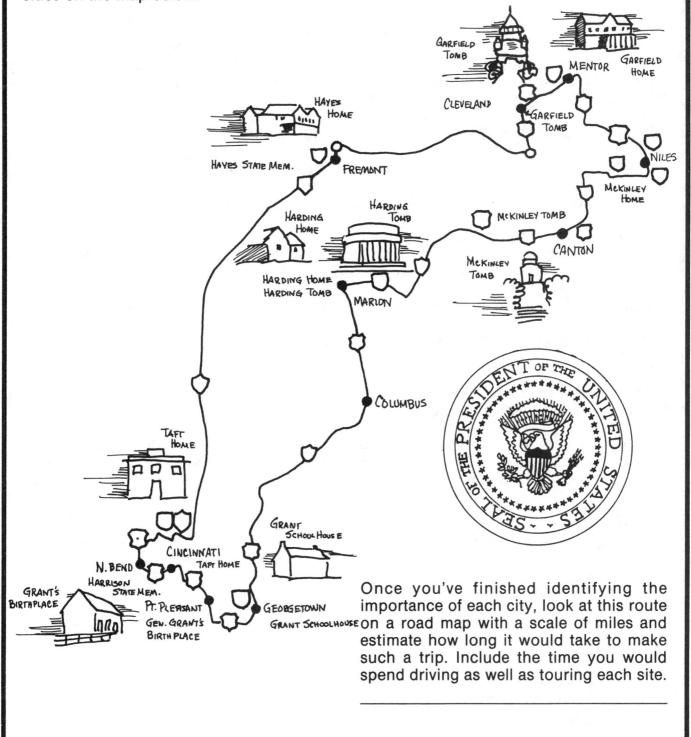

Once you've finished identifying the importance of each city, look at this route on a road map with a scale of miles and estimate how long it would take to make such a trip. Include the time you would spend driving as well as touring each site.

GA1138

OHIO'S CITIES AND INTERSTATES

Ohio's 10.8 million people make it our sixth largest state. While Ohioans live all over the state, there is a significant concentration of population in the metropolitan areas. Ohio has several large cities scattered throughout the state. Locate each of the following on your outline map with a small dot. Then print the name of the city beside the dot and place the current population figure under the name of each city.

Cleveland, Columbus, Cincinnati, Toledo, Dayton, Akron, Canton, Youngstown

1. Add together the populations of these eight cities. What total do you get?_____

2. What percent of the state's 10.8 million inhabitants live in these eight major cities? ____

3. Bear in mind that the above figures do not include the suburbs that surround these cities. Using your best "guesstimate," how many more people could be added to represent a true population figure on these eight metropolitan areas?_____

Ohio has long been recognized as a state with an excellent system of interstate highways connecting east to west and north to south. Locate these major interstate highways on your map by consulting a current road atlas—then drawing them in as accurately as you can.

Interstate 70, Interstate 71, Interstate 75, Interstate 76, Interstate 77, Interstate 80 (also Ohio Turnpike)/Interstate 90 (also Ohio Turnpike)

4. Look again at the map you've just completed and list below beside the name of each interstate any of the eight major cities (with a population near 100,000 or more) that are linked to that highway.

    Interstate 70:

    Interstate 71:

    Interstate 75:

    Interstate 76:

    Interstate 77:

    Interstate 80:

    Interstate 90:

GA1138

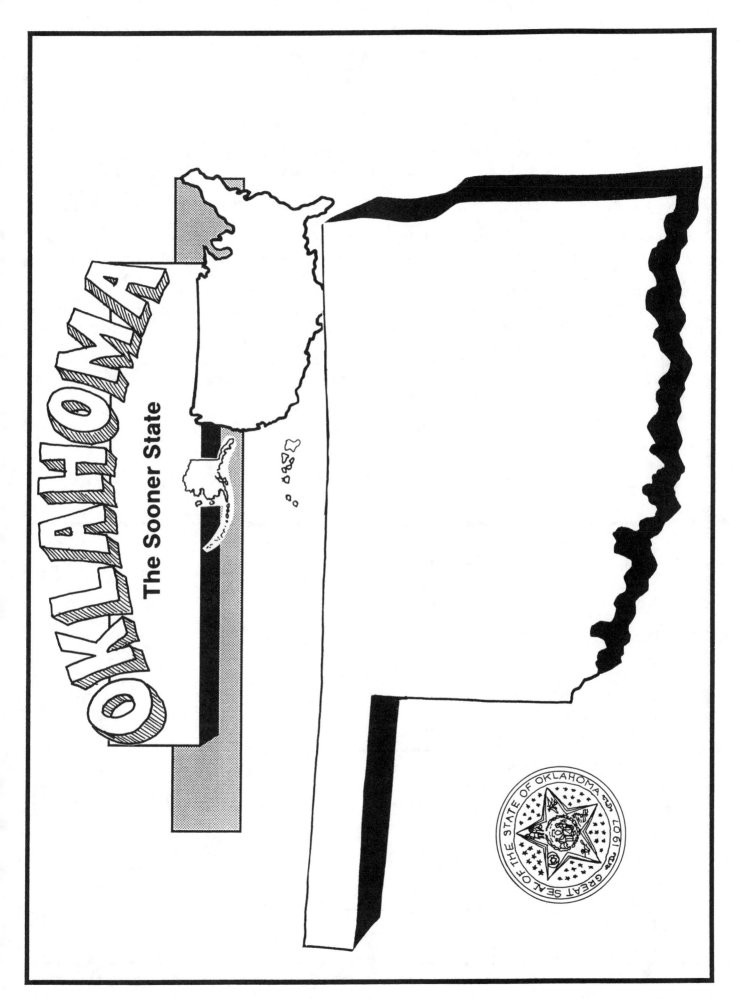

OKLAHOMA

The Sooner State

211

OKLAHOMA
THE SOONER STATE

Although Oklahoma is one of the youngest of our states, it is a land that shows evidence of prehistoric man's existence there as early as 11,000 B.C. Its recorded history began in 1541 when Spanish explorer Coronado traveled through the area. Oklahoma was a part of the Louisiana Purchase of 1803 and was later set aside as Indian Territory. A land run in the late 1800's opened the first segment of the Unassigned Lands for white settlers, and before long the state had enough people to apply for statehood. The Sooner State lies just west of the Midwest/East industrial belt, just north of the Gulf Coast states of Louisiana and Texas and just west of the agricultural Midwest. Overproduction and lack of appropriate farming methods by the early settlers left the state little more than a dust bowl during the drought of the 1930's. However, the nation's demand for oil and natural gas has brought back the economy of Oklahoma, and the careful conservation practices of recent years have restored much of the land and made the state once again a major food producer. Increased manufacturing has raised the economy further and seems to hold the key to Oklahoma's success in the future.

Before you continue with your study of Oklahoma, become familiar with these state symbols:

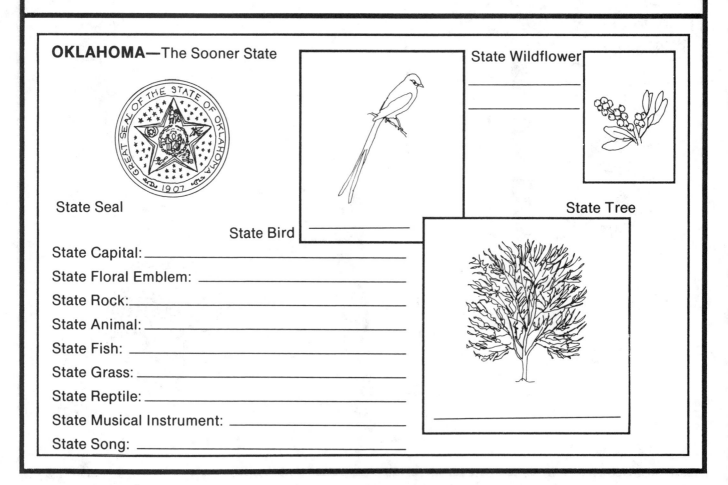

OKLAHOMA—The Sooner State

State Seal

State Bird _____

State Wildflower
_____
_____

State Tree

State Capital: _____

State Floral Emblem: _____

State Rock: _____

State Animal: _____

State Fish: _____

State Grass: _____

State Reptile: _____

State Musical Instrument: _____

State Song: _____

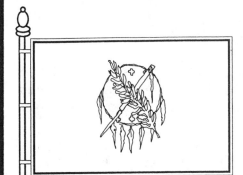

OKLAHOMA ON THE MAP

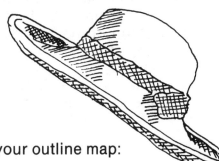

Pinpoint the locations of these Oklahoma cities on your outline map:

Oklahoma City   Stillwater
Tulsa   Ponca City
Enid   Midwest City
Broken Arrow   Norman
Muskogee   Bartlesville

Draw in these rivers that flow through Oklahoma:

North Canadian
South Canadian
Arkansas
Cimarron
Red
Washita

Trace with a broken line ---- these famous cattle trails:

Chisholm Trail
East Shawnee Trail
Great Western Trail

Draw in these modern transportation routes through Oklahoma:

I-40; Will Rogers Turnpike; I-35; H.E. Bailey Turnpike; Indian Nation Turnpike

Locate the following tourist attractions:

Ouachita National Forest
Chickasaw National Recreation Area
Will Rogers Memorial (Claremore)
Woolaroc Museum (Bartlesville)
Washita Battlefield
Fort Sill
National Cowboy Hall of Fame
Indian City, U.S.A. (Anadarko)

GA1138

OKLAHOMA COWBOYS

Oklahoma is the home of the American cowboy. His image is firmly etched in American folklore. The stereotyped image that has been perpetuated by Hollywood Western movies is actually a blend of the working cowboys, infamous outlaws and the show cowboys. Each had an impact on the history of Oklahoma.

1. Working Cowboy—America's working cowboy began on the plains of Texas. Research the life of this American hero and describe below reasons for Oklahoma's importance to him.

_____

_____

_____

_____

2. Outlaws—With the coming of cattlemen and settlers to Oklahoma came more than a fair share of outlaws and thieves. Law enforcement was inadequate and the landscape offered many hiding places for bank and train robbers who roamed the area almost at will. Below are the scrambled names of four of the most notorious. Unscramble the names of these villains and choose one for further research. Create a short "four-statement report" on this outlaw and share it with other members of your class.

   a. WLRAMO EORBTHRS _____

   b. LLIB ODIOLN _____

   c. EORS NDUN _____

   d. LLBEE RSATR _____

3. Show Cowboys—The lives and adventures of those who lived the early West have been portrayed successfully by Hollywood to the delight of several generations of Americans. The idea that such a venture could be so successful began with the live Wild West shows that were so popular during the early 1900's. Three of the more popular originated in Oklahoma on these three ranches: the Pawnee Bill Ranch, the Mulhall Ranch and the Miller 101 Ranch. Choose one and make four statements that describe it in the space below.

_____

_____

_____

_____

OKLAHOMA INDIANS

The word *Oklahoma* is derived from two Indian words, *Okla* meaning "people" and *humma* meaning "red." Indians have had a lasting impact on Oklahoma with much of their culture still in evidence today. Scientists estimate that a hunter-agricultural civilization lived in the area more than 11,000 years ago and have identified the spearheads of a primitive tribe of Indians known as the Cloves. The Golden Age of Oklahoma's prehistory, 500 to 1300 A.D., is represented by the Spiro Mounds site on the banks of the Arkansas River in eastern Oklahoma. The artifacts found there show that the Spire People were highly skilled artisans with a fairly sophisticated society.

With the arrival of Coronado in 1541 comes the beginning of a recorded history of the Oklahoma Indians. Research their story and write down two statements about each of the following:

Plains Indians met by Coronado _____

_____

Osage _____

_____

Quapaw _____

_____

The Five Civilized Tribes

Choctaw _____

_____

Chickasaw _____

_____

Cherokee _____

_____

Creek _____

_____

Seminole _____

_____

Make one statement about each of the following great Indians:

Sequoyah _____

Geronimo _____

Chief Black Kettle _____

Jim Thorpe _____

GERONIMO   JIM THORPE

GA1138

OKLAHOMA SONS AND DAUGHTERS

Hidden below in the maze of letters are the names of seventeen persons that history links to the state of Oklahoma. To help you search them out, find answers to the clues below the maze. Once you've done this, circle the letters that spell each name in the word search.

```
O I C R E G I T Y N N H O J N R A
S U W A T C O H C I Y A D T I E L
A L I R S E Q U O Y A H E O L H F
B E L L E S T A R R T H F I O C A
H D L S E E P R O H T M I J O S L
T S R T G E R O N I M O S R D T F
N E O E L L A S A L T A D O L I A
I H G U F Y M R D E Y H T F L M B
D P E S E M I N O L E I E F I K I
W S R L E L T T E K K C A L B R L
I I S L L I B E E N W A P I O A L
J O S E P H O K L A H O M B I M M
M A R I A T A L L C H I E F Y L W
```

_____ Rancher who was given his name by Indians when he saved them from starvation one winter

_____ He was the first white man to venture into what is now Oklahoma.

_____ He claimed the land from France when he claimed all of Louisiana in 1682.

_____ The most peaceful tribe removed of the Five Civilized Tribes

_____ The last of the five tribes removed who gave up only after raging a seven-year war in Florida

_____ Cherokee Indian who stands as one of America's most honored

_____ Famous Apache warrior

_____ Famous Rear Admiral during World War II from Oklahoma

_____ America's most decorated World War I hero

_____ One of America's best-loved entertainers, this humorist was born in Oologah.

_____ Oklahoma Indian who became one of America's greatest athletes

_____ Famous outlaw killed in an ambush by Marshal Heck Thomas

_____ Famous Cheyenne chief

_____ Oklahoma Indian who became one of America's great artists

_____ William Henry Murray's nickname. (He was governor of Oklahoma during the 1930's.)

_____ Famous female outlaw sent to prison by Judge Parker for stealing horses

_____ Oklahoma Indian who was once the world's premier ballerina

GA1138

OREGON

The Beaver State

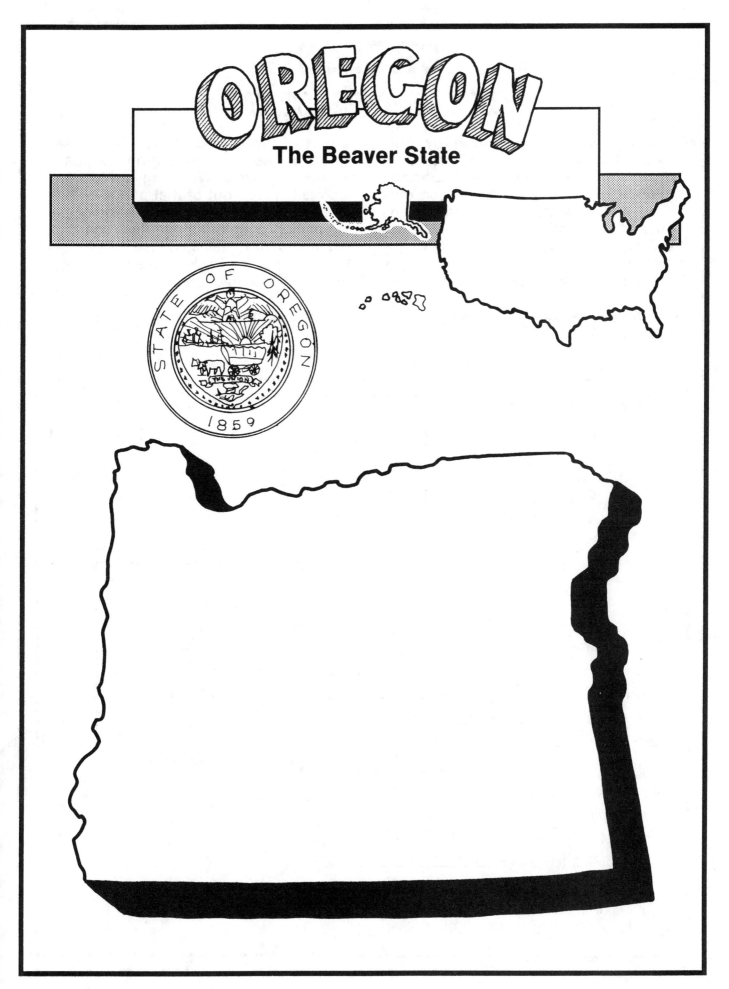

GA1138

OREGON
THE BEAVER STATE

Of all the western trails used by gold seekers, missionaries and immigrants, the Oregon Trail was the most important. Beginning in 1841 and lasting for over twenty years, it was the route traveled by thousands of immigrants on their way to the West. This wave of immigrants finally caused England to loosen her hold on the Old Oregon Territory, and in 1846 it became a part of the United States. The present states of Oregon, Washington and Idaho, as well as parts of Wyoming and Montana were all carved out of that parcel of land. Today Oregon boasts a population of over 2.5 million people. Its beautiful coastline, legendary mountains, dense forests and beautiful scenery make it one of America's top vacation attractions.

To begin your study of Oregon, research these few basic facts and report your findings in the blank spaces below.

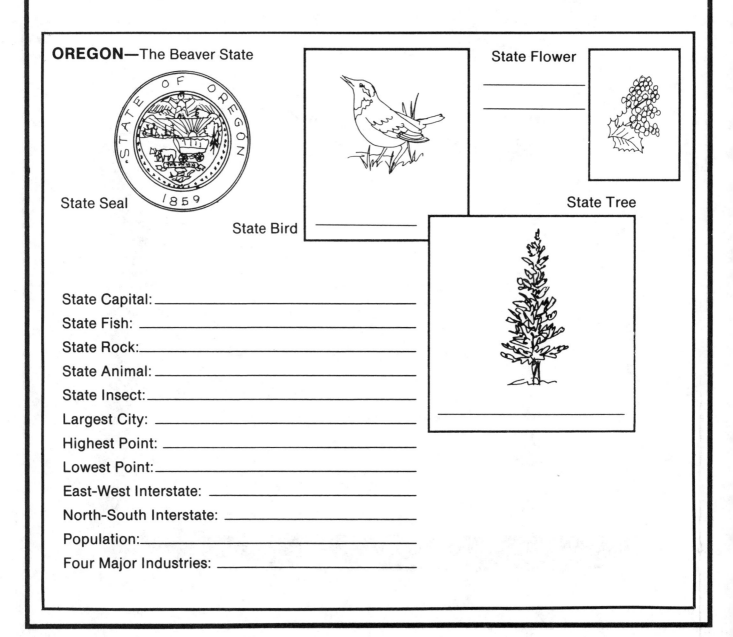

OREGON—The Beaver State

State Seal

State Bird _____

State Flower
_____
_____

State Tree

State Capital: _____

State Fish: _____

State Rock: _____

State Animal: _____

State Insect: _____

Largest City: _____

Highest Point: _____

Lowest Point: _____

East-West Interstate: _____

North-South Interstate: _____

Population: _____

Four Major Industries: _____

GA1138

TIME LINING OREGON'S HISTORY

Below are several events that have been significant in the history of Oregon. The years in which the events occurred are found on the time line. Match the letter of each event that corresponds to the appropriate date.

a. Oregon Territory is organized on August 14. (Abraham Lincoln is asked to be governor of the Territory of Oregon.)

b. First school in the Pacific Northwest at Fort Vancouver. Teacher is John Ball, a member of Wyeth's party. Same year, first timber to be shipped from Oregon is sent to China.

c. Nez Percé War

d. Sir Francis Drake sails north to the southern part of Oregon.

e. Oregon celebrates its centennial as a state.

f. The Tillamook Burn, one of the nation's worst forest disasters, wipes out 240,000 acres of Oregon's finest timber.

g. President Jefferson negotiates the purchase of Louisiana from France. American interests now turn to this new land of Louisiana and the unknown wilderness beyond it called Oregon Country.

h. Freeway completed connecting Salem and Portland

i. Captain James Cook visits the northwest coast on a voyage of discovery and through the sea otter trade with China starts heavy fur trading by many nations in this area.

j. Jedediah Smith, fur trapper, reaches the Pacific Northwest from California, becoming the first party to come overland from California.

k. February 14: Congress ratifies Oregon state constitution and Oregon becomes a state. This is the formal birthday of the state. June 3: Congressional proposal to admit Oregon into the Union is accepted by the state. John Whiteaker becomes the first elected governor of Oregon. Ladd and Tilton Bank, first in the state, was founded.

l. Transcontinental railroad is completed.

SIR FRANCIS DRAKE

OREGON'S TIME LINE

1980 • 1961 • 1959 • 1933 • 1883 • 1877 • 1864 • 1859 • 1848 • 1846 • 1844 • 1833 • 1828 • 1811 • 1804-1806 • 1803 • 1793 • 1778 • 1765 • 1579

TIME LINING OREGON'S HISTORY

m. Treaty between the United States and Great Britain established the Oregon boundary at 49 degrees north latitude. The first newspaper, *Oregon Spectator*, is printed at Oregon City.

n. Jane Barnes, first white woman to land in the Pacific Northwest, arrives at Fort George.

o. "Ouragon," first known use of Oregon, is called so by Major Robert Rogers.

p. Mt. St. Helens erupts with cataclysmic force in southwestern Washington, devastating 200 square miles of popular forestland and triggering destructive ash, floods, mud flows and river silt. The busy Columbia River is temporarily closed to deep-draft ships at Portland and Vancouver.

q. Salem becomes the state capital by popular vote. Transcontinental telegraph lines into Portland via California are first existent.

r. National election slogan "54-40 or Fight" is proof of growing American interest in Oregon. The first American taxes on the Pacific Coast were collected on a voluntary basis.

s. Captains Lewis and Clark and party travel from St. Louis to the mouth of the Columbia River.

t. Sir Alexander Mackenzie canoes down the Bella Coola River to the Pacific Ocean, becoming the first white man to cross the North American continent.

GA1138

OREGON ON THE MAP

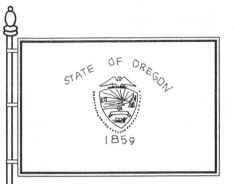

The Cascade Mountains, extending the length of the entire state from north to south, have a towering influence on Oregon's climate and weather patterns. Marine air coming in off the Pacific Ocean creates a mild rainy climate west of the Cascades. East of the mountains, the climate is drier, with more sunshine and greater temperature changes. Because there are climate changes throughout the state, geographers have divided the state into seven different regions.

On your outline map draw in those seven regions using the map below as a guide for the boundaries of each region.

Label the following regions:

Northeastern Oregon
Southeastern Oregon
Central Oregon
Southern Oregon
Willamette Valley
Portland/Columbia Gorge
Coast

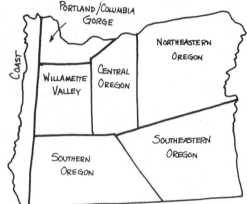

Once you've drawn the lines that define these regions, pinpoint the location of the largest city in each region. Place a dot on the appropriate location for each of these cities:

Eugene
Portland
Coos Bay
Medford
Bend
Pendleton
Ontario

Oregon is also well-known for its natural wonders in Crater Lake National Park within its boundaries as well as the Cascade Mountains (including Mt. Hood) and a portion of the Columbia River. Draw these on your map.

The old Oregon Trail, which brought thousands of settlers to the West, ends at Oregon City. Find where this famous path cut through Oregon and indicate with a dotted line.

The Marine climate that tempers much of Oregon has blessed the land with thousands of acres of natural beauty, many of which have been turned into national forests and state parks. Look at a map of Oregon and find several. Then locate at least four and show them on your outline map.

GA1138

OREGON'S CITIES AND TOWNS

Find the location of each of the following and indicate in the blank provided.

_____ 1. Site of the Oregon State Fair, 47 miles south of Portland

_____ 2. The city where Oregon State University is located, 29 miles southwest of Salem

_____ 3. The "Dungeness Crab Capital of the World," 54 miles west of Corvallis

_____ 4. City closest to Azalea State Park, the site of the annual Azalea Festival

_____ 5. Site of the traditional Pear Blossom Festival, 12 miles northwest of Ashland

_____ 6. Home of the Strawberry Festival, approximately 14 miles southeast of Albany

_____ 7. The site of the West's largest cheese plant, approximately 58 miles west of Portland

_____ 8. This city is atop a subterranean reservoir of high pressure steam, believed to be one of the world's richest stores of geothermal energy, approximately 140 miles south of Bend.

_____ 9. Home of the Peter Britt Music Festival, 7 miles west of Medford

_____ 10. Host of the Miner's Jubilee in July where the world championship porcupine sprint races are held, approximately 100 miles southeast of Pendleton

_____ 11. Home of the Oregon Shakespearean Festival, 65 miles west of Klamath Falls

_____ 12. Site of the Oregon Bach Festival, approximately 44 miles south of Albany

_____ 13. World Championship Timber Carnival, 50 miles south of Newberg

_____ 14. Site of the Rhododendron Festival, approximately 52 miles west of Eugene

_____ 15. Umpqua Valley's largest urban center, 70 miles southwest of Eugene

_____ 16. Central Oregon's largest city, approximately 40 miles southwest of Madras

_____ 17. Oregon's "tallest town" at 4800 feet, it is at the highest elevation of any incorporated city, located less than 10 miles from Goose Lake.

_____ 18. The Round-Up City, surrounded by cattle ranches, celebrates with its annual Round-Up week in September, located about 52 miles northwest of La Grande.

_____ 19. The site of the first permanent European-American settlement in Oregon Country, 35 miles northwest of Clatskanie

_____ 20. The home of Western Oregon State College, 23 miles north of Corvallis

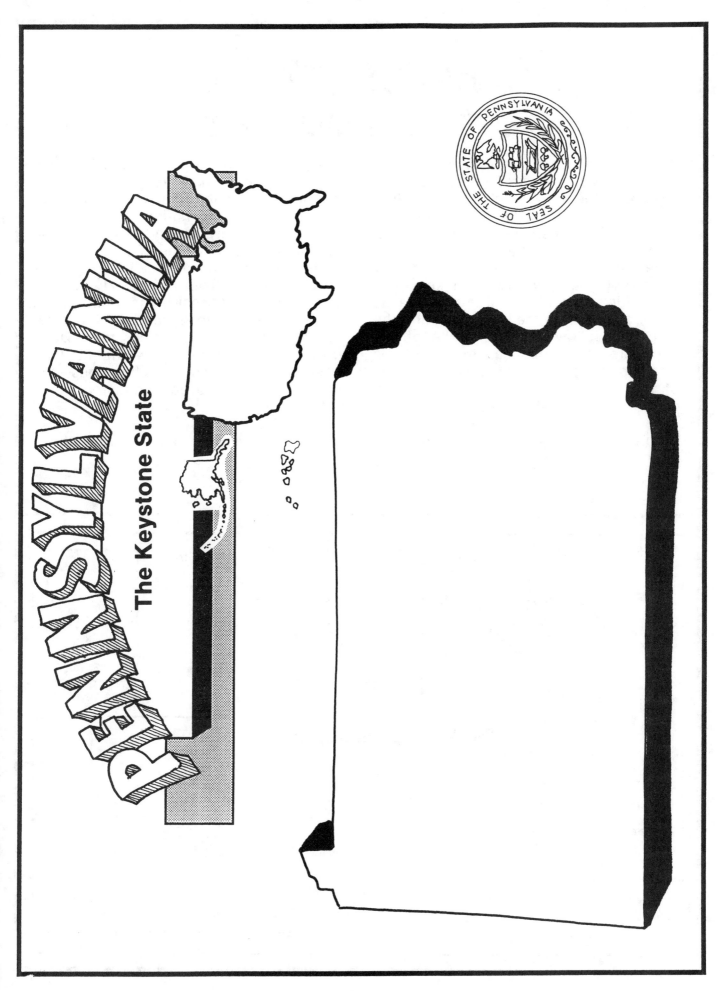

PENNSYLVANIA

The Keystone State

223

PENNSYLVANIA
THE KEYSTONE STATE

Pennsylvania bears the nickname of The Keystone State because of its historical position in the north-south coastal arch of the original thirteen colonies. It remains today one of America's favorite vacation lands for those seeking a touch with America's past. Several landmarks in Philadelphia are part of what is known as the nation's most historical square mile. Its importance during the Revolution and the time that followed make it one of the cornerstones of America. But the city is also important as a link in the megalopolis of the northeastern seaboard. In stark contrast to the culture of history of Phil-adelphia is Pittsburgh, America's "steel city." It played a major role in turning the northeastern United States into the industrial leader of the nation. Pennsylvania produces roughly twenty percent of the nation's pig iron and steel. The state is one of four states officially called commonwealth. Forests cover about sixty percent of the state, and the soil in the southeastern corner of the state is some of the most fertile farmland in the United States. Deep underground in Pennsylvania lie vast deposits of anthracite and bituminous—the hard and soft coal used in industry.

Before continuing with your study of Pennsylvania, become familiar with these Pennsylvania symbols:

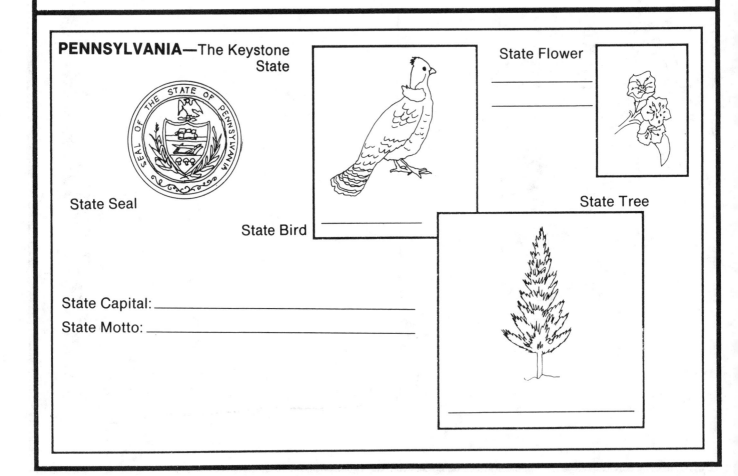

PENNSYLVANIA—The Keystone State

State Seal

State Bird

State Flower

State Tree

State Capital: _____

State Motto: _____

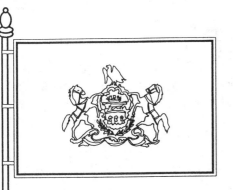

PENNSYLVANIA ON THE MAP

Locate the following cities on your outline map of Pennsylvania:

Philadelphia	Pittsburgh	Bethlehem
Allentown	Reading	Wilkes-Barre
Scranton	Johnstown	Lancaster
Harrisbrug	Carlisle	Erie
Altoona	State College	York

Locate the Allegheny National Forest.

Locate these rivers: Allegheny, Susquehanna, Schuylkill, Monongahela and Ohio.

Find the locations of these tourist attractions and pinpoint the location of each on your outline map:

Hawk Mountain Bird Sanctuary
Roadside America
Strasburg Railroad
Gettysburg National Military Park
Flagship *Niagara*
Rockville Bridge
Pine Creek Gorge
Pennsylvania Farm Museum of Landis Valley
Longwood Gardens
Valley Forge National Historical Park
Ephrata Cloisters

Pennsylvania has several mountain ranges. Show the following on your outline map. Using these symbols ᴧᴧᴧ, draw the Pocono Mountains, Endless Mountains, Appalachian Mountains, Blue Mountains, Tuscarora Mountains and the Allegheny Mountains.

GA1138

HISTORIC PENNSYLVANIA

Pennsylvania advertises itself to tourists as the place "where America began." Within its borders are battlefields, monuments, cemeteries, museums, shrines, parks and courtyards that give testament to the significance of the events that have happened there and the people who made them happen. The list below is out of order, but does give you an idea of some of the importance of Pennsylvania to American history. Your task is to find the sequence in which they took place. Simply place the letter *A* in the blank beside the earliest event and proceed on through the letter *M* for the most recent happening.

1. _____ King Charles II granted Pennsylvania to William Penn.

2. _____ The Second Continental Congress met in Philadelphia.

3. _____ The Battle of Gettysburg was the turning point in the Civil War.

4. _____ The Dutch from New Netherland captured New Sweden from the Swedes.

5. _____ William Penn granted the Charter of Privileges.

6. _____ Congress adopted the Declaration of Independence.

7. _____ Swedish settlers established a capital on Tinicum Island, near present-day Philadelphia.

8. _____ The Constitution was signed and adopted in Philadelphia.

9. _____ The English took control of Pennsylvania from the Dutch.

10. _____ The first steamboat on the Ohio River was launched at Pittsburgh.

11. _____ The nation's first nuclear power reactor began producing electricity at Shippingport.

12. _____ The First Continental Congress met in Philadelphia.

13. _____ Edwin Drake drilled the nation's first commercially successful oil well near Titusville.

WILLIAM PENN

GA1138

KEYSTONE "KEYS"

Below are the names of several people who have distinguished themselves in Pennsylvania through their achievements in various walks of life. Answer each clue in the blank space provided. Then find and circle the name in the word search.

```
M E A O O T M O T T Y H L E M T A O
A I M P S J A M E S B U C H A N A N
R G O R O K N A A K D H O S L O O R
I E N H Y T C D L G A N I L E L H E
A N G E O R G E M A R S H A L L A D
N R U D E D S U W A L Y P S Y E S L
A A B E N J A M I N W E S T B M R A
N C E D G A R A L L A N P O E W K C
D W A T T U N L E U M A S L E P R
E E R Y O S S H I E S S H A O R M E
R R E T T U R S A M O H T O T D R D
S D A B R A H A M L I N C O L N O N
O N W W A C O E P H U R T I S A A A
N A T S L E S E E E R U O E S A L X
T O S L O H B E N F R A N K L I N E
B F G O W T T O N P N E D T O T L L
E G E O R G E W A S H I N G T O N A
```

_____ English Quaker who received the land from King Charles II

_____ He made a famous speech on a battleground called Gettysburg.

_____ He set up the first iron forge on the creek near Pottstown.

_____ He is credited with starting the steel industry in 1732 at Coventry Forge.

_____ He made a fortune in steel and gave a lot of it away to build libraries.

_____ He wrote, printed and sold *Poor Richard's Almanac*.

_____ He lived in Philadelphia where he wrote "The Raven" and "Annabel Lee."

_____ He made a fortune in the manufacture of Coke and aluminum.

_____ U.S. President born in a log cabin near Mercerberg

_____ He won the 1953 Nobel peace prize for helping to rebuild Europe after World War II.

_____ Pennsylvania-born American painter

_____ He spent a bitter winter at Valley Forge.

_____ Famous Philadelphia sculptor

_____ Female singer who "belonged to Philadelphia"

AMERICA'S HISTORIC SQUARE MILE

Independence National Historical Park in Philadelphia is the most historic square mile in America. A complete tour of the park includes twenty-six sites. The map below shows the location of fourteen of the most significant. Note their locations on the map. Then jot down a brief statement that explains the significance of each.

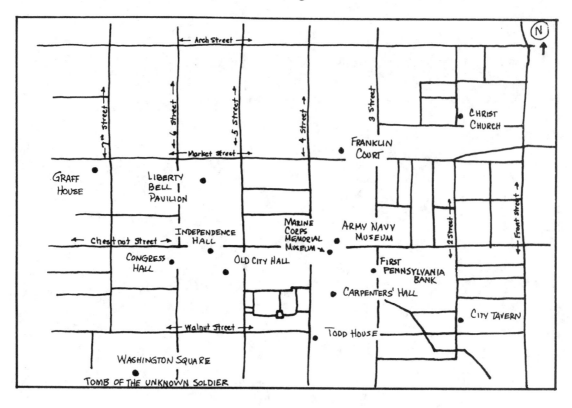

Liberty Bell Pavilion _____

_____

Independence Hall _____

_____

Army-Navy Museum _____

_____

Carpenters' Hall _____

_____

City Tavern _____

_____

Congress Hall _____

_____

Franklin Court _____

_____

Graff House _____

_____

Marine Corps Memorial Museum _____

_____

Old City Hall _____

_____

Todd House _____

_____

Christ Church _____

_____

First Pennsylvania Bank _____

_____

Tomb of the Unknown Soldier _____

GA1138

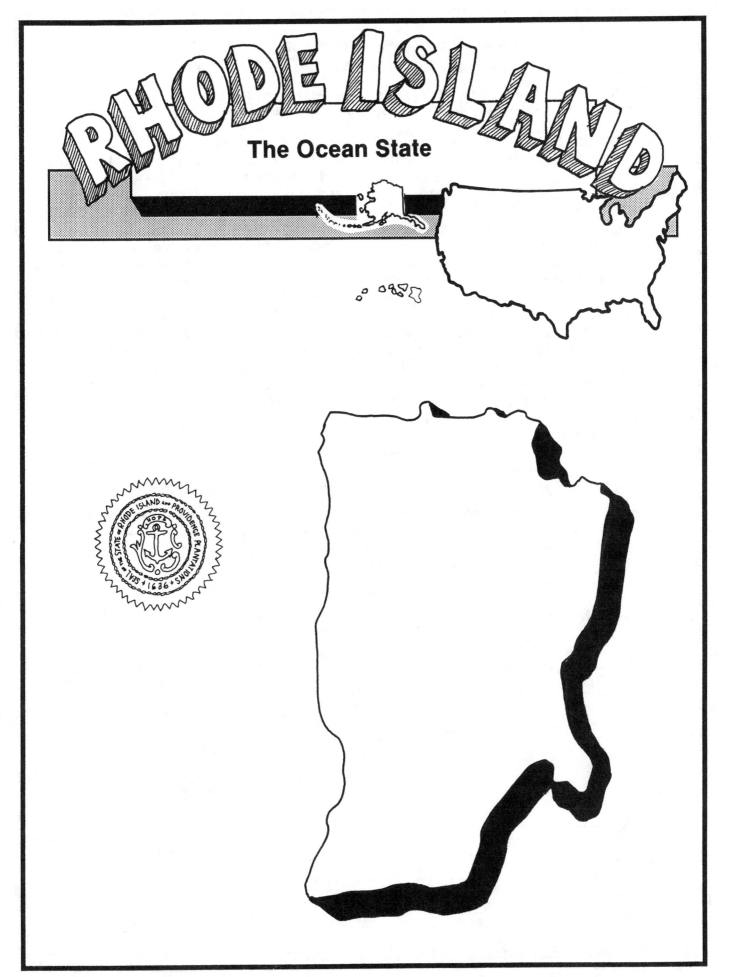

RHODE ISLAND

The Ocean State

GA1138

RHODE ISLAND
THE OCEAN STATE

Rhode Island's 1214 square miles makes it America's smallest state in land area. Its greatest distance from north to south is 48 miles; from east to west the greatest distance is 37 miles. Its coastline however, measures over 400 miles with all the bays and inlets along the 70 miles of Atlantic shoreline. Its small size has not kept it from being significant historically, and the state has long served as a barometer of forecasts and trends to the future for much of the entire nation. It started its tradition as a leader in 1647 when its charter was the first to guarantee colony members complete religious freedom. Rhode Island was also the first colony to declare itself free from England during the American Revolution. Narragansett Bay with its fishing and waterpower potential is the state's greatest resource. Without many other resources, the tiny state developed one of the earliest industrialized regions along the eastern seaboard. Manufacturing today is Rhode Island's chief source of income and its largest employer. The production of jewelry, electrical machinery, electronics, plastics, metal products, instruments, chemicals and boat building rank highest on its list of job supporters. More recently the tourism industry has become important to the state, providing over 24,000 jobs and generating over a billion dollars in revenue. Its rank of 20th in income/capita gives strong evidence that its size is not important to its success. The state has integrated well into the flow of the East Coast megalopolis.

Before continuing your study of Rhode Island, find each of the following symbols:

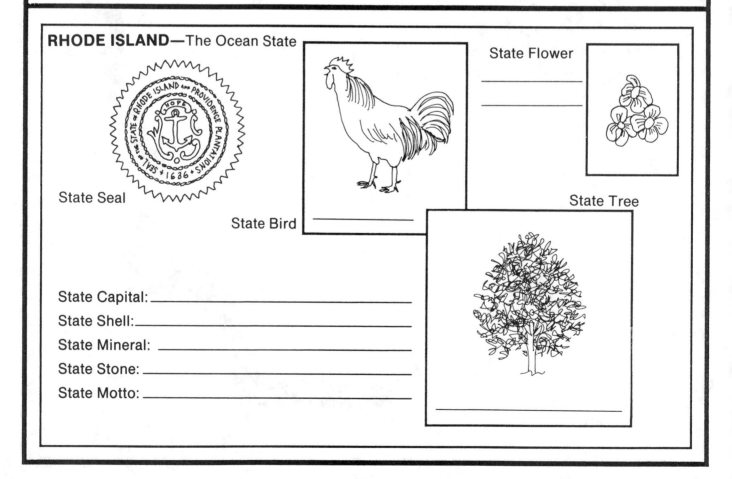

RHODE ISLAND—The Ocean State

State Seal

State Bird _____

State Flower
_____
_____

State Tree

_____

State Capital: _____

State Shell: _____

State Mineral: _____

State Stone: _____

State Motto: _____

230

A DRIVE THROUGH HISTORY

Small in size, Rhode Island has more than its share of historical shrines that stand as preserved monuments to America's precious and storied past. Since none of the sites are far in distance from any of the others, a trip through Rhode Island is a touch with the past that is well worth the time and effort. To give yourself a better perspective when you locate these historic shrines, begin by pinpointing on your outline map these locations:

Providence	Warwick
Newport	Pawtucket
Woonsocket	Cranston
Bristol	Westerly
Narragansett Bay	Seekonk River

Find out from an atlas or travel guide of Rhode Island the location of each of the following; then mark the letter that corresponds to that historic landmark on its correct location on your outline map. Jot down a one-liner by each to describe its historical significance.

a. The State House _____

b. White Horse Tavern _____

c. Slater Mill _____

d. Friends Meeting House _____

e. Gilbert Stuart Birthplace _____

f. Smith's Castle _____

g. Redwood Library _____

h. First Unitarian Church _____

i. General Nathanael Greene Homestead _____

j. First Baptist Church in America _____

k. Old School House _____

l. Brown University _____

m. Old Colony House _____

The above sites are but a few of the historic landmarks of Rhode Island's past. Assume you are entering the state from the southwest on I-95. Decide the order (by letter) in which you would visit the above sites if you were taking a drive through Rhode Island's history.

_____

GA1138

RHODE ISLAND SONS AND DAUGHTERS

Rhode Island is justifiably proud of her famous sons and daughters. People associated with this tiny state have made significant contributions in the arts, music, business and sports world. Below are descriptions of some of their most noteworthy achievements. Your task is to find the missing names.

1. _____ Brown University graduate who made his first fortune in oil.

2. _____ South County resident who won 1929 Pulitzer prize for *Laughing Boy.*

3. _____ She wrote the inspiring "Battle Hymn of the Republic."

4. _____ This Providence poetress was probably the subject of Edgar Allan Poe's famous lyric poem "Annabel Lee."

5. _____ Pawtucket native who authored *Main Street USSR* and is a news correspondent for NBC.

6. _____ A former professional baseball player who became an actor and was formerly a host on *Good Morning, America.*

7. _____ The only composer to win the Congressional Medal of Honor, this Providence native wrote patriotic songs including "Over There" and "You're a Grand Old Flag."

8. _____ This famous Rhode Island sister team consisted of Jackie Gleason's stage wife and Steve Allen's real wife.

9. _____ This real-life "Rocky" began his boxing career in Rhode Island.

10. _____ The nickname of the Providence College basketball team that has produced many famous NBA "Rhode Island Sons."

11. _____ He was the hero of the Battle of Lake Erie in 1813.

12. _____ Revolutionary War general who was second in command to George Washington.

13. _____ The first woman to establish a town in America, she started Portsmouth.

14. _____ He was the foremost painter of the portraits of George Washington, John Adams, Thomas Jefferson, James Madison and James Monroe.

15. _____ The Father of the American Textile Industry.

232

GA1138

RHODE ISLAND'S FOUNDING FATHER

Below are listed several events in the life of Roger Williams, the founder of Rhode Island. Research his life and arrange by number the events in the order they occurred.

1. _____ He was assigned a church in Salem when he refused to join the congregation in Boston.

2. _____ He grew up in the old Holborn section of London near Smithfield plain, where religious dissenters were burned at the stake.

3. _____ He found some disagreement with the Pilgrims and returned to Salem.

4. _____ He founded the settlement of Providence after buying the land from the Indians.

5. _____ His proficiency in transcribing long sermons brought him to the attention of Sir Edward Coke, Chief Justice of the King's Bench.

6. _____ His courtship of Jane Whalley was brought to an end by her aunt, Lady Barrington.

7. _____ He was ordered banished from Massachusetts and told he would be deported to England if he did not denounce his beliefs.

8. _____ He wrote his first book *A Key into the Language of America.*

9. _____ After Charterhouse School, he furthered his education at Pembroke Hall in Cambridge University.

10. _____ He left the church of Salem for Plymouth where he was made welcome by the Separatist Pilgrims.

11. _____ He founded the First Baptist Church in America.

12. _____ He accepted the post of chaplain to Sir William Masham at Otes in Essex.

13. _____ He sought sanctuary with his Indian friends in the Narragansett country.

14. _____ He stayed on during the burning of Providence in King Philip's War.

15. _____ He married Mary Barnard at High Laver Church on December 15, 1629.

16. _____ He established a successful trading post near Wickford.

17. _____ His last year's were spent in the office of town clerk.

18. _____ His open opposition to the Established Church of England led him to set sail on the *Lyon* for New England.

GA1138

RHODE ISLAND TRIVIA

Below are scrambled words that, when rearranged, will satisify the clues that describe some interesting Rhode Island trivia. Research the clues, find the correct answer from the list and place the corresponding letter in the space provided.

a. UROTO UYSNAGGEO
b. RGANRANATTSE REAPC
c. LHAMEP TERTSE
d. ATCWH LIHL OSERRT
e. OOPL
f. ILESTTTO
g. NHOJ EKNENYD

h. NAN & EOHP
i. RENWOPT
j. TATSE PCAITLO
k. RXETTNO
l. SUNREYR
m. ANYV
n. ROEHTDOE AFRNCIS NEREG

1. _____ Saddle horse bred in Rhode Island during Colonial period, it was the first breed of American horse.

2. _____ This sport was played for the first time in America at Newport in 1876.

3. _____ The first discount department store in America started in 1953

4. _____ The oldest Jewish house of worship in America

5. _____ It houses the famous painting by Gilbert Stuart of George Washington.

6. _____ Even though farmland accounts for only eleven percent of Rhode Island's land area, this crop is important to the economy and accounts for over one third of the agriculture income.

7. _____ Virtually the first of American business conglomerates

8. _____ It operates the nation's oldest carousel in Westerly, built in 1850.

9. _____ This Newport street was the first in America illuminated by gaslight.

10. _____ U.S. President married in St. Mary's Church in Newport in 1952

11. _____ Newport was the birthplace of this branch of the U.S. military.

12. _____ Southeastern New England's principal airport in Warwick

13. _____ The first torpedo boat in America, it was built in 1887 in Bristol.

14. _____ "The Sailing Capital of the World," it was home to the America's Cup for fifty-three years.

GA1138

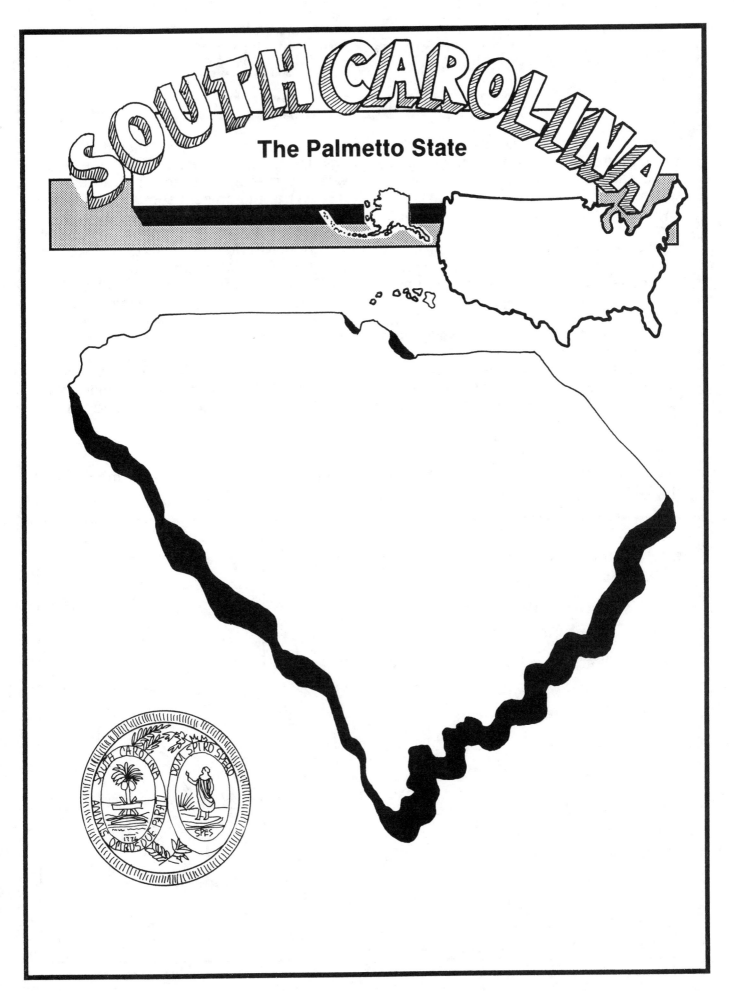

SOUTH CAROLINA

The Palmetto State

235

GA1138

SOUTH CAROLINA
THE PALMETTO STATE

Although smallest in size of the southern states, South Carolina is an important state to the nation's economy. It is one of the leaders in textiles and tourism and has developed a diversified economy. South Carolina is also rich in history and has been the site of many significant chapters in the story of America. It all began shortly after Columbus discovered the Americas with a group of Spanish explorers unsuccessfully attempting to establish a colony at the present site of Georgetown. A few years later (1562) a group of French Huguenots tried again near the present-day Paris Island Marine Corps Base near Beaufort. But this attempt failed as well, and the first permanent colony was founded by eight nobles who were the lords proprietors as a result of land "given" them by King Charles II. The time was 1670 and the place was Albemarle Point, later moved across the river to the present site of Charleston. German, Scotch-Irish and Welsh settlers soon followed. South Carolina was one of the original thirteen colonies that broke ties with England and fought for their freedom during the Revolution. Important battles were fought in South Carolina, and the entire bloody Civil War began there with the firing on Fort Sumter. Because much of the war was fought in the South, the aftermath was one of destruction and ruin, but South Carolinians rebuilt their state and today enjoy a healthy and rising economy.

Before continuing your study of South Carolina, find out about these symbols and emblems:

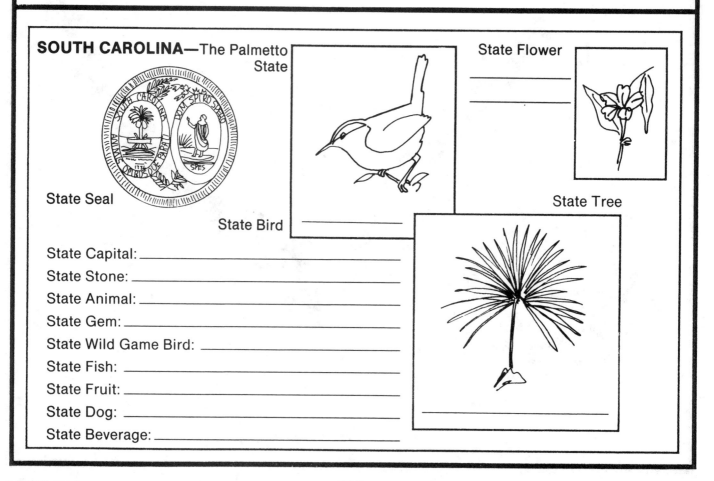

SOUTH CAROLINA—The Palmetto State

State Seal

State Bird _____

State Flower
_____
_____

State Tree

State Capital: _____

State Stone: _____

State Animal: _____

State Gem: _____

State Wild Game Bird: _____

State Fish: _____

State Fruit: _____

State Dog: _____

State Beverage: _____

GA1138

SOUTH CAROLINA CITY SLEUTH

Find out the South Carolina city that answers each of the clues below. Then locate each of the mystery cities on your outline map.

1. This South Carolina city, hosts the "Southern 500" every year on Labor Day weekend, located 78 miles northeast of the capital.

   _____

2. This "Gateway to the Low Country" is only 41 miles southeast of Columbia and has a fruit contained in its name.

   _____

3. The sun and fun capital of the Grand Strand, located 143 miles east-by-southeast of Columbia, has less than 30,000 in population with over 300,000 people there in the summer months.

   _____

4. This beautiful old port city is the oldest city in South Carolina, located 112 miles southeast of Columbia.

   _____

5. Spanish explorers discovered this area 100 years before the Pilgrims landed at Plymouth Rock. In the 19th century this city, located 134 miles southeast of Columbia, was called "the wealthiest, most aristocratic and cultivated town of its size in America."

   _____

6. Located 164 southeast of Columbia, this island covers 42 square miles and is situated between the Intercoastal Waterway and the Atlantic Ocean, one of the most popular resorts on the East Coast.

   _____

7. Home of the Thoroughbred Hall of Fame, training grounds for champions Kelso and Pleasant Colony, located 56 miles southwest of Columbia

   _____

8. Oldest inland city in South Carolina, major British garrison of Lord Cornwallis, famous battleground during American Revolution, located 124 miles northwest of Charlestown

   _____

9. York County's largest city, named for a cut made through white flinty rock during construction of the Columbia to Charlotte railroad, located 95 miles west of Greenville

   _____

10. This charming town in northwestern South Carolina was called Calhoun until 1943 when it changed its name to honor the prestigious land grant college that bears its name—133 miles northwest of Columbia.

    _____

11. The Textile Center of the World, the largest city in northwestern South Carolina, located on Intereste 85—182 miles northwest of Florence

    _____

12. Once a way station known as Lowry's Turnout, located on the stagecoach route from Charleston to Augusta, this town in southwestern South Carolina was renamed after the man who bought the station—56 miles south of Columbia.

    _____

13. Largest peach-producing area in the state, located off Interstate 85 in northwest part of state, 93 miles northwest of Columbia

    _____

14. "The Birthplace of the Confederacy," located in western South Carolina, the Secession Document was first presented here—189 miles northwest of Columbia, birthplace of John Calhoun.

    _____

GA1138

SOUTH CAROLINA SCRAMBLE

Read each clue below and jot down the correct answer in the space provided, or unscramble the letters to satisfy the clues.

1. _____ ORASCELHTN—The oldest city in South Carolina

2. _____ OTOCNT—The crop that "wore out" the soil

3. _____ ORFT ETSUMR—The Civil War began here

4. _____ PINSA—The country from which the first explorers in South Carolina came

5. _____ OUMCLBIA—The largest city in South Carolina

6. _____ RNADEW NCOJKAS—The President of the United States born in South Carolina

7. _____ EHCPA—South Carolina ranks second in the production of this fruit.

8. _____ ITHLON DAHE ILNSAD—One of South Carolina's favorite vacation areas

9. _____ OFRT RLOMUTEI—The first American victory in the Revolution

10. _____ ELBU GDRIE—Mountains in northwestern area of South Carolina

11. _____ SASSARAFS IANOMUTN—Highest point in South Carolina

12. _____ OHJN ACLUOHN—He was Vice President, Secretary of War, a U.S. senator, and a native South Carolinian

13. _____ IDEPNOMT—It geographically covers much of the northern part of South Carolina.

14. _____ BATOOCC—Still one of South Carolina's leading crops

15. _____ AABLECRBKD—One of history's most notorious pirates hanged on Charleston's Execution Dock

16. _____ ONSAEBYS—One of the state's leading cash crops

17. _____ RTMYLE HAEBC—South Carolina's largest resort area

18. _____ LTTBAE TA SOCWEPN—One of the turning points in the Revolutionary War

19. _____ RNSICFA AMIRNO—One of South Carolina's two national forests

20. _____ XTTESLIE—South Carolina ranks only behind North Carolina in this industry.

238

SOUTH CAROLINA'S ECONOMY

Below is a map showing where the state's leading farm, mineral and forest products are produced. On the basis of the information provided on this map and nothing else, answer the questions that follow as (t) true, (f) false or (–) not enough information to supply a conclusion.

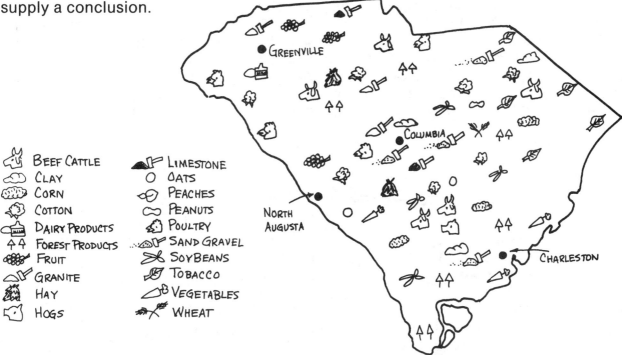

Beef Cattle
Clay
Corn
Cotton
Dairy Products
Forest Products
Fruit
Granite
Hay
Hogs

Limestone
Oats
Peaches
Peanuts
Poultry
Sand Gravel
Soybeans
Tobacco
Vegetables
Wheat

1. _____ Most of the tobacco is grown in the eastern half of the state.
2. _____ The beef cattle industry is more important to South Carolina than dairy cattle.
3. _____ Most of the forest products are found in the northwest.
4. _____ Granite is a bigger industry than cotton in South Carolina.
5. _____ Vegetables and truck farming is an important industry in southeastern South Carolina.
6. _____ Limestone is a bigger industry than tourism.
7. _____ Of the economy factors included on the map, corn would appear to be the most important industry in South Carolina.
8. _____ Dollars to the economy from manufacturing and tourism are not included in this map.
9. _____ Limestone is important to the area around Charleston.
10. _____ The Atlantic coastal area seems well suited to the growth of cotton.
11. _____ Dairy products are found near the Greenville area.
12. _____ More people are employed in manufacturing than any other industry.
13. _____ Cotton is not as important to South Carolina as tobacco.
14. _____ Forest products are produced in several parts of the state.
15. _____ South Carolina is a leading state in the peach industry.
16. _____ Grain farming is important to central South Carolina.
17. _____ The products on this map do not include all products of South Carolina.
18. _____ The symbols would suggest that tobacco is more important than corn.
19. _____ The wholesale and retail trade is more important than agriculture.
20. _____ Mining is less significant in South Carolina than agriculture.

GA1138

SOUTH CAROLINA—BEAUTIFUL PLACES

Sandy beaches, rolling hills, historic forts and cities, stately mansions, elegant resorts and warm climate all add up to the kind of vacation millions of Americans save their money for every year. South Carolina has all of the above. As a result, tourism is big business in South Carolina. Its state Division of Tourism is responsible for creating advertising brochures and flyers that show the state in its finest hour in an attempt to entice vacationers to come to South Carolina. Create your own four-page 4" x 8½" folder that will attract visitors to South Carolina. Investigate all the pluses the state has to offer; then lay out your folder using photos or rough drawings as well as creating advertising copy that will emphasize your points. Share your folder with other members of your class.

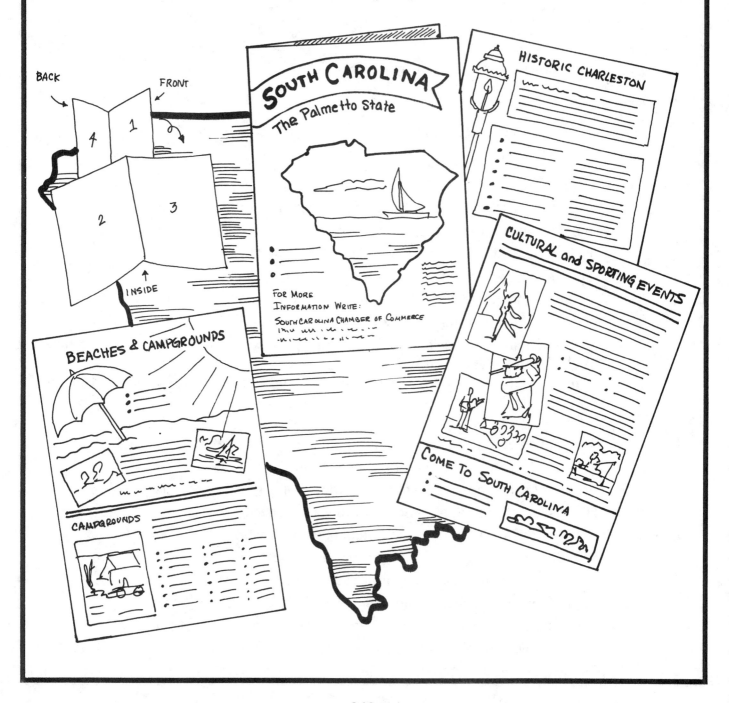

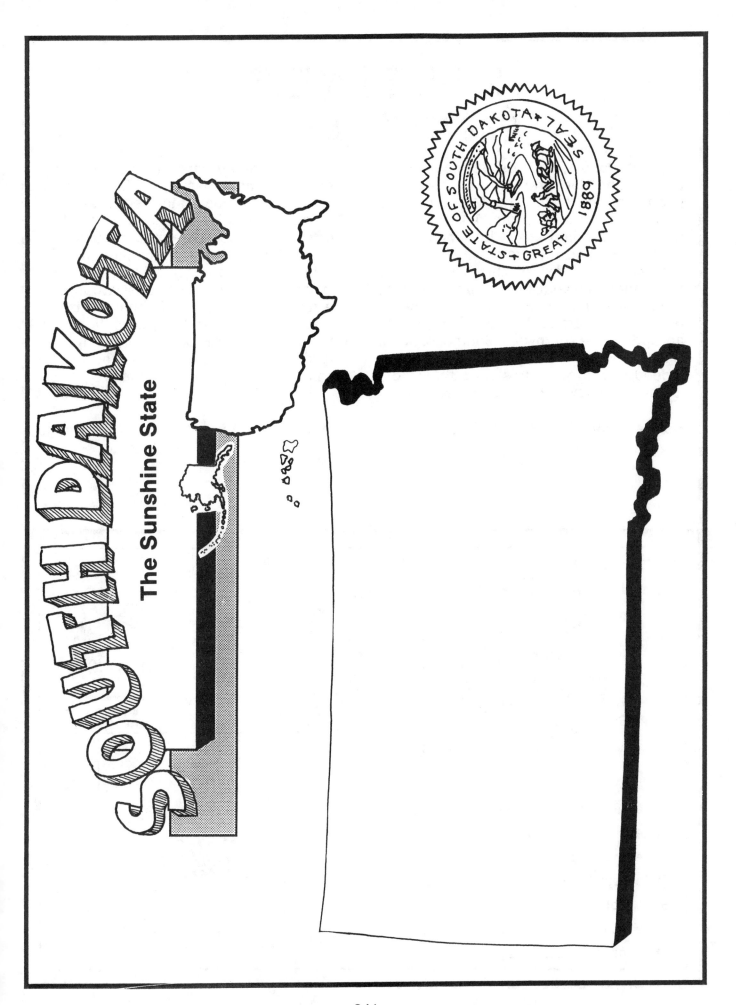

The Sunshine State

241

GA1138

SOUTH DAKOTA
THE SUNSHINE STATE

In South Dakota, the Midwest and the West come together dramatically near the middle of the state. The Missouri River (locate on a map of South Dakota) seems to be the dividing line, with lands to the east resembling the prairie grasslands of the Midwest. West of the Missouri the population thins out and the land becomes visibly drier with more cattle ranches and fewer grain farms. The Black Hills rise abruptly in the southwest. Southeast of the Black Hills are the rugged Badlands. It is indeed a land of contrasts. South Dakota is one of the few states with a greater rural population than urban. Likewise its economy leans more heavily on agricultural products than manufactured products. Several projects have been completed to harness the Missouri River Basin into better use for South Dakota, including hydro-electric power, flood control and irrigation projects. Its showpiece tourist attraction, the four faces at Mount Rushmore, bring thousands of tourists and millions of dollars into South Dakota annually. Its future appears strong and will no doubt lean more heavily toward industry.

Before continuing your study of South Dakota, familiarize yourself with the following:

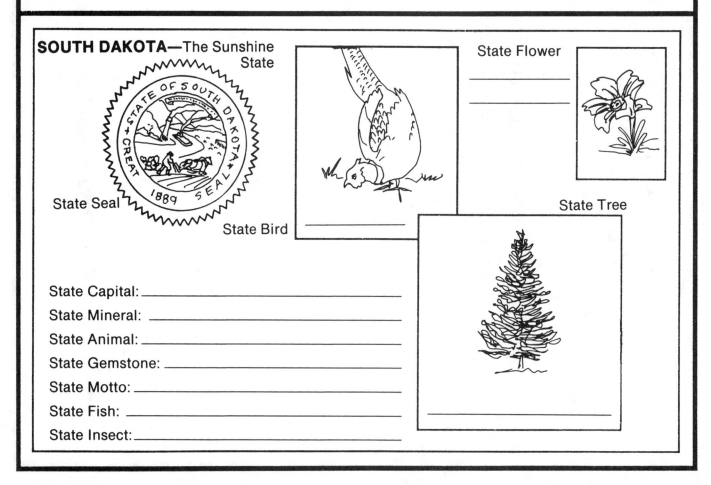

SOUTH DAKOTA—The Sunshine State

State Seal

State Bird

State Flower
_____
_____

State Tree

State Capital: _____

State Mineral: _____

State Animal: _____

State Gemstone: _____

State Motto: _____

State Fish: _____

State Insect: _____

GA1138

PLACES ON THE WAY TO THE FACES

South Dakota's greatest tourist attraction is Mount Rushmore, the world's largest mountain carving. But there are several other sites to see and places to visit on the way to getting there that make a vacation to South Dakota all the more fun. Find out about each of the attractions below and jot down a short identifying statement; then pinpoint the location of each site on your outline map.

Glacial Lakes _____

Corn Palace _____

Wall Drug _____

Keystone _____

Crazy Horse Memorial _____

Deadwood _____

Badlands National Park _____

Little Town on the Prairie _____

Jewel Cave _____

Mammoth Site _____

Wind Cave _____

Custer State Park _____

When you've finished making your identifying statements and locations on the map, go back through the list and number the sites in the order in which you would visit them on your way to Mount Rushmore (depending upon where you live).

GA1138

FOUR FACES IN STONE

The Black Hills of South Dakota provide the backdrop for Mount Rushmore, the world's largest mountain carving. These four 60-foot high faces that are 500 feet up commemorate four of our greatest Presidents. The sculptor Gutzon Borglum began drilling into the 6000-foot mountain in 1927. The project took fourteen years and cost a mere $1 million, though it's now deemed priceless. Research the history behind this shrine to democracy, including Borglum's reasons for undertaking the project, the Presidents whose faces appear on the mountain and its designation as a national monument. Report your findings in the space below.

244

SOUTH DAKOTA TIME LINE

Below are listed several important events in the history of South Dakota. Find out when each occurred; then record the letter corresponding to that event next to the appropriate date on the time line at the bottom of the page.

a. Congress established the Dakota Territory.

b. South Dakota became the 40th state.

c. Titan missiles became operational in South Dakota.

d. South Dakota suffered through the great drought.

e. Robert Cavelier, Sieur de la Salle, claimed for France all land drained by the Mississippi including land now called South Dakota.

f. Legendary Wild Bill Hickok was shot in Deadwood while playing cards in a saloon.

g. First permanent settlement established at what is now Fort Pierre

h. The Missouri River Basin Project was approved by Congress.

i. The United States acquired South Dakota through the Louisiana Purchase.

j. Gold was discovered in the Black Hills.

k. The *Yellowstone* came up the Missouri River to Fort Tecumseh, proving that steamships could travel the upper Mississippi.

l. Gutzon Borglum started Mount Rushmore National Memorial.

m. Sitting Bull, the great Sioux Indian chief, was killed by Indian police when they came to arrest him.

n. Armed and angry Indians seized the village of Wounded Knee and remained in control for seventy-one days.

o. Francois and Louis-Joseph La Vérendrye were the first white men to visit what is now South Dakota.

p. Laramie Treaty ended the Red Cloud War.

q. Lewis and Clark passed through South Dakota on their exploration of Louisiana.

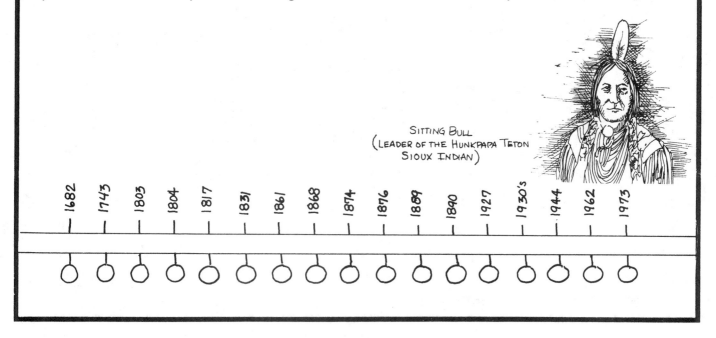

SITTING BULL
(LEADER OF THE HUNKPAPA TETON
SIOUX INDIAN)

1682 1745 1805 1804 1817 1831 1861 1868 1874 1876 1889 1890 1927 1930's 1944 1962 1973

GA1138

LITTLE TOWN ON THE PRAIRIE

DeSmet, South Dakota, is the "Little Town on the Prairie" made famous by author Laura Ingalls Wilder's pioneer adventure books. It is the setting that set Laura writing and includes the subjects of many of the adventures she wrote about in her books. Imagine yourself, for a moment, thrust back in the 1880's into the setting of DeSmet. Using your own characters (names included), describe a day or an incident that might have happened to you during this period of Americana. You can talk about floods, school days, work, fun times or anything else you choose. But make the narrative as realistic as you can. Remember that you're into a time period of over 100 years ago. Reading one of the "Little House" books could really put you into the spirit. When you have finished, share your "stories" with other members of the class.

THE INGALLS HOME

LAURA INGALLS WILDER

GA1138

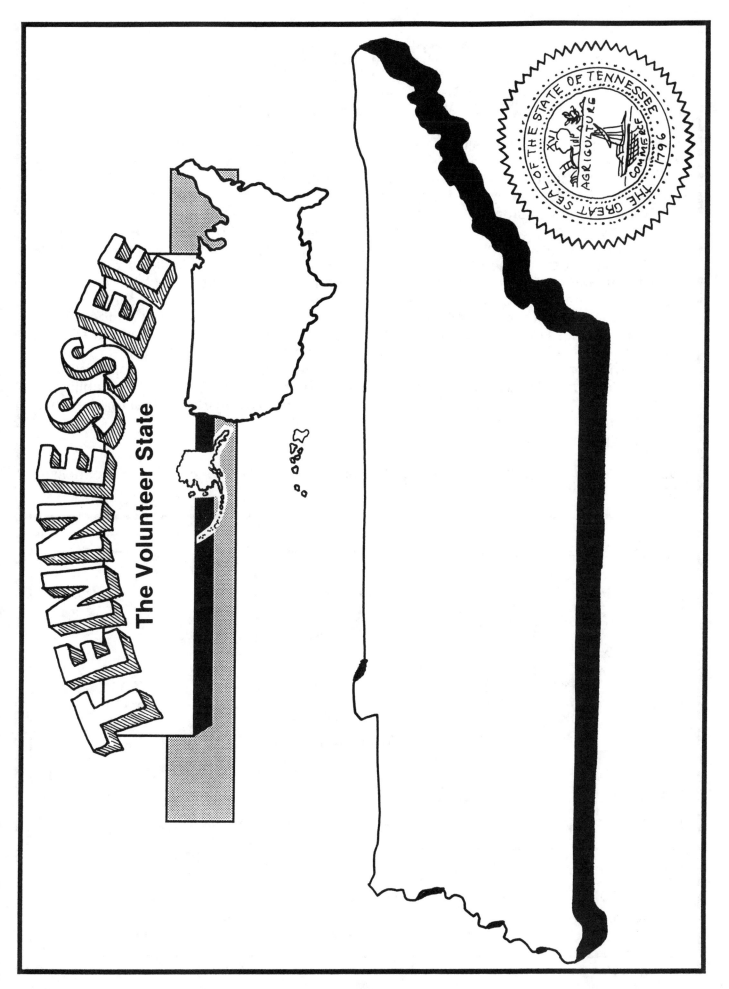

TENNESSEE

The Volunteer State

247

TENNESSEE
THE VOLUNTEER STATE

From the Blue Ridge Mountains of eastern Tennessee with peaks of over 6000 feet to the Mississippi bottom in the far west (with an elevation of less than 300 feet), Tennessee is a land of contrasts. The people themselves are also a study of contrasts. Dating back to the Civil War, those living in the eastern part of the state remained loyal to the Union, while those in the central part of the state sided with the South. People in the West were a mix of both loyalties. Tennessee was the last state to leave the Union and the first to rejoin when the war was over. Several generations later, the people in those areas still harbor some of those ties with the past. Its scenic beauty, historic significance and wide variety of parks and other attractions make it a favorite of thousands of vacationers every year. The city of Nashville is the capital of country music, but it has a lot of other appeal as well. During the 1930's the Tennessee Valley Authority was created to improve navigation on the rivers of Tennessee. The results of the ambitious project were improved flood control, the generation of hydroelectricity and the conservation of land. Thousands of permanent jobs were created and the project became a showpiece to the world of what can be done by man in his quest to control nature. Tennessee's future appears to be bright but could hinge on its ability to continue to serve as a pivotal link between North and South.

Before proceeding with your study of Tennessee, research the symbols of Tennessee called for below.

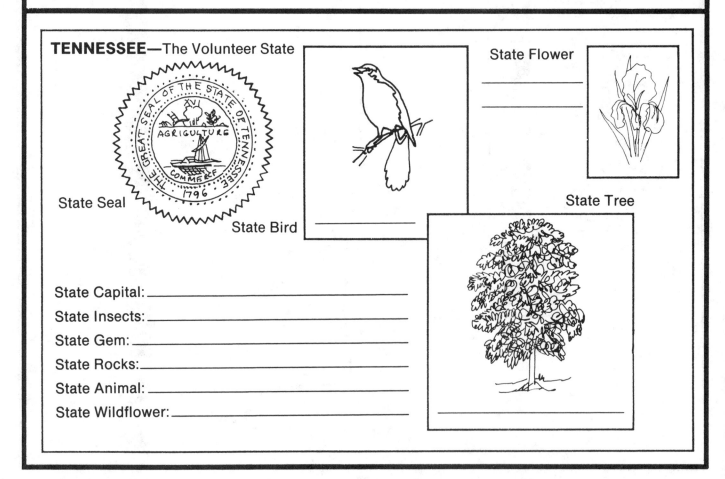

TENNESSEE—The Volunteer State

State Seal

State Bird

State Flower

_____

_____

State Tree

State Capital: _____

State Insects: _____

State Gem: _____

State Rocks: _____

State Animal: _____

State Wildflower: _____

GA1138

TENNESSEE TIME LINE

Below are some of the more important events in the history of Tennessee. Find out when each took place and put the letter of the event that corresponds to the date on the time line.

a. John Scopes was convicted of teaching evolution in a public school.

b. France surrendered to Great Britain all claims to lands east of the Mississippi.

c. Tennessee became the 16th state on June 1.

d. A severe epidemic of yellow fever wiped out over one fourth of the population of Memphis.

e. Tennessee became the last state to secede from the Union on June 8.

f. Robert Cavelier, Sieur de la Salle, claimed the Mississippi River Valley for France.

g. Nashville settlers signed the Cumberland Compact.

h. Chickasaw Indians sold their land east of the Mississippi to the U.S. government.

i. A new constitution gave all male citizens 21 and older the right to vote.

j. The federal government began construction of the atomic energy center at Oak Ridge.

k. Hernando de Soto of Spain led the first white expedition into Tennessee.

l. Tennessee became the first state readmitted to the Union on July 24.

m. Congress created the Tennessee Valley Authority.

n. The Cherokee Indians were forced out of Tennessee.

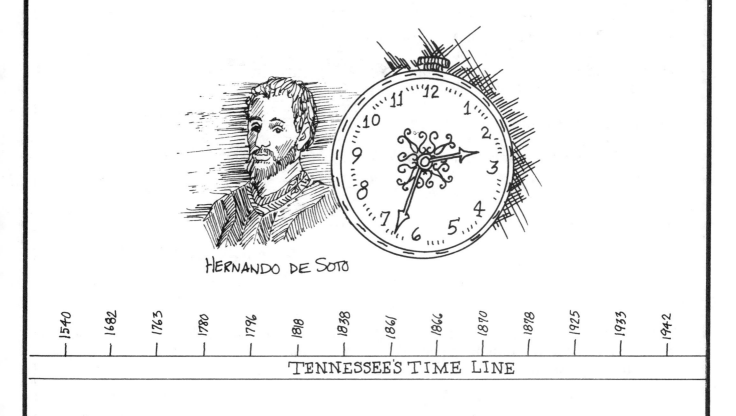

HERNANDO DE SOTO

1540   1682   1763   1780   1796   1818   1838   1861   1866   1870   1878   1925   1933   1942

TENNESSEE'S TIME LINE

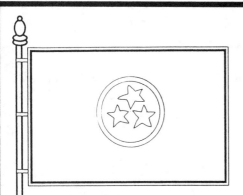

A DRIVE THROUGH THE PAST

MAGEVNEY HOUSE

Tennessee has an abundance of landmarks, homesteads, shrines and museums that provide vital links to the people and events that have shaped its history. Listed below are some of the most significant. Find out the location of each and pinpoint by labeling on your outline map.

Historic Jonesborough District
Davy Crockett Birthplace Park
Andrew Johnson National Historic Site
Sycamore Shoals State Historic Area
Blount Mansion
Sam Houston Schoolhouse
Cades Cove
Chickamauga and Chattanooga National
   Military Park
The Hermitage
Tennessee State Capital
Sam Davis Home
Shiloh National Military Park
James K. Polk Ancestral Home
Fort Donelson National Battlefield
Wynnewood
Alvin York's Farm and Grist Mill
The Carter House
Chucalissa Prehistoric Indian Village
Meriwether Lewis Monument
Cumberland Gap National Historic Park

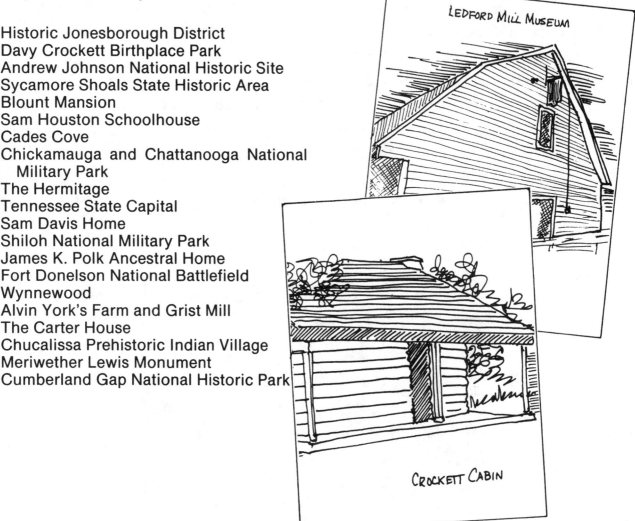

LEDFORD MILL MUSEUM

CROCKETT CABIN

When you've finished locating the above historical sites, choose one that sounds especially interesting. Research the history behind the significance of the landmark and share your information with other members of your class.

GA1138

A MILESTONE EXPERIMENT

In 1933 Congress created the Tennessee Valley Authority to develop methods for conserving the resources of the valley region, to speed along the region's economic development and to use the valley's resources in the event of war. What was accomplished from those original goals has spread far outside the valley. Research the accomplishments of the TVA and summarize your findings in the space below. Include in your discussion something about the dams that were built, the hydroelectricity produced, the flood control that has resulted and the other activities that have occurred.

NORRIS DAM

GA1138

FOLLOW THE MOCKINGBIRD

Tennessee has many attractions other than those associated with history that attracts tourists to the Volunteer State. Several of the more important ones are located on the map below. Your task is to find the location of each from other sources. Then place the number that corresponds to each attraction (on the map) in the blank space provided.

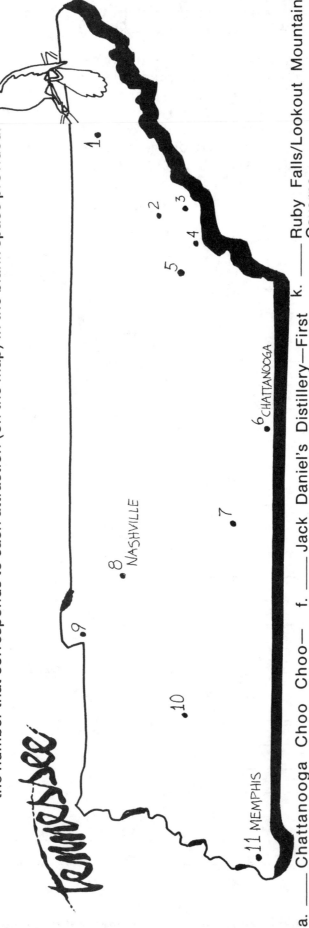

a. ____ Chattanooga Choo Choo—Complex of restaurants, shops, gardens and accommodations

b. ____ Pigeon Forge—Resort community-site of Dollywood

c. ____ Beale Street—Birthplace of the Blues

d. ____ Casey Jones Village—Museum and home of the legendary engineer

e. ____ The Parthenon—Exact size replica of the ancient temple of Greece

f. ____ Jack Daniel's Distillery—First registered distillery in United States

g. ____ Country Music Hall of Fame and Museum

h. ____ Bristol International Raceway—Famous half-mile NASCAR track

i. ____ Great Smoky Mountains National Park—The most visited national park in America

j. ____ TVA's Land Between the Lakes—Massive outdoor recreation area

k. ____ Ruby Falls/Lookout Mountain Caverns

l. ____ Mud Island—Museum and park that tells the story of the mighty Mississippi

m. ____ Gatlinburg—Smoky Mountain resort town noted for its crafts

n. ____ Tuckaleechee Caverns—Greatest sight under the Smokies

o. ____ Graceland—Home and estate of Elvis Presley

p. ____ Grand Ole Opry/Opryland USA—Famous radio show is performed here plus well-known theme park

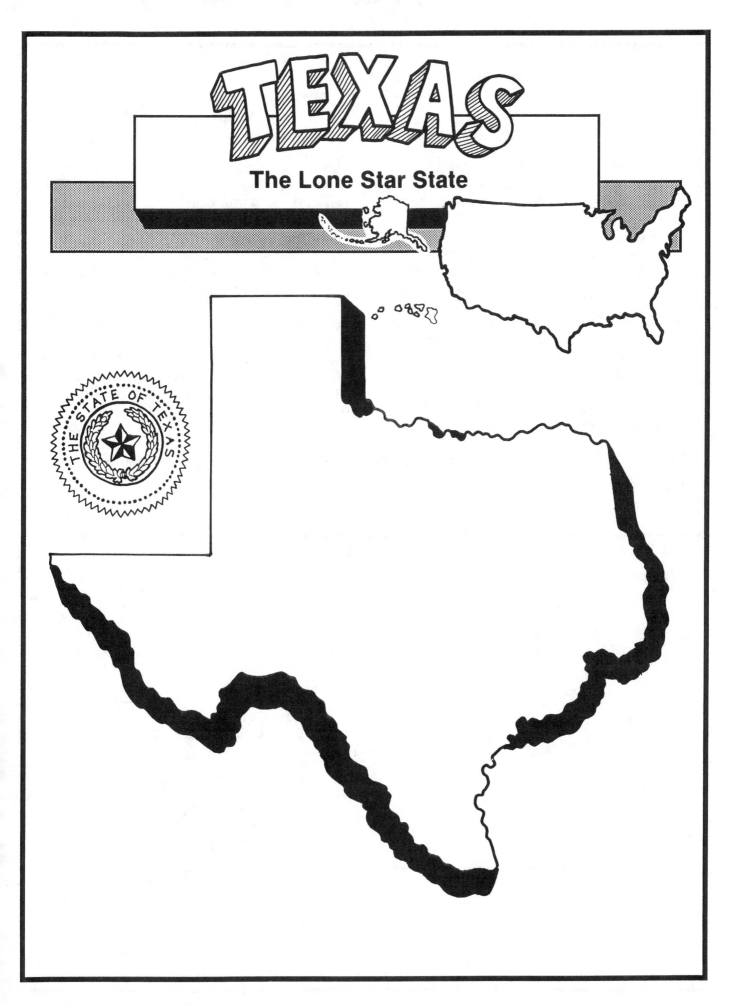

TEXAS
The Lone Star State

253

TEXAS
THE LONE STAR STATE

With the exception of Alaska, Texas is our largest state. Its huge size covers over a quarter-million square miles with its north-south boundaries 800 miles apart and its east-west borders spanning 770 miles. The vast size and wealth of Texas make it at times seem more like a nation than a state. It was at one time a separate nation, apart from the United States. Its location between the Rocky Mountains and the Gulf of Mexico makes its land routes valuable as a connection between the sea and the north and west. Texas' wealth has spread to nearly every sector of the ecomony, with its vast reserves of oil and natural gas production leading the way. Underground pipelines pump them in their unrefined state to various parts of the country, but refining them into consumer goods is also big business in Texas. Some people have a stereotyped image of Texas as a state filled with cowboys and ten-gallon hats. While cattle ranching is important to the Texas economy, Texas today is a state highly dependent upon high technology and wide diversification. Its significant Hispanic and black population has been somewhat below the rest of the state in educational and income achievements, but the futures of both look brighter in light of recent statistics.

Before beginning your study of this amazing state, familiarize yourself with the symbols of Texas asked for below.

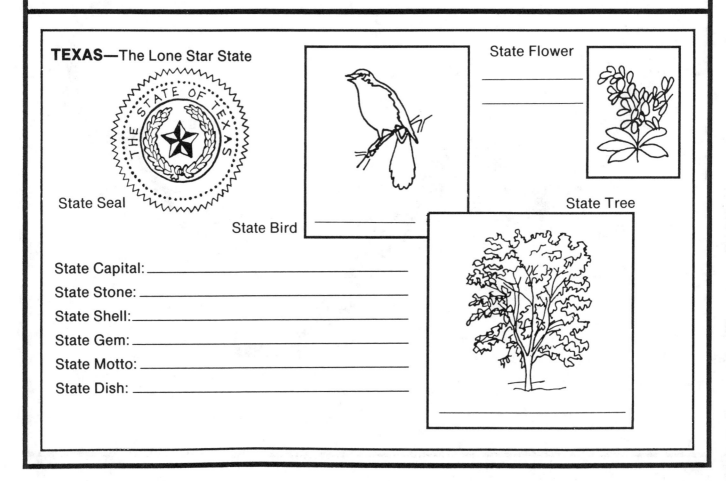

TEXAS—The Lone Star State

State Seal

State Bird

State Flower

State Tree

State Capital: _____

State Stone: _____

State Shell: _____

State Gem: _____

State Motto: _____

State Dish: _____

GA1138

WHAT TO DO WITH THE MAP

With its vast size and rich history, there are many things to see in Texas. In fact, one could travel far and wide (Texas is both) just visiting its many interesting sights. Thousands of tourists do so every year. Below is a list of some of the most popular locations. Find out about each and jot down a brief statement that identifies the reason for the place's popularity. Then pinpoint its location on your outline map.

The Alamo _____

Lyndon B. Johnson Space Center_____

Padre Island National Seashore_____

Six Flags over Texas _____

Mission San Jose _____

Astroworld _____

Fair Park _____

La Villita _____

Aquarena Springs _____

Big Bend National Park _____

San Jacinto Monument_____

Texas Memorial Museum_____

Guadalupe Mountains National Park _____

Lyndon B. Johnson Library/Museum_____

Texas Ranger Hall of Fame_____

Once you've finished making your identifying statements and have pinpointed their locations, go back through the list and decide which place you would like to visit most. Justify your decision by explaining the reasons for your choice.

_____

_____

_____

_____

_____

_____

_____

_____

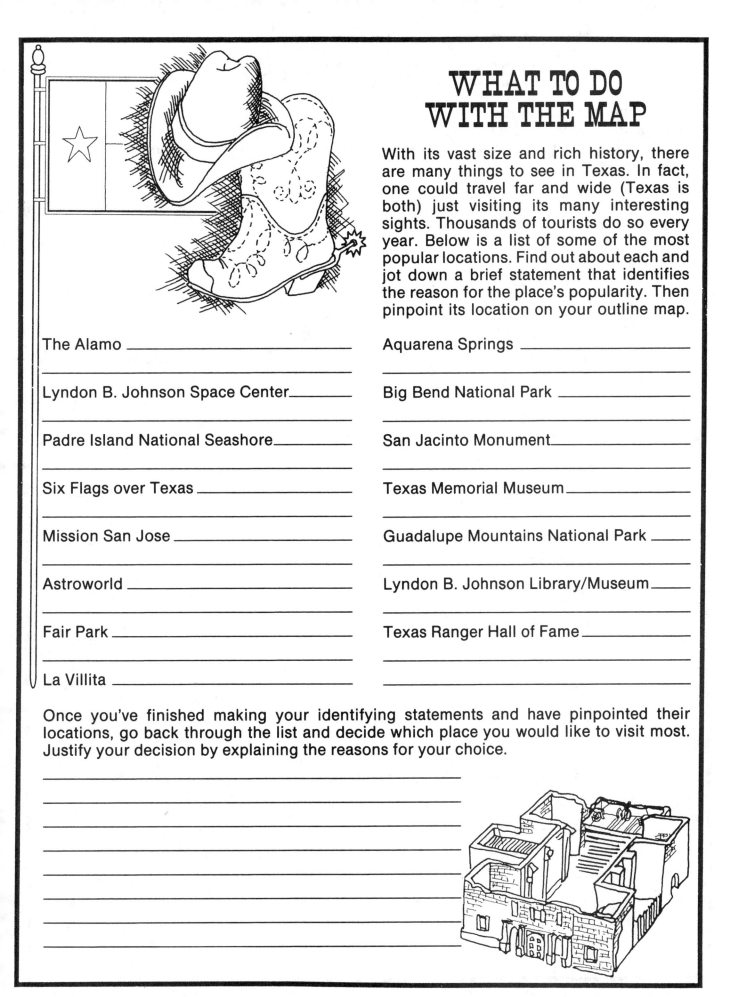

GA1138

SIX FLAGS OVER TEXAS

During the four centuries of recorded history in the area that became Texas, many flags have flown. Below are the six flags of the nations that have exercised actual domination over or staked claims to Texas. Under each flag jot down a brief explanation that properly identifies the flag.

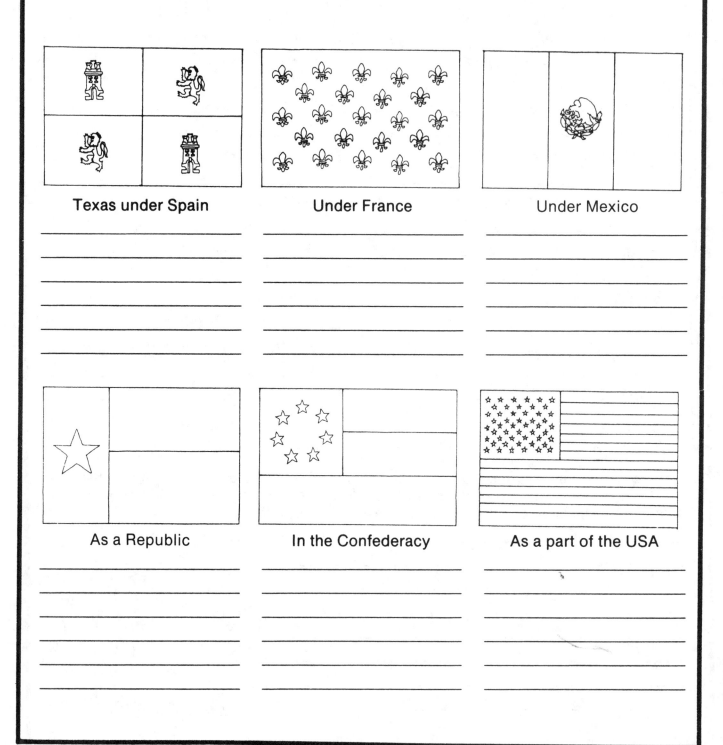

Texas under Spain

Under France

Under Mexico

As a Republic

In the Confederacy

As a part of the USA

GA1138

TEXAS TIME LINE

Below are several important dates in the history of Texas. Research the date when each event took place and record the letter next to that event on the correct line indicator on the time line at the bottom of the page.

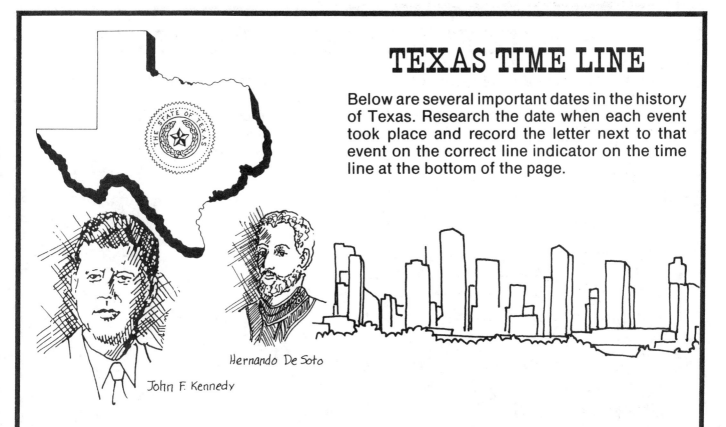

Hernando De Soto

John F. Kennedy

a. Texas seceded from the Union and joined the Confederacy.
b. Alonso Alvarez de Pineda of Spain arrived on Texas coast.
c. Francisco Vasquez de Coronado traveled across part of west Texas.
d. Construction began on the Manned Spacecraft Center at Houston.
e. Texas became the 28th state.
f. Spaniards established a mission at the present-day San Antonio.
g. Cabeza de Vaca and three survivors of a shipwreck landed on Texas coast and explored.
h. President Kennedy was assassinated in Dallas.

i. The Texas Revolution began.
j. The Lucas Well at Spindletop was discovered.
k. Congress readmitted Texas into the Union.
l. Hernando de Soto explored in northeast Texas.
m. Texas became the Republic of Texas.
n. The Texas Centennial Exposition celebrated 100 years of Texas independence.
o. Robert de la Salle founded Fort Saint Louis, a French settlement on the Texas coast.
p. Manned Spacecraft Center renamed the Lyndon B. Johnson Space Center

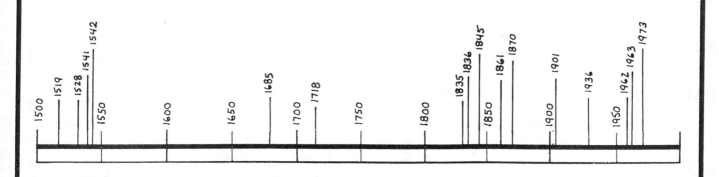

GA1138

THE EYES OF TEXAS

Below are clues that help identify men who have helped to shape the history of Texas. Read each clue carefully, then fill in the letters that spell his name in the empty boxes that correspond to the numbered clue.

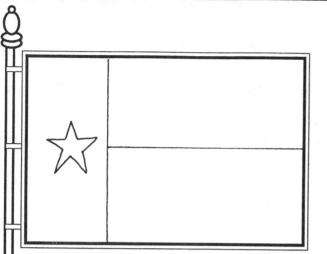

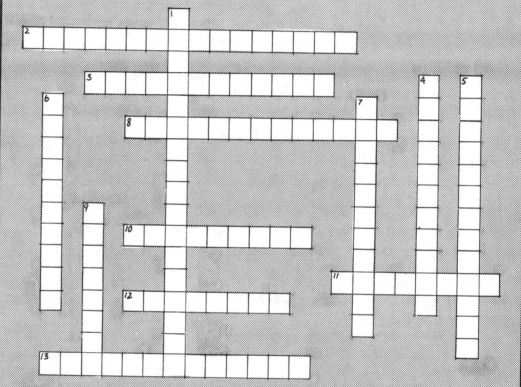

Across

2. U.S. President born in Dension
3. Legendary hunter from Tennessee who fought at the Alamo
8. U.S. President born near Stonewall
10. This leader from Mexico won the Battle of the Alamo.
11. He led the attack on the Mexican army at San Antonio and won.
12. He traveled across part of west Texas looking for gold.
13. Often referred to as the "Father of Texas"

Down

1. First governor of Texas
4. He and his men were defeated near Goliad, all forces in Texas taken prisoner and executed under Santa Anna.
5. He signed a letter vowing to "never surrender" the Alamo.
6. After the Texas Declaration, he was made Commander in Chief.
7. U.S. President assassinated in Dallas in November 1963
9. During the Battle of the Alamo, he fought Santa Anna's men from his sickbed.

GA1138

UTAH

The Beehive State

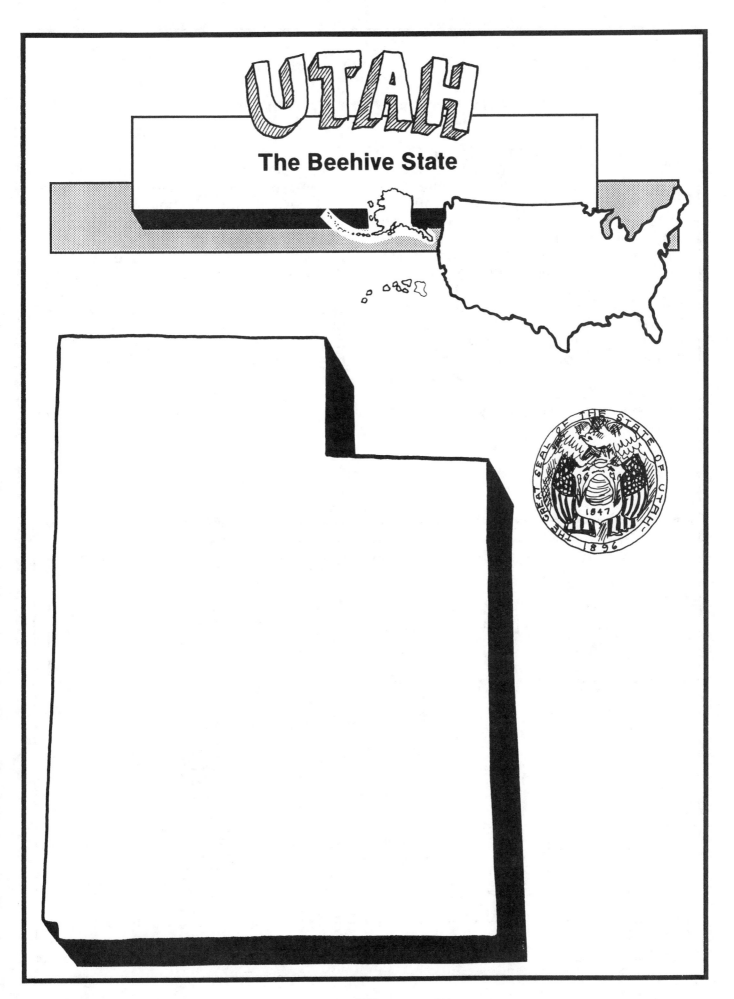

259

GA1138

UTAH
THE BEEHIVE STATE

During the settling of the early West, Utah served as a pathway for thousands on their way to "The Land Beyond." Some were attracted by the natural beauty enough to stay. The followers of Brigham Young, leader of the Mormon Church, built Salt Lake City and transformed the harsh desert landscape into a livable environment that today thrives as Utah's largest and most important city. It still serves as the centerpiece of the Mormon religion. Utah is also rich in mineral deposits with major deposits of copper, petroleum, gold, silver, uranium, magnesium, salt and coal. Its many unusual landforms and other geologic wonders of time draw thousands of tourists annually. With five national parks and several more national monuments, tourism has become big business to the Utah economy. During the winter months the steep slopes of Utah's mountains and the plush resorts have turned Utah into a favorite for skiers in recent years. Utah's past image as a mere pathway to the West has been transformed into one of thriving business and industry and a state with a bright and promising future.

Before you begin your study of Utah, familiarize yourself with the symbols of the Beehive State called for below.

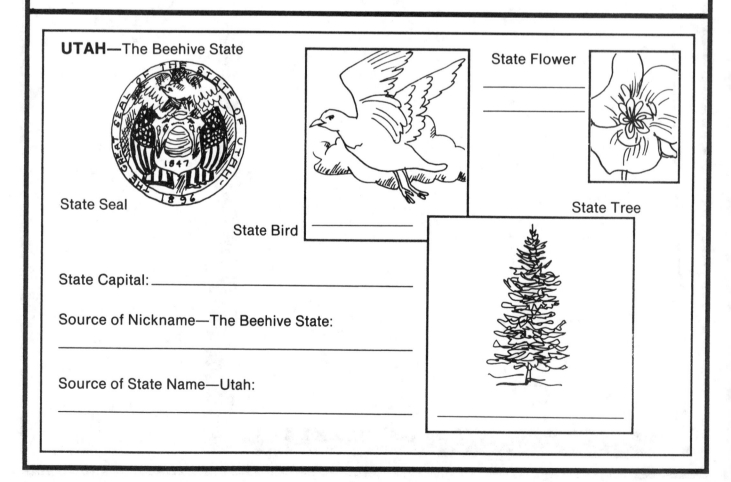

UTAH—The Beehive State

State Seal

State Bird _____

State Flower
_____
_____

State Tree
_____

State Capital: _____

Source of Nickname—The Beehive State:
_____

Source of State Name—Utah:
_____

260

GA1138

UTAH MAP STUDY

Locate these Utah cities on your outline map:

Provo	Bountiful	Midvale
Salt Lake City	Brigham City	Orem
Pleasant Grove	West Valley City	Tooele
American Fork	Layton	West Jordon
Sandy	St. George	Murray
Ogden		

Draw in these rivers:

Colorado	Weber	Virgin
Sevier	Strawberry	White
Green		

Locate these Utah tourist attractions:

Golden Spike National Historic Site
Dinosaur National Monument
Cedar Breaks National Monument
Glen Canyon National Recreation Area
Hovenweep National Monument
Natural Bridges National Monument
Arches National Park
Bryce Canyon National Park
Canyonlands National Park
Capitol Reef National Park
Zion National Park
Timpanogos Cave National Monument
Rainbow Bridge National Monument

GA1138

NEWS FLASH!

Below are several "headlines" that tell the story of Utah's past. Find out when each took place; then cut them out, arrange them in the order in which they occurred and glue to another sheet of paper.

1.

2.

3.

4.

5.

6.

7.

8.

9.

10.

11.

12.

GA1138

UTAH'S NATURAL TREASURES

No state has a greater number of natural treasures than the five national parks found in Utah, each one providing the tourist spectacular scenery and a look at some of nature's most unique geologic masterpieces. Below is a description of each park. Find out from other sources what each park has to offer, then match each of these five parks (Capitol Reef, Zion, Canyonlands, Bryce Canyon and Arches) to the best description below.

1. Located along the eastern edge of Paunsagunt Plateau, the result of fifteen million years of volcanoes, faults and uplifts. The 35-mile drive gives the traveler plenty of time to view the delicate sandstone pinnacles, spires and hoodoos. Special vantage points include Fairyland View, Sunset Point, Inspiration Point and Paria View. Pink Cliffs can be seen from Rainbow Point at the southern end of the park.

   _____

2. Located in southwestern Utah, the Virgin River winds its way through the park, contains Gateway to the Narrows, guided horseback trips, weekend concerts at the Obert C. Tanner Amphitheater, paved road provides excellent view of the park's massive canyons, deserts, streams, waterfalls and hanging gardens.

   _____

3. Covers almost a quarter-million acres of towering cliffs and eroded landscape, located in the heart of Utah's slickrock country, park was named after a rock outcrop that is capped with white sandstone strongly resembling a famous building in Washington, D.C. Location of Waterpocket Fold, a 100-mile bulge in the earth's crust containing pockets eroded in the rock that catch thousands of gallons of water each rainfall.

   _____

4. Contains the world's largest concentration of sandstone arches, created by the combined erosive forces of wind and water. Over 200 arches inside the park's boundaries. North and South Windows, Fiery Furnace, Balanced Rock and Devil's Garden are among the main attractions.

   _____

5. The Green and Colorado Rivers are the main architects in this park dividing it into three districts: The Needles, Island in the Sky and the Maze. The Needles are rock pinnacles banded in orange and white. Island in the Sky contains an observation tower for views of the rest of the park. The Maze has maze-like canyons, tall standing rocks and colorful sandstone.

MONUMENT VALLEY STATE PARK

GA1138

A MORMON OASIS

In the late 1840's Brigham Young led his followers of the Mormon faith into the wastelands near the Great Salt Lake. Through hard work, perseverance and ingenuity, the Mormons established the groundwork for the beautiful city of Salt Lake that stands there today. With a population of over 160,000, it remains today the centerpiece of the Mormon religion. Why did they come? From where did they come? Why were the Mormons persecuted wherever they went? What is the significance of Carthage, Illinois, to the Mormon faith? Who was Joseph Smith? How did Brigham Young become the leader? What is the official name of the Mormon church? Why did the church split into two factions? To answer these and other questions, trace the history of the Mormon religion and summarize your findings below and on another sheet of paper.

SALT LAKE CITY SKYLINE

GA1138

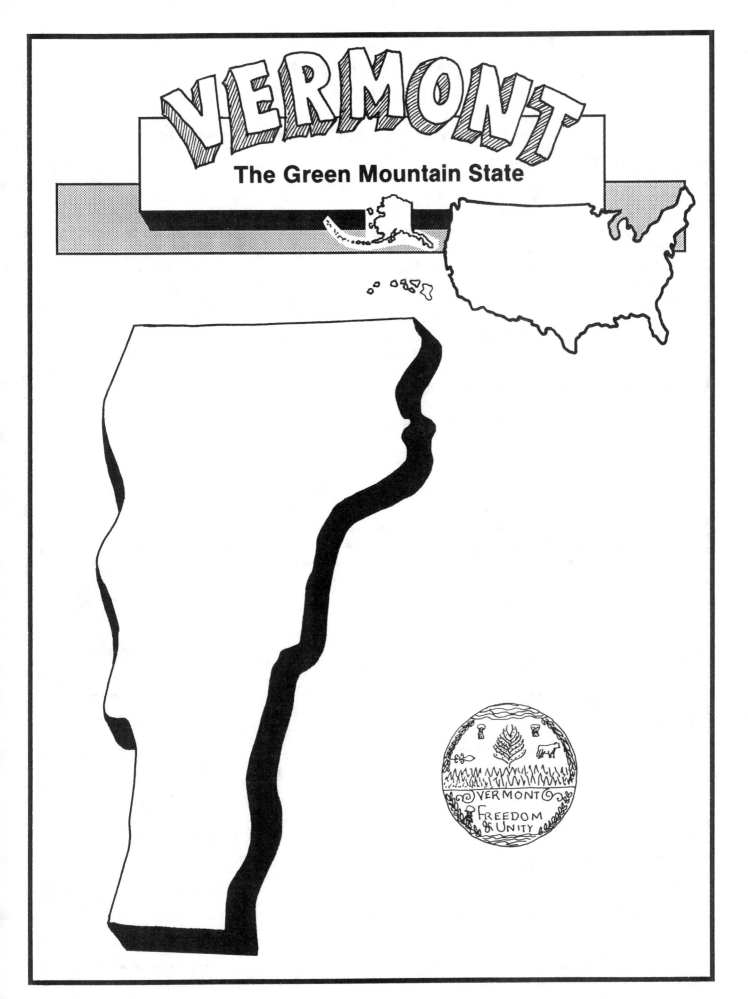

VERMONT
The Green Mountain State

VERMONT
THE GREEN MOUNTAIN STATE

Vermont is a rural state where almost seventy percent of the residents live outside the cities and towns. By this standard, it is the most rural state in America. It is a state in which visitors can almost feel thrust back into another era where life was less hectic and everything moved at a much slower pace. Its natural charm and beauty make it a hit with thousands of vacationers each year and is especially popular in the fall when nature's changing colors put on a spectacular show that many feel cannot be equaled elsewhere. Added to this are the many excellent ski resorts found throughout the Green Mountains thus making tourism very important to Vermonters. Manufacturing remains the chief economic activity with farm products accounting for about twenty percent of the value of products produced. It is the only New England state without a coastline on the Atlantic, but water does border more than half the state. Forests cover about seventy-five percent of the state, with the maple syrup and wood industries important to the state. Vermont granite and marble also contribute significantly to the economy.

To begin your study of Vermont, identify each of the following:

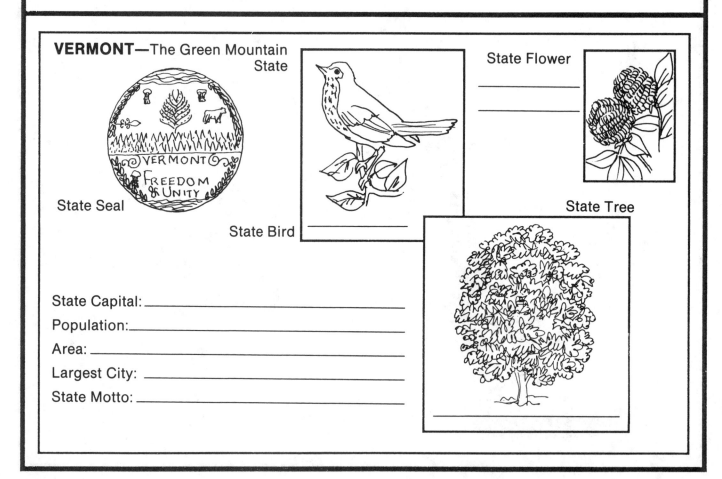

VERMONT—The Green Mountain State

State Seal

State Bird

State Flower
_____
_____

State Tree

State Capital: _____

Population: _____

Area: _____

Largest City: _____

State Motto: _____

GA1138

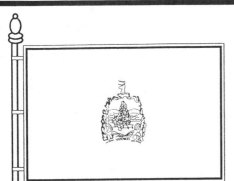

WHAT TO DO WITH THE MAP

Vermont has six main land regions even though it is one of our smallest states. Label the following on the outline map and define the region by using a different map pencil for each region:

White Mountains
Green Mountains
Vermont Valley

Taconic Mountains
Western New England Upland
Champlain Valley

Pinpoint the locations of these Vermont cities:

Montpelier
Burlington
Middlebury
Rutland

Springfield
Brattleboro
Newport
Saint Albans

Locate the following:

Connecticut River
Lake Champlain
Green Mountain National Forest
White River

Black River
West River
Batten Kill River

Create your own map symbols that depict these major products that are important to the economy of Vermont. Also sketch in each on the map where the product is found in great numbers.

Granite

Sand and Gravel

Forest Products

Potatoes

Maple Syrup

Poultry

Dairy Cattle

GA1138

FALL FOLIAGE

Mother Nature turns the Vermont landscape into a palette of beautiful colors, and thousands of tourists arrive to witness the show. This changing of seasons is a beautiful time of year regardless of where it takes place. But perhaps nowhere else in America is the show as grand as it is in Vermont. Find out the scientific explanation for this annual extravaganza and find out, too, the reason for its being more dramatic in Vermont. Discuss completely the mysteries behind both questions in the space below.

GA1138

WAR IN VERMONT

1. Samuel de Champlain was probably the first white man to explore what is today Vermont. He arrived in 1609 and claimed the land for France. During the French and Indian War, Lake Champlain became an important battleground. Read about this early historical event and report the significance of the outcome in the space below.

_____
_____
_____
_____

2. Ethan Allen, a native Vermonter, played an important role in early history during the American Revolution. Read about the deeds of Ethan Allen and his Green Mountain Boys and summarize your findings below.

_____
_____
_____
_____

3. Find out the significance of the Battle of Bennington fought during the American Revolution. Although the battle is regarded as a Vermont battle, it was actually fought elsewhere. Report your findings in the space below.

_____
_____
_____
_____

4. Although Vermont is not regarded by historians as a battleground during the Civil War, there were incidents in St. Albans that were at least connected to the war. Find out what happened there and report your findings below.

_____
_____
_____
_____

GA1138

BEAUTIFUL VERMONT

Because Vermont's beautiful scenery and rustic charm attract thousands of tourists annually, it is important for the department of tourism to create flyers and brochures that present what the state has to offer in its most favorable light. Its many historic sites, the mountains, the skiing, villages, the covered bridges and red barns, the green meadows and the "laid back" way of life of the people themselves all suggest life in America during another era, a tranquil, more peaceful time. In the panels below you see some ideas for the creation of a travel folder on Vermont. Create your own six-page Vermont vacation guide that includes your own ideas on advertising Vermont. Create your own copy. You may either draw rough sketches for illustrations, use photos, or you may use pictures from magazines. Make pages 4" x 8", staple together and share with other members of the class.

GA1138

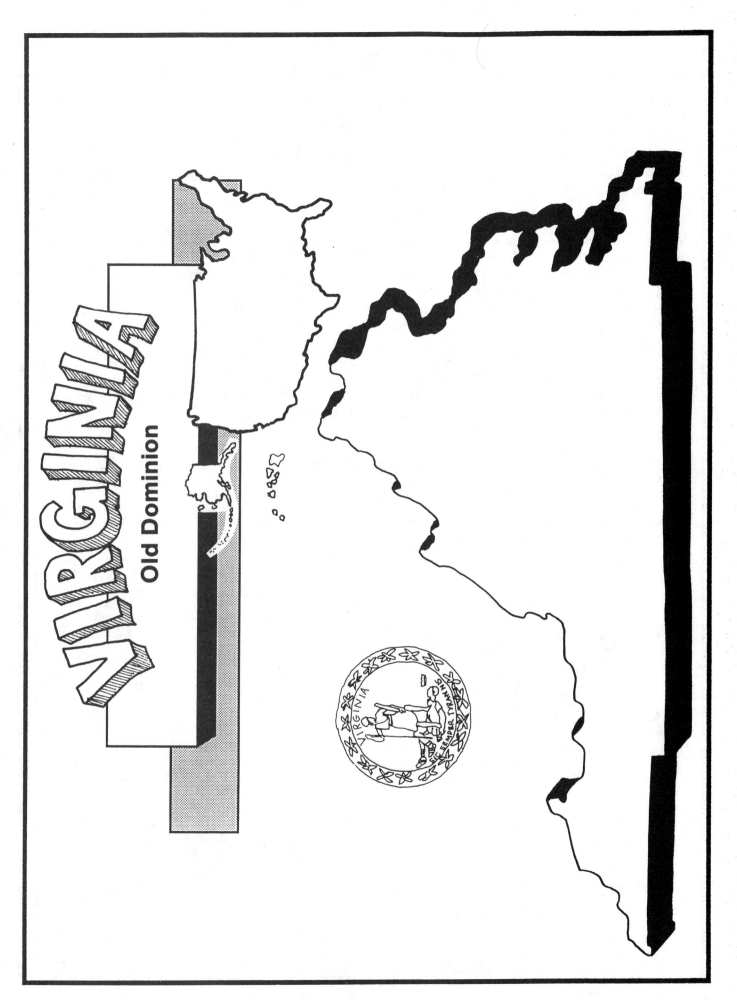

VIRGINIA

Old Dominion

271

VIRGINIA
OLD DOMINION

No other state can compare historically with the significance of Virginia. Throughout the unfolding of the American story, Virginia has played host to some of the most important events. It all started with Jamestown in 1607, the first permanent English settlement in America. Through the American Revolution and the Civil War, Virginia soil was the scene of the important battles. Cornwallis surrendered at Yorktown ending the Revolution. The Civil War ended with Lee's surrender at Appomattox. Virginia has been called the Mother of Presidents because eight U.S. Presidents were born there. The state has also been called Mother of States because all or part of eight other states were created out of territory once claimed by Virginia. Virginia's proximity to the nation's capital makes it important in supplying much of the governmental work force that runs the machinery of our huge political system. At one time the state was largely a rural state, but it now serves as the southern anchor of the giant industrial corridor that stretches north as far as Boston. Its strong ties to the South continue to make it a pivot between northern and southern manufacturing states. Virginia has significant resource wealth, and additional revenue comes from the millions of tourists attracted annually to the historical sites and beautiful scenery.

Before continuing with your study of Virginia, identify the symbols called for below.

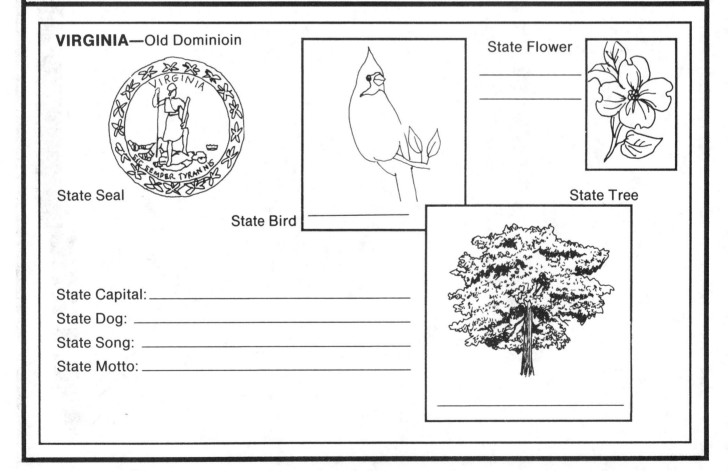

VIRGINIA—Old Dominioin

State Seal

State Bird _____

State Flower _____

State Tree

State Capital: _____

State Dog: _____

State Song: _____

State Motto: _____

_____

272

GA1138

VIRGINIA ON THE MAP

Using a map of Virginia from a good atlas, find each of the following. Then create your own set of coordinates for use on your outline map of Virginia and pinpoint the location of each of the following using those coordinates.

Lynchburg
Richmond
Williamsburg
Staunton
Fredericksburg
Harrisonburg
Alexandria

Martinsville
Roanoke
Norfolk
Newport News
Fairfax
Charlottesville

Locate also:

Shenandoah National Park
Chesapeake Bay
Potomac River
York River
James River

Virginia has an excellent network of interstate highways connecting major cities and other points of interest. Draw in and label these major highways: I-64, I-95, I-81, I-66, I-85, I-77.

MONTPELIER

GA1138

MOTHER OF PRESIDENTS

No fewer than eight U.S. Presidents were born in Virginia. No other state can claim birthrights to as many, giving Virginia claim to the unofficial nickname Mother of Presidents. Four of our first five Presidents were born there. The clues given below are sketchy, but with a little ingenuity and research and counting of letters you should be able to figure them out.

1. The Father of the Constitution
2. His policy to protect South America from European colonization may have been his most noted accomplishment.
3. He designed the campus of the University of Virginia.
4. Wakefield, southeast of Fredericksburg, was his birthplace.
5. Staunton was his birthplace.
6. A war hero during the Spanish-American War
7. He was one of our shorter Presidents at 5'4" tall.
8. He served the shortest term of any elected President.

Find the birthplace of each of the eight U.S. Presidents born in Viriginia and pinpoint the location of the birth of each with his initials on your outline map.

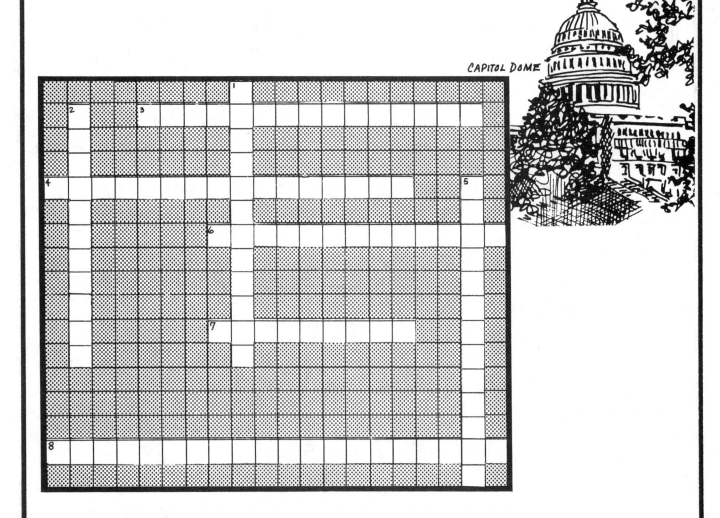

CAPITOL DOME

GA1138

WHERE A NATION WAS BORN

The oldest part of America lies within a triangle that includes Jamestown—America's first permanent English settlement, Colonial Williamsburg—the largest restored 18th century town in America, and Yorktown—where the Revolution ended and the nation began. There is indeed a lot of American history stored up in these few carefully preserved precious square miles. Colonial taverns, elegant plantations, victory monuments and famous battlefields lie within this triangle. Research the stories behind this historical land and describe the landmarks and reasons for its being so significant to America's history.

GA1138

WHAT MIGHT HAVE BEEN

The story of America continues to unfold daily with the events that occur—some of them significant, some not so significant—but all of them are a part of the continuing story. It's been that way since that first band of settlers landed at Jamestown in 1607. Our current position on the time line of American history has been determined by the events of our past. If certain events had happened differently, or not at all, that current picture might be different. Speculate on the events below that took place in historic Virginia and decide how you think the cause of history might have been affected if they had turned out differently.

- If the Virginia Company of London had not met the supply ships of Lord De La Warr coming from England. Remember the colonists who had survived were on their way back to England.

  _____
  _____
  _____
  _____

- If John Rolfe had not introduced the colonists to a method of successfully curing tobacco

  _____
  _____
  _____
  _____
  _____

- If Lord Cornwallis had won the Battle at Yorktown

  _____
  _____
  _____

- If Virginia had not seceded from the Union during the Civil War

  _____
  _____
  _____

- If Grant had been forced to surrender to Lee at Appomattox Court House to end the Civil War

  _____
  _____
  _____

GA1138

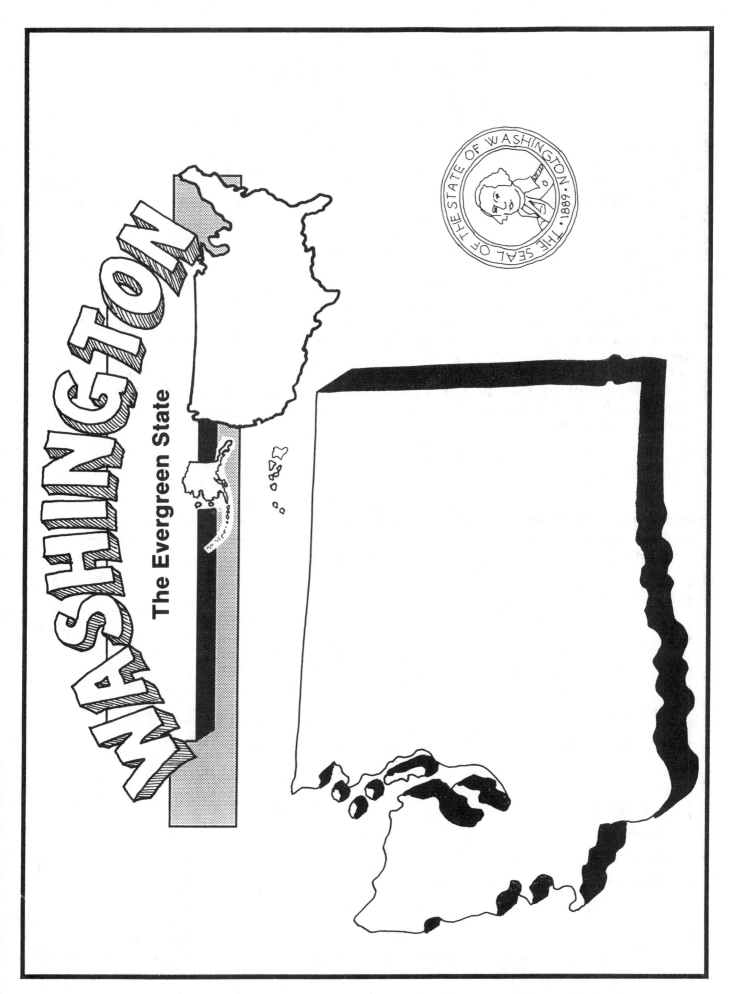

WASHINGTON

The Evergreen State

THE SEAL OF THE STATE OF WASHINGTON · 1889 ·

277

WASHINGTON
THE EVERGREEN STATE

Washington serves as an important trade and transportation link between the mainland United States and Alaska, northwestern Canada as well as Japan and other Asian countries that trade with the U.S. It is also a state whose economy is a mix between industry and agriculture. Its aircraft, shipbuilding and aerospace manufacturers pour millions of dollars annually into the state's coffers, but Washington is also well-known for its fruit, potatoes, wheat and sugar beets. The breathtaking beauty and rugged geography of Washington have made tourism and related industries important factors in the state's economy. Perhaps its greatest resource is water. Puget Sound, the Pacific Ocean and the inland waters of the Snake and Columbia Rivers all play a vital role in the manner in which Washington sustains its livelihood. The location on Puget Sound has made Seattle the key port city of the Northwest, and the hydroelectric power generated on the Snake and Columbia Rivers powers most of the state's factories and also serves as sources for water in areas where irrigation is necessary. In the future, Washington's location will continue to serve it well as a major shipping center to and beyond the Great Northwest, but its heavy reliance on government contracts makes it on occasion somewhat vulnerable and uncertain.

Before you continue with your study of Washington, become familiar with the state symbols indicated below.

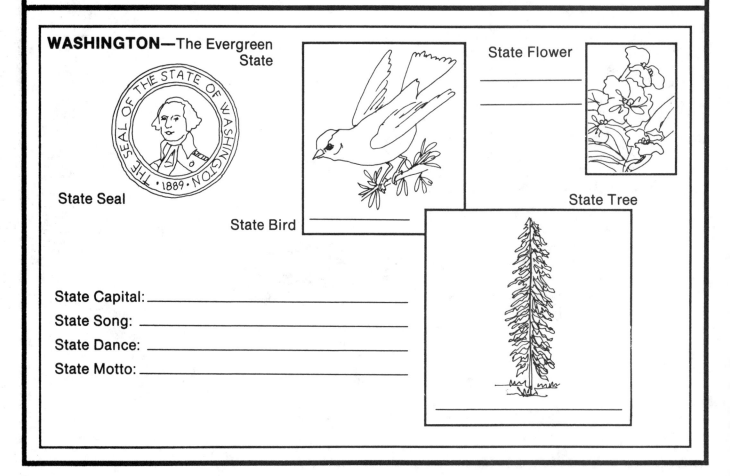

WASHINGTON—The Evergreen State

State Seal

State Bird _____

State Flower
_____
_____

State Tree

State Capital: _____

State Song: _____

State Dance: _____

State Motto: _____

278

THE GREAT OUTDOORS

MOUNT RAINIER

Since more than one third of the state is national forests or parklands, Washington is one of those states that attracts thousands of tourists annually to its great outdoors. The spectacular scenery of the towering Cascade Mountains, the jungle-like forests of the Olympic Peninsula and the sparkling coastal waters combine to make it a vacation favorite. If its parks and forests are not enough, Washington also has its share of historical sites. On your outline map of Washington, draw in and label the following:

National Forests

Colville	Olympic
Gifford Pinchot	Umatilla
Mt. Baker-Snoqualmie	Wenatchee
Okanogan	

National Parks

Mount Rainier
North Cascades
Olympic

National Historic Sites

Whitman Mission
Fort Vancouver

Locate also three of these wildernesses:

Trapper Creek
Indian Heaven
William O. Douglas

Mt. Baker
Boulder River
Goat Rocks

Pasayten
Glacier Peak
Alpine Lakes

GA1138

FACT OR FICTION

Decide which of the statements below are really facts about the state of Washington and which are merely fiction. Then write your choices in the blank spaces provided.

1. _____ On the average, December is the driest month.

2. _____ Winters are usually milder in the west than in the east.

3. _____ Washington is the downspout of the nation.

4. _____ Over eighty percent of Washington is rain forest.

5. _____ Washington is one of the only two states with a maximum speed limit of 55 miles per hour.

6. _____ Halibut ranks high on the list of seafood exports for Washington.

7. _____ Chinook, sockeye, chum, pink and silver are all varieties of salmon found in Washington.

8. _____ Hell's Canyon is North America's deepest river gorge.

9. _____ Abraham Lincoln was invited to be the first governor of the Oregon Territory (of which Washington was part), but he declined.

10. _____ The official folk song of Washington is "Roll on Columbia" by Woody Guthrie.

11. _____ Seattle's most spectacular view is atop the Space Needle.

12. _____ The University of Washington is located in Tacoma.

13. _____ Washington is the only state named for a President.

14. _____ More rain falls east of the Cascades than west.

15. _____ Wine, cheese, processed fish and apples are all products of Washington.

16. _____ The boundary dispute with England over the ownership was settled without bloodshed.

17. _____ Even though there is snow in Washington, skiing is not an important sport because the snow is so wet.

18. _____ The Klondike gold rush of the 1890's brought prosperity to the Puget Sound area.

19. _____ Water from the Columbia River helps to irrigate parts of southeastern and central Washington.

20. _____ Washington has more than 3000 varieties of flowers that are native to the state.

GA1138

SEQUENCING WASHINGTON HISTORY

Below is a list of several events that are significant to the history of Washington. Find out about each and arrange them in the order in which they occurred by placing a #1 in the blank space next to the event that happened first. Proceed on through #15, in the blank next to the event that happened most recently.

_____ The Oregon Territory is created and Abraham Lincoln is asked to be governor. He refuses and Joseph Lane accepts.

_____ Opening of the Panama Canal helps trade with the East Coast.

_____ England, Spain and Russia all claim to own the Northwest Territory.

_____ Washington becomes the 42nd state.

_____ Lewis and Clark reach Washington and the Pacific Ocean.

_____ Mount St. Helens cataclysmic explosion devastates 150,000 acres of surrounding landscape.

_____ The Alaskan gold rush attracts the world's attention to the Pacific Northwest and turns Seattle into the embarkment point for gold seekers.

_____ Captain Robert Gray names the Columbia River after his ship.

_____ President Millard Fillmore signs a bill creating the Washington Territory which includes the present state of Washington, northern Idaho and western Montana.

_____ Work is completed on Grand Coulee Dam—the largest man-made structure in the world.

_____ John Jacob Astor organizes the Pacific Fur Company.

_____ President Roosevelt signs a bill to create Olympic National Park.

_____ Washington celebrates its centennial with a year-long schedule of events.

_____ Arguments with England over the ownership for the Oregon Territory are settled when the 49th parallel is fixed.

_____ Seattle hosts the World's Fair, a celebration that puts Puget Sound on the map for many first-time visitors.

GA1138

WASHINGTON CROSSWORD

Below are clues to words that satisfy the number of letters required to fill the boxes in the crossword puzzle.

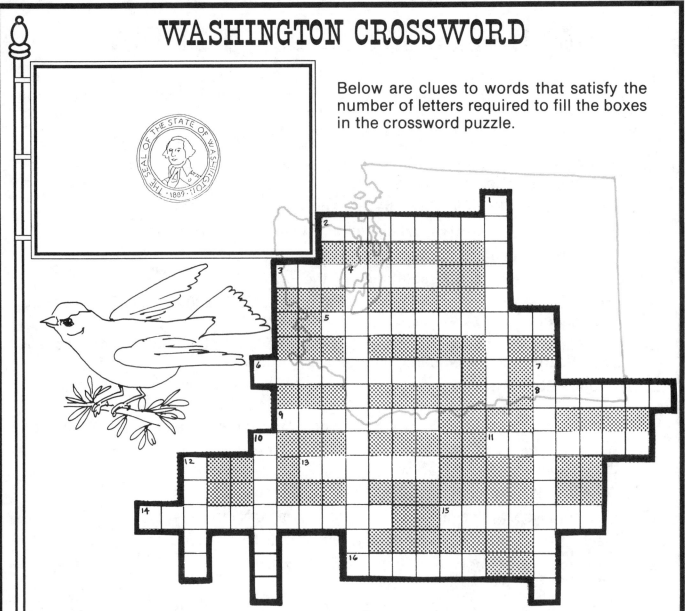

Across

2. Important river in Washington
3. Washington's westernmost national park
5. Body of water on which Seattle is located
6. Well-known Washington painter
8. Washington produces a large crop of this fruit.
9. The location of a compass with a 500-foot needle
11. It has the nation's highest yield per acre of wheat.
13. He founded an airplane company in Seattle in 1916.
14. The largest hydroelectric dam in the world
15. Washington's largest city in the east
16. Washington's #1 fish

Down

1. Washington's oldest city
4. It erupted on May 18, 1980.
7. City in southeastern Washington with an Indian name meaning "place of many waters"
10. The mountains that divide eastern and western Washington
12. He was perhaps the first European to see the coast of Washington.

282

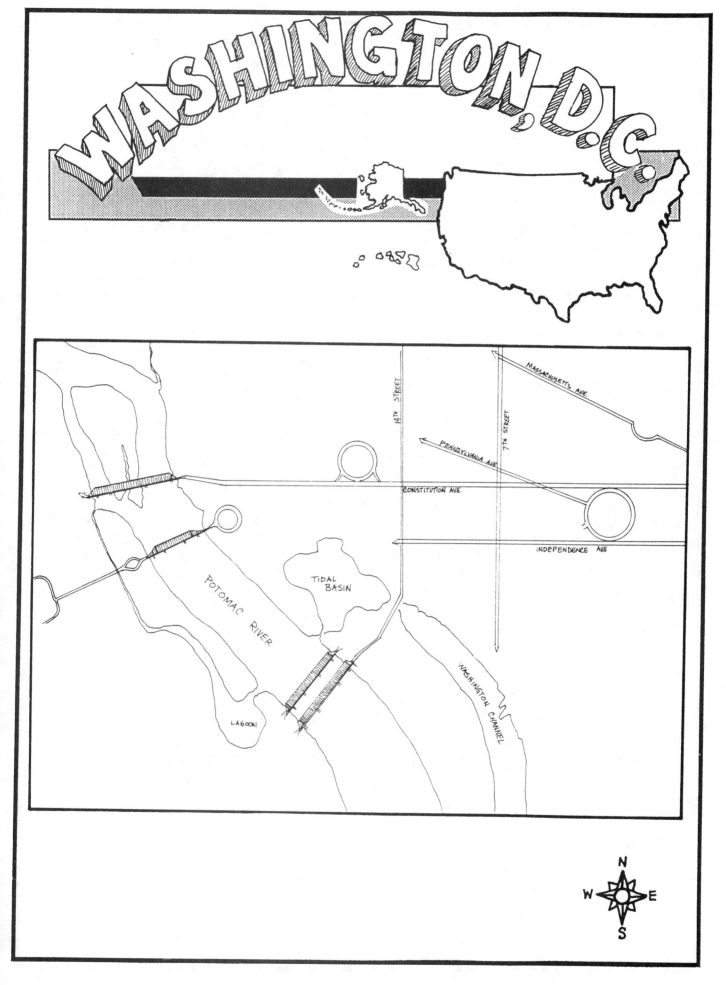

283

WASHINGTON, D.C.

As the nation's capital city, Washington, D.C., is not a part of any state. It lies between Maryland and Virginia on the east bank of the Potomac River. The city covers 67 square miles on a track of land that falls under the jurisdiction of the federal government. Every year millions of persons from all over the United States and other countries visit Washington, D.C., to see the important government buildings that are located there. Washington is also important to Americans as a symbol of our nation's unity, history and democratic ideals. It is one of our most beautiful cities and its monuments and memorials and government buildings are cherished by reminders of what living in America means. Washington is one of the few cities anywhere that was designed before it was built. The site was chosen by President George Washington in 1791, and Pierre Charles L'Enfant, a French engineer, was lured to draw up plans for the city. In 1800

Washington replaced Philadelphia as the nation's capital. The special commission formed to plan the city named it in honor of George Washington, the young country's first President. The *D.C.* in the city's name stands for District of Columbia. Many of the monuments and government buildings are located in the west-central part of the city. The U.S. Capitol is the geographic center of Washington's streets. Streets extend from the Capitol in all directions like the spokes of a wheel. The city is divided into four sections—Northwest, Northeast, Southwest and Southeast—and every address in Washington is followed by one of four abbreviations that tells what section of the city it is in. Below is a map of the Washington metropolitan area which also includes counties and cities in Maryland and Virginia. Find a good map of the Washington area and label all sections of the city and surrounding cities, counties and outlying areas.

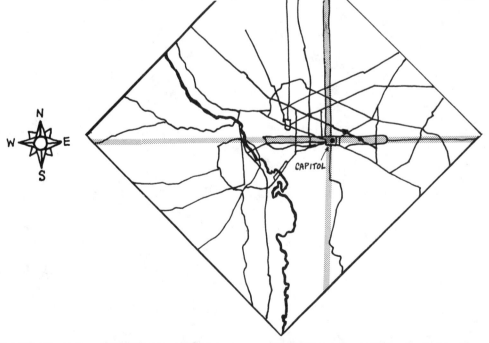

284

CAPITAL TOUR

Below are clues that will help you to identify several of the major attractions of our nation's capital. Read each clue carefully and place the name of the attraction in the space provided. Then create your own symbol for each attraction and use that symbol to pinpoint its location on your outline map of the Washington, D.C., area.

1. _____ Here lie the remains of 175,000 American soldiers who fought from the Revolutionary War to the present.

2. _____ The historically significant playhouse where Abraham Lincoln was assassinated on Good Friday, April 14, 1865

3. _____ The largest bronze statue ever cast, this 78-foot memorial commemorates the Marines who have died since 1775.

4. _____ Classical dome, colonnades and quotes from the Declaration of Independence highlight this memorial to our third U.S. President.

5. _____ 1600 Pennsylvania Ave., 132 rooms, the home of every U.S. President since 1800

6. _____ The meeting place for the highest court in the land

7. _____ The tallest masonry structure in the city, this majestic obelisk stands 555 feet as a monument to our first President.

8. _____ The original documents of the Declaration of Independence, the Constitution and the Bill of Rights are stored here.

9. _____ Grecian temple-like memorial overlooking the massive Reflecting Pool on the National Mall

10. _____ The world's largest office building with 3.7 million square feet, it houses the headquarters for the Secretary of Defense, Army, Navy, Air Force and Coast Guard.

11. _____ Our nation's largest library with over 84 million items in 470 languages

12. _____ Under this 180-foot white dome our lawmakers make the rules and laws under which we live.

13. _____ Modern V-shaped memorial inscribed with the names of the 58,156 people who either died or remain missing in the most recent confrontation for the United States

14. _____ Contains over 3000 animals including the giant pandas, Ling-Ling and Hsing-Hsing, given to the United States by China in the early 1970's.

15. _____ Splendid 19th century mansion near Georgetown containing extensive Byzantine collection, Garden Library, Rare Book Room and Music Room. The house is surrounded by an estate with ten acres of terraced gardens.

16. _____ The place where billions of U.S. dollars are printed every year

17. _____ Spectacular 14th century Gothic cathedral—second largest in the United States

CAPITAL TOUR

18. _____ Over fifty acres of rolling, shaded lawn with a six-acre lake in the middle. A memorial in the middle of an island in the lake commemorates the signers of the Declaration.

19. _____ Popularly known as the "Castle," it is the oldest of the Smithsonian museums and houses the information center and the crypt of founder James Smithson.

20. _____ The headquarters of the Federal Bureau of Investigation

List below the five sites that would be "musts" on your own personal tour of our nation's capital.

_____

_____

_____

_____

_____

JEFFERSON MEMORIAL

CAPITOL DOME

LINCOLN MEMORIAL

GA1138

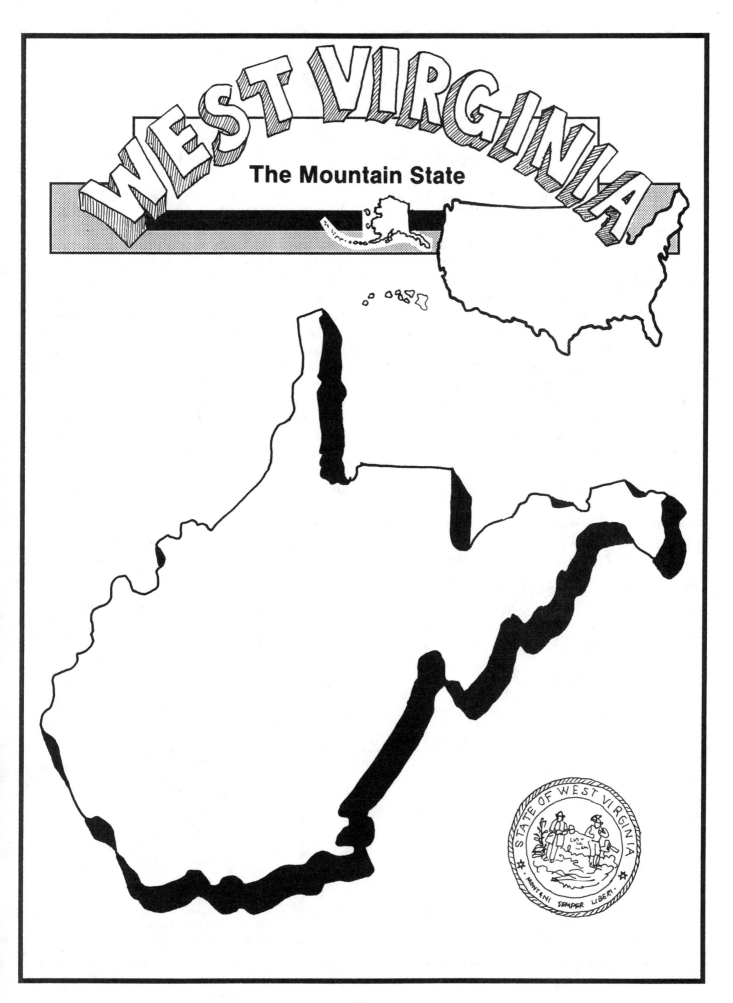

WEST VIRGINIA

The Mountain State

STATE OF WEST VIRGINIA
MONTANI SEMPER LIBERI

WEST VIRGINIA
THE MOUNTAIN STATE

On June 20, 1863, Abraham Lincoln signed the papers that made the 450,000 Virginians living west of the Blue Ridge Mountains the new state of West Virginia. The rugged terrain of the area had led to the development of an economy based on industry and small-scale farming, this being in stark contrast to the large plantation culture found in the eastern part of the state. As a result of several differences, the people in the west part of the state wanted a state of their own. These differences reached the boiling point at the onset of the Civil War when the sympathies of the plantation owners were with the South and the "West" Virginians remained loyal to the Union. Lincoln's signature, supported by Congress, was the official action necessary to recognize West Virginia. Its mountainous terrain remained an obstacle to transportation, trade and communication. Agriculture was limited to subsistence farming in isolated valleys. Coal, natural gas, oil and high-grade sand were developed to a degree, but mechanization left many workers out of jobs. In more recent times, many of the once-famous country roads have been turned into an efficient network of interstates that connect the state with surrounding states and the nation. Fine hardwood furniture built from native oak, cherry, walnut and ash as well as vast coal reserves offer a bright outlook for the future of this state that is finally emerging from the economic shadow of its more prosperous neighbor.

Before continuing with your study of West Virginia, find the symbols called for below.

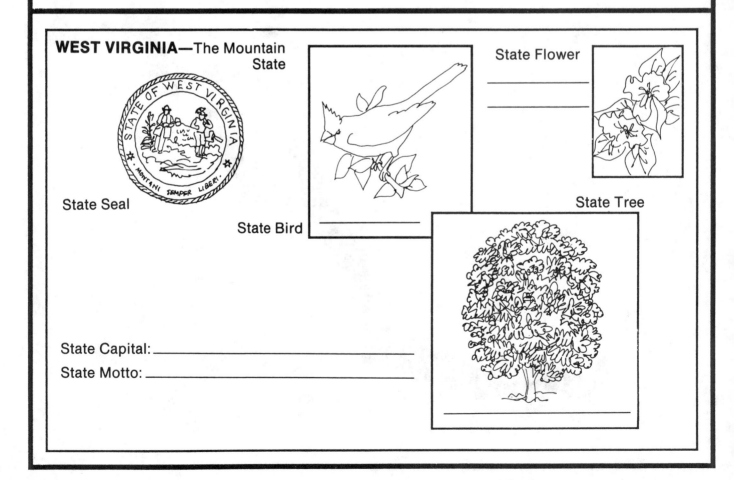

WEST VIRGINIA—The Mountain State

State Seal

State Bird _____

State Flower
_____
_____

State Tree

State Capital: _____

State Motto: _____

GA1138

WEST VIRGINIA ON THE MAP

Create a system of your own coordinates for your outline map that will help you to be more accurate in locating the cities listed below. Base your system on those you find on the atlas or road map you use for reference.

Charleston	Weirton
Huntington	Wheeling
Clarksburg	St. Albans
Buckhannon	Oak Hill
Morgantown	Parkersburg
Moundsville	Martinsburg
Elkins	Beckley

Locate these West Virginia rivers:

Greenbrier	Potomac
West Fork	Cheat
Elk	Ohio
Kanawha	Monongahela
New	Guyandotte

Draw in the Allegheny and Blue Ridge Mountains.

Draw in and label these interstate highways that have been important to West Virginia's economy by making it more accessible to surrounding states: I-64, I-77, I-79, I-70.

Draw in and label these national forests:

George Washington
Jefferson
Monongahela

BLACKWATER FALLS

GA1138

WEST VIRGINIA HISTORY

While students seldom remember historical dates for very long, it is important in the study of history to place significant events in the order in which they occurred. The main reason for this is that often one event is either the direct or indirect result of other events that have already taken place. So it is with the history of West Virginia as well. Each date in the time line below corresponds to an event significant to the history of West Virginia. Find out when each took place. Then when you are finished, arrange the events in chronological order in the blank spaces below, beginning with #1 beside that which happened first.

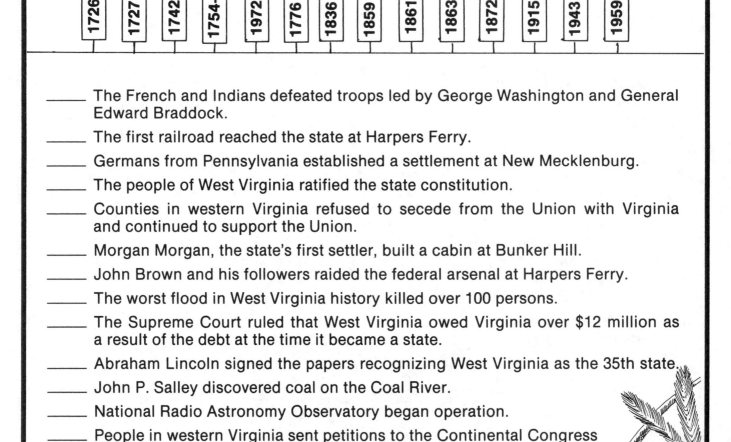

Time line dates: 1726 | 1727 | 1742 | 1754-55 | 1972 | 1776 | 1836 | 1859 | 1861 | 1863 | 1872 | 1915 | 1943 | 1959

_____ The French and Indians defeated troops led by George Washington and General Edward Braddock.

_____ The first railroad reached the state at Harpers Ferry.

_____ Germans from Pennsylvania established a settlement at New Mecklenburg.

_____ The people of West Virginia ratified the state constitution.

_____ Counties in western Virginia refused to secede from the Union with Virginia and continued to support the Union.

_____ Morgan Morgan, the state's first settler, built a cabin at Bunker Hill.

_____ John Brown and his followers raided the federal arsenal at Harpers Ferry.

_____ The worst flood in West Virginia history killed over 100 persons.

_____ The Supreme Court ruled that West Virginia owed Virginia over $12 million as a result of the debt at the time it became a state.

_____ Abraham Lincoln signed the papers recognizing West Virginia as the 35th state.

_____ John P. Salley discovered coal on the Coal River.

_____ National Radio Astronomy Observatory began operation.

_____ People in western Virginia sent petitions to the Continental Congress asking for a separate government.

_____ Geologists found vast salt deposits in West Virginia.

GA1138

PLACES TO SEE IN WEST VIRGINIA

West Virginia has been blessed with more than its share of places to visit. There are several attractions that are significant historically, but others are popular for their charm and natural beauty. Many of the state's more popular attractions are listed below. Jot down a brief identifying statement for each; then mark the letter that corresponds to each on the map in the location that is appropriate.

a. Berkeley Springs

b. Monongahela National Forest

c. Harpers Ferry National Historical Park

d. Jackson's Mill

e. National Radio Astronomy Observatory

f. Seneca Rock

g. Cass Scenic Railroad

h. Charles Town

i. White Sulphur Springs

j. Pricketts Fort

k. Carnifex Ferry Battlefield

l. Watoga

m. Blackwater Falls

n. Canaan Valley

o. Pinnacle Rock

FOR FURTHER RESEARCH . . .

Find out through the use of outside references the answers to the following questions:

1. What was the name chosen by the western counties of Virginia in 1861, when they approved the formation of a new state?

_____

2. Why did the U.S. Supreme Court order West Virginia to pay Virginia almost $12,400,000?

_____

3. Why was it a "natural" for Virginia to vote for secession?

_____

4. What is the state's most important mining product?

_____

5. The easternmost part of West Virginia lies in the Shenandoah Valley, one of the best apple-growing regions in the United States. What two well-known apple varieties were first grown here?

_____

6. What native West Virginian authored *The Good Earth*, winning a Pulitzer prize in 1932 and a Nobel prize in 1938?

_____

7. He invented a machine for making bottles, thus giving a tremendous boost to the Charleston glass industry.

_____

8. What is the highest point in West Virginia?

_____

9. How many senators are in West Virginia, and how many members of the house of delegates?

_____

10. Where was the first capital of West Virginia?

_____

GA1138

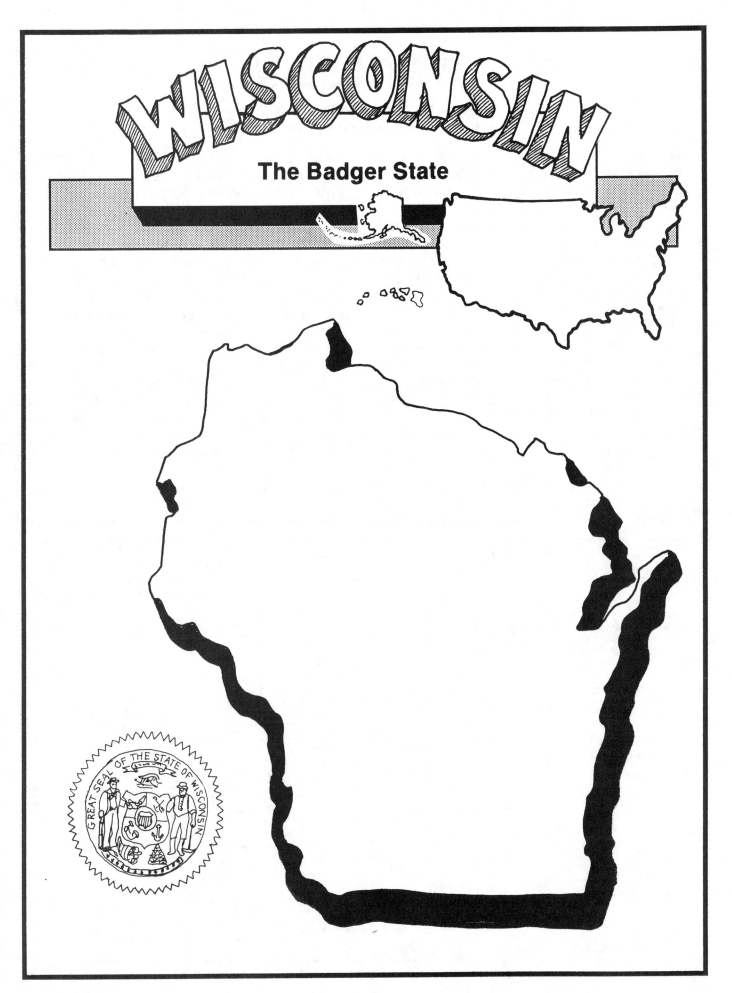

WISCONSIN

The Badger State

GA1138

WISCONSIN
THE BADGER STATE

Wisconsin has become known as America's Dairyland as it is the nation's leading producer of milk, butter and cheese products. While agriculture provides thousands of jobs, the value of its manufactured goods is much greater than its farm products. More than one fourth of Wisconsin's jobs and one third of all wages are generated through industry. Gasoline engines, turbines, canned vegetables and processed dairy products lead the list. Its thick forests covering over half of the state make the paper industry important to Wisconsin; and metal forging, cutlery and hardware also contribute to the state's economy. Wisconsin enjoys an enviable position of balance between manufacturing, agriculture and tourism that gives the state a progressive economy that does not rely too heavily on any one area of income. The natural beauty and recreational resources attract millions of vacationers every year. Almost 15,000 lakes dot the state to the delight of water sports enthusiasts. Energy supplies and some of the raw materials used in manufacturing are often imported, but the state has become an important producer of a wide variety of consumer products. An important reform movement called Progressivism started in the early 1900's and earned Wisconsin a reputation as a model state. It also has consistently been known as a leader in educational innovations. With its balanced economy and progressive outlook, the future of Wisconsin is a bright one indeed.

Before proceeding with your study of Wisconsin, become familiar with these symbols:

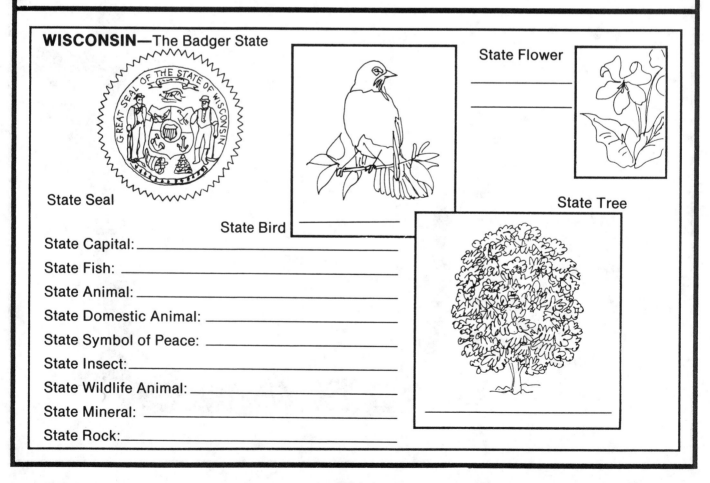

WISCONSIN—The Badger State

State Seal

State Bird

State Flower

State Tree

State Capital: _____

State Fish: _____

State Animal: _____

State Domestic Animal: _____

State Symbol of Peace: _____

State Insect: _____

State Wildlife Animal: _____

State Mineral: _____

State Rock: _____

GA1138

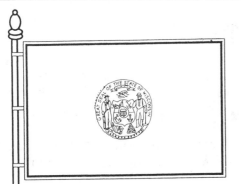

WISCONSIN RECREATION

Wisconsin is truly a land of variety and almost unlimited recreation opportunity. In fact, tourism now ranks as the second greatest revenue producer behind heavy industry. Thirteen percent of the state's work force is employed in tourism with almost two thirds of the people they serve coming from outside Wisconsin. They come to see the 15,000 inland lakes and 20,000 miles of rivers with shorelines ranging from sandy beaches to rugged, rocky coastlines. They travel over 100,000 miles of toll-free roads to over fifty state parks, two national forests and eight state forests. They come to fish, to hunt, to swim, to hike, to bike, to play golf and to enjoy many water sports, and in the winter they turn to cross-country skiing and snowmobiling and ice fishing.

Find and locate the following recreational facilities on your outline map.

These national forests:

Chequamegon National Forest
Nicolet National Forest

These state parks:

Willow River	Heritage Hill	Harrington Beach
Big Bay	Pattison	Nelson Dewey
Peninsula	Council Grounds	Hartman Creek
Buckhorn	Wildcat Mountain	Copper Falls

These state trails:

Bearskin
Tuscobia
Buffalo River
Ahnapee
Sugar River

These other national treasures:

Apostle Islands National Lakeshore
Ice Age National Scientific Reserve
St. Croix National Scenic Riverway

GA1138

HISTORICAL WISCONSIN

While the scenic beauty of Wisconsin has helped to propel it to a high rank on the list of the nation's tourists, it is also a land of history. The rich diversity of its cultural heritage and ethnic past combined with several historical buildings and monuments account for at least a portion of the tourist trade that annually descends on Wisconsin, especially during the summer months. Several of those sites are found on the map below. Find out about each and jot down a brief statement that will identify its signficance to Wisconsin history.

1. Circus World Museum _____
_____

2. Madeline Island Historical Museum _____
_____

3. Old Wade House _____
_____

4. Old World Wisconsin _____
_____

5. Pendarvis_____
_____
_____
_____

6. Stonefield Village _____
_____
_____
_____

7. Villa Louis _____
_____
_____
_____

Find the location of the following: the State Historical Museum, Wisconsin State Capital, Little Norway, Door County, Taliesin and locate them on the map.

GA1138

WISCONSIN TIME LINE

Below are several events that are significant to the history of Wisconsin. The dates when those events took place are on the time line below. Find out when each took place; then write the letter that corresponds to each event in the circle next to the proper date.

A. England received Wisconsin region from France as a result of French and Indian War.

B. Wisconsin became the 30th state.

C. William Hoard organized the Wisconsin Dairymen's Association.

D. Jolliet and Marquette traveled through the Wisconsin area.

E. The nation's first kindergarten was started at Watertown.

F. Groseilliers and Radisson visited Wisconsin.

G. Wisconsin became part of the United States.

H. Congress created the Wisconsin Territory.

I. Jean Nicolet, a French explorer, was the first white man to visit what is now Wisconsin.

J. The Progressive era of Robert La Follette began.

K. The French defeated the Fox Indians.

L. Ringling Brothers started the first circus in Baraboo.

M. Swiss immigrants introduced commercial cheese making.

N. The first practical typewriter was designed by Milwaukee inventors.

O. Robert La Follette was defeated as the Progressive candidate for President.

P. The Peshtigo forest fire killed 1200 people and destroyed millions of dollars of property.

Q. The state legislature created the University of Wisconsin System.

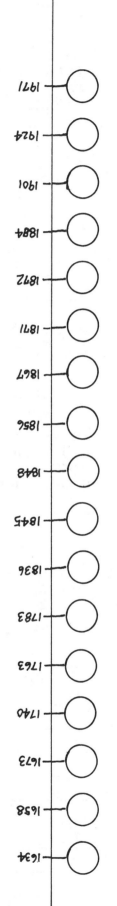

GA1138

FOR FURTHER RESEARCH...

1. Wisconsin has long been noted as a leader in public education and for its innovations that have served as a model for other states to follow. Research the system of public education in Wisconsin and jot down in the space below reasons for its distinction as a leader.

_____

_____

_____

_____

_____

_____

_____

_____

_____

_____

2. Wisconsin has a dramatic geological history that dates back to the Ice Age. In 1791 the Ice Age National Scientific Reserve was established by the federal government to preserve Wisconsin's glacial landforms. Find out about the Ice Age Trail and explain its path in the space below.

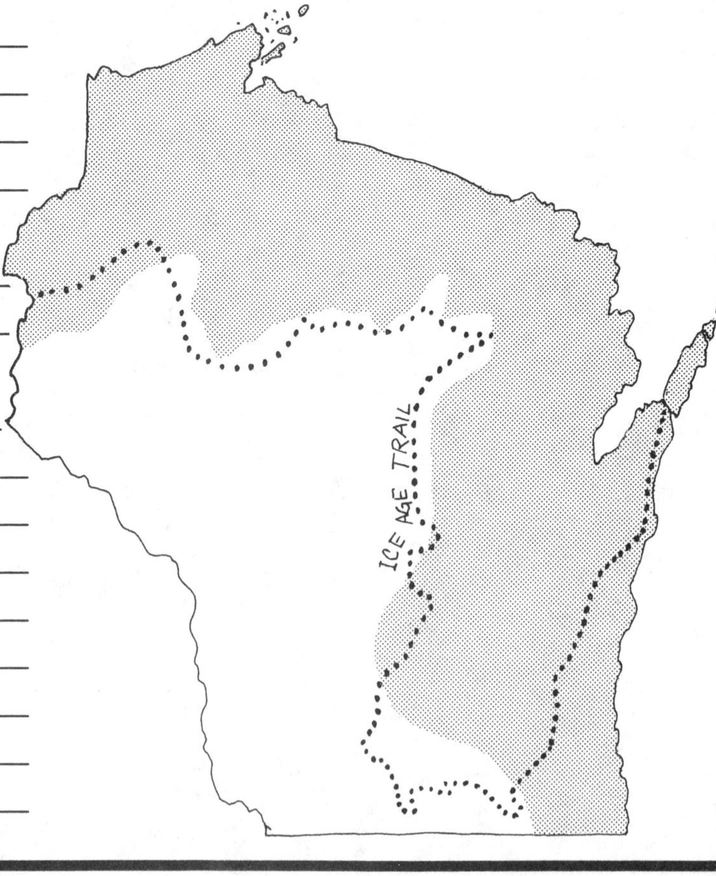

_____

_____

_____

_____

_____

_____

_____

_____

_____

_____

_____

_____

_____

_____

_____

ICE AGE TRAIL

GA1138

WYOMING

The Equality State

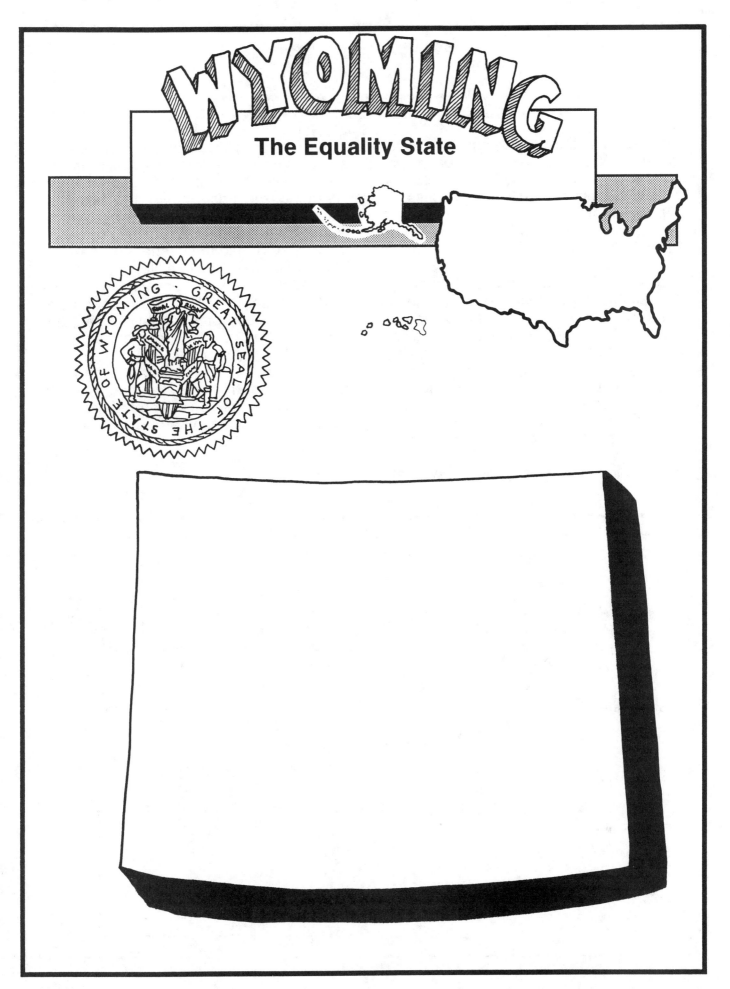

GA1138

WYOMING
THE EQUALITY STATE

Because of its harsh landforms and environments, Wyoming was long regarded as a place to "pass through" rather than one in which people wanted to stay. Thousands of prospectors traveled the Oregon Trail on their way to California during the Gold Rush. The crossing of the Union Pacific brought many permanent residents to the area, and in 1868 the Territory of Wyoming was established by Congress. The majestic beauty of Yellowstone and the Grand Teton National Park as well as Jackson Hole and several other favorite ski resorts makes tourism a huge drawing card to Wyoming businessmen. This state is one of America's leading mineral producers with huge deposits of coal, natural gas, oil, uranium and iron ore. While crop farming is not big in the Wyoming economy due to the terrain and the climate, sheep and cattle ranching does make an important contribution. Wyoming remains one of the last true landmarks of the famed American cowboy. Dude ranches and rodeos help to re-create the true spirit and atmosphere of the early West. Each year in late July, Cheyenne celebrates its Frontier Days, including the world's largest outdoor rodeo, huge parades and top-notch country entertainment. As the nation's energy supplies continue to dwindle, Wyoming's vast mineral deposits give it a promising hope for the future. Its huge size, harsh terrain and sparse population will probably always keep it from becoming an urbanized area.

Find and identify these Wyoming symbols:

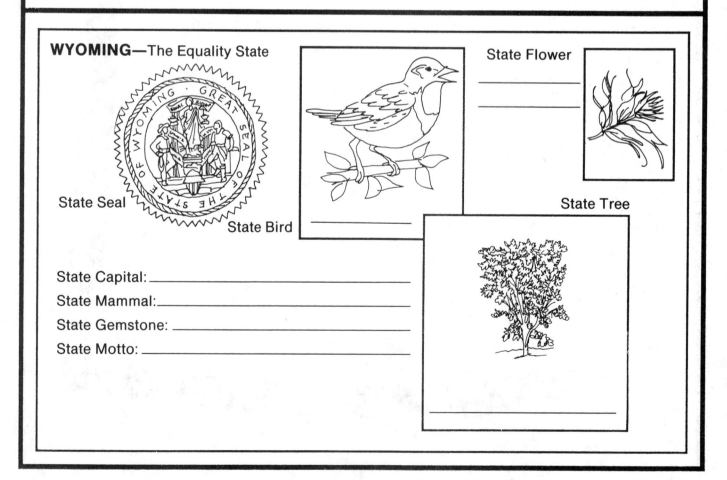

WYOMING—The Equality State

State Seal

State Bird

State Flower

State Tree

State Capital: _____

State Mammal: _____

State Gemstone: _____

State Motto: _____

300

GA1138

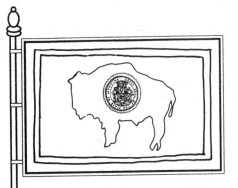

WYOMING MAP STUDY

Pinpoint the location of each of the following on your outline map of Wyoming.

These major recreation areas:

Yellowstone National Park
Grand Teton National Park
Devils Tower National Monument
Fossil Butte National Monument
Bighorn Canyon National Recreation Area
Flaming Gorge National Recreation Area
Hot Springs State Park

YELLOWSTONE AREA

These historial sites:

Ft. Laramie National Historic Site
Ft. Bridger State Historical Site
Oregon Trail Ruts National Historic Landmark
Independence Rock
Old Trail Town
South Pass City
Buffalo Bill Historical Center
J.C. Penney House
Ft. Caspar

These Wyoming cities:

Cheyenne	Buffalo	Sheridan	Gillette
Casper	Jackson	Rock Springs	Marbleton
Laramie	Thermopolis	Cody	Wheatland
Medicine Bow	Sundance	Shoshoni	Saratoga

Draw in these Wyoming rivers:

Little Missouri	Yellowstone	Wind
Snake	Bighorn	Green

Draw in these major transportation arteries:
Interstate 80, Interstate 25, Interstate 90

GA1138

INSIDE WYOMING

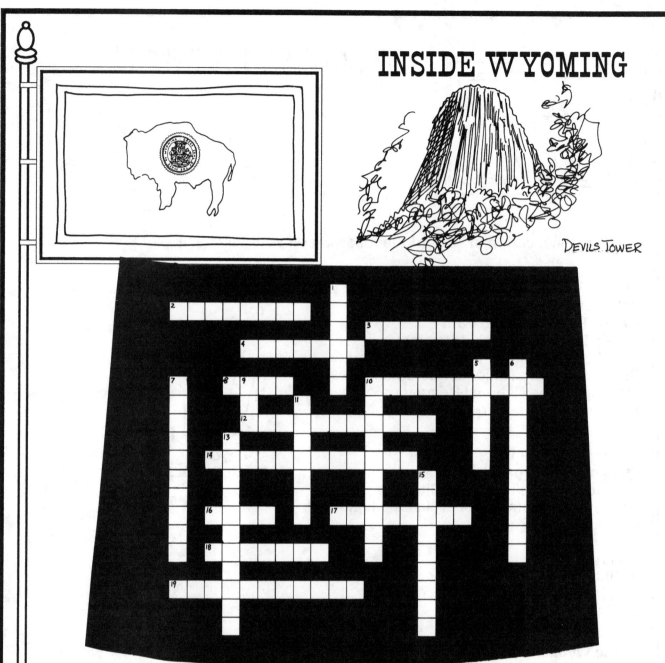

DEVILS TOWER

Read each of the clues below and find the proper answer that will fit into the puzzle.

Across

2. World's first national forest
3. Wyoming is second in the production of this mineral used to produce energy.
4. One of the main industries of Wyoming
8. Wyoming is second in the production of this mineral.
10. Green River is the county seat.
12. State motto
14. Symbol on Wyoming license plate
16. State gemstone
17. State capital
18. Wyoming heads U.S. production of this mineral as well.
19. Nation's first national monument

Down

1. Mineral used in the production of wallboard
5. Fremont County's county seat
6. The nation's first national park
7. Wyoming's state bird
9. Number of representatives from Wyoming in the House
10. One of Wyoming's top agricultural crops
11. The highest point in Wyoming is _____ Peak.
13. Hero of historical museum in Cody
15. Wyoming leads the nation in the production of this mineral.

GA1138

OUTDOOR AMERICA

In 1872 Congress established the first national park in the world in the northwest corner of a land known as Yellowstone. Over 3472 square miles were set aside to be protected for the enjoyment and recreation of those who would visit there. But our National Park System, which spends millions of dollars annually on the maintenance of its treasures, has more goals than satisfying vacationers who travel there. Find out about our National Park System. Why was Yellowstone established? Who deserves most of the credit for the birth of our national parks? What are the major goals of the Park System? What purpose do park rangers serve? Under what federal departments are our national parks financially dependent? How much money does it cost to maintain our Park System? Do you think the money is being well spent? Would our nation be as well off if we didn't have any national parks? Define your findings and feelings into a few well-chosen paragraphs on a separate sheet of paper and share with other members of your class.

GA1138

WYOMING FLORA AND FAUNA

With over 340 species of birds, 78 species of fish, over 100 species of mammals and over 1000 species of vascular plants, Wyoming is truly an outdoor wonderland of living things. This tremendous variety of wildlife can be attributed to an extremely diverse topography. Wyoming is one of the few places left where such numbers of animals can still be seen from the highways. A trek of a few hundred yards will reward the hiker with a look at several different varieties of wildflowers. This fantastic display of nature's finest has made Wyoming a photographer's paradise. Thousands of photographs are taken every year. Your task in this assignment is to find some of those that have been published in magazines and travel folders, identify them and mount them onto a 24" x 36" sheet of poster board. The photos you choose can be all of animals, all of plants or a combination of both. The important thing to remember is to make certain all photos represent wildlife found in Wyoming. It's also important to identify each by gluing a small piece of index card (bearing the identification) beneath the photo.

DEVILS TOWER

304

GA1138

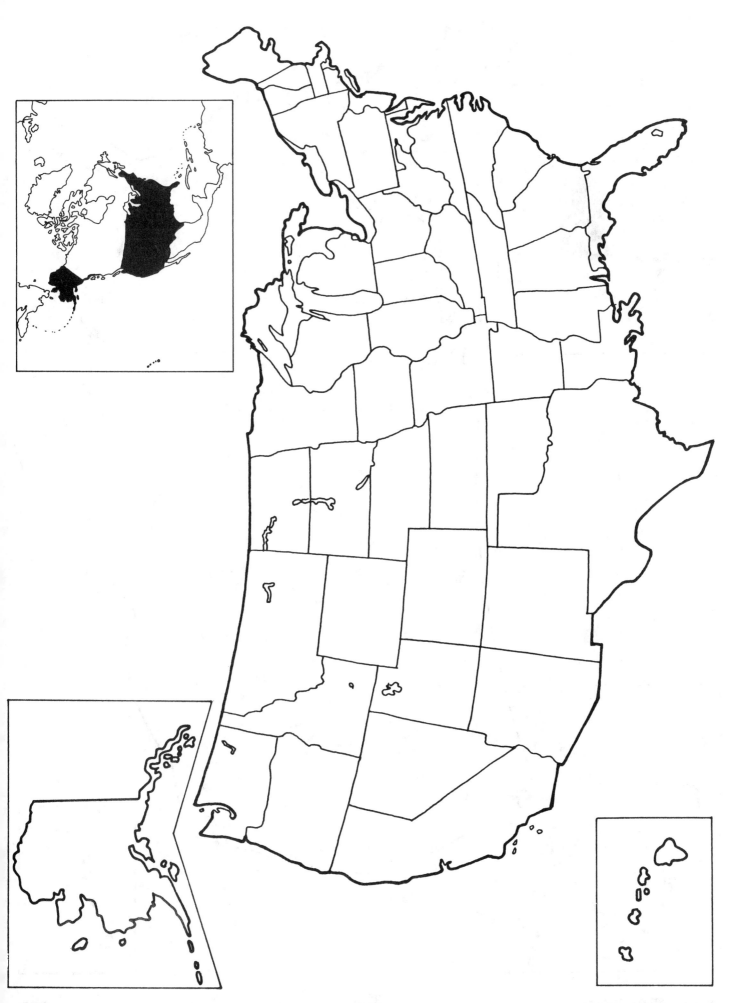

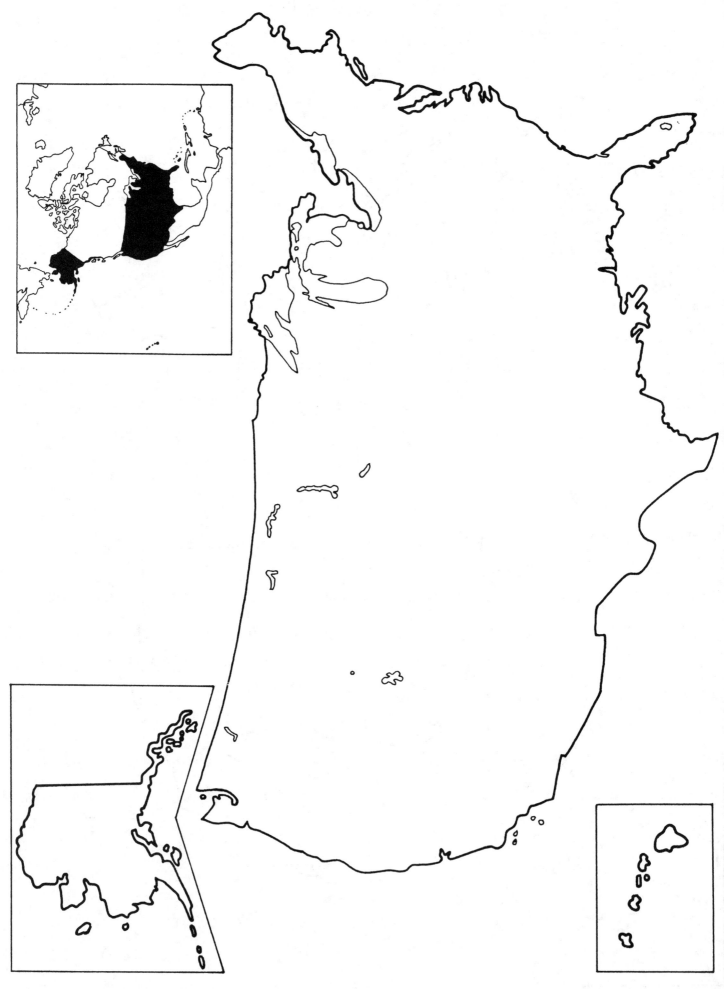

306

ANSWER KEY

Alabama—The Heart of Dixie, Page 2

State Capital: Montgomery
State Bird: Yellowhammer
State Flower: Camellia
State Tree: Southern Pine
State Song: "Alabama"
State Motto: "We Dare Defend Our Rights"

Alabama on the Map, Page 3

4, 5, 2, 8, 6, 1, 7, 3

Notable Alabamians, Page 6

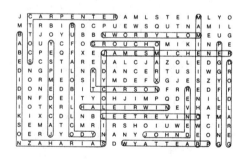

Alaska—The Last Frontier, Page 8

State Capital: Juneau
State Flower: Forget-Me-Not
State Bird: Willow Ptarmigan
State Tree: Sitka Spruce
State Fish: King Salmon
State Gem: Jade
State Mineral: Gold
State Sport: Dog Mushing
State Motto: "North to the Future"

Totem Poles, Page 10

1. T	9. T
2. T	10. T
3. F	11. F
4. T	12. F
5. T	13. T
6. F	14. T
7. F	15. T
8. T	16. T

Arizona—The Grand Canyon State, Page 14

State Capital: Phoenix
State Flower: Saguaro (Giant Cactus)
State Bird: Cactus Wren
State Tree: Paloverde
State Gem: Turquoise
Largest City: Phoenix
State Motto: "Ditat Deus" (God enriches)
Official State Neckwear: Bola Tie

City Cross, Page 17

Across	Down
1. Tempe	1. Tucson
3. Flagstaff	2. Phoenix
4. Cave Creek	7. Winslow
5. Prescott	9. Red Rock
6. Mammoth	10. Snowflake
8. Casa Grande	11. Payson
12. Lupton	14. Yuma
13. Alpine	

Arkansas—The Land of Opportunity, Page 20

State Capital: Little Rock
State Bird: Mockingbird
State Flower: Apple Blossom
State Tree: Pine
State Fruit: South Arkansas Vine Ripe Pink Tomato
State Instrument: Fiddle
State Beverage: Milk
State Insect: Honeybee
State Gem: Diamond
State Motto: "Regnat Populus" (The People Rule)

Capital to Capital, Page 22

1. Olympia, WA, 2303 miles	7. 1078 miles (Trenton)
2. Jackson, MS, 264 miles	8. 477 miles (Austin)
3. 1369 miles	9. Arizona (Phoenix)
4. 1091 miles	10. Charleston, WV
5. Salem, OR, 2186 miles	11. Columbia, SC
6. Oklahoma City, OK, 344 miles	12. Des Moines, IA

Arkansas Agriculture, Page 23

1. T	11. T
2. T	12. F
3. F	13. F
4. T	14. T
5. F	15. T
6. F	16. T
7. F	17. F
8. T	18. T
9. T	19. F
10. F	20. F

California—The Golden State, Page 26

State Capital: Sacramento
State Tree: California Redwood
State Flower: Golden Poppy
State Bird: California Valley Quail
State Animal: Grizzly Bear
State Reptile: Desert Tortoise
State Marine Mammal: California Gray Whale
State Mineral: Gold
State Insect: California Dog-Face Butterfly

California on the Move, Page 28

1. When the earth shifts and the two plates move in different directions, the result is a breakup at the earth's crust.
2. Schools and some homes have been built to withstand strong tremors.
3. Most of the buildings were destroyed by either fire or the earthquake with thousands of lives lost.
4. Soon

Colorado—The Centennial State, Page 32

State Capital: Denver
State Flower: Columbine
State Bird: Lark Bunting
State Tree: Blue Spruce
State Animal: Bighorn Sheep
Largest City: Denver
Population: 3.5 million
State Motto: "Nil sine Numine" (Nothing Without Providence)
Major Manufactures: Steel, film, rubber products, construction
Other Important Sources of Income: Agriculture, livestock, mining, tourism

Colorado's History, Page 34

7, 3, 8, 1, 2, 5, 4, 6, 9

Famous Sons and Daughters, Page 35

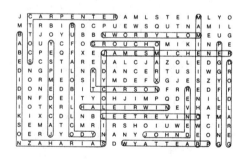

Rocky Mountain High, Page 36

1. F	6. T	11. T
2. F	7. T	12. T
3. F	8. F	13. T
4. F	9. T	14. T
5. F	10. F	15. F

Connecticut—The Constitution State, Page 38

State Capital: Hartford
State Bird: Robin
State Flower: Mountain Laurel
State Tree: White Oak
Largest City: Hartford
Highest Point: Mt. Frissell—2380 feet
Lowest Point: Long Island Sound Shoreline—Sea level
Area: 5009 square miles

Connecticut's Heritage, Page 39

a. Site of 1781 massacre of Americans by British soldiers under direction of traitor Benedict Arnold
b. The home of the famous author during the late 1800's
c. Restored to look like whaling village of 1800's
d. Old gristmill built in 1650
e. Family home built by Nathan's father in 1776
f. Where Nathan taught school from 1773 to 1774
g. New England's oldest stone house built as a stronghold, meeting hall and minister's home
h. National Historic Landmark beautifully restored with period furnishings
i. Rare mid-18th century cut-stone house with stone outdoor bake oven
j. Well-restored colonial house authentically furnished
k. One hundred classic trolleys, oldest operating suburban line in U.S.A.
l. History of fife and drum music in America, with emphasis on Revolutionary and Civil war periods
m. Known as Knapp's Tavern during Revolution, it was the meeting place of war leaders.
n. Home of the only colonial governor to support the war for independence
o. Resting place of Uncas, Mohegan chief who gave original land for settlement of Norwich
p. First government-operated lighthouse in Connecticut
q. Outstanding example of colonial architecture
r. Birthplace of American Episcopacy, historic early 18th century house museum, period furnishings
s. Display of early fire fighting equipment
t. Center chimney colonial housed Hession prisoners during Revolutionary War

Looking into Connecticut, Page 40

1. In colonial America travelling salesmen were so shrewd, stories arose accusing them of selling wooden nutmegs. The stories became so widespread that the state earned the nickname.
2. Hartford is the main headquarters for over 50 insurance companies.
3. Eli Whitney showed the advantage of using interchangeable parts in gunmaking. Whitney's methods led to high-speed assembly line production of today.
4. The large states wanted representation in Congress to be determined by population. The small states wanted equal representation among all states. Roger Sherman authored a plan to create a two-house legislature that would make both large states and small states happy. The result was the present Congress we have with a Senate and a House of Representatives.
5. Because it's along the East Coast, because it lies close to New York and Boston, because its inhabitants are among the highest paid in the U.S., and because of the desirability of the land itself.
6. The Fundamental Orders of 1639 was the first Constitution in the colonies written and approved by the people themselves.

Connecticut Hero Hunt, Page 41

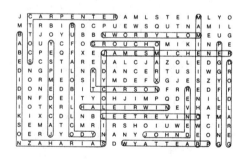

GA1138

Delaware—The First State, Page 44

State Capital: Dover
State Bird: Blue Hen Chicken
State Tree: American Holly
State Flower: Peach Blossom
State Bug: Ladybug
State Fish: Weakfish (sea trout)
State Mineral: Sillimanite
State Motto: "Liberty and Independence"
State Song: "Our Delaware"

Delaware's Storied Past, Page 46

a.	4	i.	8
b.	7	j.	12
c.	10	k.	15
d.	1	l.	3
e.	5	m.	6
f.	11	n.	13
g.	14	o.	9
h.	2		

Delaware—Small Wonder, Page 47

1. 45 miles, 60 minutes
2. 26 miles, 35 minutes
3. 100 miles; 2 hours, 13 minutes
4. 33 miles, 44 minutes
5. 29 miles, 39 minutes
6. 36 miles, 48 minutes
7. 65 miles; 1 hour, 27 minutes
8. 19 miles, 25 minutes
9. 43 miles, 57 minutes
10. 34 miles, 45 minutes
11. 34 miles, 45 minutes
12. 35 miles, 47 minutes

Florida—The Sunshine State, Page 50

State Capital: Tallahassee
State Bird: Mockingbird
State Tree: Sabal Palm
State Flower: Orange Blossom
State Beverage: Orange Juice
State Saltwater Fish: Sailfish
State Freshwater Fish: Largemouth Bass
State Animal: Florida Panther
State Saltwater Mammal: Porpoise
State Reptile: Alligator
State Marine Mammal: Manatee
State Song: "Old Folks at Home"

Florida Time Track, Page 53

a.	1813	i.	1966
b.	1740	j.	1565
c.	1845	k.	1986
d.	1783	l.	1674
e.	1513	m.	1821
f.	1763	n.	1865
g.	1961	o.	1586
h.	1835	p.	1928

Florida's Future . . ., Page 54

1. Because of its position as a melting pot for retirees from the North, immigrants from northern states and millions of tourists from the North
2. Cold weather, fluctuating market price, consumer demand, to name a few
3. Answers will vary. Should include environmental problems, overbuilding, poor, homeless, overpopulation, refugees which result in water problems, sewage problems, etc.
4. Answers will vary.

Georgia—The Peach State, Page 56

State Capital: Atlanta
State Flower: Cherokee Rose
State Bird: Brown Thrasher
State Tree: Live Oak
Largest City: Atlanta
State Song: "Georgia on My Mind"
State Motto: "Wisdom, Justice and Moderation"

Georgia on the Map, Page 57

1.	Atlanta	10.	Cordele
2.	Augusta	11.	Macon
3.	Savannah	12.	Valdosta
4.	Marietta	13.	Athens
5.	Dalton	14.	Albany
6.	Rome	15.	Americus
7.	Moultrie	16.	Waycross
8.	Milledgeville	17.	Gainesville
9.	Decatur	18.	Griffin

1. Savannah River
2. Alapaha River
3. Oconee River
4. St. Marys River
5. Suwannee River
6. Flint River
7. Okefenokee Swamp
8. Lake Sidney Lanier
9. Chattahoochee National Forest
10. Oconee National Forest

Georgia Crossword, Page 58

Across	Down
1. Cotton	1. Clayton
4. Carter	2. De Soto
5. Stone Mountain	3. Oglethorpe
7. Harris	6. Masters
9. Sherman	8. Augusta
11. De Aviles	10. Mitchell
13. Whitney	12. Low
14. Savannah	

Georgia on My Mind, Page 60

1. Atlanta
2. Jekyll Island
3. Hoagy Carmichael
4. Marta
5. Albany
6. Dahlonega
7. Augusta
8. Peachtree Street
9. Savannah
10. Robert E. Lee, Stonewall Jackson, Jefferson Davis
11. Valdosta
12. Perry
13. Six Flags over Georgia
14. Callaway Gardens
15. Columbus
16. Lookout Mountain

Hawaii—The Aloha State, Page 62

State Capital: Honolulu
State Tree: Kukui
State Flower: Hibiscus
State Bird: Nene (Hawaiian Goose)
State Motto: "Ua mau ke ea o ka aina i ka pono" (The life of the land is perpetuated in righteousness.)
Chief Products: Sugarcane, pineapple, beef cattle, fishing, mining, food products, clothing
Largest City: Honolulu

Islands from the Sea, Page 64

1. Hot lava burst through a large crack in the ocean floor. As the lava cooled it hardened into cone-shaped piles. Later the process was repeated over and over. After millions of years of this, the lava flows reached above the water level and the islands were formed. Years later the lava broke up and soil was formed.
2. Answers will vary. Should include spores carried by winds, seeds clinging to bird feathers, seeds stuck on floating logs and birds being blown off course and any other plausible theory (since answer is mostly speculative).
3. Hawaii still has two active volcanoes that continue to erupt. Mauna Loa and Kilauea Crater erupt and create an additional buildup of lava.

Trade Winds and Tropical Breezes, Page 65

1. The trade winds come from the northeast bringing moisture from the ocean. As they blow onto the mountains along the northeast coast, they are pushed upward. The clouds become cool and can no longer hold the moisture, so there is rain. The leeward side is much drier because there is little moisture left.
2. The winds keep the temperature fairly constant all year long. Temperatures in the lowlands average about 77° F in July and 71° F in January.

Hawaiian Talk, Page 66

yes	feast
eat	thanks
hello	toward the sea
no	newcomer
work	bird
sleep	mountain
angry	chant
dance	family
food	flower
child	hole
sugarcane	woman
wreath/garland	fresh water

Idaho—The Gem State, Page 68

State Capital: Boise
State Flower: Syringa
State Tree: Western White Pine
State Bird: Mountain Bluebird
State Horse: Appaloosa
State Gemstone: Garnet
State Motto: "Esto Perpetua" (Let it be perpetual.)

Idaho's Story Retold, Page 70

1.	1877	9.	1860
2.	1805	10.	1862
3.	1963	11.	1834
4.	1855	12.	1905
5.	1890	13.	1863
6.	1892, 1899	14.	1951
7.	1809	15.	1959, 1961, 1968
8.	1860		

Illinois—The Prairie State, Page 74

State Capital: Springfield
State Tree: White Oak
State Flower: Violet
State Bird: Cardinal
Largest City: Chicago
State Insect: Monarch Butterfly
State Mineral: Fluorite
State Animal: White-Tailed Deer
State Song: "Illinois"
State Slogan: Land of Lincoln

A Sweep Through History, Page 76

a.	1763	f.	1858	k.	1893	p.	1809	u.	1968
b.	1787	g.	1865	l.	1886	q.	1844	v.	1717
c.	1818	h.	1837	m.	1820	r.	1860	w.	1783
d.	1673	i.	1864	n.	1778	s.	1847	x.	1800
e.	1832	j.	1871	o.	1699	t.	1848	y.	1889

Tourism in Illinois, Page 77

1. to visit friends and relatives
2. 17%
3. California
4. $8,662,000
5. $4 billion
6. $300+
7. 65%—from $183 to $303

The Windy City, Page 78

a. Picasso Sculpture in Daley Center
b. Board of Trade
c. Old Water Tower
d. John Hancock Building
e. Sears Tower

Indiana—The Hoosier State, Page 80

State Capital: Indianapolis
State Bird: Cardinal
State Flower: Peony
State Tree: Tulip Tree
State Song: "On the Banks of the Wabash"

Indiana Time Line, Page 83

1.	p	9.	e
2.	c	10.	b
3.	f	11.	g
4.	i	12.	h
5.	l	13.	d
6.	a	14.	m
7.	k	15.	j
8.	n	16.	o

The Greatest Spectacle in Sports, Page 84

Across	Down
2. Johncock	1. Vukovich
4. Sneva	3. Harroun
6. Clark	4. Sachs
7. Shaw	5. Hanks
9. Unser, B.	8. Andretti
11. Ward	9. Unser, A.
13. Foyt	10. Rose
14. Mears	12. Rahal
15. Hanks	
16. Hill	

GA1138

Iowa—The Hawkeye State, Page 86

State Capital: Des Moines
State Flower: Wild Rose
State Bird: Eastern Goldfinch (Wild Canary)
State Tree: Oak
Population: 2.9 million (ranks 27th)
Largest City: Des Moines
Area: 56,290 square miles (ranks 25th)
State Motto: "Our liberties we prize and our rights we will maintain."
Meaning of Iowa: "Beautiful Land"

Iowa Trivia, Page 87

1. 7
2. Mesquakie
3. Burlington
4. 95
5. Bix Biederbecke
6. Covered bridges
7. Britt
8. Register's Annual Great Bicycle Ride Across Iowa
9. Indianola
10. Knoxville
11. August
12. Mount Pleasant
13. The Drake Relays
14. Stone City
15. Kalona
16. Pella or Orange City

"IQ"—Iowa Quotient, Page 88

Across
2. Missouri
6. Lewis
7. Mason City
10. Des Moines
11. Cyclones
12. three
13. Newton
14. Hawkeyes

Down
1. John Wayne
2. Mississippi
3. West Branch
4. WHO
5. ACT
8. Joliet
9. Corning

Iowa's Greatest Resource—Her Land, Page 90

1. Cedar Rapids
2. $400 per acre
3. $184,000
4. $224,000
5. $544,000
6. $320,000
7. Council Bluffs

Kansas—The Sunflower State, Page 92

State Capital: Topeka
State Bird: Western Meadowlark
State Flower: Sunflower
State Tree: Cottonwood
State Song: "Home on the Range"

Kansas, Crossroads of America, Page 95

Across
2. Missouri
3. Eisenhower
5. Brown
6. Pike
8. Jayhawkers
11. Lawrence
13. Curtis
14. Mt. Sunflower

Down
1. Hickok
2. Mennonites
4. Higley
7. Kansas
9. Robinson
10. Wheat
12. Frémont

For Further Research. . ., Page 96

1. In 1854 Congress passed the Kansas-Nebraska Act, giving both the North and South the right to decide whether Kansas would be a slave or free state. There was violence and bloodshed between the two forces trying to populate the new territory.
2. Responses here will no doubt vary. Accept reasonable answers.
3. The coming of the railroad brought Texas cattlemen to drive their herds to connect them to eastern markets.
4. Kansas has a reputation as a progressive, innovative state that includes several highlights in history where Kansas took the role as "leader."

Kentucky—The Bluegrass State, Page 98

State Capital: Frankfort
State Bird: Kentucky Cardinal
State Flower: Goldenrod
State Tree: Kentucky Coffeetree
State Fish: Kentucky Bass
State Wild Animal: Grey Squirrel
State Motto: "United We Stand, Divided We Fall"
State Song: "My Old Kentucky Home"

Kentucky Time Line, Page 99

a. 1774
b. 1792
c. 1815
d. 1750
e. 1825
f. 1978
g. 1767
h. 1861-1865
i. 1775
j. 1809
k. 1955
l. 1904-1909
m. 1944
n. 1936
o. 1963

A Frontier Legend, Page 101

1. In a cabin near Reading, Pennsylvania
2. Quaker
3. Tick-Licker
4. John Finley
5. North Carolina
6. Rebecca Bryan
7. Cumberland Gap
8. Boonesborough
9. The Wilderness Road
10. Answers will vary.

The Most Exciting Two Minutes in Sports, Page 102

[word search puzzle solution]

Louisiana—The Pelican State, Page 104

State Capital: Baton Rouge
State Bird: Brown Pelican
State Flower: Magnolia
State Tree: Bald Cypress
State Gemstone: Agate
State Insect: Honeybee
State Fossil: Petrified Palmwood
State Dog: Catahoula Leopard
State Motto: "Union, Justice and Confidence"

Louisiana's Past, Page 106

Across
1. Jazz
2. Creoles
3. Cajuns
6. De Soto
7. Napoleon
9. La Salle
11. Van Cliburn
13. Mardi Gras
14. Mississippi

Down
1. Jackson
3. Crozat
4. Bienville
5. Louis Armstrong
8. Parishes
10. Law
12. Audubon

Maine—The Pine Tree State, Page 110

State Capital: Augusta
State Bird: Chickadee
State Tree: White Pine
State Flower: White Pine Cone and Tassel
Largest City: Portland
State Animal: Moose
State Gem: Tourmaline
State Fish: Landlocked Salmon
State Insect: Honeybee
State Cat: Maine Coon Cat
State Motto: "Dirigo" (I direct.)

Crossing Maine's History, Page 111

1. John Smith
2. Hannibal Hamlin
3. John Cabot
4. Edmund Muskie
5. Ferdinando Gorges
6. Benedict Arnold
7. Franklin Pierce
8. Leif Ericson
9. David Ingram
10. Popham Colony
11. George Waymouth
12. Hanson Gregory

A Search Through Maine, Page 113

[word search puzzle solution]

Maryland—The Old Line State, Page 116

State Capital: Annapolis
State Flower: Black-Eyed Susan
State Tree: White Oak (Wye Oak)
State Bird: Baltimore Oriole
Largest City: Baltimore
State Song: "Maryland, My Maryland"
State Motto: "Fatti Maschii Parole Femine" (Manly Deeds, Womanly Words)

Maryland's Past, Page 120

5, 7, 9, 3, 11, 1, 8, 13, 4, 12, 16, 17, 2, 6, 14, 18, 20, 10, 15, 19

Massachusetts—The Bay State, Page 122

State Capital: Boston
State Bird: Chickadee
State Flower: Mayflower
State Tree: American Elm
Largest City: Boston

Massachusetts Time Line, Page 124

a. 3
b. 8
c. 10
d. 7
e. 1
f. 9
g. 13
h. 14
i. 16
j. 2
k. 5
l. 12
m. 17
n. 6
o. 18
p. 15
q. 4
r. 11
s. 19

Massachusetts Name Hunt, Page 125

Freedom Trail, Page 126

1. Site of many pre-Revolution protests by angry colonists
2. In 1770 five patriots were killed when British soldiers fired into a mob of colonists.
3. Seat of the colonial government
4. On Milk Street
5. Anti-British speeches were given here that inspired the Boston Tea Party.
6. Meeting place for Boston writers in the 1800's
7. The Boston Latin School opened in 1635 and stood until 1922.
8. Stands near the old City Hall
9. Samuel Adams and Paul Revere are buried here.
10. U.S. military stored gunpowder here during the War of 1812.
11. Capitol of Massachusetts
12. Nation's first Unitarian church
13. Oldest house in Boston built in 1670
14. A park with bronze tablets telling Boston's history to 1918
15. Lanterns hung here to warn patriots of an attack.
16. Has graves that date back to 1660.

Michigan—The Great Lake State, Page 128

State Capital: Lansing
State Bird: Robin
State Flower: Apple Blossom
State Tree: White Pine
Largest City: Detroit
State Song: "Michigan, My Michigan"
State Fish: Brook Trout
State Motto: "Si quaeris peninsulam amoenam, circumspice" (If you seek a pleasant peninsula, look about you.)

Michigan's People, Page 130

1. Henry Ford
2. Jacques Marquette
3. Tecumseh
4. Gabriel Richard
5. Ransom Olds
6. Glenn Seaborg
7. Gerald Ford
8. John Jacob Astor
9. Ralph Bunche
10. William Beaumont
11. Walter Chrysler
12. Sojourner Truth
13. Bruce Catton
14. William Durant
15. Charles Lindbergh

Michigan Time Table, Page 131

13, 5, 12, 7, 10, 8, 1, 2, 4, 14, 3, 11, 15, 6, 9

Center Stage, Page 132

Minnesota—The Gopher State, Page 134

State Capital: St. Paul
State Tree: Norway (Red) Pine
State Flower: Pink and White Lady's-Slipper
State Bird: Common Loon (Great Northern Diver)
State Fish: Walleye Pike
State Grain: Wild Rice
State Fungus: Morel Mushroom
State Gemstone: Lake Superior Agate
State Motto: "L'E toile du Nord" (The Star of the North)

What to Do with the Map, Page 135

1. Split Rock Lighthouse—Built in 1910, the historic old lighthouse saw nearly sixty years of service serving as a sentinel for Minnesota's inhospitable Lake Superior shoreline.
2. Lindbergh House—Located in Charles A. Lindbergh State Park, two miles south of Little Falls. Lindbergh House was the childhood home of the famous aviator Charles A. Lindbergh—the first to fly solo over the Atlantic.
3. James J. Hill House—Located in St. Paul, the Hill mansion is a very imposing sandstone edifice built in 1891 by the "Empire Builder," the founder of the Great Northern Railroad.
4. Forest History Center—Deep in the woods of northern Minnesota, the center is an authentically constructed turn-of-the-century logging camp.
5. Jeffers Petroglyphs—The carvings of almost 2000 representations of human figures, weapons and animals (some as old as 3000 B.C.) that present definition to our past.
6. Oliver H. Kelley Farm—Family farm of the man who founded the Patrons of Husbandry, better known as the Grange.

7. Comstock House—The home of two important Minnesotans—Soloman (a leading political figure and entrepreneur) and Ada Comstock (the first dean of women at the University of Minnesota).
8. Fort Snelling—The guardian of American interests in the upper Northwest. The fort was the center of government policy and administration during the years prior to Minnesota's statehood.
9. North West Company Fur Post—Reconstructed trading post that served as wintering quarters for Montreal-based company that traded with Ojibwe Indians.
10. Grand Mound—An immense mound of earth, the monument of the Laurel Indians. It is the largest prehistoric burial mound in the upper Midwest.

Famous Minnesotans, Page 136

Across
1. Mondale
3. Garland
7. Neiman
8. Lange
9. Schultz
10. Mayos
11. Lindbergh
13. Hill
15. Severeid
16. Burger

Down
2. Dylan
4. Anderson
5. Fitzgerald
6. Bly
12. Humphrey
14. Lewis

Mississippi—The Magnolia State, Page 140

State Capital: Jackson
State Bird: Mockingbird
State Flower: Magnolia
State Tree: Magnolia
Largest City: Jackson
State Song: "Go Mis-sis-sip-pi"

All Roads to Jackson, Page 141

Cleveland-Jackson 127
Greenwood-Jackson 96
Clarksdale-Jackson 151
Southaven-Jackson 198
Tupelo-Jackson 170
Greenville-Jackson 115
Starkville-Jackson 125
Columbus-Jackson 147
Vicksburg-Jackson 44
Clinton-Jackson 10
Pearl-Jackson 5
Meridian-Jackson 93
Laurel-Jackson 84
Hattiesburg-Jackson 88
Moss Point-Jackson 181
Biloxi-Jackson 165
Gulfport-Jackson 157
Pascagoula-Jackson 184
Natchez-Jackson 102

Mississippi Time Line, Page 143

a. 1861
b. 1763
c. 1964
d. 1939
e. 1540
f. 1863
g. 1798
h. 1870
i. 1781
j. 1699
k. 1960
l. 1936
m. 1817
n. 1969
o. 1858

Molders of Mississippi, Page 144

1. Jefferson Davis
2. Stephen D. Lee
3. John A. Quitman
4. William Faulkner
5. Elvis Presley
6. Eudora Welty
7. Laurence Jones
8. Jimmie Rodgers
9. Leontyne Price
10. L.Q.C. Lamar
11. Jean Baptiste Bienville

Missouri—The Show Me State, Page 146

State Capital: Jefferson City
State Bird: Bluebird
State Flower: Hawthorn
State Tree: Flowering Dogwood
State Musical Instrument: Fiddle
State Song: "Missouri Waltz"
State Insect: Honeybee
State Rock: Mozarkite
State Mineral: Galena

Missouri History, Page 148

a. 2
b. 5
c. 7
d. 1
e. 9
f. 14
g. 3
h. 8
i. 10
j. 13
k. 4
l. 12
m. 6
n. 11

Famous Missourians, Page 149

Spirit of St. Louis, Page 150

1. Gateway Arch
2. Laclede's Landing
3. Busch Memorial Stadium
4. St. Louis Zoo
5. Union Station
6. *President*
7. Grant's Farm
8. Six Flags over Mid-America
9. The Muny
10. Jewel Box
11. Missouri Botanical Garden
12. Missouri Historical Society

Montana—The Treasure State, Page 152

State Capital: Helena
State Bird: Western Meadowlark
State Flower: Bitterroot
State Tree: Ponderosa Pine
State Grass: Bluebunch Wheatgrass
State Fish: Blackspotted Cutthroat Trout
State Gemstones: Agate and Sapphire
State Animal: Grizzly Bear
State Motto: "Oro y Plata" (Gold and Silver)
Largest City: Billings

Montana Math, Pages 153-154

1. 1,527,116 acres
2. 10,999 feet
3. 3.6; 56.4; 2.4; 5.1; 4.0; 1.8; 20.4; 1.9; 4.5; Total near 100%
4. 174.5; 608; 257.2; 198.29 students
5. $218.18
6. 29.7%
7. 21.1% increase; 2000

Nebraska—The Cornhusker State, Page 158

State Capital: Lincoln
State Bird: Western Meadowlark
State Flower: Goldenrod
State Tree: Cottonwood
State Insect: Honeybee
State Gem: Blue Agate
State Rock: Prairie Agate
State Grass: Little Blue Stem
State Motto: "Equality Before the Law"

Nebraska's Past, Page 160

15, 10, 1, 6, 9, 3, 11, 14, 5, 7, 4, 12, 8, 2, 13

Nebraska Search, Page 162

GA1138

Nevada—The Silver State, Page 164
State Capital: Carson City
State Flower: Sagebrush
State Tree: Single-Leaf Piñon
State Bird: Mountain Bluebird
Largest City: Las Vegas
State Motto: "All for Our Country"

Nevada History, Page 167
5, 1864
10, 1936
2, 1843-45
7, 1907
3, 1859
11, 1951
8, 1910
1, 1776
12, 1971
4, 1861
6, 1877-81
9, 1931

Our Driest State, Page 168
1. Most of the rivers that flow into lakes and streams have no outlets. In the summer many of them dry up under the hot desert sun.
2. Built during the Depression (1931-1936), the massive structure is 725 feet high and 1244 feet long. The reservoir created by the dam is Lake Mead, one of the largest man-made lakes. It is 115 miles long and provides much of the Southwest with electricity and water.
3. Most of the irrigated farms are near river valleys. Water is also pumped from wells to irrigate crops from overhead sprinklers. Chief crops are alfalfa seed, barley, hay, oats and wheat.

New Hampshire—The Granite State, Page 170
State Capital: Concord
State Bird: Purple Finch
State Tree: White Birch
State Flower: Purple Lilac
State Gem: Smoky Quartz
State Rock: Granite
State Motto: "Live Free or Die"
State Animal: White-Tailed Deer
State Insect: Ladybug
State Amphibian: Red-Spotted Newt

Famous Sons and Daughters, Page 172
1. Daniel Webster
2. Franklin Pierce
3. Leonard Wood
4. Harlan Stone
5. Alan Shepard
6. Edna Dean Proctor
7. Walter Kittredge
8. Horace Greeley
9. Mary Baker Eddy
10. Salmon Chase
11. Edward MacDowell
12. Robert Frost
13. John Mason

New Hampshire Time Capsule, Page 173
a. 3
b. 2
c. 9
d. 5
e. 13
f. 10
g. 14
h. 12
i. 4
j. 11
k. 8
l. 1
m. 6
n. 7

Wildlife in New Hampshire, Page 174

New Jersey—The Garden State, Page 176
State Capital: Trenton
State Bird: Eastern Goldfinch
State Flower: Purple Violet
State Tree: Red Oak
Largest City: Newark
State Animal: Horse
State Insect: Honeybee
State Motto: "Liberty and Prosperity"

New Jersey Map Mysteries, Page 177
1. Trenton
2. Menlo Park
3. Bayonne
4. Newark
5. South Orange
6. Jersey City
7. East Orange
8. Paterson
9. Hoboken
10. Camden
11. Elizabeth
12. Passaic
13. Perth Amboy
14. New Brunswick
15. Atlantic City
16. Princeton

First in New Jersey, Page 178
1. f
2. g
3. j
4. m
5. n
6. h
7. d
8. l
9. q
10. a
11. b
12. c
13. o
14. p
15. s
16. i
17. e
18. r
19. k
20. t

Crossing in New Jersey, Page 179
Across
2. Crane
4. Wilson
8. Washington
11. Freneau
14. Rockefeller
15. Inness
17. Woolman
19. Cleveland
20. Mey
21. Edison

Down
1. Morris
3. York
5. Lenox
6. Cooper
7. Singer
8. Whitman
9. Verrazano
10. Hudson
12. Berkeley
13. Roebling
16. Einstein
18. Morse

New Mexico—The Land of Enchantment, Page 182
State Capital: Santa Fe
State Bird: Road Runner
State Flower: Yucca Flower
State Tree: Piñon or Nut Pine
Largest City: Albuquerque
State Motto: "Crescit Eundo" (It grows as it goes.)

A Spanish Past, Page 185
Across
4. Onate
6. Mendoza
9. Rodriguez
10. Pike
13. Popé
14. Vial
15. Vargas

Down
1. Coronado
2. Pershing
3. Marcos
5. Espejo
7. Esteban
8. Granada
11. Peralta
12. Calhoun

Lost Pueblos, Page 186

New York—The Empire State, Page 188
State Capital: Albany
State Bird: Bluebird
State Tree: Sugar Maple
State Flower: Rose
State Fruit: Apple
State Fish: Brook Trout
State Gem: Garnet
State Animal: Beaver
State Motto: "Excelsior" (Ever upward)
Population: 17,558,165
Area: 49,576 square miles
Largest City: New York City (nation's largest)

Time Capsule: New York, Page 189
1. 1609
2. 1755
3. 1735
4. 1890
5. 1827
6. 1664
7. 1524
8. 1781
9. 1550's
10. 1788
11. 1901
12. 1825
13. 1900
14. 1931
15. 1831
16. 1763
17. 1626
18. 1614
19. 1625

New Yorkers of the 20th Century, Page 190
1. Theodore Roosevelt
2. George Meany
3. George Eastman
4. Susan Anthony
5. Irving Berlin
6. Arthur Miller
7. Langston Hughes
8. Samuel Gompers
9. Jerome Kern
10. Margaret Mead
11. Leonard Bernstein
12. Franklin Roosevelt
13. Nelson Rockefeller
14. Gene Sarazen
15. Jonas Salk
16. Sugar Ray Robinson
17. Duke Ellington

Attracting Tourists to New York, Page 192
1. a
2. e
3. j
4. b
5. h
6. c
7. f
8. i
9. d
10. g

North Carolina—The Tar Heel State, Page 194
State Capital: Raleigh
State Flower: Flowering Dogwood
State Bird: Cardinal
State Tree: Pine
Population: 5.9 million
State Motto: "Esse quam videri" (To be, rather than to seem)
Most Important Agricultural Crop: Tobacco
Highest Point: 6684 feet
Lowest Point: Sea level (0) along Atlantic Coast
Largest City: Charlotte

Early History of North Carolina, Page 196
1. d
2. a
3. i
4. b
5. k
6. c
7. g
8. h
9. e
10. f
11. l
12. j

For Further Research. . ., Page 197
1. During the Civil War, North Carolina fought with the Confederacy. During one fierce battle some of the Confederate troops retreated, leaving the North Carolina soldiers to fight alone. The North Carolinians supposedly threatened to put tar on the heels of the other troops so they would not abandon the cause.
2. Because of the islands, reefs and sandbars that make up the treacherous coastline along North Carolina, the seas are among the most dangerous in the world. Many ships have been wrecked along this area by the rough seas and difficult current.
3. The leader, John White, went back to England for supplies and returned in 1590 to find the colony completely vanished. It became known as the "Lost Colony."
4. Major universities are located at Durham (Duke), Raleigh (North Carolina State) and Chapel Hill (University of North Carolina)—all three within a few miles of each other, all three spending many dollars annually on scientific research.

GA1138

Mileage Master, Page 198

1. 91 miles	9. 215 miles
2. 352 miles	10. 81 miles
3. 28 miles	11. 63 miles
4. 144 miles	12. 199 miles
5. 93 miles	13. 69 miles
6. 220 miles	14. 75 miles
7. 178 miles	15. 111 miles
8. 203 miles	

North Dakota—The Flickertail State, Page 200

State Capital: Bismarck
State Bird: Western Meadowlark
State Tree: American Elm
State Flower: Wild Prairie Rose
State Fish: Northern Pike
State Motto: "Liberty and Union, Now and Forever, One and Inseparable."

North Dakota on the Map, Page 201

```
T  S  I (S  K  R  O  F  D  N  A  R  G) E  T  K  B
A  H  O  N (A  D  E (D (T  O  N  I  M) G (R) M  Y
H  Y  B  N  L  L  F (E  N  S  T  A  S  F  E  I  T
N  O  I  K  L  L  O  V  O  N  W (B) C  F  D  V  L
(M  I  S  S  O  U  R  I  R  I  V  E  R) U  R  U  D
P  R  M  M  R  T  T  L  U  K  H  A  O  O  I  L  N
(B  M  A  O  A  C  Y  S  R  C  I  C  S  N  O  L  W
(O  G  R  A  F) T  A  L  U  I  I (H) B  W  E  P  E
W  O  C  P  I  S  T  A  L  D  E  T  Y  R  A  U
M  R  K  S  E  E  E  K  L  S  E  T  D  S  A  M  C
A  A (N  W  O  T  S) E  M  A  J) B  O  Y  B  T  H
(N  A  P  O  L  E  O  N) D  O  Y  S  A  W  O  I  T
(T  H  E  O  D  O  R  E  R  O  O  S  E  V  E  L  T)
```

North Dakota Time Capsule, Page 202

1. 1804-1806	6. 1951	11. 1989
2. 1861	7. 1818	12. 1812
3. 1889	8. 1968	13. 1682
4. 1738	9. 1803	14. 1956
5. 1915	10. 1863	15. 1986

North Dakota Trivia, Page 204

1. Unlike other domed capital buildings, it's in a skyscraper.
2. A North American ground squirrel
3. Red River Valley, The Drift Prairie, The Great Plains
4. wheat, flaxseed, sunflower seeds
5. 212 miles, 360 miles, 17th
6. 3506 ft. at White Butte; 750 ft. in Pembina County
7. 652,717 (1980 census), 46th (1980 census)
8. 2, 1, 53, 106
9. Northern Pacific Railroad
10. lignite coal

Ohio—The Buckeye State, Page 206

State Capital: Columbus
State Flower: Scarlet Carnation
State Bird: Cardinal
State Tree: Buckeye
State Stone: Flint
State Insect: Ladybug
State Beverage: Tomato Juice
State Motto: "With God, all things are possible."
State Fossil: Isotelus Trilobite
State Animal: White-Tailed Deer
State Wildflower: White Trillium
Population: 10.8 million (ranks 6th)
Largest City: Cleveland, 575,000

Famous Ohioans, Page 207

1. Cy Young	14. Tecumseh
2. Edwin M. Stanton	15. Benjamin Harrison
3. Ulysses S. Grant	16. James Garfield
4. Harvey S. Firestone	17. John D. Rockefeller
5. William McKinley	18. John Sherman
6. Horace Mann	19. Joseph Strauss
7. Annie Oakley	20. William Henry Harrison
8. Zane Grey	21. Rutherford B. Hayes
9. Warren G. Harding	22. George Custer
10. John Brown	23. Clarence Darrow
11. John Chapman	24. John Bingham
12. Daniel Beard	25. John Clem
13. Barney Oldfield	

Ohio Counties, Page 208

1. Scioto	6. Defiance
2. Cuyahoga	7. Auglaize
3. Wyandot	8. Licking
4. Medina	9. Columbiana
5. Champaign	10. Perry

Presidental Tour, Page 209

16 hours, 25 minutes

Ohio's Cities and Interstates, Page 210

1. 2,518,088 (depends on census used)
2. 23%
3. Accept reasonable answers.
4. Interstate 70: Columbus, Dayton
   Interstate 71: Akron, Cincinnati, Cleveland, Columbus
   Interstate 75: Cincinnati, Dayton, Toledo
   Interstate 76: Akron, Youngstown
   Interstate 77: Akron, Canton, Cleveland
   Interstate 80: none directly
   Interstate 90: Cleveland

Oklahoma—The Sooner State, Page 212

State Capital: Oklahoma City
State Bird: Scissor-Tailed Flycatcher
State Tree: Redbud
State Wildflower: Indian Blanket
State Floral Emblem: Mistletoe
State Rock: Barite Rose Rock
State Animal: American Buffalo
State Fish: White Bass
State Grass: Indian Grass
State Reptile: Mountain Boomer (Collared Lizard)
State Musical Instrument: Fiddle
State Song: "Oklahoma!"

Oklahoma Cowboys, Page 214

1. The cattle were in Texas. The market was in the East. The closest way to get the cattle there was to drive them through Oklahoma to the railroads in Kansas. Before long huge ranches sprang up in Oklahoma as well.
2. a. Marlow Brothers
   b. Bill Doolin
   c. Rose Dunn
   d. Belle Starr

Oklahoma Sons and Daughters, Page 216

```
O  I  C (R  E  G  I  T  Y  N  N  H  O  J) N  R  A
S  U (M  A  T  C  O  H  C) I  Y  A  D  T  I  E  L
A  L  I  R (S  E  Q  U  O  Y  A  H) E  O  L  H  C
(B  E  L  L  E  S  T  A  R  R) T  H  F  I  O  C  A
H  D  L  S  E (E  P  R  O  H  T  M  I  J) O  S  T
T  S  R  T (G  E  R  O  N  I  M  O) S  R  D  T  A
N  E  O (E  L  L  A  S  A  L) T  A  D  O  L  I  M
I  H  G  U  F  Y  M  R  D  E  Y  H  T  M  K  F
D  P  E (S  E  M  I  N  O  L  E) I  E  F  I  R  A
W  S  R  L (E  L  T  T  E  K  K  C  A  L  B) I  B
I  I  S (L  L  I  B  E  E  N  W  A  P) I  O  A  I
(J  O  S  E  P  H  O  K  L  A  H  O  M  B  I) M  M
(M  A  R  I  A  T  A  L  L  C  H  I  E  F) Y  L  W
```

Oregon—The Beaver State, Page 218

State Capital: Salem
State Flower: Oregon Grape
State Tree: Douglas Fir
State Bird: Western Meadowlark
State Fish: Chinook Salmon
State Rock: Thunderegg
State Animal: Beaver
State Insect: Oregon Swallowtail (Butterfly)
Largest City: Portland
Highest Point: 11,235 ft.—Mt. Hood
Lowest Point: Sea Level, Pacific Ocean
East-West Interstate: I-84
North-South Interstate: I-5
Population: Approximately 2.7 million
Four Major Industries: Timber products, fishing, textiles, tourism, agriculture or high technology

Time Lining Oregon's History, Pages 219-220

a. 1848	k. 1859
b. 1833	l. 1883
c. 1877	m. 1846
d. 1579	n. 1814
e. 1959	o. 1765
f. 1933	p. 1980
g. 1803	q. 1864
h. 1961	r. 1844
i. 1778	s. 1804-1806
j. 1828	t. 1793

Oregon's Cities and Towns, Page 222

1. Salem	11. Ashland
2. Corvallis	12. Eugene
3. Newport	13. Albany
4. Brookings	14. Florence
5. Medford	15. Roseburg
6. Lebanon	16. Bend
7. Tillamook	17. Lakeview
8. Klamath Falls	18. Pendleton
9. Jacksonville	19. Astoria
10. Baker	20. Monmouth

Pennsylvania—The Keystone State, Page 224

State Capital: Harrisburg
State Bird: Ruffed Grouse
State Flower: Mountain Laurel
State Tree: Hemlock
State Motto: "Virtue, Liberty and Independence"

Historic Pennsylvania, Page 226

1. D	8. I
2. G	9. C
3. L	10. J
4. B	11. M
5. E	12. F
6. H	13. K
7. A	

Keystone "Keys," Page 227

```
M (E  A  O  O  T  M  O  T  T  Y  H  L  E  M (I  A  O
A  I  M  P  S (J  A  M  E  S  B  U  C  H  A  N  A  N
R  G  O  R  O  K  N  A  A  K  D  H  O  S  L  O  O  R
I  E  N  H  Y  T  C  D  L  G  A  N  I  L  E  L  H  E
A (G  E  O  R  G  E  M  A  R  S  H  A  L  L) A  D
N  R  U  D  E  D  S  U  W  A  L  Y  P  S  Y  E  S  A
A  C (B  E  N  J  A  M  I  N  W  E  S  T) B  M  R  C
N  C (E  D  G  A  R  A  L  L  A  N  P  O  E) W  K  C
D  W  A  T (T  T  U  N  L  E  U  M  A  S) L  E  P  R
E  E  R  Y  O  S  S  H  I  E  S  S  H  A  O  R  M  E
R  R  E  T  T  U  R  S  A  M  O  H  T) O  T  D  R  D
S (A  B  R  A  H  A  M  L  I  N  C  O  L  N) O  N
O  N  W  W  A  C  O  E  P  H  U  R  T  I  S  A  A  X
N  A  T  S  L  E  S  E  E  R  U  O  E  S  A  L  L
T  O  S  L  O  H (B  E  N  F  R  A  N  K  L  I  N) E
B  F  G  O  W  T  T  O  N (P  N  E  D  T  O  T  L  L
E (G  E  O  R  G  E  W  A  S  H  I  N  G  T  O  N) A
```

America's Historic Square Mile, Page 228

Liberty Bell Pavilion—Houses our nation's most hallowed symbol of liberty

Independence Hall—Declaration of Independence was adopted here and the U.S. Constitution was written here.

Army-Navy Museum—Museum housed in 18th century home depicts development of Army and Navy.

Carpenters' Hall—First Continental Congress met here.

City Tavern—Famous Revolutionary War tavern where members of First and Second Congresses gathered

Congress Hall—Where U.S. Congress met from 1790-1800

Franklin Court—Area once owned by Ben Franklin, it is now a tribute to him.

Graff House—House where Thomas Jefferson lived when he wrote the Declaration of Independence

Marine Corps Memorial Museum—Early history of the Marine Corps

Old City Hall—Home of the U.S. Supreme Court, 1791-1800

Todd House—Home of Dolley Todd, who later became Dolley Madison

Christ Church—Worship center since 1695

First Pennsylvania Bank—Descendent of the Bank of North America, the nation's first commercial bank.

Tomb of the Unknown Soldier—Only tomb in U.S. erected to the memory of the unknown Revolutionary War soldier

GA1138

Rhode Island—The Ocean State, Page 230

State Capital: Providence
State Flower: Violet
State Bird: Rhode Island Red
State Tree: Red Maple
State Shell: Quahog
State Mineral: Bowenite
State Stone: Cumberlandite
State Motto: "Hope"

A Drive Through History, Page 231

a. second largest unsupported marble dome in the world
b. oldest tavern in America
c. birthplace of American industry
d. oldest meeting house in New England
e. home of the famous portrait painter of five Presidents
f. site where Roger Williams traded with the Indians
g. nation's oldest library in continuous use
h. houses largest bell cast by Paul Revere
i. home of George Washington's second in command
j. famous church of Roger Williams
k. nation's oldest
l. nation's seventh oldest university
m. nation's second oldest capital building

Rhode Island Sons and Daughers, Page 232

1. John D. Rockefeller
2. Christopher La Farge
3. Julia Ward Howe
4. Sarah Helen Whitman
5. Irving R. Levine
6. David Hartman
7. George M. Cohan
8. Audrey and Jane Meadows
9. Rocky Marciano
10. Friars
11. Oliver Hazard Perry
12. Nathanael Greene
13. Anne Hutchinson
14. Gilbert Stuart
15. Samuel Slater

Rhode Island's Founding Father, Page 233

1. 8	7. 11	13. 12
2. 1	8. 15	14. 17
3. 10	9. 3	15. 6
4. 13	10. 9	16. 16
5. 2	11. 14	17. 18
6. 5	12. 4	18. 7

Rhode Island Trivia, Page 234

1. b	8. d
2. e	9. c
3. h	10. g
4. a	11. m
5. j	12. n
6. l	13. f
7. k	14. i

South Carolina—The Palmetto State, Page 236

State Capital: Columbia
State Bird: Carolina Wren
State Flower: Yellow Jessamine
State Tree: Palmetto
State Stone: Blue Granite
State Animal: White-Tailed Deer
State Gem: Amethyst
State Wild Game Bird: Wild Turkey
State Fish: Striped Bass
State Fruit: Peach
State Dog: Boykin Spaniel
State Beverage: Milk

South Carolina City Sleuth, Page 237

1. Darlington	8. Camden
2. Orangeburg	9. Rock Hill
3. Myrtle Beach	10. Clemson
4. Charleston	11. Greenville
5. Beaufort	12. Bamberg
6. Hilton Head Island	13. Spartanburg
7. Aiken	14. Abbeville

South Carolina Scramble, Page 238

1. Charleston	11. Sassafras Mountain
2. Cotton	12. John Calhoun
3. Fort Sumter	13. Piedmont
4. Spain	14. Tobacco
5. Columbia	15. Blackbeard
6. Andrew Jackson	16. Soybeans
7. Peach	17. Myrtle Beach
8. Hilton Head Island	18. Battle at Cowpens
9. Fort Moultrie	19. Francis Marion
10. Blue Ridge	20. Textiles

South Carolina's Economy, Page 239

1. t	6. –	11. t	16. t
2. t	7. f	12. t	17. –
3. f	8. t	13. t	18. –
4. f	9. f	14. t	19. –
5. t	10. f	15. –	20. t

South Dakota—The Sunshine State, Page 242

State Capital: Pierre
State Bird: Ring-Necked Pheasant
State Flower: American Pasqueflower
State Tree: Black Hills Spruce
State Mineral: Rose Quartz
State Animal: Coyote
State Gemstone: Fairburn Agate
State Motto: "Under God the People Rule"
State Fish: Walleye
State Insect: Honeybee

South Dakota Time Line, Page 245

a. 1861	j. 1874
b. 1889	k. 1831
c. 1962	l. 1927
d. 1930's	m. 1890
e. 1682	n. 1973
f. 1876	o. 1743
g. 1817	p. 1868
h. 1944	q. 1804
i. 1803	

Tennessee—The Volunteer State, Page 248

State Capital: Nashville
State Bird: Mockingbird
State Flower: Iris
State Tree: Tulip Poplar
State Insects: Firefly and Ladybug
State Gem: Tennessee River Pearl
State Rocks: Limestone and Agate
State Animal: Raccoon
State Wildflower: Passion Flower

Tennessee Time Line, Page 249

a. 1925	h. 1818
b. 1763	i. 1870
c. 1796	j. 1942
d. 1878	k. 1540
e. 1861	l. 1866
f. 1682	m. 1933
g. 1780	n. 1838

Follow the Mockingbird, Page 252

a. 6	i. 4
b. 2	j. 9
c. 11	k. 6
d. 10	l. 11
e. 8	m. 3
f. 7	n. 5
g. 8	o. 11
h. 1	p. 8

Texas—The Lone Star State, Page 254

State Capital: Austin
State Tree: Pecan
State Flower: Bluebonnet
State Bird: Mockingbird
State Stone: Petrified Palmwood
State Shell: Lightning Whelk
State Gem: Topaz
State Motto: "Friendship"
State Dish: Chili

Texas Time Line, Page 257

a. 1861	i. 1835
b. 1519	j. 1901
c. 1541	k. 1870
d. 1962	l. 1542
e. 1845	m. 1836
f. 1718	n. 1936
g. 1528	o. 1685
h. 1963	p. 1973

The Eyes of Texas, Page 258

Across	Down
2. Dwight Eisenhower	1. Pinckney Henderson
3. Davy Crockett	4. James Fannin
8. Lyndon Johnson	5. William Travis
10. Santa Anna	6. Sam Houston
11. Ben Milam	7. John Kennedy
12. Coronado	9. Jim Bowie
13. Stephen Austin	

Utah—The Beehive State, Page 260

State Capital: Salt Lake City
State Bird: Sea Gull
State Flower: Sego Lily
State Tree: Blue Spruce
Source of Nickname—The Beehive State: Brigham Young called the land "Deseret." This Mormon word means "honeybee" and stands for hard work on the part of the Mormons when they transformed the desert into Salt Lake City.
Source of State Name—Utah: Named for the Ute Indians who lived there.

News Flash! Page 262

1. 1848	7. 1913
2. 1896	8. 1860
3. 1890	9. 1952
4. 1824	10. 1850
5. 1869	11. 1849
6. 1847	12. 1964

Utah's Natural Treasures, Page 263

1. Bryce Canyon
2. Zion
3. Capitol Reef
4. Arches
5. Canyonlands

Vermont—The Green Mountain State, Page 266

State Capital: Montpelier
State Bird: Hermit Thrush
State Flower: Red Clover
State Tree: Sugar Maple
Population: Approximately 500,000 (48th)
Area: 9614 square miles (43rd)
Largest City: Burlington—37,712
State Motto: Freedom and Unity

War in Vermont, Page 269

1. As a result of the British gaining control of this land, the French were driven out of this area as well as most of the rest of the land they claimed in North America.
2. He, along with Benedict Arnold and more than eighty Green Mountain Boys, captured Fort Ticonderoga in 1775 and held the fort until 1777 when the British drove them out.
3. Battle of Bennington was actually fought on New York soil. It marked the end of British occupation in northern colonies.
4. In 1864 Confederate soldiers robbed banks before fleeing into Canada.

Virginia—Old Dominion, Page 272

State Capital: Richmond
State Flower: Flowering Dogwood
State Tree: Flowering Dogwood
State Bird: Cardinal
State Dog: Foxhound
State Song: "Carry Me Back to Old Virginia"
State Motto: "Sic Semper Tyrannis" (Thus always to tyrants)

GA1138

Mother of Presidents, Page 274
1. James Madison
2. James Monroe
3. Thomas Jefferson
4. George Washington
5. Woodrow Wilson
6. Zachary Taylor
7. John Tyler
8. William Henry Harrison

Washington—The Evergreen State, Page 278
State Capital: Olympia
State Bird: Willow Goldfinch
State Flower: Coast Rhododendron
State Tree: Western Hemlock
State Song: "Washington, My Home"
State Dance: Square Dance
State Motto: "Alki" (Bye and Bye)

Fact or Fiction, Page 280
1. fiction	11. fact
2. fact	12. fiction
3. fiction	13. fact
4. fiction	14. fiction
5. fiction	15. fact
6. fact	16. fact
7. fact	17. fiction
8. fact	18. fact
9. fact	19. fact
10. fact	20. fact

Sequencing Washington History, Page 281
6, 10, 1, 8, 3, 14, 9, 2, 7, 12, 4, 11, 15, 5, 13

Washington Crossword, Page 282

Across	Down
2. Columbia	1. Vancouver
3. Olympic	4. Mount St. Helens
5. Puget Sound	7. Walla Walla
6. Mark Tobey	10. Cascade
8. Apples	12. Drake
9. Seattle	
11. Palouse	
13. Boeing	
14. Grand Coulee	
15. Spokane	
16. Salmon	

Washington, D.C., Pages 285-286
1. Arlington National Cemetery
2. Ford's Theatre
3. Marine Corps War Memorial
4. Jefferson Memorial
5. White House
6. Supreme Court Building
7. Washington Monument
8. National Archives
9. Lincoln Memorial
10. Pentagon
11. Library of Congress
12. United States Capitol
13. Vietnam Veterans Memorial
14. National Zoological Park
15. Dumbarton Oaks
16. The Bureau of Engraving and Printing
17. The National Cathedral
18. Constitution Gardens
19. Smithsonian Institution Building
20. J. Edgar Hoover Building

West Virginia—The Mountain State, Page 288
State Capital: Charleston
State Flower: Rhododendron
State Tree: Sugar Maple
State Bird: Cardinal
State Motto: "Montani Semper Liberi" (Mountaineers Are Always Free)

West Virginia History, Page 290
4, 6, 2, 10, 8, 1, 7, 14, 11, 9, 3, 13, 5, 12

Places to See in West Virginia, Page 291
a. health resort city noted for the health-related qualities of its spring water which is always 74.5⁰ F
b. located entirely within West Virginia
c. significant to beginning of Civil War
d. family farm where Confederate General Stonewall Jackson spent his boyhood
e. center for the study of radio waves from space
f. landmark with many colorful layers of rock
g. state-owned scenic railroad powered by a steam locomotive through beautiful mountain country
h. John Brown Gallows, Harewood and Mordington
i. famous resort town, home of the Greenbrier
j. reconstructed frontier town rebuilt much as it was in 1774, when it was originally built
k. site of a major battle during Civil War
l. West Virginia's largest state park offers many recreational facilities.
m. sparkling water from the Blackwater River plunging from a height of five stories
n. unique mountain valley resort 3200 feet above sea level
o. striking geological formation

For Further Research. . ., Page 292
1. Kanawha
2. It determined that to be West Virginia's part of Virginia's debt at the time the new state was formed.
3. With its large wealthy plantations, the sympathies would lean toward the South and slave-holding.
4. Bituminous coal
5. Grimes Golden, Golden Delicious
6. Pearl Buck
7. Michael J. Owens
8. Spruce Knob, 4863 ft.
9. 34 senators, 100 members in house of delegates
10. Wheeling

Wisconsin—The Badger State, Page 294
State Capital: Madison
State Bird: Robin
State Tree: Sugar Maple
State Flower: Wood Violet
State Fish: Muskellunge
State Animal: Badger
State Domestic Animal: Dairy Cow
State Symbol of Peace: Mourning Dove
State Insect: Honeybee
State Wildlife Animal: White-Tailed Deer
State Mineral: Galena
State Rock: Red Granite

Historical Wisconsin, Page 296
1. Baraboo—forty acres of circus acts, trained animals, circus memorabilia and the largest collection of circus wagons restored to original condition. Ringling Brothers started here.
2. La Pointe—The site of former American Fur Company, now a museum housed in four pioneer structures surrounded by a cedar stockade.
3. Greenbush—Built in 1850 to serve immigrants traveling in Wisconsin, it has been restored with period furniture.
4. Eagle—Vast outdoor museum that contains houses and other structures built in 1800's by immigrants to Wisconsin.
5. Mineral Point—Complex of restored miners' homes who came from Cornwall, England. Rich in Cornish history and tradition.
6. Cassville—the estate of Wisconsin's first governor, Nelson Dewey. Now it's a turn-of-the-century restored village.
7. Prairie du Chien—art and literary treasures of Hercules Louis Dousman, frontiersman and trader who built a lavish mansion.

Wisconsin Time Line, Page 297
1634 I, 1658 F, 1673 D, 1740 K, 1763 A, 1783 G, 1836 H, 1845 M, 1848 B, 1856 E, 1867 N, 1871 P, 1872 C, 1884 L, 1901 J, 1924 O, 1971 Q

For Further Research. . ., Page 298
1. Answers will vary, but should include some of the following: nation's first state to open a kindergarten; students in elementary and secondary schools score consistently higher on national tests than the national average; the University of Wisconsin System consists of 13 campuses, 13 two-year schools and serves 160,000 students, the U W-Extension System serves more than a million people by bringing its resources to individuals and groups; the state operates its own educational TV stations; its vocational, technical and adult education system serves almost 450,000 people.
2. When the great Wisconsin glacier retreated from the state 10,000 years ago, it left behind a trail of debris. The trail is on the dividing line and follows a line of 1000 miles through bowl-shaped depressions, snake-like ridges and elongated rounded hills.

Wyoming—The Equality State, Page 300
State Capital: Cheyenne
State Flower: Indian Paintbrush
State Bird: Meadowlark
State Tree: Plains Cottonwood
State Mammal: Bison
State Gemstone: Jade
State Motto: "Equal rights"

Inside Wyoming, Page 302

Across	Down
2. Shoshone	1. Gypsum
3. Uranium	5. Lander
4. Tourism	6. Yellowstone
8. Coal	7. Meadowlark
10. Sweetwater	9. Oné
12. Equal rights	10. Sugar beets
14. Bucking horse	11. Gannett
16. Jade	13. Buffalo Bill
17. Cheyenne	15. Bentonite
18. Soda ash	
19. Devils Tower	

GA1138